"FRAUD INVESTIGATION: CRIMINAL PROCEDURE AND INVESTIGATION"

by

Sally Ramage

iUniverse, Inc.
New York   Bloomington

Fraud Investigation: Criminal Procedure and Investigation

Copyright © 2009 by Sally Ramage

All rights reserved. No part of this book may be used or reproduced by any means, graphic, electronic, or mechanical, including photocopying, recording, taping or by any information storage retrieval system without the written permission of the publisher except in the case of brief quotations embodied in critical articles and reviews.

iUniverse books may be ordered through booksellers or by contacting:

iUniverse
1663 Liberty Drive
Bloomington, IN 47403
www.iuniverse.com
1-800-Authors (1-800-288-4677)

Because of the dynamic nature of the Internet, any Web addresses or links contained in this book may have changed since publication and may no longer be valid. The views expressed in this work are solely those of the author and do not necessarily reflect the views of the publisher, and the publisher hereby disclaims any responsibility for them.

ISBN: 978-1-4401-1645-2 (sc)
ISBN: 978-1-4401-1646-9 (ebk)

Library of Congress Control Number: 2009921067

Printed in the United States of America

iUniverse rev. date: 01/27/2009

Table of Contents

Preface. vii
Table of Cases xv
Table of Statutes xx
Table of Regulations xxii
Table of Treaties & Conventions & Foreign Laws xxiii
Glossary of Acronyms xxv
Glossary of Accounting Terms. xxvi
Glossary of Electronic Terms. xxix
Glossary of Legal Terms. xxxix
Chapter 1- Introduction To Fraud Law 1
Chapter 2-An analysis of the Fraud Act 2006 36
Chapter 3- Other legislation that deals with fraud. 108
Chapter 4- Conspiracy to defraud, attempted fraud,
               incitement to fraud 130
Chapter 5- Common frauds, detection and prevention . . 142
Chapter 6- Bribery and corruption in corporations,
               government and authorities 193
Chapter 7- Regulatory fraud- money laundering,
               cartels and other corporate fraud 204
Chapter 8- Analysis of organised crime for cross
               -border fraud 280
Chapter 9- Legal awareness 298
Chapter 10- Investigating and prosecuting authorities. . . 321
Chapter 11- Analysis of Theft Acts 1968 and 1978 369
Chapter 12- Investigation of electronic fraud 403
Chapter 13- Police fraud investigations- policies and
               management 439
Chapter 14- The Serious Fraud Office investigation
               procedure 456
Chapter 15 -Sentencing in fraud cases. 492
Bibliography 509

"FRAUD INVESTIGATION: CRIMINAL PROCEDURE AND INVESTIGATION"

Preface

This is a very special book. It has been written to assist police detectives who investigate fraud. It is therefore a manual on fraud law and fraud investigation procedures. Apart from the author's academic qualifications, all gained from United Kingdom universities, this book is the fruit of practical work experience, giving insight into business practices, forensic practices, interviewing of clients, and good practical legal research methodologies. This book is not the fruit of an academic exercise, let this be clear. The author, Sally Ramage, BA (Hons), MBA, MPhil, has first-hand experience of accountancy and finance work with listed companies, small companies, medium-sized companies, sole traders, as well as university law teaching experience, legal writing, legal editing and report writing as can be seen at website http://www.sallyramage.net.

There are fifteen chapters in this book preceded by some *vital* glossaries of accounting terms, acronyms, electronic terms and legal terms. These glossaries are the gems in this book, as are the case studies. So as not to interrupt the chapters with notes referring to the glossaries, it is left to the reader to refer to the glossary when he or she needs clarification of a word or term. If the glossary does not contain the explanation, then it will be found in the Oxford English dictionary.

A brief synopsis of the contents follows.

Table of Statutes

It must be emphasised that simply reading a copy of a statute will not enlighten a person unless he knows its purpose, its explanation and how it fits in with other relevant statutes. It is therefore hoped that this comprehensive book will assist the police fraud investigator by preparing him in his attempt to pursue the crime of fraud. The analogy of running at speed with sharp, open scissors in one's hands, as in the Word publishing software, is one which illustrates that an officer may possibly trip over and wound himself, should he run before he can walk in this area of law. Better to study a comprehensive manual first.

Table of Cases

Caselaw is extremely important and according to the English doctrine of precedent, a previous decision is to be treated as an authority, if it is analogous to a present dispute before a court, if it was decided by a court which, according to the riles of the doctrine, has the status to make decisions which will be deemed to be authoritative, and if the decision has not been abrogated by a statute or a court which has the power to overrule prior decisions. When a court has to deal with a precedent decision, the doctrine prescribes that if the precedent is a decision of a superior court, then it *must* follow that precedent in the present case. If the precedent is one of its own previous decisions, then, subject to certain exceptions in which it may depart from it, it must follow the precedent. If the precedent is a decision of a court inferior to it, in the judicial hierarchy, then it is not bound to follow the precedent but may do so if it chooses.

Chapter 1- Introduction to Fraud Law

This chapter contains the essential fact that the Fraud Act 2006 is **not** retrospective. Therefore, offences committed before 15 January 2007, when the Fraud Act came into force by The Fraud Act 2006 (Commencement) Order 2006, Statutory Instrument 2006/3200, will have to be prosecuted under the relevant statutes in force at the time of the commission of the crime, such as the Theft Act 1968, Theft Act 1978, or using the common law charge of conspiracy to defraud.

Chapter 2- The Fraud Act 2006

This chapter explains and analyses the Fraud Act 2006, a statute at once simple yet complex. The United Kingdom now has a statutory fraud offence, a dishonesty-based crime, which is committed by making a false representation (as per section 2); failure to disclose information (as per section 3); abuse of financial trust (as per section 4); possessing an article useable to commit fraud (as per section 6); making, adapting or supplying such an article (as per section 7); participating in fraudulent businesses (as per sections 9 and 10) and obtaining services dishonestly (as per section 11). The idea of a statutory fraud crime was moot for many years. The Fraud Bill in the 2002 Law Commission Report No.276 followed several Law Commission Reports, namely, the 1987

Law Commission Report No. 104, "Conspiracy to defraud"; the 1994 Law Commission Report No. 228, "Conspiracy to defraud", the 1999 Law Commission Report No. 154, "Illegal consideration"; the 1999 Law Commission Report No. 261 "Company Directors: Regulating Conflicts of Interest and Formulating a Statement of Duties"; the 2000 Law Commission Report No. 265, "Fraud and deception"; the 2001 Law Commission Report No. 160, "Conversion" , and others.

Chapter 3- Other current legislation that deals with fraud

This chapter deals with other current legislation that deals with fraud.

It gives essential explanations of statutes which deal with fraud, apart from the Fraud Act 2006, as well as the civil law system, used mainly for 'breach of contract' type frauds. The civil system is used because the standard of proof is lower than for a criminal fraud case and because assets seized go immediately to the claimant instead of the Crown, as in a criminal case. In this respect, the true amount of fraud is unknown because crime statistics reveal only criminal prosecutions.

Chapter 4- Conspiracy to defraud, attempted fraud, incitement to fraud

Conspiracy to defraud and the criminal offence of 'attempt' are explained. The procedure under which the common law offence of 'conspiracy to defraud' is important to note and the criteria that must be met in order to be able to use the charge of 'conspiracy to defraud' since the Fraud Act 2006 came into force on 15 January 2007.This chapter also tackles the difficulties encountered if the criminal offence of 'attempt' is used.

Chapter 5- Common frauds, detection and prevention

Common frauds, detection and prevention, is a chapter which is full of different examples of fraud. Although these are factual differences of types of fraud in the country and on the internet, this chapter is one to dip into if you need to see whether a certain fraud is a common fraud and if there is similar fact caselaw. It is here that a sound and rigorous explanation is made of the *actus reus* and the *mens rea* of a crime.

Chapter 6- Bribery and corruption in corporations, government and authorities

Bribery and Corruption are both urgent issues, in view of the fact that, following the Law Commission's Consultation Paper, titled "Reforming Bribery", the consultation has been responded to and closed. A Draft Bribery Bill is expected soon from the criminal law team at the Law Commission, namely, Christina Hughes, Raymond Emson, Simon Tabbush, Clare Wade, Sophie McWilliam, Joanna Dawson, Peter Melleney, and Marie-Aimee Brajeux, headed by Jeremy Horder, Law Commissioner until the year 2010. The findings of the OECD as regards bribery and corruption in the United Kingdom were examined in this chapter, as well as the OECD recommendations.

Chapter 7- Regulatory fraud- money laundering, cartels and other corporate fraud

This chapter deals with regulatory fraud. It is a complex chapter and difficult to grasp, but it is necessary to be aware of how regulatory agencies control the markets; how they treat fraud and how the police fit into the regulatory legal system.

Chapter 8- Analysis of organised crime for cross -border fraud

Organised crime and cross-border fraud are explained in this chapter. The law relating to cross-border and organised crime is much bandied in the media with no good depth of legal explanation. Therefore this chapter serves to explain laws relating to the urgent matter of organised crime.

Chapter 9- Legal awareness

Legal Awareness, is vital, as it is of no use pursuing a matter without being aware of what other laws may be breached if certain conduct persists, unnecessarily quashing a good case.

Chapter 10- UK investigating and prosecuting authorities

This comprehensive yet concise explanation of the relevant investigation and prosecuting agencies is the pride and joy of this book. This chapter gives a good 'helicopter' view of the combating of fraud in the country, and globally - essential to understanding that other countries governments mostly have the same aims and objectives of putting a stop to fraud.

Chapter 11- Analysis of Theft Acts 1968 and 1978

The Theft Acts 1968 and 1978 are included in this book for completeness and to remind us that these laws are still very important, especially when a fraud discovered today, was committed years ago.

Chapter 12- Investigation of electronic fraud

The investigation of electronic fraud is a topic that is not included in other criminal law books. This chapter gives the reader the 'nuts and bolts' of collecting and examining electronic evidence, even though the courts in this country are not yet up to speed on electronic evidence. There are still no English law rules on electronic discovery. However, organisations which have systems and policies in place, serve as the status quo for electronic evidence discovery. All forms of legislation are classed as documents and in the case of *R v Spens* [1993] Cr. App. R. 194, C.A., the City Code on Takeovers and Mergers, the court decided, sufficiently resembled legislation to be regarded as demanding construction by a judge. The City Code of Takeovers and Mergers was therefore treated by the court as a form of consensual agreement between parties with penal consequences. Following this logic, agencies which have policies in place for the treatment of their electronic documents, (where no legislation is in place), their Policies might be argued to be similarly classed.

Chapter 13- Police fraud investigations- policies and management

(contributed by Manchester Police Authority, Chief Detective Inspector).

Chapter 14- SFO investigation procedures.

Includes the important Attorney General's guidelines for disclosure in criminal cases.

Chapter 15 -Sentencing in fraud cases

Sentencing is a chapter, as per guidelines from the Criminal Appeals Procedure and brings a fitting closure to the writings in this fraud law book for the police.

TABLE OF CASES

Abdul Ghafar v Chief Constable of West Midlands Police [2000] C.A. 12th May 2000 315
Abou-Rahmah and another v City Express Bank of Lagos and others [2006] EWCA Civ 1492 56
Aldrich v Norwich Union Life Insurance Co Ltd [1998] CLC 1621 50
Ali and others [2005] EWCA Crim 87, [2005] All ER (D) 16 (Jun) 215
Armitage v Nurse [1998] Ch 241, [1997] 2 All ER 705 127
Attorney-General's Ref. (No 1 of 1991) [1993] QB 94) 120
Barlow Clowes International Ltd v Eurotrust International Ltd, 10th October 2006, Privy Council 55
Basher v DPP [1993] unreported 98
Bowman v Fels [2005] EWCA Civ 226, [2005] All ER (D) 115 (March) 216
Chant v Brown (1862) 9 Hare 790 102
Churchill Car Insurance v Victor Kelly, Feb 2007 175
Commissioners of Revenue and Customs v Khawaja, Chancery Division, The Times, 20 October 2008. 383
Cooper v Slade 1851 200
Cox-Johnson v Cox-Johnson and Others [2007] unreported 175
Crouther's Case (1599) Cro. Eliz 654 11
Derry and others v Peek (1886-90) All ER Rep 1 47
DPP v Bignell [1998] 1 Cr App R8 121
DPP v Kent and Sussex Contractors Ltd and R v ICR Haulage Ltd. 88
DPP v McKeown, DPP v Jones [1997] 2 Cr App R, 155, HL 120
DPP v Ray [1973] 374
Duckitt and ors v Ferrand and ors [2001] PLR 155, CA 127
Eurofood IFSC Ltd, Re: C-341/04 [2006] All ER (D) 20 (May) 487
Gary Harper v The Director of the Assets Recovery Agency (SPc 507) [2005] 218

Global Projects Management Ltd v Citigroup Inc and others [2005] EWHC 2663 (Ch), [2005] All ER (D) 182 (Oct) 165
Healy v Brown and another, 25th April 2002 96
International Business Machines Corp v Phoenix International (Computers) Ltd [1995] 1 All 412 102
IRC v Duke of Westminster [1936] AC1 179
Izodia v Royal Bank of Scotland International Limited [2006] JLR 346 178
Kansal v UK [2004] App.No. 21413/02; 27 April 2004 302
Kent Pharmaceuticals and Ors v The Director of the SFO and Ors [2004] EWCA (Civ) 1494. 462, 483
K Ltd v National Westminster Bank plc [2006] EWCA Civ 1039 218
MacNiven v Westmoreland Investments Ltd [2001] UKHL 6, [2001] STC 237 179
National Westminster Bank plc v Angeli Luki Kotonou [2006] EWHC 1785 61
National Westminster Plc v Rabobank Nederland [2006] EWHC 2332 (Comm) 304
Norris v Government of the US [2007] EWHC 71 (Admin), [2007] All ER (D) 199 (Jan) 252
Pamplin v Express Newspapers Ltd [1985] 2 All ER 185, [1985] 1 WLR 689 101
Pulvers v Chan – [2007] EWHC 2406 (Ch) 147
Rafsanjan Pistachio Producers Cooperative v Bank Leumi (UK) plc [1992] 1 Lloyds Report 513 136
Raja Munawar Khan v The Director of the Assets Recovery Agency (SpC 503) [2006] 218
Re Arrows (no.4) [1994] 3 All ER 814. 329
Re Barot [2007] Crim LR 741 : (2008) 1 Cr App R (S) 31 : Times, May 23, 2007 316
Re Diamond Commodities, Secretary of State for Business Enterprise and Regulatory Reform v Farndell , Ch.D., 19 March 2008, Case No. 1547 of 2007 112

Re H (Minors) (Sexual Abuse Standard of Proof) [1996] AC 563 112
Rio Tinto Zinc Corp v Westinghouse Electric Corp [1978] 1 All ER 434 197
R (on the application of UMBS Online Ltd v Serious Organised Crime Agency & Revenue & Customs, 2007] All ER (D) 35 (May). 248
Royal Brunei Airlines v Tan; Twinsectra Ltd v Yardley [2002] UKHL 12 55
R v (1) Chesterfield Justices (2) Chief Constable of Derbyshire, ex parte Bramley [1999] unreported 307
R v Adams [1995] WLR 52 PC 63
R v Adaway [2004] EWCA Crim 2831 314
R v Alladice [1988], 99
R v Andrew Regan [2002-2003] unreported 198
R v. Asghar [1974] 1 WLR 148
R v Asif Butt and others [2005] unreported 339
R v B. Clowes [1994] 2 All ER 316 55
R v Bellman [1989] A.C. 836 the House of Lords 370
R v Berenger (1814) 3 M & S 67, 105 ER 536 51
R v Bowden [1995] All ER 14
R v Bow Street Magistrates Court and Allison (AP) Ex parte Government of the United States of America (Allison) [2002]2 AC 216 120
R v Bryce [1992] 4 All ER 572 313
R v Callen [1992] 13 Cr.App.R. (S.) 60 498
R v Charles Forsyth [2004] unreported 90
R v Chief Constable of West Midlands Police, ex parte Wiley [1995] AC 274 306
R v Commissioners of Inland Revenue, ex parte H [2002] EWHC 2164 (Admin). 309
R v Condron [1997] 1 Cr.App.R. 185 301
R v Crick [1981] 3 Cr App Rep (S.) 275 75
R v Davis, Ellis, Gregory, Simms and Martin [2006] EWCA Crim. 19 May 2006 313
R v Dealey, CA Crim Div [1997] STC 217. 358

R v Dhjillan [1996] UKHL 13 374
R v Doherty [2006] EWCA Crim. (25 October 2006) 314
R v Dryden [1995] All ER 314
R v Duff [2002] Manchester Crown Court 214
R v Ellames [1974] 3 All ER 130 77
R v Firth (1989) 91 Cr App Rep 217, [1990] Crim. LR 326. 58
R v Freeman and Hodgkinson [2003] unreported 89
R v Ghosh [1982] QB 1053 41
R v Gomez [1993] HL 88
R v Goodwin and Unstead [1997] STC 22, CA. 357
R v Greenberg [1972] unreported 374
R v Gunawardena [1990] 2 All ER 477 and R v Hedworth [1997] 1 Cr App R 421. 7
R v H [2007] UKHL7 6
R v Hall [1891] 1 QB 747 14
R v Hollinshead [1985] 2 All ER 769, [1985] 3 WLR 159 77
R v ICR Haulage Ltd [1944] 1 All ER 691 136
R v J. F .Alford Transport Ltd., [1997] 2 Cr. App. R. 326 94
R v Lennon [2006] EWCH 1201, 11 May 2006 122
R v Loosley, Attorney General's Reference No.3 [2002] 314
R v Mason [1991]12 Cr.App.R. (S.) 737 497
R v McDonnell [1966] 1 All ER 193 136
R v McNamara [2006] VSCA 267 (4 December 2006). 94
R v Montila [2004] 1 WLR 3141. 43
R v Naci Vedat Natji, 2002 EWCA Crim 271 200
R v Nadir [1993] 4 All ER 513 98
R v Newcastle -upon-Tyne Magistrates' Court, ex parte Still [1996] EWHC Admin 75 315
R v Peter Lavender [2002] unreported 125
R v Peter Young [2003] unreported 93
R v Philippe Roux [1998] Unreported. 342
R v Preddy [1996] 3 All ER 481 373
R v Ray [1974] AC 370 House of Lords 376
R v Rees [2000] LTL 20 October 318

R v Said Mubarak Ahmed and others [2008] EWCA 1386. 362
R v Secretary of State for the Home Department, ex parte Fininvest Spa, [1997] 1 All ER 942 195
R v Sharma [2006] EWCA Crim 16, [2006] 2 Cr App R (S) 416 5
R v Smith [1992] 95 Cr App R 191 301
R v Terence Richmond [1992], unreported 199
R v Trustees of CW Cheyney [2005] unreported 128
R v Waddon, 6 April 2000, the Court of Appeal 120
Sears Group Properties Plc v Andrew Scrivener [1998] unreported 130
Solo Industries UK Ltd v Canara Bank [2001] 1 WLR 1800, CA. 136
Sowerby v Charlton [2006] 1 WLR 568 160
Squirrell Ltd v National Westminster Bank Plc [2005] EWHC 664 (Ch), [2005] 2 All ER 784) 217
Stoke-on-Trent City Council v Walley [2006] EWCA Civ 1137 160
SW v UK (1996) 21 EHRR 363 8
Taylor v Hamer [2002] EWCA Civ. 1130 40
The Hellespont Ardent [1997] 2 Lloyd's. Rep. 547 88
The Herald Free Enterprise [1987] unreported 94
Three Rivers District Council v Bank of England (No 5) [2003] QB 1556 and (No 6) [2005] 1 AC 610 304
Tsang Ping-nam v R [1981] 1 WLR 1462 314
USA v Gary Steven Mulgrew, Giles Robert Hugh Darby and David John Bermingham,[2006] Cr. No. H-02-0597 63
Van Colle v Chief Constable Hertfordshire Constabulary [2006] EWHC 360 (QB) 314
Westminster City Council v Croyalgrange Ltd [1986] 83 Cr. App. R 155 at 164. HL 40
Wilson v Inyang [1951] 2 All ER 237 57
Younghusband v Luftig [1949] 2 KB 354 90

TABLE OF STATUTES

Aiders and Abettors Act 1861 108
Anti-Terrorism, Crime, and Security Act 2001 14, 16
Aviation Security Act 1982 liv
Bills of Exchange Act 1882 91
Civil Partnership Act 2004 8
Companies Act 1985 xl, xliv, xlvii, li, liv, 82, 260, 403, 458, 465, 521
Companies Act 2006 xli, xlix, liv, lv, 38, 260, 273, 277, 343, 344, 502
Computer Misuse Act 1990 lii, 117, 118, 121
Consumer Credit Act 1974 116, 159
Consumer Credit Act 2006 116
Copyright, Designs, and Patents Act 1988 108
Criminal Attempts Act 1981 139, 141
Criminal Evidence (Witness Anonymity) Act 2008 318
Criminal Justice Act 1987 xlvi, 6, 196, 302, 326, 327, 328, 403, 458, 465
Criminal Justice Act 1993 xlii, xlviii, lv, 4, 97, 108, 130, 133, 134, 135, 335, 336, 381, 382, 461, 483, 502
Criminal Justice Act 2003 103, 325, 330, 384, 494, 496
Criminal Justice (International Co-operation) Act 1990) 196
Criminal Justice (Terrorism and Conspiracy) Act 1998 24
Criminal Law Act 1977 8, 24
Criminal Procedure and Investigations Act 1996 6, 311, 403, 468
Criminal Procedure (Attendance of Witnesses) Act 1965 477
Criminal Procedures (Insanity and Unfitness to Plead) Act 1991 92
Customs and Excise Management Act 1979 xlii, xliv, xlvi, xlvii, xlviii, li, lii, 10, 351, 358
Data Protection Act 1998 458, 463, 465, 484
Electronic Communications Act 2000 86

Enterprise Act 2002 xlv, lii, 250, 252, 340, 502
Extradition Act 2003 20, 21, 252
Financial Services and Markets Act 2000 xl, xli, xlii, xlviii, li, 108, 210, 334, 335, 340, 458, 465
Fraud Act 2006 v, ix, x, 1, 3, 4, 9, 10, 36, 41, 54, 73, 78, 81, 82, 83, 89, 93, 96, 106, 130, 132, 140, 147, 339, 369, 370, 371, 372, 373, 374, 380, 390, 402, 496, 507
Honours (Prevention of Abuses) Act 1925 14, 24, 367
Human Rights Act 1998 302, 412, 454, 522
Insolvency Act 1986 xli, xliii, xliv, xlv, xlvi, xlviii, lv, lvi, 109, 110, 207, 343, 403
Internationally Protected Persons Act 1978 liv
Interpretation Act 1978 lvi, 210
Magistrates Courts Act 1980 477
Official Secrets Act 1911 468
Official Secrets Act 1989 468
Pensions Act 2004 124
Piracy Act 1837 xl, xliii, l, li, lii, liii, liv
Police and Criminal Evidence Act 1984 xlii, xliii, xlvi, li, liii, 97, 98, 299, 308, 309, 351, 358, 404
Police and Justice Act 2006 119, 120, 121, 122, 123, 283, 317
Political Parties Elections and Referendum Act 2000 366
Prevention of Corruption Act 1906 xlii, liii, 11, 16, 199, 200
Prevention of Corruption Act 1916 lv, 16, 200, 201
Proceeds of Crime Act 2002 xlii, xlv, xlvi, 16, 34, 54, 61, 100, 103, 105, 108, 150, 206, 209, 211, 216, 217, 218, 219, 288, 310, 403, 447, 489, 502
Public Bodies Corrupt Practices Act 1889 xxxix, xl, xliii, lii, lv, 14, 200
Public Interest Disclosure Act 1998 364, 365
Regulation of Investigatory Powers Act 2000 13, 318, 358, 458, 465, 489
Regulatory and Sanctions Act 2008 13

Regulatory Enforcement and Sanctions Act 2008 13, 336
Representation of the People Act 1983 14
Sale of Offices Act 1809 14
Security Services Act 1989 461, 468
Serious Crimes Act 2007 108, 447, 489
Serious Organised Crime and Police Act 2005 106, 489
Statute of Frauds 1677 82
Taxes Management Act 105, 218, 309, 403
Terrorism Act 2000 77, 100, 103, 105, 209, 211
Theft Act 1968 ix, xl, xli, xlii, xliii, xlvii, xlviii, xlix, l, li, lii, liii, liv, lv, lvi, 2, 75, 76, 134, 139, 307, 370, 371, 372, 373, 374, 377, 379, 380, 381, 384, 389, 390, 391, 392, 394, 395, 396, 397, 398, 399, 400, 401, 402, 503
Theft Act 1978 ix, xlix, 1, 2, 89, 134, 370, 374, 375, 376, 377, 378, 379, 388, 401, 402, 502
Trade Marks Act 1994 108
Unfair Contracts Terms Act 1977 46
Value Added Tax Act 1994 xlvi, 108, 351

TABLE OF REGULATIONS

Cancellation of Contracts Concluded away from Business Premises Regulations 1987 115
Cancellation of Contracts Made in a Consumer's Home or Place of Work etc Regulations 2008' 115
Channel Tunnel (Security) Order, SI 1994 570 xlviii, lii, liv
Council Regulation 1346/2000/EC (the regulation) on insolvency proceedings 487
Directive 89/592 [1989] OJ L 334/30) on insider dealing 336
Directive 2003/6/EC on market abuse 340
Directive 2005/60/EC of the European Parliament (3rd money laundering directive) 101
FSMA 2000 (Regulated Activities) Order 2001 regulating electronic money 241

Payments and Miscellaneous Amendments) Regulations 2005 124
Police (Conduct) Regulations 1999 364
Police (Discipline) Regulations 1985 364
SI 2005/2151 Occupational Pension Schemes (Fraud Compensation Payments and Miscellaneous Amendments) Regulations 2005 124
SI No. 1503, The Home Information Pack Regulations 2006. 45

TABLE OF TREATIES & CONVENTIONS & FOREIGN LAWS

Council Directive 2001/115/EC on Electronic Invoices 87
Council of Europe Convention on the Prevention of Terrorism 2005 32
Council of Europe International Convention on Cyber-crime 2001 80
European Convention on Human Rights 1950 7, 132
European Convention on Mutual Assistance in Criminal Matters 1959 196
Foreign Corrupt Practices Act 1977 (USA) 21
Identity Theft and Assumption Deterrence Act 1998 (USA) 84
International Anti-bribery and Fair Competition Act 1998 (USA) 21
OECD Anti-Bribery Convention 1999 25
OECD Convention on Bribery of Foreign Public Officials 1997 15
United Nations Vienna Convention on the Law of Treaties 1969 xxv, 33
United Nations Vienna Narcotics Convention 1984 220, 226, 228, 229, 231
US v Stringer, 408 F. Supp. 2d 1083 (D. Or. 2006) 293

GLOSSARY OF ACRONYMS

ACPO- Association of Chief Police Officers
ACSA- Anti-terrorism, Crime and Security Act
AML- Anti-money laundering
CA- Companies Act
CLA- Criminal Law Act
CJTCA- Criminal Justice (Terrorism and Conspiracy) Act
EA-extradition act
EAW-European Arrest Warrant
EU-European Union
FATF- Financial Action Task Force
FCPA- Foreign Corrupt Practices Act (US)
FIU-Financial Intelligence Unit
HIP- Home Information Pack
NYSE- New York Stock Exchange
OECD- Organisation for Economic Co-operation and Development
PBPCA- Prevention of Public Bodies Corruption Act
PCA- Prevention of Corruption Act
POCA- Proceeds of Crime Act
SAR- Suspicious Activity Report
SEC- Securities Exchange Commission (US)
SFO-Serious Fraud Office
TI-Transparency International
UK-United Kingdom
US-Untied States
VCLT- Vienna Convention on the Law of Treaties

GLOSSARY OF ACCOUNTING TERMS

Card-based money

These are products that employ a card or other electronic voucher for authentication, or to store the electronic money or a record of it on the card or voucher. A closed scheme or system contains a single issuer of electronic money. There may be multiple distributors or resellers, who purchase electronic money from the issuer for onward sale to consumers. An open scheme or system allows the participation of multiple issuers of electronic money, which means that there is a need for the clearing and settlement of transactions. Digital coin products are unaccounted products where the product is distinguished by (a) a fixed denomination; (b) a unique digit string or serial number, and (c) the value residing in the electronic coin itself. The coin is usually discarded as soon as the electronic money is spent or redeemed.

Cartel

A cartel is a group of companies which have entered into an agreement to fix their price or to share the market so that they can raise prices by removing and/or reducing the competition around. There are price-fixing cartels, bid-rigging cartels and market sharing cartels. Cartels have been in operation for centuries and it is only now that they have been criminalized. The word cartel, though centuries old, was first used in the year 1879 to designate private market-control mechanisms of entrepreneurs.

Electronic money

Electronic money is defined as: *'monetary value, as represented by a claim on the issuer, which is :(a) stored on an electronic device; (b) issued on receipt of funds; and (c) accepted as a means of payment by persons other than the issuer.'* Electronic money is therefore a prepaid means of payment that can be used to make payments to multiple persons, where the persons are distinct legal or natural entities. It can be card based or account based and used entirely online. Accounted products are those that record centrally every transaction that takes place within the system. Such recording need not be in real time, and may be subject to cycles of clearing and settlement. Unaccounted products do not involve the central recording of every transaction, although transactions may be recorded at the point of sale, or point of transfer of value. Accounted products may also comprise electronic vouchers that are not intended to be reloaded once used.

Electronic Money Association

(EMA) is the trade body representing electronic money issuers and payment service providers.

Electronic money purse

Electronic money purse is a store of electronic money, which may be in an account, on a card or other device.

Long Firm fraud

Long Firm Fraud is the common term used for outfits which set up as firms , usually retail businesses, who seduce suppliers into complacency by buying stock, initially very small amounts and paying promptly, gaining a record of being good customers.

Merchant

A merchant is a natural or legal person that uses electronic money to transact in the course of business.

Payment Service Provider

(PSP) is defined in Article 2(5) of Regulation (EC) No 1781/2006 as "a natural or legal person whose business includes the provision of transfer of funds services".

Redemption

Redemption is the process whereby a customer submits electronic money to the issuer for exchange at par value, for cash, cheque or a fund transfer drawn on the issuer's account. Server-based products are products where the value held by a customer is held centrally on a server under the control of the issuer. Customers access their purses remotely, usually online.

Wire Transfer Regulation

WTR is Regulation (EC) 1781/2006 on information on the payer accompanying transfers of funds.

GLOSSARY OF ELECTRONIC TERMS

Access token

In Windows, an internal security card that is generated when users log on. It contains the security IDs (SIDs) for the user and all the groups to which the user belongs. A copy of the access token is assigned to every process launched by the user.

BIOS

Basic Input Output System. The set of routines stored in read-only memory that enable a computer to start the operating system and to communicate with the various devices in the system such as disk drives, keyboard, monitor, printer, and communication ports.

Buffer

An area of memory often referred to as a "cache," used to speed up access to devices. It is used for temporary storage of data read from or waiting to be sent to a device such as a hard disk, CD-ROM, printer, or tape drive.

Click

A portable disk drive is also known as a PocketZip disk. The external drive connects to the computer via the USB port or a PC card, the latter containing a removable cartridge slot within the card itself.

CD-R

Compact disk-recordable. A disk to which data can be written but not erased.

CD-RW

Compact disk-rewritable. A disk to which data can be written and erased.

Compressed file

A file that has been reduced in size through a compression algorithm to save disk space. The act of compressing a file will make it unreadable to most programs until the file is uncompressed.

Cookies

Small text files stored on a computer while the user is browsing the Internet. These little pieces of data store information such as e-mail identification, passwords, and history of pages the user has visited.

CPU

Central processing unit. The computational and control unit of a computer. Located inside a computer, it is the "brain" that performs all arithmetic, logic, and control functions in a computer.

Deleted file

If a subject knows there are incriminating files on the computer, he or she may delete them in an effort to eliminate the evidence. Many computer users think that this actually eliminates the information. However, depending on how the files are deleted, in many instances a forensic examiner is able to recover all or part of the original data.

Digital evidence

Information stored or transmitted in binary form that may be relied upon in court.

Docking station

A device to which a laptop or notebook computer can be attached for use as a desktop computer, usually having a connector for externally connected devices such as hard drives, scanners, keyboards, monitors, and printers.

Documentation

Written notes, audio/videotapes, printed forms, sketches, and/or photographs that form a detailed record of the scene, evidence recovered, and actions taken during the search of the scene.

Dongle

Also called a hardware key, a dongle is a copy protection device supplied with software that plugs into a computer port, often the parallel port on a PC. The software sends a code to that port and the key responds by reading out its serial number, which verifies its presence to the program. The key hinders software duplication because each copy of the program is tied to a unique number, which is difficult to obtain, and the key has to be programmed with that number.

DSL

Digital subscriber line. Protocols designed to allow high-speed data communication over the existing telephone lines between end-users and telephone companies.

Duplicate digital evidence

A duplicate is an accurate digital reproduction of all data objects contained on the original physical item.

DVD

Digital video disk. Similar in appearance to a compact disk, but can store larger amounts of data.

Electromagnetic fields

The field of force associated with electric charge in motion having both electric and magnetic components and containing a definite amount of electromagnetic energy. Examples of devices that produce electromagnetic fields include speakers and radio transmitters frequently found in the trunk of the patrol car.

Electronic device

A device that operates on principles governing the behaviour of electrons. Examples include computer systems, scanners, printers, etc.

Encryption

Any procedure used in cryptography to convert plain text into cipher text in order to prevent anyone but the intended recipient from reading that data.

First responder

The initial responding law enforcement officer and/or other public safety official arriving at the scene.

Hidden data

Many computer systems include an option to protect information from the casual user by hiding it. A cursory examination may not display hidden files, directories, or partitions to the untrained viewer. A forensic examination will document the presence of this type of information.

ISDN

Integrated services digital network. A high-speed digital telephone line for high-speed network communications.

ISP

Internet service provider. An organization that provides access to the Internet. Small Internet service providers provide service via modem and ISDN, while the larger ones also offer private line hook-ups (e.g., T1, fractional T1).

Latent

Present, although not visible, but capable of becoming visible.

LS-120

Laser Servo-120 is a floppy disk technology that holds 120MB. LS-120 drives use a dual-gap head, which reads and writes 120MB disks as well as standard 3.5-inch 1.44MB and 720KB floppies.

Magnetic media

A disk, tape, cartridge, diskette, or cassette that is used to store data magnetically.

Misnamed files and files with altered extensions

One simple way to disguise a file's contents is to change the file's name to something innocuous. For example, if an investigator was looking for spreadsheets by searching for a particular file extension, such as ".XLS," a file whose extension had been changed by the user to ".DOC" would not appear as a result of the search. Forensic examiners use special techniques to determine if this has occurred, which the casual user would not normally be aware of.

Modem

A device used by computers to communicate over telephone lines. It is recognized by connection to a phone line.

Network

A group of computers connected to one another to share information and resources.

Networked system

A computer connected to a network.

ORB

A high-capacity removable hard disk system. ORB drives use magneto resistive (MR) read/write head technology.

Original electronic evidence

Physical items and those data objects that are associated with those items at the time of seizure.

Password-protected files

Many software programs include the ability to protect a file using a password. One type of password protection is sometimes called "access denial." If this feature is used, the data will be present on the disk in the normal manner, but the software program will not open or display the file without the user entering the password. In many cases, forensic examiners are able to bypass this feature.

Peripheral devices

An auxiliary device such as a printer, modem, or data storage system that works in conjunction with a computer.

Phreaking

Telephone hacking.

Port

An interface by which a computer communicates with another device or system. Personal computers have various types of ports. Internally, there are several ports for connecting disk drives, display screens, and keyboards. Externally, personal computers have ports for connecting modems, printers, mice, and other peripheral devices.

Port replicator

A device containing common PC ports such a serial, parallel, and network ports that plugs into a notebook computer. A port replicator is similar to a docking station but docking stations normally provide capability for additional expansion boards.

Printer spool files

Print jobs that are not printed directly are stored in spool files on disk.

Removable media

Items (e.g., floppy disks, CDs, DVDs, cartridges, tape) that store data and can be easily removed.

Screen saver

A utility program that prevents a monitor from being etched by an unchanging image. It also can provide access control.

Seizure disk

A specially prepared floppy disk designed to protect the computer system from accidental alteration of data.

Server

A computer that provides some service for other computers connected to it via a network.

Sleep mode

Power conservation status that suspends the hard drive and monitor resulting in a blank screen to conserve energy, sometimes referred to as suspend mode.

Stand-alone computer

A computer not connected to a network or other computer.

System administrator

The individual who has legitimate supervisory rights over a computer system. The administrator maintains the highest access to the system. Also can be known as sysop, sysadmin, and system operator.

Temporary and swap files

Many computers use operating systems and applications that store data temporarily on the hard drive. These files, which are generally hidden and inaccessible, may contain information that the investigator finds useful.

USB

Universal Serial Bus. A hardware interface for low-speed peripherals such as the keyboard, mouse, joystick, scanner, printer, and telephony devices.

Volatile memory

Memory that loses its content when power is turned off or lost.

Zip

A 3.5-inch removable disk drive bundled with software that can catalogue disks.

GLOSSARY OF LEGAL TERMS

Accused
Prosecution of Offences Act 1985 and Criminal Evidence Act 1898, s.1, in relation to any criminal proceedings, means *any person charged with an offence to which the proceedings relate (whether or not he has been convicted)*.

Actus reus
This Latin term means the act of the crime. It is one element of a crime. The establishment of *actus reus* or the existence of actus reus is essential for criminal liability to be proven. Each crime has its own *actus reus*. Examples of actus reus are: conduct of the accused; result or consequences or an omission.

Adult
Adults who appear or are brought before a magistrates' court charged with an offence triable only on indictment must always be sent forthwith to the Crown Court for trial in accordance with section 51 of the Crime and Disorder Act 1998.

Advantage
Section 1 Public Bodies Corrupt Practices Act 1889 states that every person who shall by himself or by or in conjunction with any other person, corruptly solicit or receive, or agree to receive, for himself, or for any other person, any gift, loan, fee, reward, or advantage whatever as an inducement to, or reward for, or otherwise on account of any member, officer, or servant of a public body as in this Act defined, doing or forbearing to do anything in respect of any matter or transaction whatsoever,

actual or proposed, in which the said public body is concerned, shall be guilty of a misdemeanour.

Agent

Companies Act 1985, s.434 includes *its bankers and solicitors and persons employed by it as auditors, whether these persons are or are not officers of the company or other body corporate.*

Attorney General

Public Bodies Corrupt Practices Act 1889, s.4 means *the Attorney General for England, and as respects Scotland means the Lord Advocate.*

Authorised Person

Financial Services and Markets Act 2000, s.165 *includes a person who was at any time an authorised person but who has ceased to be an authorised person.*

Business

Financial Services and Markets Act 2000, s.167 includes *any part of a business even if it does not consist of carrying on regulated activities.*

Cash

Piracy Act 1837, s7 means *notes, coins or travellers' cheques in any currency.*

Cheat

Theft Act 1968 means *an offence under section 15 of this Act.*

Child

As defined in:
Criminal Law Act 1967, s.12
Bail Act 1976, s.2
Children and Young Persons Act 1969
Children and Young Persons Act 1933, s.36
Powers of Criminal Courts (Sentencing) Act 2000, s.163

Collection

Theft Act 1968 includes *a collection got together for a temporary purpose.*

Communicate

Financial Services and Markets Act 2000, s.21 includes *causing a communication to be made.*

Company

Powers of Criminal Courts (Sentencing) Act 2000, s.132 states: "*any company which may be wound up under the Insolvency Act 1986 or the Insolvency (Northern Ireland) Order 1989 (S.I. 1989 No. 2405 (N.I. 19))*"
Companies Act 2006, s1, defines "company".
Energy Act 2004, s171 has the same meaning of "company". It states:
"In this Chapter.... "company" means— (b) an existing company; or(c)an unregistered company".
Insolvency Act 1986, Part 7 s.251 includes "*anybody corporate (whether incorporated in Great Britain or elsewhere); and references to directors and other officers of a company and to voting power at any general meeting of a company have effect with any necessary modifications*".

Criminal Justice Act 1993, Part 5 s.60: company means "anybody *(whether or not incorporated and wherever incorporated or constituted) which is not a public sector body*".

Confession

Police and Criminal Evidence Act 1984, s.73.
Proceeds of Crime Act 2002, Part 2 s.76A includes "*statement wholly or partly adverse to the person who made it, whether made to a person in authority or not and whether made in words or otherwise*".

Consideration

Prevention of Corruption Act 1906 includes "*valuable consideration of any kind*".

Consumer

Financial Services and Markets Act 2000, s.14.

Container

Customs and Excise Management Act 1979, includes "*any bundle or package and any box, cask or other receptacle whatsoever*".

Conveyance

Theft Act 1968 means "*any conveyance constructed or adapted for the carriage of a person or persons whether by land, water or air, except that it does not include a conveyance constructed or adapted for use only under the control of a person not carried in or on it*".

Copy

Police and Criminal Evidence Act 1984, s.73- "*anything onto which information recorded in the document has been copied, by whatever means and whether directly or indirectly*".

Corruptly

Public Bodies Corrupt Practices Act 1889, s.4- "*not 'dishonestly' but purposely doing an act which the law forbids as tending to corrupt*".

Debt

Insolvency Act 1986, s.351 – "*to be construed in accordance with section 382(3)*".

Debtor

Insolvency Act 1986, s.351 (a) - "*the individual making or intending to make that proposal, and (b) in relation to a bankruptcy petition, means the individual to whom the petition relates*".

Deception

Deception in the Theft Act 1968 – "*any deception (whether deliberate or reckless) by words or conduct as to factor as to law, including a deception as to the present intentions of the person using the deception or any other person*".

Director

Piracy Act 1837, Part 2 s.10 – "*a member of the body corporate*".

Customs and Excise Management Act 1979, s.4 - "*Where an offence under any enactment relating to an assigned matter which has been committed by a body corporate is proved to have been committed with the consent or connivance of, or to be attributable to any neglect on the part of any director, manager, secretary or other similar officer of the body corporate or any person purporting to act in any such capacity, he as well as the body corporate shall be guilty of that offence and shall be liable to be proceeded against and punished accordingly. In this subsection "director," in relation to anybody corporate established by or under any enactment for the purpose of carrying on under national ownership any industry or part of an industry or undertaking, being a body corporate whose affairs are managed by the members thereof, means a member of that body corporate*".

Companies Act 1985, s.733 - "*a shadow director*".

Companies Act 1985, s.733 – "*any person occupying the position of director, by whatever name called*".

Insolvency Act 1986, Part 7 s.251- "*any person occupying the position of director, by whatever name called*".

Company Directors Disqualification Act 1986, s.11 – "*any person occupying the position of director, by whatever name called*".

Document – definitions

Civil Evidence Act 1995 section 1(2).

Companies Act 1985, s.434 - "information *recorded in any form*".

Criminal Justice Act 1988, s.138 - "*anything in which information of any description is recorded, but not including any recording of sounds or moving images*".

Criminal Justice Act 1988- "*anything in which information of any description is recorded*".

Criminal Justice and Police Act 2001, Part 2 s.66 – "*information recorded in any form*".

Evidence Act 1845, s.2 - *"anything in which information of any description is recorded"*.

Enterprise Act 2002, s.202 - "*in relation to information recorded otherwise than in a form in which it is visible and legible, references to its production include references to producing it in a form in which it is visible and legible or from which it can readily be produced in a visible and legible form*".

Misuse of Drugs Regulations, SI 2001 3998 reg.2 means *"anything in which information of any description is recorded (within the meaning of the Civil Evidence Act 1995")*.

Proceeds of Crime Act 2002, Part 2 s.70 includes: information *recorded otherwise than in legible form"*.

Proceeds of Crime Act 2002, (Commencement No. 5, Transitional Provisions, Savings and Amendment) Order, SI 2002/ 333 sched.1 r.57.1- *"anything in which information of any description is recorded"*.

Road Traffic Offenders Act 1988, s.1 means *anything in which information of any description is recorded.*

Employee

Directors, managers, workers, servants, agents, contractors, agency staff, consultants and others.

Estate

Insolvency Act 1986, s.351- "*is to be construed in accordance with section 283 in Chapter II of Part IX*".

Evasion

Customs and Excise Management Act 1979, s 147 *"fraudulent evasion of duty"*.

In *R v Czyzewski, Bryan, Mitchell, Diafi and Ward*, the Court of Appeal issued revised guidelines for cases of fraudulent evasion of payment of duty on tobacco or alcohol. The guidelines follow closely the recommendations of the Sentencing Advisory Panel. 170 of the Customs and Excise Management Act 1979 (c 2), s 170 – *"fraudulent evasion of duty"*.

Unlawful conduct can be prosecuted by customs officers. Unlawful conduct is

evasion of VAT; evasion of excise and other indirect taxes and duties; and

evasion of a wide range of import and export prohibitions and restrictions.

Value Added Tax Act 1994, Paragraph 10(3) of Schedule 11 – *"seizure of evidence of fraudulent evasion of VAT"*.

Evidence

Criminal Justice Act 1987, sched.1 – *"documents and other articles"*.

Police and Criminal Evidence Act 1984, s.78 – *"all the evidence which the prosecution might seek to adduce at trial"*.

False or misleading

Proceeds of Crime Act 2002, Part 2 s.67- *"false or misleading in a material particular"*.

Family

Insolvency Act 1986, s.351- *"the persons (if any) who are living with him and are dependent on him"*.

Money Laundering Regulations 2007-Regulation 14 - *"Regulated persons must carry out 'enhanced' CDD, and 'enhanced' on-going monitoring, in certain specified circumstances and in any other situation which presents a higher risk of money laundering or terrorist financing. Among the specified circumstances set out in the Regulations are where the customer has not been personally present for identification purposes and where the client is a 'politically exposed person' (or an immediate family member or known close associate of such a person). A 'politically exposed person' is an individual who, in the preceding year, has exercised 'a prominent public function' in a state or institution outside the UK."*

Fraudulent

Companies Act 1985 s458 - *"Punishment for fraudulent trading:*
If any business of a company is carried on with intent to defraud creditors of the company or creditors of any other person, or for any fraudulent purpose, every person who was knowingly a party to the carrying on of the business in that manner is liable to imprisonment or a fine, or both. This applies whether or not the company has been, or is in the course of being, wound up".
Telecommunications (Fraud) Act 1997, s1. Customs and Excise Management Act 1979, s.170: "Without prejudice to any other provision of the Customs and Excise Acts 1979, if any person is, in relation to any goods, in any way knowingly concerned in any fraudulent evasion or attempt at evasion".

Goods

Powers of Criminal Courts (Sentencing) Act 2000, s.132 – *"money and every other description of property (within the meaning of the Theft Act 1968) except land, and includes things severed from the land by stealing.* Theft Act 1968, includes *money and every other description of property except land, and includes things severed from land by stealing".*

Channel Tunnel (Security) Order, SI 1994 570 Part 1 art.2 - *"goods or burden of any description and includes baggage, stores and mail".*

Customs and Excise Management Act 1979 – *"stores and baggage".*

Inside information

Criminal Justice Act 1993, Part 5 *s.56*

Insolvency

Insolvency Act 1986, Part 7 s.247 – *"the approval of a voluntary arrangement under Part I".*

Investigator

Financial Services and Markets Act 2000, s.169 – *"a person appointed under subsection (1) (b)".*

Financial Services and Markets Act 2000, s.171- *"a person conducting an investigation under section 167".*

Investment

Financial Services and Markets Act 2000, s.21 – *"any asset, right or interest".*

Financial Services and Markets Act 2000, s.22 – *"any asset, right or interest".*

Financial Services and Markets Act 2000, s.25 – *"any asset, right or interest".*

Legal privilege

Criminal Justice and Police Act 2001, Part 2 s.66 – *"shall be construed in accordance with section 65"*.

Knowledge

Criminal Justice Act 1967 - *"wilfully shutting one's eyes to the truth"*.
International Criminal Court Act 2001, s.66 – *"awareness that a circumstance exists or a consequence will occur in the ordinary course of events"*.

Letter
Companies Act 2006, s1000 (1).

European Communities Act 1972, Part 5 s.85 – *"any communication in written form on any kind of physical medium to be conveyed and delivered otherwise than electronically to the person or address indicated by the sender on the item itself or on its wrapping (excluding any book, catalogue, newspaper or periodical); and includes a postal packet containing any such communication"*.
Criminal Justice (International Co-operation) Act 1990, *Part 1, s3 (9).*

Liability

Theft Act 1978 – *"legally enforceable liability"*.

Loss

Theft Act 1968 – *"a loss by not getting what one might get, as well as a loss by parting with what one has"*.

Forgery and Counterfeiting Act 1981 – "*not getting what one might get as well as parting with what one has*".

Malicious

Malicious Communications Act 1988, s1.

Meeting

Piracy Act 1837, Part 2 s.10 – "*a meeting of three or more persons, whether or not the public are admitted*".
Public Order Act 1936, s.2 – "*a meeting held for the purpose of the discussion of matters of public interest or for the purpose of the expression of views on such matters*".

Mens Rea

This Latin term is used for one of the elements of a crime. To prove a crime, in many cases, it is necessary that the defendant has committed the act with the relevant mens *rea* or degree of blame-worthiness required for that offence. The different degrees of *mens rea* vary with the seriousness of the crime. The jury must decide whether the accused carried out the crime with intent.

Money

Theft Act 1968 – "*money expressed in a currency other than sterling or in the European currency unit (as defined in Council Regulation No. 3320/94/EC or any Community instrument replacing it)*".

Obtain

Theft Act 1968 – "*obtaining for another or enabling another to obtain or to retain*".

Officer

Companies Act 1985, s.733 - "*a director, manager or secretary*".

Community Order (Electronic Monitoring of Requirements) (Responsible Officer) Order 2001.Statutory Instrument 2001 No. 2233.

Criminal Appeal Act 1968 – "*a director, manager, secretary or other similar officer of the body, or a person purporting to act in any such capacity*".

Criminal Appeal Act 1968 – "*an officer of a police force or a customs and excise office*".

Criminal Justice Act 1988, s.139 - "*a director, manager, secretary or other similar officer of the body, or a person purporting to act in any such capacity*".

Financial Services and Markets Act 2000, s.165 – "*an officer of the Authority and includes a member of the Authority's staff or an agent of the Authority*".

Financial Services and Markets Act 2000, *s.400.*

Piracy Act 1837, Part 2 s.10.

Police and Criminal Evidence Act 1984 (Application to Customs and Excise) Order, SI 1985 1800 art.2 – "*a person commissioned by the Commissioners for Her Majesty's Revenue and Customs under section 6(3) of the Customs and Excise Management Act 1979*".

Theft Act 1968 – "*director, manager or secretary. An auditor of a company was held to be an officer within section 84 of the Larceny Act 1861*" as in R *v Shacter* [1960] 2 Q.B. 252, 44 Cr. App. R. 42, CCA.

Organisation

Piracy Act 1837, Part 2 s.10 – "*any association or combination of persons*".
Public Order Act 1986, s.148 – "*any institution, trust, undertaking or association of persons*".

Owner

Ownership implies authority and responsibility.
Theft Act 1968, s 12(7) (b) – "*a person in possession of the conveyance under a hiring or hire-purchase agreement*".
Channel Tunnel (Security) Order, SI 1994 570 Part 1 art.2 – "*a lessee*".
Customs and Excise Management Act 1979 – "*the operator of the aircraft*".
Customs and Excise Management Act 1979 – "*in relation to a pipe-line, means (except in the case of a pipe-line vested in the Crown which in pursuance of arrangements in that behalf is operated by another) the person in whom the line is vested and, in the said excepted case, means the person operating the line*".

Person under investigation

Enterprise Act 2002, s.202 – "*meaning given in section 192(2)*".

Person

Public Bodies Corrupt Practices Act 1889, s.7.

Premises

Computer Misuse Act 1990 – "*land, buildings, movable structures, vehicles, vessels, aircraft and hovercraft*".

Criminal Justice and Police Act 2001, Part 2 s.39 - "*any vehicle*".

Criminal Justice and Police Act 2001, Part 2 s.66 - "*any vehicle, stall or moveable structure (including an offshore installation) and any other place whatever, whether or not occupied as land*".

Piracy Act 1837, Part 2 s.10 – "*any place and in particular includes - (a) a vehicle, (b) an offshore installation within the meaning given in section 44 of the Petroleum Act 1998 , and (c) a tent or moveable structure*".

Police and Criminal Evidence Act 1984 (Application to Customs and Excise) Order, SI 1985 1800 sched.1 – "*any place and, in particular, includes - (a) any vehicle, vessel, aircraft or hovercraft; (b) any offshore installation; and (ba) any renewable energy installation; (c) any tent or movable structure*".

Police and Criminal Evidence Act 1984 - "*any place*".

Pensions Fraud

The Pensions Regulator has powers to require any person to provide him with relevant documents if he believes that person has information relating to non-compliance with the new requirements. He also has the ability to send inspectors to the personal pension provider's and the employer's premises to investigate any possible non-compliance.

Principal

Prevention of Corruption Act 1906 – "*an employer*".

Procure

Theft Act 1968 – "*no more than 'cause' or 'bring about'*".

Property

Aviation Security Act 1982 - "*any land, buildings or works, any aircraft or vehicle and any baggage, cargo or other article of any description*".

Channel Tunnel (Security) Order, SI 1994 570 Part 1 art.2 - "*any land, building or works, any train or other vehicle and any goods or other article of any description*".

Piracy Act 1837, Part 2 s.10 – "*property wherever situated and whether real or personal, heritable or moveable, and things in action and other intangible or incorporeal property*".

Theft Act 1968 includes *money and all other property, real or personal, including things in action and other intangible property.*

Prospectus

Companies Act 2006, Schedule 15, section 1272, "*Transparency obligations and related matters: minor and consequential amendments*", section 1:"

Companies Act 1985, s.735.

Protected person

Internationally Protected Persons Act 1978, s.1 – "*in relation to an alleged offence, any of the following, namely - (a) a person who at the time of the alleged offence is a Head of State, a member of a body which performs the functions of Head of State under the constitution of the State, a Head of Government or a Minister for Foreign Affairs and is outside the territory of the State in which he holds office; (b) a person who at the time of the alleged offence is a representative or an official of a State or an official or agent of an international organisation of an inter-governmental character, is entitled under international law to special protection from attack on his person, freedom or dignity and does not fall within the preceding paragraph; (c) a person who at the time of the alleged offence is a member of the family of another person mentioned in either of the preceding paragraphs and - (i) if the other person is mentioned in paragraph (a) above, is accompanying him, (ii) if the other person is mentioned in paragraph (b) above, is a member of his household".*

Public body

Prevention of Corruption Act 1916, s.2 – *"in addition to the bodies mentioned in the last-mentioned Act, local and public authorities of all descriptions (including authorities existing in a country or territory outside the United Kingdom) [and companies which in accordance with Part V of the Local Government and Housing Act 1989 are under the control of one or more local authorities]".*
Public Bodies Corrupt Practices Act 1889, s.7.

Receive

Theft Act 1968 – *"handle".*

Regulated market

Criminal Justice Act 1993, Part 5 s.60 – *"any market however operated, which, by an order made by the Treasury, is identified (whether by name or by reference to criteria prescribed by the order) as a regulated market for the purposes of this Part".*

Shadow director

Companies Act 2006, s251.
Insolvency Act 1986, Part 7 s.211- *"false representation to creditors".*

Trustee

Insolvency Act 1986, s.351 – "*the trustee of the bankrupt's estate*".

United Kingdom

Interpretation Act 1978, s.1 – "*Great Britain and Northern Ireland*".

Valuable security

Theft Act 1968 – "*any document creating, transferring, surrendering or releasing any right to, in or over property, or authorising the payment of money or delivery of any property, or evidencing the creation, transfer, surrender or release of any such right, or the payment of money or delivery of any property, or the satisfaction of any obligation*".

Writing

Interpretation Act 1978, s.15 – "*typing, printing, lithography, photography and other modes of representing or reproducing words in a visible form, and expressions referring to writing are construed accordingly*".

CHAPTER 1- INTRODUCTION TO FRAUD LAW

1.1.1. The Fraud Act 2006

The UK has a new fraud offence in the Fraud Act 2006. The defects of the old law of theft resulted in the Fraud Act 2006. This new offence of fraud is much simpler and it is a more general offence. It targets the nature of fraudulent behaviour, rather than particular instances of such behaviour. The Fraud Act 2006, in force since 15th January 2007, is *not retrospective* and so the Theft Acts 1968 and 1978 are still applied in those cases coming to court for frauds committed before January 2007.

The concept of fraud is not directly defined by the Fraud Act but by implication, it is confined to conduct falling within sections 2, 3 and 4 which provide three different ways of committing the offence of fraud. These are fraud by false representation, fraud by failing to disclose information and fraud by abuse of position.

The Fraud Act is largely based on recommendations of the Law Commission (Report on Fraud, Law Commission, No.276, 2002, for instance). The medley of individual offences based on deception in the Theft Acts 1968 and 1978 has been replaced by a new wide-ranging offence of fraud. This overcomes a number of problematic features of the old law. As an instance, the fraud offence of obtaining services dishonestly (section 11 Fraud Act) replaces and extends the former offence of obtaining services by deception under section 1 of the Theft Act 1978.

The Theft Act 1978 s 1(1) focuses on the word "services", which is defined in s1(2). The section in the statute uses the words "confer a benefit", a matter of contention. The definition also states that the benefit is payable and this is another issue.

This Theft Act 1978 s1 offence of 'obtaining services by deception' could also mean 'obtaining property by deception' since property is a benefit, thus overlapping with Theft Act 1968, s15 and caused such confusion that a new Theft Act 1968 s 1(3) was enacted to cover the difficulties. Also merely omitting to do an act was insufficient grounds to activate the offence. The new offence of fraud by obtaining services dishonestly, dispensed with the problems of proving deception. The former theft offence was not successful in convicting criminals of illegally defrauded cash machines, because one cannot deceive a machine. The new offence will succeed.

1.1.2. The scale of fraud in the UK

In March 2008, it was estimated that the UK has £361 billion of consumer assets at risk of online fraud, according to a reputable survey. UK consumers have a collective £361 billion exposure to online fraud, amounting to £10,077 per vulnerable internet user in online banking, shopping and gaming accounts. The survey revealed that 78% of respondents said they were worried about ID theft. Of those polled, 65% said they share personal data with their online bank, 58% with web retailers and 31% with social networking sites. The popularity of internet banking continues to grow, but so does cyber crime. There have been attacks on online banking systems, as well as credit and debit cards. There has been a recent wave of 'phishing' emails, which attempt to get people to disclose account and credit card information. Individuals have also been targeted by phishing emails purporting to be offering refunds on their taxes if they supply information to a fake Inland Revenue website.

1.2. Fraud offences before the Fraud Act

Before the Fraud Act 2006, fraud was prosecuted under many headings. As to serious fraud, that was usually prosecuted as offences of conspiracy to defraud, corruption, insider dealing, offences against the Securities Act, etc. The Home Office sets out what it considers are offences of fraud in its Report, "Counting Rules for Recorded Crime". These Counting Rules were last amended in April 2008. They can be found on the Home Office website.

Even though the UK now has a Fraud Act, there are still problems of assessing exactly where the geographical fraud hotspots are to be found and exactly how much fraud is suffered and perpetrated in the UK. One reason for this is that different police forces around the country log charges differently. They do not all follow the Counting Rules.

> **Point to Note: New rules on treating plastic card and cheque fraud**
>
> Since 15 January 2007 when the Fraud Act came into force, there have been two major changes in relation to police recording plastic card and cheque fraud.
>
> There is a new rule for counting such fraud as simply *one economic crime against each credit card account* rather than counting every single fraud committed with that credit card. Financial institutions are now the first point of contact for account holders who wish to report such a fraud offence. The public must inform their financial institution who will report the economic crime to the police via a central recording point in each police force.

Even though the UK had a Serious Fraud Office since the year 1987, English law did not prescribe the constituents of fraud, neither was 'serious fraud' defined, although it is commonly expected to consist of a complex embezzlement, a "long firm fraud", corporate fraud or organised financial crimes.

The Criminal Justice Act 1993 makes provision for jurisdiction issues in relation to certain offences of dishonesty and blackmail. The SFO often use the charge of "conspiracy to defraud" in cases of "misleading the markets" and "insider trading." "Insider trading" is very difficult to prosecute. The new UK Fraud Act 2006 does not model the fraud offence on the offence of conspiracy to defraud which was considered too wide, although the offence of 'conspiracy to defraud' remains as a common law fraud offence. A statutory fraud offence was called for because it could be argued that there is no fraud if there is no fraud offence.

1.3.1. Abolishing the conspiracy to defraud offence

After much debate in Parliament as to whether or not the offence should be abolished, it was decided not to abolish it for the time being. The Attorney General said that the position would be reviewed after three years of the implementation of the Fraud Act 2006, i.e. after January 2010.

1.3.2. Cases which may use the 'conspiracy to defraud charge'

The Attorney General's Guidance, issued 7th January 2007, states that the offence of 'conspiracy to defraud' may be used in the following types of cases:

(i) Conduct that can more effectively be prosecuted as conspiracy to defraud. This includes cases where various types of criminality are found

(ii) Conduct that can only be prosecuted as conspiracy to defraud. This category includes conduct which is not covered by any statutory provision, but which would amount to conspiracy to defraud.

(iii) Whenever a conspiracy to defraud charge is to be used, the prosecutor must set out the reason for using that charge and how that charge will add to the evidence likely to be called by the prosecution and defence, and the justification for using the charge. The prosecutor must then provide the Attorney General with a record, which can be used during later deliberations as to the fate of the common law offence of conspiracy to defraud.

Caselaw

***R v Sharma* [2006] EWCA Crim 16, [2006] 2 Cr App R (S) 416**

The defendant was convicted of conspiracy to defraud. The fraud in which he was engaged obtained about £179,000, paid into a company account of which the defendant was the sole signatory. (This case was a guideline judgement on confiscation orders).

Caselaw

R v H [2007] UKHL7

The use of the charge of conspiracy to defraud is not without its problems as this caselaw reveals. The defendant was charged, with others, with conspiracy to defraud and a preparatory hearing under s 7 of the 1987 Act was ordered. Section 9(1) of the 1987 Act provided that at a preparatory hearing 'the judge may exercise any of the powers specified in this section'. Under sub-s (3) (b), (c) he could determine any question as to the admissibility of evidence and any other question of law relating to the case. Section 9(11) provided that any appeal lay to the Court of Appeal from any order or ruling of a judge under sub-s (3)(b) or (c) with leave of the judge or the Court of Appeal. In the course of the preparatory hearing ordered under s 7 of the Criminal Justice Act 1987 the defendant made an application under s 8^c of the Criminal Procedure and Investigations Act 1996 for disclosure of documents in the possession of the prosecution. The judge refused the application and the defendant applied for leave to appeal under s 9(11). The Court of Appeal considered, in the light of prior authority of the Court of Appeal, that it had no jurisdiction to hear the appeal. It granted leave to appeal to the House of Lords and certified questions of general public importance, namely: (i) whether, for an appeal to lie to the Court of Appeal under the provisions of s 9(11) of the 1987 Act from an order or ruling made during the course of a preparatory hearing held under s 7(1), the order or ruling itself had to be for one of the purposes set out in s 7(1); (ii) if so, whether an order or ruling in determination of an application for

> disclosure under s 8 of the 1996 Act could fall within one of those purposes; and (iii) in any event, whether an order or ruling in determination of an application for disclosure under s 8 of the 1996 Act could be the subject of an appeal under the provisions of s 9(11) of the 1987 Act. The House of Lords dismissed the appeal for the following reasons: (1) The purposes set out in s 7(1) of the 1987 Criminal Justice Act were to be broadly and purposively construed in order to produce an efficient and expeditious disposal of the criminal proceedings in question overruling *R v Gunawardena* [1990] 2 All ER 477 and *R v Hedworth* [1997] 1 Cr App R 421.

1.3.3. Article 7 Human Rights and the charge of conspiracy to defraud

The use of the charge of conspiracy to defraud is subject to the general principles relating to all common law offences. These general principles are that, where a statutory alternative exists, there must be boundaries to common law offence usage. Article 7 of the European Convention on Human Rights 1950, controls the growing use of common law offences outside their established bounds.

Article 7 states:

> *"No one shall be held guilty of any criminal offence on account of any act or omission which did not constitute a criminal offence under national or international law at the time when it was committed. Nor shall a heavier penalty be imposed than the one that was applicable at the time the criminal offence was committed. This Article shall not prejudice the trial and punishment of any person for*

any act or omission which, at the time it was committed, was criminal according to the general principles of law recognised by civilised nations."

> **Caselaw**
>
> In *SW v UK* (1996) 21 EHRR 363, the court ruled that Article 7 did not prohibit *"the gradual clarification of rules of criminal liability through judicial interpretation from case to case, provided that the resultant development is consistent with the essence of the offence and could be reasonably foreseen"*.

1.3.4. Statutory 'conspiracy'

The Criminal Law Act 1977 creates a statutory offence of conspiracy. Statutory conspiracy is in essence an agreement by two or more parties to commit a crime and it is committed as soon as the agreement is concluded irrespective of what, if anything is actually done in pursuance of it. The charge of conspiracy can only be brought in respect of an agreement to commit indictable or summary offences. Conspiracy is triable only on indictment *even if* it relates to a summary offence, when the consent of the Director of Public Prosecutions must first be fully agreed. The offence of conspiracy is committed at the moment of the agreement, whether or not the substantive offence is carried out. An agreement is a decision which is made between at least two persons to commit a crime. A person can be charged with conspiracy even if the other conspirators are unknown (Criminal Law Act 1977, s 5(8)). However, a husband and wife cannot commit conspiracy nor can two civil partners registered under the Civil Partnership Act 2004.

1.3.5. *Actus reus* of 'conspiracy'

The *actus reus* of a 'conspiracy' is the forming of the agreement that a course of conduct is to be pursued. The course of conduct must amount to or involve the commission of any offence or offences by *one* or more of the parties to the agreement. In a statutory 'conspiracy' the offence in this context would be a conspiracy to commit the section 1 Fraud Act offence.

1.3.6. *Mens Rea* of conspiracy

The *mens rea* of 'conspiracy' is the intention to carry out the offence. The Law Commission stated:

> *"What the prosecution ought to have to prove is that the defendant agreed with another person that a course of conduct should be pursued which would result, if completed, in the commission of a criminal offence, and further, that they both knew any facts they would need to know to make them aware that the agreed course of conduct would result in the commission of the offence".*

In this regard, section 1(2) Fraud Act provides the requirement for *mens rea*. Section 1(2) Fraud Act 2006 states that the different ways of committing the fraud offence are by false representation, failing to disclose information and abuse of position.

1.4. Statutory fraud needs no proof of deception

The new statutory offence of fraud does not require proof of deception. The concept of dishonesty in the new fraud offence emphasises the act of the perpetrator and need not be proved to have caused the loss in question. The offence of fraud can mean making a positive misstatement, or dishonestly making a false representation, or dishonestly failing to disclose information to another. In all cases, it is not necessary that any onsequence be brought about by the fraud.

1.5. Fraud by making a false instrument

The Fraud Act 2006 makes it an offence to make a false instrument, the intention being that the maker or another, shall induce a third party to accept it as genuine to his prejudice. It is also an offence to make a copy of a false instrument, or to use an instrument which the user knows or believes to be false. It is a dogma in English law that the document must purport to be that which it is not. It must 'tell a lie about itself' as distinct from containing dishonest assertions about the details of transactions.

1.6. The offence of 'fraudulent evasion'

Fraudulent evasion of indirect taxation or duty is contrary to section 170 of the Customs and Excise Management Act 1979. The UK Customs and Excise Act is the Code used by Customs Officers. This creates two offences:

(i) Knowingly acquiring possession of goods on which duty has not been paid.

(ii) Being knowingly concerned in any fraudulent evasion or attempt at evasion of any duty chargeable on goods.

The maximum penalty on summary conviction is the prescribed sum or three times the value of the goods, whichever is greater, and/or imprisonment for six months. On indictment, the penalty is a fine in any amount and/or imprisonment for seven years. This offence can be committed by using a false statement or by concealment. It is not affected by the Fraud Act.

1.7. The Fraud of Corruption

Corruption is not mentioned in the Fraud Act but is one of the charges used by the Serious Fraud Office. The Serious Fraud Office can bring charges of corruption contrary to the Prevention of Corruption Act 1906, as in the recent IKEA corruption trial in October 2007, in which two former IKEA staff were found guilty of taking bribes. *R v Adam David Hauxwell-Smith* (Case No T 20057504) and *R v John Brown* (Case No. T 20057505- unreported) were sentenced to three and two years imprisonment respectively.

1.8. The fraud offence of 'misfeasance in public office'

Misfeasance in public office is a contemporary topic of criminal law. It is both a common law misdemeanour and a civil tort. The criminal offence dates back to at least the year 1599 when a constable was indicted for refusing to pursue a felon (see *Crouther's Case* (1599) Cro. Eliz 654). In recent years misfeasance in public office has enjoyed something of a revival, recently emerging in the political domain as a mechanism to deal with police officers who transgress and public officials whose behaviour is on the margins of corrupt practice. It is a topic that will feature more often because the public are demanding more transparency.

1.9. Elements of the offence of 'misfeasance in public office'

Misfeasance in public office is both a common law misdemeanour and a tort. The elements of the offence of misconduct in public office are: a public official who in the course of or in relation to his public office, wilfully and intentionally and culpably misconducts himself. A public official culpably misconducts himself if he wilfully and intentionally neglects or fails to perform a duty to which he is subject, by virtue of his office or employment, without reasonable excuse or justification. To amount to a criminal offence the neglect must be wilful and not merely inadvertent and it must be culpable in the sense that it is without reasonable cause or justification. However, misfeasance is a complicated subject, impinging on employment law, with possible consequent civil actions against the police. The matter is being addressed in a future 2008-9 Bill, having recently been studied by the Law Commission.

1.10. Issue flowing from 'misfeasance' - breach of confidentiality

Amongst an employee's duties is the supervision of the company's procedures and practices, necessary to ensure compliance with the regulatory requirements imposed from time to time by the Financial Services Authority. Suppose an employee of a company leaves his employment, following which time, he has a telephone conversation with the company's Chief Executive during the course of which they discussed the question of a payment to be made to this former employee in connection with the termination of his employment. Suppose during the course of the conversation, the ex-employee threatens to report the Chief Executive Officer ("CEO") to the Financial Services Authority ("FSA") for breaches of regulations said to have occurred and to the Inland Revenue for alleged misfeasance on the part of the Directors of the company and clients in respect of tax frauds. Should such a case go to court, the company might contend that the threatened disclosure would result in the ex-employee making use of confidential documents and information. The company might seek an injunction to restrain any disclosure and an *Anton Piller Order* to remove any of its documents from the former employee's home. This would be contrary to public interest for employees to be inhibited by threat of legal proceedings from disclosing matters that are in the province of the relevant authorities to investigate.

> **Point to Note: List of regulatory requirements**
>
> Local authorities need to make a list of all the regulatory requirements that will have to be set out as to the level of sanction that ought to be imposed for 'misfeasance in public office'. Under the UK Regulatory and Sanctions Act 2008, the council's officers can use any of the civil sanctions available only if they are satisfied to the criminal standard of proof that there is a case to go ahead on that basis.

To establish 'misfeasance' it is necessary to carry out investigations, some of which may have to be covert and must comply with the Regulation of Investigatory Powers Act 2000. Authorisation to carry out covert surveillance can be given only in a case where it is desired to prevent or detect crime.

> **Point to Note: No covert surveillance investigation in relation to misfeasance**
>
> By the Regulatory Enforcement and Sanctions Act 2008, 'misfeasance' is dealt with by way of civil sanction. Therefore covert surveillance could *not* be used to investigate cases in relation to misfeasance, malingering and moonlighting by employees of public authorities. The Investigatory Powers Tribunal, set up under the 2000 Regulation of Investigatory Powers Act, said that such activities of public employees are *not* susceptible to being dealt with under RIPA. Such acts are outside its sphere and must be dealt with in common law.

1.11.1. Bribery and misconduct in public office

The *common law* offences of bribery and misconduct in public office, as well as in the Prevention of Corruption Acts 1889 and 1916, the Sale of Offices Act 1809, the Honours (Prevention of Abuses) Act 1925, and the Representation of the People Act 1983, are the many ways of prosecuting bribery and corruption. The Anti-Terrorism, Crime, and Security Act 2001 extends the law on corruption to include bribery of foreign officials and agents by UK nationals.

In *R v Bowden* [1995] All ER, Mr Barker submitted that as with *R v Hall* [1891] 1 QB 747, the common law offence of bribery cannot apply to local authority employees since their position was covered by the Public Bodies Corrupt Practices Act 1889, which prescribes, in summary, offences of bribery by officers of local authorities who corruptly solicit or receive or agree to receive bribes, and by other persons who give promises or offer such bribes to such officers.

1.11.2. Proposed new bribery offence

The Law Commission, on 29 November 2007, published a mammoth report on bribery. In this 337-page report, the Law Commission proposed a new offence of bribery, criminalising both the active and the passive forms of bribery, and making no distinction between private and public sector bribery. The new offence would consist of two elements: an advantage conferred or promised by, or received or solicited from the payer; and an improper act or omission performed or promised by, or solicited from, the recipient. The improper act or omission must involve a breach of a relationship of trust or a breach of a duty to act impartially or in the best interests of another. In addition, the payer, in conferring the advantage, must either intend that the advantage should be the primary reason for the recipient doing an improper act, or he must foresee a serious risk that the advantage will create the primary reason for the recipient to do an improper act. The new offence will have similar extra-territorial effect to the Anti-terrorism, Crime and Security Act 2001 and will, in addition, apply to acts done abroad by foreign nationals resident in England and Wales.

1.11.2. Present offence of bribery of foreign public officials

The 1997 Organisation for Economic Cooperation and Development, ("OECD") Convention on Bribery of Foreign Public Officials, ratified by the UK, requires the Parties to outlaw, in their domestic laws, acts of bribery committed by their nationals or committed in their territory and directed towards the public officials of another foreign state. The Convention also requires that the Party bribing a foreign public official be punished by effective, proportionate, and dissuasive criminal penalties comparable to those that apply to their own public officials. Parties are required to facilitate mutual legal assistance between them and cannot invoke "bank secrecy" to deny mutual legal assistance. The OECD Convention requires Parties to regulate accounting and record –keeping and impose effective and dissuasive penalties for omissions and falsifications in accounts, records, financial statements, and similar reports.

> **Case Study**
>
> A company officer from a country party to the OECD Convention, country X, arrives in a foreign country, country Y, to negotiate a business deal on behalf of his company. He meets public officials from country Y and offers, promises and pays a substantial amount to the public officials to award his company the business contract in question. The company officer would be caught by the Convention because he is a resident of country X.
>
> The OECD website is at http://www.oecd.org.

A very recent OECD survey found that British companies are among the worst offenders for bribing foreign officials. Some 37 of the 55 companies which the World Bank publicly blacklists and has disbarred from participating in its contracts because of evidence of corruption, are domiciled in the United Kingdom. At present in the UK, as well as the common law offence of bribery, the principle statutes dealing with bribery are the Public Bodies Corrupt Practices Act 1898, The Prevention of Corruption Act 1906, the Prevention of Corruption Act 1916, Part 12 of the Anti-Terrorism, Crime, and Security Act 2001, the Proceeds of Crime Act 2002 and the common law offence of bribery. The core rationale for the UK law then in 1889, as today, is clear - namely to prevent corruption from enabling a public official to abuse his or her position, and to prevent a party from using corruption to obtain an advantage.

1.11.3. Proposed new 'bribery of foreign public officials' offence

As to bribery in respect of foreign public officials, the Law Commission proposed that, in order to obtain business, retain business, or obtain or retain a business advantage, the payer must give, offer or agree to give an advantage to or for any person, being an advantage to which the recipient or the intended recipient is not legitimately entitled, and the payer must do so and must intend to influence that person or another person in respect of any act or omission by that person or another person in his or her capacity as a foreign public official; or must realize that there is a serious risk that the advantage will influence that person or another person in respect of any act or omission by that person or another person in his or her capacity as a foreign public official; or must intend to influence a third party to use their influence over another person in respect of any act or omission by that person or another person in his or her capacity as a foreign public official. No account would be taken, in determining whether an advantage is "legitimately due", of the fact that the advantage may be customary, or perceived to be customary in the circumstances, or whether such payments are officially tolerated. It is proposed that the offence of bribing a foreign public official would only apply to the payer, i.e. that it would be targeted on the supply side.

Facilitation payments to domestic public officials that would involve a breach of legal or equitable duty would be prohibited, as they are now. Companies making facilitation payments could be prosecuted under the proposed bribery offence. All existing statutory and common law bribery offences will be abolished. The consent of the Director of Public Prosecutions or the Director of the Serious Fraud Office would be required for prosecutions of bribery under the proposed offence. Bribery of a foreign official is an offence which does *not* come under a Statute of Limitation in the UK.

> **Point to Note: OECD definition of 'foreign public official'**
>
> "*Foreign public official means any person holding a legislative, administrative or judicial office of a foreign country, whether appointed or elected; any person exercising a public function for a foreign country, including for a public agency or public enterprise; and any official or agent of a public international organisation*".

1.11.4. Defences to the proposed bribery offence

One defence would be that the advantage was reasonable in order to avoid what the payer reasonably believed to be an imminent danger of physical harm to him, herself, or another. The second defence would be that the payer reasonably believed that conferring the advantage was legally required. It will be up to the payer to prove that he or she reasonably believed this.

> **Points to Note: Environmental checklist for bribery**
>
> (i) Policies, training, and structures, put in place by top management to prevent bribery.
>
> (ii) Where a company does business is important. Check whether business is being transacted with country with low ratings on the Transparency International (TI) Corruption Perceptions Index and/or World Bank Governance Indicators list.

(iii) Check whether business is transacted within a high risk industry.

High risk industries are oil and gas producers; oil equipment, services, and distribution; chemicals; industrial metals; mining; construction and materials; aerospace and defence; and utilities.

(iv) Check whether company is involved with government contracts.

(v) Check whether company needs a licence for its business.

(vi) Check whether payments to/from the company are by cash.

(vi) Check whether payments are being made to a country other than the intermediary's country.

(viii) Check whether payments are made to personal and/or business residence.

(ix) Check out the company for lapses in normal business compliance procedures.

(x) Check whether company has due diligence procedures.

(xi) Check whether it appears that the company has a compliance culture in line with written procedure.

(xii) Check for strong financial control underpinning the compliance programme.

(xiii) Check for transparent and accountable controls on the delegation of authority.

(xiv) Check for third party payment controls.

1.11.5. Bribery offence committed by a company

As companies undergo greater globalisation, the extra-territorial reach of national economic regulation, particularly from the US, is increasingly impacting on life in the UK boardroom. For instance, BAE Systems is the subject of an anti-corruption probe by the US Department of Justice. The current fast-track extradition arrangements between the US and UK mean senior executives are at risk when doing transactional or banking business with the US.

1.12.1. Extradition of suspects

The Extradition Act 2003 ("EA 2003") came into force in January 2004. Under EA 2003, two categories of country are recognised: Category 1 countries are in Europe; and Category 2 countries consist of some EU countries and those outside the EU with which the UK has extradition arrangements. The United States is a Category 2 territory. Slightly different procedures and safeguards apply to the two categories. One of the main differences is that Category 2 countries must show *prima facie* evidence before a suspect is extradited from the UK. However, certain Category 2 countries, known as designated territories, are exempted from this evidential obligation. The US is one such designated territory. Other Category 2 countries which are exempt include Albania, Azerbaijan, Moldova and Serbia and Montenegro. Extradition to Category 1 countries no longer requires the *prima facie* evidence safeguard.

Therefore, exactly the same risks apply to British businessmen who have cross-border dealings in the EU as apply to those who have dealings in the US. Traditionally, those wanted for extradition from the UK used to enjoy the safeguard of "dual criminality", i.e. the relevant conduct had to be an offence in both the UK and the requesting State. It is now possible for suspects to be extradited to a Category 1 State under a European Arrest Warrant (EAW) for conduct which is considered to be a crime in the requesting state, but which is not a crime in the UK. Category 1 States can request extradition from the UK if they can satisfy a British court that the conduct in question falls into part of a "framework list" set out in Extradition Act 2003, Schedule 2, which is derived from the European Framework Decision of the Council of the European Union 2002/JHA on the EAW and the surrender procedures between Member States. Fraud is included in the list of extraditable offences, as are offences of racism, xenophobia, corruption, and "computer-related crime."

1.12.2. The long arm of the US law as regards extradition

The US Foreign Corrupt Practices Act 1977 (FCPA) was enacted in wake of investigations by the US Security Exchange Commission (SEC) which revealed that hundreds of US companies had paid bribes totalling more than $300 million to foreign government officials, politicians and political parties. All US citizens and firms, including foreign companies whose shares are quoted on the New York Stock Exchange (NYSE), are subject to the FCPA. Its anti-bribery provisions make it unlawful to bribe foreign officials to obtain or retain business. "Foreign official" includes any officer or employee of a foreign government or any person acting in an official capacity. Also included are foreign political parties, candidates for foreign political office and any intermediaries where it is known that the payments are destined for such officials. Later amendments by way of the US International Anti-bribery and Fair Competition Act 1998 brought the US into line with the OECD's Convention on Bribery to make it plain that it is a crime to make or offer payments to any foreign official to secure any improper advantage.

The United States' FCPA applies to all foreign people who commit an act in furtherance of a foreign bribe while in the US and include the acts of US businesses and nationals in furtherance of unlawful payments that take place wholly outside the US. A wire transfer passing through a US bank would be sufficient to found US jurisdiction.

1.12.3. Implications of extradition laws for global companies

The FCPA has three broad implications for US companies as well as any other public company listed on the NYSE. (1)Its anti-bribery provisions outlaw the making of illicit payments to foreign officials for commercial benefit. (2)Its accounting provisions require public companies to make and keep books and records that accurately reflect the transactions of the corporation and put in place strict accounting controls aimed at uncovering and deterring corruption. (3)The company itself as well as employees, is at risk of prosecution for infringement of the FCPA's provisions anywhere in the world. Recently the US attorney general has announced that to give greater pause to the management of organisations, for every case brought against a corporation there will be a parallel case brought against individuals. No doubt it is hoped that the jailing of individuals will bring the message home.

1.13.1. UK adopted UN Corruption Convention

In the year 2003, the United Kingdom adopted the United Nations Convention against Corruption. This Convention includes measures to prevent corruption; criminalises corruption; provides for international cooperation in prosecution and asset recovery. However, there have been few UK prosecutions for corruption. Overall, in all countries, the level of enforcement is low and outside the twenty countries that are signatories to this Convention, there is little or no anti-corruption enforcement (see http:www.transparency.org for a report that gives statistics on prosecutions)

The difficulty in proving corruption is the complex paper trail, the main feature of such an investigation. International standards and agreements help to prohibit corruption. There is an obvious reluctance on the part of domestic investigative agencies to investigate any party other than a foreign party, the reason being, the realities of commerce, because many business people still view bribes as "commission payments" necessary for commerce in some parts of the world. Such persons see anti-bribery regulation as harmful to national business interests.

The UK has recently signed up to various international obligations in its effort to combat financial crime. The UK is a member of the Financial Action Task Force (FATF). The EU Anti-Money Laundering (AML) Directives have a direct impact on both the investigation of financial crime and the legislative framework. The political furore caused by the decision of the director of the Serious Fraud Office (SFO) to abandon an investigation into alleged corruption involving British Aerospace (BAE) and Saudi Arabia has brought into focus the potential conflict between the UK national interest and its international criminal law commitments.

1.13.2. Defining Corrupt Acts

The definition of a corrupt act in statute and at common law is wide. The 1889 Public Bodies Corrupt Practices Act ("PBCPA") section 1, makes it an offence to corruptly make or receive a payment, the purpose of which is to act as an inducement or reward for any member, officer or servant of a public body, doing or forbearing to do anything in respect of any matter or transaction in which the public body is concerned. The 1906 Prevention of Corruption Acts ("PCA"), section 1 created the offence of corruptly paying or accepting a bribe to or as an agent. In both the statutory offences and under common law 'corruptly' does not mean dishonestly but, rather, purposely doing an act that the law forbids as tending to corrupt.

With the exception of the passing of the Honours (Prevention of Abuses) Act 1925, introduced to deal with the specific problem of the sale of peerages, for most of the remainder of the 20th century the statute law relating to corruption did not alter. Jurisdiction was territorial and, under both Acts, corruption could be prosecuted only if the offence had taken place in the UK and only with the consent of the Attorney General.

1.13.3. Legislation that assists prosecution of corruption

Two relatively recent Acts have significantly extended the jurisdiction of the English criminal courts to prosecute corruption offences, namely the Criminal Law Act 1977 (CLA 1977) as amended by the Criminal Justice (Terrorism and Conspiracy) Act 1998 (CJ(TC)A 1998) and the Anti-Terrorism, Crime and Security Act 2001 (ACSA 2001). CJ (TC) A 1998 inserted a new section into CLA 1977. Under s 1A, conspiracies to corrupt people overseas are triable under English criminal law provided certain conditions are satisfied and there is a sufficient connection with the UK. There will be sufficient connection with the UK if a party does something in the UK in relation to the conspiracy before its formation, or a party joins the conspiracy in the UK, or the party does or omits to do anything in the UK as part of the conspiracy. In addition, ACSA 2001, s 109 specifically gives extra-territorial effect to corruption offences and applies if any UK national or UK company does anything in a country or territory outside the UK that would, if done in the UK, constitute an offence at common law or under PBCPA 1889 or PCA 1906. While CJ (TC) A 1998 was driven by the government's attempt to remedy perceived deficiencies in the criminal law against overseas terrorism, the ACSA 2001 was a specific legislative response to the coming into force of the Organisation for Economic Co-operation and Development (OECD) Anti-Bribery Convention (the Convention) on 15 February 1999.

The Convention has 36 signatories, and Article 5 forbids any State, when investigating allegations of corruption, from taking into account considerations of the national economic interest, the potential effect upon relations with another State, or the identity of the natural or legal persons involved.

1.13.4. Corruption by company and personnel

Both the officer and the company may be charged with and convicted with the offence of corruption. English law does not even require that the officer acted with intent to benefit the company. English law makes no distinction in terms of liability between the various types of company. All are liable. Private sector companies are liable whether they are formed with a view to commercial activities or not. State corporations are also liable. Whether a corporation has limited liability or not makes no difference to the applicability of corporate criminal liability or the amount of penalty, which may be imposed. In reality though, corporations are not prosecuted for fraud, but directors of those companies are prosecuted instead.

The Higgs Report constitutes the latest review of governance standards for UK corporations. It recommended changes to the Combined Code for Companies, but these have not yet been implemented.

1.13.5. Prevention of Corruption Procedures

(i)   Corruption Control Policy

Have in place corruption prevention strategies, policies, procedures and systems to minimise corruption. Those policies, procedures and systems must respond, and be proportionate, to the corruption risks faced by the organisation.

(ii)   Responsibility Structures

There is clear accountability and responsibility for implementation and monitoring of any corruption prevention strategies. This accountability must be made known to staff. The responsibility for the prevention of corruption rests with senior management.

(iii)   Corruption Risk Assessment

Corruption risk assessments must be undertaken as required. The corruption risk

Assessments quantify the level, nature and form of the risks to be managed. Actions must be taken by the department to mitigate the risks identified in the corruption risk assessments.

(iv)   Employee Awareness

Employees must have access to the corruption prevention policies so they understand the ethical behaviour required of them in the workplace. Training programs in ethical behaviour are must be provided by the department. The training will deal with the corruption risks faced by individuals in their workplaces. Every employee has a responsibility to contribute to eliminating corruption

(v) Customer, Community & Supplier Awareness

Customers, the community and suppliers must understand that corrupt dealings/transactions are not acceptable.

(vi) Notification Systems

Policies, systems and procedures in place must encourage reporting of suspected wrongdoing. Corruption notification systems give the complainant the opportunity to report the suspected wrongdoing anonymously. Policies, systems and procedures must give equal opportunities to managers, staff, students, contractors, consultants, customers and suppliers to notify the organisation of suspected wrongdoing.

(vii) Detection Systems

Data is to be monitored and reviewed to ensure that irregularities and warning signals are picked up at an early stage and flagged for further review. Regular internal audits/reviews will examine samples of medium and high-risk decision-making. An established Audit & Risk Management Committee will make decisions based on risk about key systems and decisions to be audited with outcomes reported to the Audit & Risk Management Committee at regular intervals.

(viii) External Notification Systems

Policies clearly identify the nature of suspected wrongdoings and must require reporting to the police or to other appropriate external agencies.

(ix) Investigation Systems

Investigations undertaken are to be consistent with widely used and recognised investigation standards. Where appropriate expertise is not available internally, external assistance is to be sought. Procedures and other appropriate support (including training where required) are to be provided to staff undertaking investigations.

(ix) Conduct & Disciplinary Systems

All employees are to be given information so that they understand that corruption will not be tolerated and that perpetrators will face disciplinary action. Employees must have access to written information to assist them to understand their ethical obligations.

1.13.6.1. Police corruption and prevention safeguards

The Home Office is like any other large organisation and corruption raises its head, even here. There have been a few recent instances of police corruption in England and Wales. To prevent police corruption, ACPO had set out its strategies to prevent corruption. The ACPO strategy is a dynamic process and will be continuously refined as knowledge and understanding increases. It will identify and develop good practice for the benefit of Chief Constables and is designed to enable both corruptors and those vulnerable to corruption to be identified and confronted.

ACPO aims to prevent corruption by promoting knowledge and understanding; using intelligence to prevent corruption; to detect corruption and mutual assistance between forces. An understanding of corruption, its motivation, processes and areas of vulnerability is essential to its prevention. The issues are complex and have been subject of considerable study throughout the world. The ACPO strategy will ensure Chief Officers have a sophisticated understanding of corruption and are aware of the benefits of training for all police officers and employees. This search for knowledge will go beyond corruption and include issues relevant to ethics, integrity and the maintenance of standards.

1.13.6.2. Opportunist instances for Police corruption

The opportunities for corruption within the Police Service are many and are increased when policies, processes, procedures, supervision and leadership are weak. It is self evident that many of the weaknesses can be identified and good practice suggested minimising the dangers. Experience has demonstrated the key role of intelligence in any strategy. Recent investigations have shown that on almost every occasion corruption is, by its very nature, a *secret* process that is mutually beneficial to both corruptor and corrupted. Invariably a known criminal plays an active role. On rare occasions when there is no benefit to the criminal he/she is not in a position to make a public complaint. There is also evidence that frequently colleagues of a corrupt officer suspect his/her activity.

Using ACPO's best practice in the use of existing police intelligence systems, it is hoped that this will detect areas of possible corruption and produce intelligence-led solutions where corruption is identified. The investigation of acts of police corruption is difficult, not least because the possible suspect may be trained in methods of surveillance and detection. Added to that are high levels of probability that the evidence of colleagues or criminals may be necessary to bring charges.

1.13.6.3. Method of apprehending corrupt officers

A covert and proactive approach has proved to be one effective method. Organised criminals do not recognise police boundaries, neither do corrupt police officers. Corruption enquiries are resource intensive and sometimes require specialist skills not readily available to all forces. Frequently there is difficulty in using a covert response as those charged with the investigation will be known to the suspect. There is a need for the concept of mutual assistance to be used in the investigation of suspected offences of corruption. The vast majority of police officers and support personnel act with honesty and integrity. When properly informed they will challenge corruption and support prevention policies which can only enhance their professional reputations.

1.13.6.4. Cost of police corruption

The cost of police corruption is considerable. It can prevent successful prosecutions, result in wrongful convictions and render police operations ineffective. Police corruption can grow under the influence of one corrupt police officer who remains unrecognised or unchallenged and infects whole work groups. The financial penalties to any Police Force can be massive. Failure to deal with corruption effectively will erode trust in the Police Services of England and Wales and allow criminality to flourish within and outside Police Forces. Community based policing can be infected if there is police corruption as community based policing involves police at all levels of the community. If corruption infects the community policing system, it will ultimately result in breach of trust, the opposite goal to that intended by community policing.

1.14.1. How the international anti-fraud body FATF rates UK fraud

The FATF, an international anti-fraud agency, provides technical assistance and expertise to those countries which need help to improve their national procedures and measures in order to bring them in line with agreed standards. The Financial Action Task Force sets international standards to combat money laundering and financing terrorism. The FATF has 40 Recommendations and 9 Special Recommendations on the Financing of Terrorism. These are not Treaty-based, but they have been endorsed by 175 national jurisdictions worldwide and represent the global reference for the prevention of money -laundering.

Since 1980, the FATF has worked to combat money laundering as a major threat to the rule of law.(You will come across the work of the FATF again in Chapter 7). Taking as a first stage the criminal fraud of money laundering, a look at the FATF 2007 Report on UK reveals the very urgent need to vigorously investigate and prosecute fraud in the UK. Money laundering is the processing of criminal proceeds in order to disguise their illegal origin. To stop money laundering is directly to stop future criminal activity from affecting legitimate economic activities. Money laundering provides organised crime with cash flow and capital, and it is an incentive to commit new criminal acts.

1.14.2. Black -list of Money-Laundering countries

The FATF has compiled a list of countries which are not co-operative (NCCT's) and it publishes and maintains this list in its detailed and public annual report. (See its web page at http://www.fatf-gafi.org). The FATF puts countries on this list if they fail through inadequate or no supervision of offshore banking, if they have strict bank secrecy laws, if they have no suspicious transaction reporting system, if they have no requirement that the effective owners of companies be identified and an absence of mutual legal assistance provision.

1.14.3. Recent Conventions to combat money laundering fraud

The UK has adopted two other Conventions since the New York terrorist outrage of 11 September 2001. These are:-the 2005 Council of Europe Convention on the Prevention of Terrorism and the 2005 Council of Europe Convention on Laundering, Search, Seizure and Confiscation of the Proceeds from Crime and the Financing of Terrorism.

1.14.4. UK has some poor anti-money laundering procedures- OECD Report

According to the OECD Report on UK money laundering crime, UK authorities should make more direct obligations to obtain information on the intended purpose and nature of the business relationship, to specify the procedures for on-going due diligence in compliance with the FATF Recommendations. The OECD must require that financial institutions maintain documents and other data up-to-date and relevant by undertaking more regular reviews; implement enforceable obligations regarding politically exposed persons while correspondent banking rules are generally compliant as regards FATF; implement enforceable requirements (regarding introduced business) that the financial institutions be satisfied that the introducer will make ID and other relevant documentation available upon request. Note that recently implemented UK Money Laundering Regulations 2007 do not require that financial institutions satisfy themselves that the third party is regulated and supervised (in accordance with FATF Recommendations 23, 24 and 29).

The UK does, however, have a reasonably comprehensive legal structure to combat money laundering. This money laundering offence, though, is broad, as it tried to cover the elements of the Vienna and Palermo Convention. The Palermo Convention 2000, named the United Nations Convention against Transnational Organized Crime, is a convention against transnational organized crime. It has two protocols, namely: Protocol to Prevent, Suppress and Punish Trafficking in Persons, especially Women and Children; and Protocol against the Smuggling of Migrants by Land, Sea and Air.

The Vienna Convention on the Law of Treaties (VCLT) 1969 codified the pre-existing customary international law on treaties and entered into force in 1980. The VCLT has been ratified by 108 states as at May 2007.

1.14.5. OECD criticism of poor financial crime reporting in the UK

The report criticises the UK for not releasing public reports on statistics, typologies and trends, as well as information regarding its Financial Investigating Unit's activities in a manner required by the FATF standards. It states that the UK must increase its FIU staff, especially its analytical staff, in line with the objective set out in the SARs ("Lander") review.

1.15. Organised Crime

The FATF estimated that the total quantified organised crime market in the UK is worth about £15 billion per year, as follows: drugs (50%); excise fraud (25%); fraud (12%); counterfeiting (7%); organised immigration crime (6%). The following typologies are currently those of most concern to UK law enforcement:

(i) cash/value couriering;

(ii) abuse of gatekeepers;

(iii) abuse of money transmission agents (including 'Hawala' and other alternative remittance systems);

(iv) cash- rich businesses;

(v) front-companies;

(vi) high- value assets and property;

(vii) abuse of bank accounts and

(viii) over-the-counter financial sector products.

1.16. The proceeds of crime

Estimated total recoverable criminal assets per annum are £4.75 billion, of which it is estimated that £ 2.75 billion is sent overseas. Cash remains the mainstay of most serious organised criminal activity in the UK. The introduction of the Proceeds of Crime Act 2002 (POCA) has had a positive impact on the UK's ability to restrain, confiscate and recover proceeds of crime and the UK's FIU appears to be a generally effective .FIU measures for domestic and international cooperation are generally comprehensive but there is a very high threat to the UK from serious organised crime and contingent money laundering.

1.17. Conclusion to Chapter One

The simple and general statutory offence of fraud targets the nature of fraudulent behaviour rather than particular instances of such behaviour. The intention of the Government initially, was to abolish the common law offence of 'conspiracy to defraud' when the fraud offence was first introduced in the Fraud Bill 2006. However, the Government's consultation produced strong support for its retention, at least until January 2010, by which time it will be seen how effective the Fraud Act is. Fraud is a moving target and there are new methods, techniques and vehicles for fraud being identified by the authorities every day. Fraud may appear to be discreet and non-violent but this criminal activity is a direct threat to the values of democracy, human rights and the rule of law. It constitutes social harm.

Society has an interest in protecting people and things. Social harm, i.e. the negation, endangering or destruction of an individual, group or state interest deemed socially valuable, is what fraud is.

Further Reading- Chapter 1

D. Leigh, "Law lords: fraud office right to end bribery investigation in BAE case
Reversal of earlier ruling brings condemnation from anti-corruption campaigners", The Guardian, 31 July 2008.

Association of Police Officers, "Oversight and Scrutiny of Professional Standards Matters", 25/06/2007

Association of Police Officers," Enhancing Accountability", 20/09/2006

M. Levi and J. Burrows, "Measuring the Impact of Fraud in the UK", British Journal of Criminology, May 2008; 48: 293 - 318.

CHAPTER 2-
AN ANALYSIS OF THE FRAUD ACT 2006

2.1.1. Introduction

Until the 2006 Fraud Act was introduced, English criminal law did not include a statutory offence of 'fraud' or a specific definition of that term. Instead, a series of separate offences (e.g., obtaining property by deception, obtaining a money transfer by deception, obtaining a pecuniary advantage by deception, procuring the execution of a valuable security by deception, obtaining services by deception and evasion of liability by deception) sought to cover the same ground. This Diaspora of highly specific offences gave rise to a number of difficulties in practice. In particular, conduct which would generally be regarded as dishonest or fraudulent might not fit neatly into one of the specific offences. This very detailed legislative approach also tended to promote defences of a highly technical nature.

The 2006 Fraud Act was passed in order to simplify the law and to enhance the prospects of successful prosecutions in future fraud cases. It does not over-ride all other statutes that could be used to prosecute fraud, but sits alongside them, only repealing certain sections, (see Schedule 3 Fraud Act), mainly of the Theft Acts 1968 and 1978 ,that conflict with its meaning.

2.1.2. The offences in the 2006 Fraud Act

The 2006 Fraud Act seeks to classify fraud into three general categories. First of all, it creates an offence of 'positive' fraud, i.e., where the defendant makes a statement designed to make a gain or to cause a loss. Secondly, a 'negative' fraud offence is created, which criminalizes the deliberate withholding of information with a view to securing a gain or inflicting a loss. The Act also creates an 'abuse of position' fraud which affects those who seek to take advantage of a position of trust or confidence.

2.2.1. (FA 2006 s2) Section 2 Fraud Act- Fraud by false representation

The elements of the offence are that the Defendant: (i) made (ii) a false representation (iii) dishonestly (iv) knowing that the representation was or might be untrue or misleading (v) with intent to make a gain for himself or another, to cause loss to another or to expose another to risk of loss. The offence is complete as soon as the Defendant makes a false representation, provided that it is made with the necessary dishonest intent.

Fraud differs from Theft Act deception offences in that it is immaterial whether or not anyone is aware of the representation, deceived or any property actually gained or lost. Section 2(2) (a) states that a representation may be false by either being 'untrue' or 'misleading'. Examples of false representation offences are: false representation on mortgage application forms, loan application forms, life insurance forms or company directors' indemnity insurance forms.

> **Points to Note: Directors Liability Insurance does not cover criminal fines**
>
> Companies Act (CA) 2006 sections 232 to 238 enables companies to provide insurance and indemnity to directors of the company and any associated company. The Companies Act 2006 section 235 permits companies to provide qualifying pension scheme indemnities which indemnify directors of a company that is a trustee of an occupational pension scheme against liability incurred in connection with the company's activities as trustee to the scheme. But neither indemnity can be provided to cover criminal fines, regulatory penalties or costs incurred by the director in defending criminal proceedings in which he is convicted. But the qualifying pension scheme indemnity will enable a company to indemnify a director in respect of liability incurred by that director to the company. Companies Act 2006 section 206 allows funds to be advanced to a company director to meet the defence costs of any regulatory investigation or action and there is no requirement to repay advances for defending regulatory proceedings.

Such false representation may be *'express'* or *'implied'* (Section 2 (4)). It can be stated in words or communicated by conduct. There is no limitation on the way in which the representation must be expressed. It could be written, spoken, posted on a 'phishing' website, spoken into a Dictaphone or sent by email.

For example, a representation is implied by conduct when a person uses a credit card dishonestly. By tendering the card, he is falsely representing that he has the authority to use it for that transaction. A representation can be made through body language - a nod of the head, presence in a restricted area implying the right to be there (including presence within a secure computer system) or being dressed or wearing identification that implies a certain status or right to be present. A representation can be about identity - using a false identity to open a bank account.

A false representation may be made in the art world. An example of this would be when the Defendant who sells works of art, tells a customer that he has a Matisse painting for sale, when in fact it is not a real Matisse painting. There is always a risk that the paintings in the Defendant's shop which are displayed as originals might not be so. Many competent art dealers will acknowledge that there is always a risk that a painting might be a forgery. The dealer, who actually thinks that a painting he is selling to a customer might be a forgery but sells it as an original, acts dishonestly. A reputable art dealer would have followed some sort of procedure to ascertain whether the painting is an original. There would be other indications of his knowledge as to this fact, such as the purchase price, the place of purchase, the name of the person he bought it from, the date he bought it, the insurance he took out to protect it, his shop security systems, etc. If these things are not satisfactory, then it can be said that the art dealer had shut his eyes to an obvious means of knowledge, as in the case *Westminster City Council v Croyalgrange Ltd*.

Caselaw

Westminster City Council v Croyalgrange Ltd [1986] 83 Cr. App. R 155 at 164. HL

The House of Lords, in their decision, said: "*It is always open to the tribunal of fact, when knowledge on the part of a defendant is required to be proved, to base a finding of knowledge on evidence that the Defendant had deliberately shut his eyes to the obvious or refrained from inquiry because he suspected the truth but did not want to have his suspicion confirmed.*"

Other relevant caselaw to false representation show the variety of circumstances in which this offence occurs.

Caselaw

Taylor v Hamer [2002] EWCA Civ. 1130

The buyer had carried out a physical inspection of the property, in order to discover all that the buyer could about the property before committing to a purchase. On inspecting the property the buyer noticed some old flagstone paving in the garden. However, after the buyer had inspected the property, but before the exchange of contracts, the seller had the flagstones lifted and moved to a new property, covering the area with grass seeds. principle of caveat emptor because she had intentionally made a material alteration to the property and then had attempted to conceal this alteration from the potential buyer of the property; the seller was also found to have lied about the flagstones being present at the property during some part of the transaction The principle of *caveat emptor* had no application in this case as the buyer had been induced to enter into the contract by fraud. The seller was ordered to replace the flagstones at the property or pay to the buyer in damages a sum equivalent to the cost of doing so.

> **Caselaw**
>
> *R v Ghosh* [1982] QB 1053
>
> The defendant was a consultant at a hospital. He falsely claimed fees in respect of an operation that he had not carried out. He claimed that he thought he was not dishonest by his standards because the same amount of money was legitimately payable to him for consultation fees. The defendant's conviction under s15 was affirmed by the Court of Appeal.
>
> On the basis of the court's decision, the jury, applying their own standards, must judge the defendant's actions and beliefs and decide whether he was honest or dishonest. If the jury find that according to their standards he was dishonest, they must then establish whether the defendant knew that ordinary people would regard such conduct as dishonest. This judgment set a two-stage test. The first question is whether a defendant's behaviour would be regarded as dishonest by the ordinary standards of reasonable and honest people. If answered positively, the second question is whether the defendant was aware that his conduct was dishonest and would be regarded as dishonest by reasonable and honest people. This is the test of dishonesty in the Fraud Act 2006.

A false representation can be made by omission - for example, a defendant who omitted to mention previous convictions or County Court Judgments on a job application form. That Defendant would be representing himself as being of good character or financial probity when the opposite was the case. There is a potential for the offence to be complete when the Defendant failed to correct a false impression after a change in circumstances from the original representation, if the representation may be regarded as a continuing series of representations.

A representation can be made to a machine (Section 2 (5)), for example, where a person enters a number into a 'CHIP and PIN 'machine or a bank 'ATM'. Providing false credit card details to the voice activated software on the cinema telephone line is the same as providing false credit card details to the man who works in the ticket office. Similarly, providing false credit card details to a supermarket website to obtain groceries is the same as giving false details to the assistant at the till.

It is of no relevance at all whether the false representation is believed or has any affect whatsoever on any recipient. However, evidence will be necessary to prove that the defendant communicated the false representation to a person or submitted it to a machine. Conduct short of that may be an 'attempt'. In most cases the fact that the false representation was communicated will be demonstrated by its appearance on a computer screen, its effect on the recipient or the system to which it was submitted. In some cases it will not be necessary to call evidence from a victim. Section 2 (2) defines the meaning of "false" and Section 2 (3) defines the meaning of "representation".

2.2.2. (FA 2006 s2) Definition of 'false'

A representation is defined as 'false' if it is untrue or misleading and the person making it knows that it is, or might be, untrue or misleading. The words 'might be' do not import recklessness. Actual knowledge that the representation might be untrue is required - not awareness of a risk that it might be untrue.

> **Point to Note: Knowledge is a requirement of the offence**
>
> Knowledge is a strict *mens rea* requirement. It is much stricter than 'belief', 'suspicion', or 'having reasonable grounds to suspect'. It is stricter than 'recklessness'.
>
> Therefore it may require proof of knowledge as to existing facts but it is sufficient to prove that the Defendant knew that the representation might be false. Proving only that the Defendant knew that the representation might be untrue or misleading is all that is required when the allegation involves representations as to states of mind of those other than the accused. The Defendant cannot easily be shown to know the state of another person's mind but he can be shown to know what it might be. So it is sufficient to show that the Defendant knew that his representation might be false.

> **Caselaw**: *R v Montila*
>
> The House of Lords in *Montila* said
> *"A person may have reasonable grounds to suspect that property is one thing (A) when in fact it is something different (B). But that is not so when the question is what a person knows. A person cannot know that something is A when in fact it is B. The proposition that a person knows that something is A is based on the premise that it is true that it is A. The fact that the property is A provides the starting point. Then there is the question whether the person knows that the property is A."*

2.2.3. (FA 2006 s2) Definition of 'representation'

A 'representation' means any representation as to fact or law, including a representation as to the state of mind of the person making the representation or any other person (Section 2 (3)). An example of the latter might be where a defendant claims that a third party intends to carry out a certain course of action - perhaps to make a will in someone's favour. It may be difficult to prove to the necessary standard that the Defendant knew the state of mind of a third party, but easier to prove that he knew what it might be.

2.2.4. (FA 2006 s2) – 'Phishing' as false representation

False representation frauds include crimes taking place as a result of the use of computer technologies e.g. 'Phishing'. The activity of 'phishing' is the practice of sending requests which falsely claim to originate from banks, for instance, asking customers to re-register or re-activate their accounts at a replica bank website, with the aim of using the information provided to transfer money out of these accounts. This offence will be committed not only when the Defendant knows that his representation is false or misleading, but when he is aware that it might be.

2.2.5.1. (FA 2006 s2) False representation in property transactions

Fraud by false representation will be of particular relevance for the property industry when buying and selling property, or when entering into leases, or financial transactions secured against property. The new rules impact upon all elements of a transaction, from answering replies to pre-contract enquiries to giving warranties and disclosing against those warranties.

The Fraud Act has an impact on liability for replies to contract inquiries.

This type of fraud will be committed when a person dishonestly makes a false representation to another, to benefit himself or herself or another person. When it comes to pre-contract enquiries and contracts, a seller needs to be careful, since, if the seller makes a false representation, which has the relevant intention attached to it, the seller may be guilty of fraud, even if the relevant contract be that for sale, or to grant a lease or otherwise has not yet been entered into.

2.2.5.2. Statutory HIP Home-buyers Pack prohibits false representation

The well-known principle of law, *caveat emptor* (let the buyer beware); means that a seller of property is not obliged to disclose anything about the state of the property being sold to the buyer, even if specifically asked to do so. The obligation rests with the buyer of the property to find out all they want to know about the property before committing to buy. There are a number of ways for a buyer to acquire this information, such as raising pre-contract enquiries and carrying out a physical inspection of the property. The statutory disclosure regime in force since December 2007 helps to combat false representation.

The law is to be found in Statutory Instrument 2006 No. 1503, The Home Information Pack Regulations 2006. The new statutory HIP disclosure means that every home for sale must have a Home Information Pack of valuable information such as a sale statement, local searches, evidence of title and an Energy Performance Certificate that contains advice on CO_2 emissions and fuel bills. The principle of *caveat emptor* has no application where the buyer has been induced to enter the contract by fraud.

2.2.5. 1. (FA 2006 s2) False representation fraud by market manipulation

Investor compensation for fraud has primarily to rely upon the tort of deceit. In its nature, deceit involves fraudulent representations and statements. Market manipulation comes to mind and occurs when an investor is induced to purchase a large stake in a company by reason of a false representation about its operations and financial affairs. By and by, the investments are found to be worth less than expected when the true state of affairs comes to light. In the securities market, manipulators might issue baselessly optimistic comments on internet chat rooms about the financial or operational health of the issuer to ratchet up the traded price of a stock.

2.2.5.2. There is no defence in marketing puffery.

Note that a defence cannot be made out that the false representation is mere marketing puff. Puffery refers to promotional statements and claims that express *subjective* rather than *objective* views, such that no reasonable person would take literally. All advertising regulation, both by government and self-regulation by business, imposes limitations on what, where, and how different products can be advertised, and the types of claims that can be made. In any case, dishonesty in advertising would fall under the Unfair Contracts Terms Act 1977 (amended in 2003) and is investigated and prosecuted by the Trading Standards Agency. Alternatively the company itself might, in response to a developing scandal, issue false statements to maintain the trading price of its stock. In such instances, it is conceivable that investors who have bought at a higher price can claim that a fraud was perpetrated on them. One thus needs to have evidence to show that the maker of the statement was consciously aware that the statement was untrue when it was made.

> **Caselaw**
>
> *Derry and others v Peek* 1886-90) All ER Rep 1
> To sustain an action of deceit there must be proof of fraud and nothing short of that will suffice, said the House of Lords. Fraud is proved when it is shown that a false representation has been made knowingly, or without belief in its truth, recklessly, not caring whether it is true or false. Lord Herschell said: "*I think it is important that it should be borne in mind that the common law action of deceit differs essentially from an action brought to obtain rescission of a contract on the ground of misrepresentation of a material fact*"

2.2.6. (FA 2006 s2) False representation in business investments

Directors may be sued for inaccurate statements. Directors are liable for negligent statements found in the company prospectus. In the context of accounting manipulation where there might be room for differential treatment of earnings recognition, investors cannot claim that a fraud was perpetrated on them because, even when there is an earnings restatement demanded by an auditor, the matter is one of professional misjudgement. At its narrowest, a misleading disclosure for compliance purposes is not addressed to investors even though the company may be aware that investors might rely on it.

However, if an auditor recklessly does not discover fraud the auditor can be held liable, as in the latest case in June 2008.

> ### Case Study: Company cannot sue itself for fraud committed by a director
>
> A man S set up a one-man limited company and is the only director.
>
> He borrowed money from a bank on behalf of the company. The company failed, owing the bank money. The company sued its own auditors for failing to detect and report that fraud.
>
> The Court of Appeal held that it could not. It could not rely on its own fraud.
>
> The bank made a claim against the company for all the money loaned to the company due to fraudulent statements made to the bank by the director and succeeded.
>
> The company then went into liquidation and liquidators claimed against the auditors.
>
> There is an established principle that knowledge of a director's fraud committed against a company of which he or she is director is not attributed to that company (the Hampshire Land principle). This is because the company is the primary victim of the fraud.
>
> But in this particular case, the company was *not* the primary victim of the fraud. The bank was the victim. So the fraud of the director could be attributed to the company which was, in reality the perpetrator of the fraud. In bringing a claim against the auditors, the company had to rely on its own illegal act and was unsuccessful.

2.2.7. (FA 2006 s2) False representations in the stock market

Unless a court finds that the maker of the statement intends also to address the plaintiffs, market players who rely on the disclosure will not have a claim. Others who rely on the integrity of the price formation process of the public markets will have even more difficulty lodging a claim. Amongst these will be the holder of convertible securities who, by reason of the artificially inflated prices, receives fewer shares under the conversion formula than if the prices had not been manipulated. The false representation offence protects persons to whom fraudulent statements are addressed. And the claimant has to demonstrate that he has acted upon the misrepresentation or was going to act on it. The practical implication is that investors who transacted at the manipulated prices are only able to claim if they knew of the statement and acted upon it. For those who merely relied on the integrity of the price formation process without more, their claims would fail by reason of the lack of specific reliance. One does not have a claim merely because of the price distortion produced by the manipulation; one needs to show that one has relied on the statements or acts that generated the price distortion. It targets purposeful transmission of fraudulent messages. Conduct, in its nature, tends to be more ambiguous in the message it conveys.

2.2.8. (FA 2006 s2) False representation in bidding up a share price

Take the instance of one bidding up the price of a stock. Is any message intended? Is it not possible to argue that the message is merely incidental to the conduct? In other words, at issue is first the fundamental question of whether there is a representation, and secondly, whether the injured party is an intended recipient of the message. In theory, it is possible to characterise conduct as a representation; however, pinning market manipulative conduct down as a false representation is probably practicable only where the message conveyed is clear in its context.

2.2.9. (FA 2006 s2) False representation in a 'market squeeze'

A 'market squeeze' or 'corner' is 'market abuse' by reason of one's cornering the supply of the commodity and such market manipulative conduct is, from a conceptual perspective outside the realm of misrepresentation. See caselaw *Aldrich v Norwich Union Life Insurance Co Ltd* [1998] CLC 1621 .The requirement for specific reliance establishes the chain of causation between the wrong perpetrated and the damage suffered. Securities pricing is determined by information, whether this be information concerns the issuer of the securities, or information relating to risks attaching to the income stream expected from the security. The case for prohibiting market manipulative statements is very obvious and a fraud prosecution in this area is awaited.

Caselaw

Aldrich v Norwich Union Life Insurance Co Ltd [1998] CLC 1621

Although the regulatory rules against manipulation in the U.K. have moved steadily toward formulations that ease the burdens of prosecution, the drive toward stronger regulatory protections against market manipulation does not yet translate into more robust private rights of action. In this case breach of UK Financial Services Act s 47 was held not to have an impact upon contractual obligations.

An investor injured by a market squeeze has little recourse. Similarly an investor prejudiced by the distorted price generated from a large buy order at the close of trading could do nothing about it until now. The fraud offence can be used in this case. Before the Fraud Act, this behaviour could not be prosecuted by the law on conspiracy to defraud unless there was more than one party involved in the manipulative scheme.

> **Caselaw**
>
> *R v Berenger* (1814) 3 M & S 67, 105 ER 536
>
> This was a case of criminal conspiracy. This is the earliest successful market manipulation prosecution in England. De Berenger's told blatant lies relating to Napoleon Bonaparte's death and the allies' conquest of Paris, calculated to Berenger was charged along with other members of the British aristocracy who participated in the scheme. The crime in *R v de Berenger* was conspiracy to defraud. The significance of the case lay in the prosecution not having to allege that particular purchasers had suffered loss as a result of the actions. The ratio of *R v de Berenger* consists of the holding that the criminal conspiracy is constituted by the use of wrongful means for a wrongful purpose. Here, the wrongful means is located in the false rumours, and the wrongful purpose in the creation of an inflated value of the government security.

2.2.10. (FA 2006 s2) Company Statements as false Representations

A director is liable to all persons who shall subscribe for securities on the faith of his prospectus or notice inviting subscriptions for such securities for the loss or damage they may have sustained by reason of any untrue statement in the prospectus or notice.

2.2.11. (FA 2006 s2) Fraudulent uses of stolen identity

Identity theft is unassuming in its range of fraud because by stealing an identity a sole trader or partnership can use it for: false advertising; false billing; forgery; embezzlement; false insurance claims; and internet securities fraud. On the internet, equipped with such identity, it would be easy to reveal and to identify the name and address of the primary mail server, back-up mail server, its host or external provider such as 'blueyonder.co.uk'.

Mining the internet further gives such fraudsters the multiple IP addresses and name aliases for one single server, and digging into this would reveal aliases for the bigger servers such as Microsoft, and then looking for weaknesses here will give the sole trader a list of absolutely all the information of all named hosts, sub-zones and associated Internet Provider addresses. So, just one identity theft can lead to the identity theft of thousands, using the internet as an article that equips the fraudster.

2.2.12 (FA 2006 s2) Consequences for victims

The 'fraud by false representation' offence may have consequences for borrowers seeking to raise loan facilities from their banks, and for the individuals involved in those negotiations. Some typical situations may help to illustrate the point. In order for a company to draw funds under a standard loan agreement, the borrower will be required to confirm that it is not in default in respect of any of its other borrowing arrangements (essentially a question of **fact**); that no official consents are required in order to enable it to perform its obligations under the loan agreement (essentially a question of **law**); and that there has been no material adverse change in its financial position since the date of its most recent audited financial statements (essentially a question of **opinion**).

The borrower company and the officers in charge of the negotiations on its behalf may commit the "fraud by false representation" offence if to their knowledge, any of these statements are, *or might be*, untrue and the statements are made dishonestly with a view to ensuring the drawdown of the loan. So the existence of dishonesty involves a partly objective and a partly subjective test. But it may well be possible to prove dishonesty in such a case; it would be objectively dishonest to obtain funds from a bank in this way, and those working in the borrower's treasury or finance function would be aware of that fact.

2.2.13. (FA 2006 s2) Insurance frauds by false representation

Sole traders are renowned for committing insurance fraud when the going gets tough. There is at present no immunity for whistle blowers in the United Kingdom who report that a sole trader is attempting to commit an insurance fraud. Insurance fraud is colluded with in many sectors of industry such as road accident repair sector and personal injury sector. There are no set rules for authorised agencies, which investigate insurance fraud but an ad-hoc set of individual provisions made by certain insurance companies who share information.

> **Points to Note: Lacking formal insurance claims Protocol**
>
> Were there an authorised agency in place they could have a set list of information required for disclosure such as the history of previous claims made by the insured; policy information relevant to the fraud under investigation; statement of proof of loss; policy payment records. There could be automatic sharing of insurance data with fraud investigating agencies with automatic right to receive information and immunity to anyone who reports suspected insurance fraud provided it was without malice, provided none of this information gets into the public domain unless after criminal proceedings.

2.2.14. (FA 2006 s2) Banking frauds by false representations

The 2006 Fraud Act broadens the scope of the offence of fraud as that term is generally understood. A bank may occasionally have grounds for believing that a borrower has misrepresented its financial position, or may have failed or delayed in providing material information required under the terms of the loan agreement, and that this may have prejudiced the bank in some way. Yet, in the normal course, such matters would be dealt with through negotiation. The lender, having discovered the truth, may demand additional security or other measures. Criminal law issues would arise only in the most extreme and obvious cases. This position may now change, given that the Fraud Act 2006 must be read in conjunction with the bank's anti-money laundering obligations under the Proceeds of Crime Act 2002.

2.2.15. (FA 2006 s2) Fraud by dishonest assistance through false representation

Until the decision in *R v Barlow Clowes* the test for "dishonest assistance by a solicitor" could be defined as: *"Was the solicitor dishonest by the ordinary standards of a reasonable and honest solicitor and if so, did he realise that he was dishonest by these standards?"*

The "legal test" for dishonest assistance has been considered by three main decisions.

Royal Brunei Airlines v Tan; Twinsectra Ltd v Yardley; and *Barlow Clowes International Ltd v Eurotrust International Ltd*. One area of ambiguity persisted following *Twinsectra,* and this was whether or not it was necessary for an individual to be aware that his conduct would be considered dishonest, by ordinary standards. The Privy Council in *Barlow Clowes* clarified the uncertainty in a relatively short period of time following *Twinsectra* and it was encouraging to see the courts act with such speed, given the potential consequences if the uncertainty had been allowed to persist. In *Barlow Clowes*, the defendant argued that he was not aware that his conduct would, by ordinary standards, be regarded as dishonest and he relied on a misleading paragraph in *Twinsectra* which lent some support for the argument. This argument was rejected and *Barlow Clowes* clarified matters by stating that a dishonest state of mind meant a consciousness that one is transgressing ordinary standards of behaviour; and the person need not have thought about what these standards were.

Caselaw

Abou-Rahmah and another v City Express Bank of Lagos and others [2006] EWCA Civ 1492

This matter went to the Court of Appeal at the end of 2007. The relevant facts are that the claimants were the victims of a fraud and considered that the City Express Bank of Lagos ("the bank") were liable to them for dishonest assistance, or in restitution for monies had and received. The claimants had paid money to the bank on the fraudster's instructions, and the money was then transferred on to another of the bank's clients (the co-conspirator), who were also involved in the fraud and, in short, the bank was being used as a money laundering vehicle. The bank's local manager had suspected that the co-conspirator had been involved in money laundering activities, but it was held in the lower court that he had not held suspicions around this particular transaction. The claimants appealed the decision of the lower court, arguing that the court (1) had demanded too specific a knowledge of the fraud and (2) had ignored the evidence relating to the local manager's suspicions of the co-conspirator. The Court of Appeal upheld the decision of the lower court.

The Court of Appeal decided that the local bank manager had not held any particular suspicions at the time of the transactions involving the claimants, and therefore the general suspicion held about the co-conspirator was insufficient to support a finding of dishonest assistance against the bank. The Court of Appeal reaffirmed that the test for dishonest assistance was predominantly an objective test. The decision in this case is a clear example of how difficult dishonest assistance cases can be, and how every such case is heavily dependent on its own facts.

2.2.16. (FA 2006 s2) Innocent False Representation

In some cases, a genuine mistake may negate criminal liability. However, criminal liability will not be excluded by ignorance of the law. In considering whether the accused has acted honestly, the presence or absence of reasonable grounds of belief ought to be taken into account.

> **Caselaw**
>
> *Wilson v Inyang* [1951] 2 All ER 237
>
> Inyang was an African who had lived in the United Kingdom for two years, he was charged with wilfully, and falsely using the title or description of "physician", contrary to the Medical Act 1858, section 40. He was not a registered medical practitioner, but had obtained a Diploma of the British Guild of Drugless Practitioners. He had published an advertisement in which he was referred to as "Naturopath physician, N.D, M.R.D.P." The charge was dismissed by the magistrate on the ground that he genuinely believed he was entitled to describe himself in the terms used in the advertisement. The Prosecution appealed. Lord Goddard .C.J, said that he understood the reasoning of the magistrate. For it was the magistrate who had seen the respondent, heard him and cross-examine him and so there must have been evidence enough for him to draw his conclusion that the defendant had a reasonable ground for his belief in the circumstances. Had this a European or an Englishman, the magistrate would not have found him so mistaken.

2.3.1. (FA 2006 s3) Section 3-Fraud by failing to disclose information

The *actus reus* of the S3 fraud offence is failing to disclose information to a person and being under a legal duty to disclose. The *mens rea* consists of acting dishonestly and an intention to make a gain or cause a loss. S3 fraud offence overlaps with the 2 fraud offence of false representation but S3 may be better when attention is focused directly on the existence of the duty. The S3 fraud offence is committed at the point at which failure to disclose under the duty arises and in cases where there is no positive representation for the purposes of the first branch of the offence of false representation in situations where there is a legal obligation to disclose information. The element of dishonesty is important is this S3 offence where the defendant claims he is not aware of his duty to he believed he satisfied his duty.

An example is in the case *R v Firth* (1989) 91 Cr App Rep 217, [1990] Crim. LR 326.

> **Caselaw**
>
> *R v Firth* [1989] 91 Cr App Rep 217, [1990] Crim. LR 326.
> The defendant was a consultant gynaecologist who omitted to inform a hospital that certain patients referred by him for treatment were private patients. Had the hospital known this, either he or the patients would have been charged for the services. It was held that he had evaded a liability by deception. However, it is not easy to establish that there was a deception from his mere silence. Under the new law he would be guilty of the fraud offence, provided he has a legal duty to disclose such information.

The Law Commission, in its fraud report said this about the concept of legal duty:

"Such a duty may derive from statute (such as provisions governing company prospectuses) from the fact that the transaction in question is one of the utmost good faith, (such as a contract of insurance), from the express or implied terms of a contract, from the custom of a particular trade or market, or from the existence of a fiduciary relationship between the parties (such as that of agent or principal). For this purpose there is a legal duty to disclose information, not only if the defendant's failure to disclose it gives the victim a cause of action for damages, but also if the law gives the victim a right to set aside any change in his or her legal position to which he or she may consent as a result of the non-disclosure. For example, a person in a fiduciary position has a duty to disclose material information when entering into a contract with his or her beneficiary, in the sense that a failure to make such disclosure will entitle the beneficiary to rescind the contract and to reclaim any property transferred under it".

2.3.2.1. (FA 206 s3) Fraud by failing to disclose to disclose information -duty bound to disclose

It is a question of fact in each case whether or not there is a legal duty to disclose. The liability is a strict liability as to the existence of a duty.

Under section 3 of the 2006 Fraud Act, a person commits an offence if he dishonestly fails to disclose to another person information which he is under a legal duty to disclose; and he intends thereby to make a gain (for himself or any other person) or to cause a loss to another person (or to expose that person to a risk of loss). The offence created by this section is potentially very broad, given that it creates an offence of omission, rather than commission. Legal duties can flow from many diverse sources, including legislation, contracts, relationships of trust and agency and obligations of utmost good faith. The section is not limited **to** *statutory or regulatory* disclosure obligations.

2.3.2.2. Examples of "failure to disclose" fraud offences

'Failure to disclose' is a very broad term. This may not amount to criminal offences under the old law but is a fraud under the Fraud Act. Examples are as follows: (i) A borrower who fails to disclose to a lender the occurrence of adverse events which may entitle the lender to terminate the facility, knowing that the provisions of the loan agreement require notification of such matters, commits fraud. Such a borrower exposes the lender to the risk of loss (or greater loss) because the borrower's financial position may deteriorate further before the lender discovers the true situation. (ii) A borrower who neglects to inform a lender of an occurrence which might entitle the lender to charge penalties or increase the margin on the loan, commits fraud by possibly depriving the bank of funds which it was otherwise entitled to receive. If the loan agreement required the borrower to provide the relevant information and the borrower deliberately refrained from doing so, the borrower would commit an offence, because it has deliberately inflicted a loss on the lender, or exposed it to the risk of loss. Such deliberate non-disclosure may be sufficient evidence.

2.3.3. (FA 2006 s3) Failing to disclose information- tax fraud and bank secrecy

Recently, HMRC ran a large-scale investigation to reclaim unpaid tax on interest earned in offshore accounts. Investigations focused on taxpayers who have a UK address and an offshore account, or credit cards linked to or funded by offshore accounts. HMRC plans to direct banks to freeze taxpayers' accounts up to the level of the debt owing, and for that amount to be handed over to HMRC. HMRC is demanding that banks release information about customers' accounts, including the accounts of deceased customers, as well as dormant and closed accounts. The Fraud Act widens duties of banks to also consider whether customers may have committed criminal offences in the context of loan negotiations or transactions with the bank itself. Failure to do so may mean that bank employees may be charged with fraud as well as offences under section 330 of the Proceeds of Crime Act 2002. If a bank or its employees tip-off a customer against whom a report to the authorities has been made, that is a criminal offence under the Money Laundering Regulations 2007, in force since December 2007. There are now criminal penalties for stockbrokers, lawyers, estate agents and bankers if they do not carry out multiple checks to verify the identity of the beneficial owners of trusts.

> **Caselaw**
>
> *National Westminster Bank plc v Angeli Luki Kotonou* [2006] EWHC 1785
> This case highlights the importance of representations made to induce a customer to enter into a guarantee. This case is not a landmark precedent, but is a warning to banks to be cautious when giving representations. NatWest represented to the defendant guarantor that, if he did not sign a guarantee, the borrower's account would be referred to the bank's distressed debt section but did not elaborate on the other variables that would be considered when taking that decision. The representation therefore implied that if the guarantor did sign the guarantee, the borrower's account would not be referred to the distressed debt section. The

defendant was anxious that such referral should not occur as NatWest were far more likely to agree to finance future projects if the account remained under the control of a banker with whom he had built a working relationship. The deadline of 12 July 2001 was the deadline for the defendant to sign the guarantee, which occasioned a hurried exchange of documents and finally the defendant signing the guarantee, but did not lead to NatWest altering its representation. Nonetheless, NatWest referred the borrower's account to the distressed debt section on the same day. The court held that the defendant had relied on NatWest's negligent misrepresentation and had been induced to sign the guarantee. The guarantee had to be set aside. This case highlights the importance of being careful with representations that may be given during the course of a transaction, especially at busy closings. The lesson to be learnt is that representations should be considered carefully at the time they are given and again before the time the transaction is completed.

2.4.1.1. (FA 2006 s4) Section 4- Fraud by abuse of position

The *actus reus* of the s4 fraud offence comprises abusing a position of financial trust. The *mens rea* comprises acting dishonestly and an intention by the abuse to make a gain or cause a loss. The meaning of 'position' is explained in the Law Commission's fraud report which states that the necessary relationship will be present between trustee and beneficiary, director and company, professional person and client, agent and principal, employer and employee, or between business partners. It could arise in a family situation also or in voluntary work, or in any context where the parties are not at arm's length. In nearly all cases when it arises, there will be present fiduciary duties in civil law.

The case of *R v Adams* [1995] WLR 52 PC is a successful prosecution in which directors were charged with conspiracy to defraud after they failed to disclose a secret profit made in breach of a fiduciary duty. Such offences are difficult to prosecute unless clear evidence is set out to the jury to bring clear understanding that bypasses the commercial contractual intricacies.

A successfully prosecuted case that illustrates this intricacy, conspiracy and detailed and level-headed professional planning is the "*Nat West Three Bankers*" case, Southern District of Texas, Houston Division, USA *v Gary Steven Mulgrew, Giles Robert Hugh Darby and David John Bermingham,* Cr. No. H-02-0597, prosecuted in the United States because of jurisdiction and evidence reasons, termed "*forum non conveniens*" in Private International Law. The case is set out below to show the conspiracy.

2.4.1.2. The "Nat West Three" Fraud case

This case was investigated by the FBI Enron Task Force which investigated criminal activity associated with the financial collapse of Enron Corporation in the United States. The three men were involved with an Enron "Special Purpose Vehicle (SPV)" which is a subsidiary of a company that can be excluded from the company's Group Accounts, thus hiding company liabilities.

2.4.1.3. Using existing loopholes – legal formations of companies within companies

(i) An SPV company was registered as "Rhythms NetConnections", an internet business. The purpose of "Rhythms NetConnections" was to use it to hedge risk.

(ii) "Enron Group" owned 5.4 million shares in the SPV named "Rhythms NetConnections".

(iii) In 1999, Enron Group *waived its conflict-of-interest rule* (by drafting a 'Deed of Variation' commonly drafted [with the agreement of all parties] by solicitors everywhere) to allow Enron's CEO Fastow to form an SPV company called "LJM Cayman".

(iv) The function of the SPV company "LJM Cayman" was purely to hedge Enron's risk in the SPV named "Rhythms NetConnections".

(v) A transaction was therefore facilitated. In exchange for 3.4 million Enron shares, the SPV company "LJM Cayman" transacted $64 million of its own (self-created) promissory notes to "Enron Group", in effect insuring Enron's risk by Enron itself. (In the UK, this is often done for big businesses when banks loan money needed as a guarantee in a certain business transaction and depositing the same money back into the same bank, thereby offsetting the loan. Provided there is no breach of contract or fall in value of investment (if this is the transaction) the guarantee is not called upon, but should it be called upon by a court order after a claim, say, then the transaction collapses into itself, as in the present 'credit crunch'.

(vi) The SPV company "LJM Cayman" then formed another SPV company as its own subsidiary SPV company and registered it with the name "Swap Sub".

Fraud Investigation: Criminal Procedure and Investigation

(vii) The SPV named "Swap Sub" undertook (as its 'going concern' business) to underwrite some of "Enron Group" bets, called derivative options. These derivative options legally allowed "Enron Group" the right to sell its "Rhythms NetConnection" shares at a certain price on certain dates.

(ix) The SPV named "LJM Cayman" had two limited partners, (a UK registered company can legally be a partner to other partners, they being legal persons, ie. registered companies, or natural human beings, or a mix of both)- one was named "Campsie Limited" and the other was named "Enron's Rhythms Net Bet" (ENRB).

(iix) Using the facilities of the banking group "Credit Suisse First Boston", the SPV company ENRB was registered in the Cayman Islands.

(x) Using the facilities of the banking group "Nat West" the SPV company "Campsie" was also registered in the Cayman Islands.

(xi) Gary Muldrew was a Nat West branch office managing director and he also headed the Nat West Structured Finance Group of the Nat West Greenwich office.

(xii) David John Bermingham, a solicitor, also worked at the Nat West Greenwich office and he headed the Structuring Group and reported to Mulgrew and to Darby. These three Nat West employees, Bermingham, Mulgrew and Darby, had established and registered the SPV company named "Campsie".

(xiii) Nat West Bank has a branch in Houston, Texas, USA.

2.4.1.4. The conspiracy to defraud Enron by Bermingham, Mulgrew, Darby et al

The fact was proved that these three men executed a scheme which involved creating and registering an SPV company named "Campsie" with intention to create a loss for their employer Nat West, in order to themselves advise Nat West to sell at a low price, thereby facilitating another known SPV company to buy Nat West's interest cheaply, thus giving rise via another transaction to their brief ownership and planned sale of that interest, resulting in a profit of $7.5 million to themselves.

2.4.1.5. The chain of transactions –conspiracy to defraud Enron

In sum, Nat West sold its interest in Campsie for $1 million, on the advice of the defendants who immediately bought that Nat West interest in Campsie for $250,000 in total and immediately re- sold it for $7.3 million.

(i) Prior to this stage, these three men had worked towards getting the promissory notes' liability of "LJM Cayman" paid off (equal to 3.4 million Enron shares).

(ii) The three defendants had transferred those 3.4 million Enron shares (worth $64 million LJM Cayman promissory notes) to "Nat West" and "credit Suisse", thus creating an instant paper profit of $20 million for the two banks by making derivatives transactions(bets) using these 3 .4 million Enron shares.

(iii) In October 1999, Nat West instantly richer by its half of the $20 million instant paper profit experienced takeover bids from "Bank of Scotland" and "Royal Bank of Scotland".

(iv) Immediately "Nat West" bank started to seek a purchaser for its branch at Greenwich, where the three defendants were employed.

(v) "Swap Sub", the subsidiary of "LJM Cayman", (with authority to sell 5.4 million Rhythm Net Connection shares) was sold off by "Nat West" before "Royal Bank of Scotland" acquired "Nat West".

2.4.1.6. Evidence of the conspiracy to defraud Enron

Crucial evidence consisted of many email correspondence between Bermingham, Darby and Mulgrew, showing that they planned to make their own secret profits before the acquisition of "Nat West" by "Royal Bank of Scotland".

(i) The three defendants set up an SPV company which they registered as "Southampton K Co". This company was set up to receive then divide the defrauded profit they planned to make from Enron.

(ii) Email correspondence lasted up to August 2000.

(iii) In February 2000, Bermingham and Mulgrew's emails showed that they were planning to go to the US to make a slideshow presentation to Enron's CEO Fastow about their proposed restructure of the SPV company "Swap Sub" in order to persuade the "Enron Group" CEO that such a restructure would result in an instantaneous profit to "Enron Group" of $25 million. It was based on lies, in the hope that the CEO of Enron Group would agree the restructure necessary to facilitate their plan to defraud Enron.

(iv) Bermingham and Mulgrew wrote to each other acknowledging that this proposal/presentation slides to "Enron Group" CEO, purporting to make Enron an instant profit of $25 million was not feasible. So they knew that they were going to present misrepresentations to the Enron Group CEO in order to further their ultimate goal.

(v) Email correspondence between the defendants revealed, for example, that Bermingham wrote to Mulgrew, on this unrealistic purported profit, that "*we should be able to appeal to his greed*". Mulgrew's email replied, "*Why can't we squeeze the LPs a bit more?*" (See 2.2.9 for explanation of '*market squeeze*').

(vi) The Defendants exchanged more emails on 26 February 2000, about potential tax consequences if they succeeded.

(vii) Note that the fraud was calculated to its minutiae.

For instance, the $7 million profit which Bermingham, Mulgrew and Darby received through the conspiracy was exactly the monetary limit that their own (newly registered) company, "Southampton K Co", was set up transact to, in order to cancel out the losses it would suffer in their series of transaction, in order to bear no taxes. The amount of final profit was premeditatedly calculated as the optimum non-taxable profit, illustrating the defendant's meticulous skill in planning the fraud.

2.4.1.7. Time-frame for the planned fraud

Their scheme to defraud was executed between March 2000 and July 2000.

In a meticulous way, they made the following moves: -

(i) On 4 March 2000 Fastow had dinner with Bermingham and others. Fastow told Bermingham that now was the time "to do it". Evidence in a notebook confirmed this. (ii) In March 2000, Mulgrew advised "Nat West" that" Enron Group" was offering to buy-out of Nat West's interest in "Swap Sub" at a low price of $1 million. Remember that Swap Sub can sell 5.4 million Enron shares, Swap Sub being a subsidiary of LJM Cayman, worth over $18 per Enron share, i.e. for over $97 million- yet Enron bought back its own shares valued at $7 million for $1 million).

(iii) Mulgrew advised "Nat West" that Nat West's interest was not even worth $1 million at that time.

2.4.1.8. Nat West's knowledge of intention to profit by defrauding Enron Group

(i) "Nat West" knew of the new company formed by Darby, Muldrew and Bermingham, i.e. Southampton K Co.

(ii) Knowing of the existence of the defendants' new SPV company, Nat West sold its interest in SPV company "Swap Sub" for $1 million. (Remember that "LJM Cayman" had formed a subsidiary company registered as "Swap Sub". Remember that "Swap Sub" existed in order to underwrite Enron's derivative options. These derivative options legally allowed Enron to sell its 5.4 million "Rhythms NetConnection" shares at a certain price on certain dates. Remember too, that $64 million of LJM Cayman shares were swapped for 3.4 million Enron shares).

2.4.1.9. Knowingly executing a scheme and artifice to defraud

Based on the facts as set out below, a charge of "knowingly executing a scheme and artifice to defraud" was bought in the United States against defendants Bermingham, Mulgrew and Darby.

(i) On 10 March 2000, Defendant Darby formally wrote to an Enron executive, Kopper, to confirm the sale of Nat West's interest in Swap Sub by selling it to a newly formed Enron subsidiary, a SPV company registered as "NewCo", controlled by Kopper himself.

(ii) On 14 March 2000, Bermingham went to meet Kopper in New York.

(iii) In New York on 14.3.2000, Bermingham drafted an option agreement from Kopper to Mulgrew, Bermingham and Darby, for an option to purchase "Southampton K Co". This option form agreement signed by Bermingham, Mulgrew and Darby, was to give the three defendants the right to buy all issued and outstanding equity of "Southampton K Co" for $250,000, plus interest, before 31 May 2000.

(iv) "Southampton K Co, controlled by Bermingham, Mulgrew and Darby is a partner of a company "Southampton L.P" controlled by Enron executive Kopper.

(v) On 17 March 2000, both the "Campsie" (formed by Nat West) interest in "Swap Sub" and the Credit Suisse's interest were sold to "Southampton L.P" for $1 million and 10 million respectively, making Nat West and Credit Suisse an immediate paper profit of $20 million.

Fraud Investigation: Criminal Procedure and Investigation

(vi) On 20March 2000 "Enron" and "Swap Sub" entered agreements to terminate the "Rhythms NetConnections" put options (see Glossary for explanations of accounting term).

(vii) On 27 March 2000 defendant Bermingham resigned from Nat West.

(viii) On 27 March 2000 defendant Mulgrew transferred $250,000 from his bank account into defendant Bermingham's bank account.

(ix) On 27 April 2000 the deal was done when Bermingham sent a bank draft for $251,993 (i.e. $250,000 with interest) to (Enron executive) Kopper's "Chase Bank of Texas" account

(x) On 27April 2000, defendants Mulgrew, Darby and Bermingham has instantly made an instant paper profit of $7 million on their one-day-long investment of $83 898 each ($251,993 divided by 3).

(xi) On 27 June 2000 defendant Mulgrew tendered his resignation from Nat West Bank.

(xii) On 31 July 2000, defendant Bermingham instructed "Bank of Bermuda" to transfer $2.3 million from "Southampton K Co" account to an account controlled by defendant Darby.

(xiii) On 31 July 2000 defendant Darby's employment resignation from Nat West became effective.

(xiv) On 1 August 2000, defendant Bermingham instructed "Bank of Bermuda" to transfer $390,000 from "Southampton K Co" account to defendant Bermingham's personal Nat West account.

(xv) On 8 August 2000, defendant Bermingham instructed" Bank of Bermuda" to transfer $2.38 million from "Southampton K Co" account to defendant Muldrew's personal bank account.

(xvi) On 17 August 2000, defendant Bermingham instructed "Bank of Bermuda" to transfer the remaining funds in the "Southampton K Co" bank account to the bank account of his solicitor. This solicitor's account is based in the UK.

The takeover of Nat West by the Royal Bank of Scotland for £21 billion was recommended by Nat West on 11 Feb. 2000 to its shareholders.

2.4.1.10. Fraud by 'abuse of position'

A person commits fraud if he occupies a position in which he is expected to safeguard, or not to act against, the financial interests of another person, and he dishonestly, and with the fraudulent intention, abuses that position. A person may be regarded as having abused his position even though his conduct consisted of an omission rather than an act. Where a person occupies a position of trust, such as that of an employee, he can commit fraud against his employer, without the need to trick him by using a false representation. He already has entrusted to him everything necessary to commit fraud, such as the employer's premises and monies.

2.4.2 (FA 2006 s4) British Rail employee selling his own sandwiches

In this petty case of abuse of position (as compared with the 'NatWest Three' case) the court decided that two people selling their own sandwiches in place of British Rail sandwiches were guilty of conspiracy to defraud.

(see *R v Cooke* [1986] AC 909, [1986] 2 All ER 985).

2.5. (FA 2006 s5) Section 5- meaning of gain or loss

Gain or loss extends only to gain or loss in money or other property and property means any property whether real or personal, including intangible property

2.6.1. (FA 2006 s6) Section 6- Possession of articles for use in fraud

Fraud Act 2006, section 6 overcomes issues such as those in recent United States federal cases, where the placing of computer viruses or bugs into computers is treated as the means of transporting illegal materials into those computers. Defence arguments were that the accused did not commit the offences but that the programs on the computers did so. This is called 'blaming the ghost in the machine. It is not only the possession of malicious software that is targeted here, but also possession of expertise software and hardware to facilitate illegal businesses such as hard-core pornography. An FTP server used to distribute child abuse images is one type of article.

'Article' includes any program or data held in electronic form. An article for use in fraud could be a computer as was found in a shop in 2004 by the West Midlands Police. Analysis of the computer records revealed the bulk trade of firearms on EBay. Another article is called a "denial-of-service-attack". In 2004 US police circumvented a gang who stole $215 million in total from 150,000 victims by using identity theft, fraud, counterfeit software, computer intrusions and other intellectual –property crimes by hiring computer hackers to launch 'a denial of service assault' against these victims. The attacks can cost millions in revenue and defence. Criminals who run websites to collect credit card accounts are using such an instrument. Discovery of such articles is by identifying points of responsibility. Who are the domain name registrars, domain name registrants, DNS server owners, regional internet registries, network owners, web server owners, email server owners, upstream ISP, telecommunications carriers, routes' owners, and other responsible parties?

Where mobile phones are used as articles supplied for use in frauds, it is not widely known that mobile phones contain a plethora of information both in the handset and on the accompanying Subscriber Identity Module (SIM) card contained within the handset. Criminals fear the three classifications of data, which will eventually track them – Location Information, Billing Information including call logs and Locally Stored Handset Data.

The prosecution must prove that the defendant intended the article to be used in the course of or in connection with Some future fraud, although it is not necessary to prove that he intended it to used in the course of or in connection with any specific fraud being merely enough to prove general intention to use it for some fraud.

2.7. (FA 2006 s7) Section 7- Making or supplying articles for use in frauds

The meaning of 'article' in this offence includes any program or data held in electronic form. This offence would, therefore, cover those in possession of (or the makers or suppliers of) computer programs used to generate credit card numbers or produce blank utility bills. Computer files that store data such as credit card details for fraudulent use could also be caught by the offence.

> **Caselaw**
>
> *R v Crick* [1981] 3 Cr App Rep (S.) 275
> The defendant pleaded guilty to possessing a press and making 150 poor quality coins for use in slot machines. "At one extreme is the professional forger with carefully prepared plates and elaborate machinery that manufactures large quantities of bank notes and puts them into circulation. A long sentence of imprisonment is appropriate in such cases.

2.8.1. (FA 206 s8) Meaning of 'article'

Section 8 Fraud Act above describes what 'article' can be in these electronic times. It may be any data held in electronic form. One type of data used by fraudsters is a computer-generated signature and forgers create files of these to form a database. A forger might use a scanner to save these signatures as well as with such 'articles' as computer generated signatures are other more mundane articles such as blacksmithing equipment. It is an offence (carrying a maximum of five years' imprisonment on indictment) for a person to have in his possession or under his control any article for use in the course of, or in connection with, any fraud (s 6). The offence is modelled upon going equipped under Theft Act 1968, s 25, and replaces it in so far as that offence applied to cheat. Crucially, the new offence has no requirement that the person has articles "with him while not at his place of abode".

The Solicitor General stated in the Commons debates that:

> *"The requirement that a person be outside his place of abode when going equipped may have worked in 1968, but in the modern world, with computers, fraud may be*

perpetrated by a person sitting at his computer terminal in his home. The offence should not be limited to possession outside the home".

The offence is aimed, first, at articles that are designed solely for fraud, such as credit-card cloning devices, or ATM fascia for skimming bank details; the police had complained that when they found such devices at a person's home address there was no obvious offence to charge, despite the plain ill-intent. Second, the offence includes in its scope articles that may also have a benign use—possessing an ordinary computer for use in fraud is within the ambit of the offence. This gives the section a wide scope, particularly as there is no *mens rea* on the face of the statute.

However, it is clear that the caselaw in relation to Theft Act 1968 s 25 will remain relevant. Critically 'article' includes any program or data held in electronic form, so programs for generating credit-card numbers or e-mails for use in phishing attacks should be caught by the offences.

2.8.2. Aim of section 8 Fraud Act

The offence is aimed, first, at articles that are designed solely for fraud, such as credit-card cloning devices, or ATM fascia for skimming bank details; the police had complained that when they found such devices at a person's home address there was no obvious offence to charge, despite the plain ill-intent. Second, the offence includes in its scope articles that may also have a benign use, possessing an ordinary computer for use in fraud is within the ambit of the offence. This gives the section a wide scope, particularly as there is no mens rea on the face of the statute. However, it is clear that the case law in relation to Theft Act 1968 s 25 will remain relevant.

In particular, the case of *R v Ellames* [1974] 3 All ER 130, established that *"has with him any article for use ... "* means *"has with him for the purpose (or with the intention) that they will be used ..."*, and that the prosecution has to prove that the defendant has the articles for the purpose of use in a future offence, by him, or another, though it is not necessary to establish the details of a particular contemplated fraud. Given that it was not Parliament's intention to produce a strict liability offence, a better model might have been *"possesses money or other property, and intends that it should be used for the purpose of..."* as in the Terrorism Act 2000, s 16. Critically 'article' includes any program or data held in electronic form, so programs for generating credit-card numbers or e-mails for use in phishing attacks should be caught by the offences.

2. 8.3. Making, adapting or supplying articles

Making, adapting or supplying articles for use in the course of, or in connection with, fraud is a more serious offence and carries 10 years' imprisonment (s 7).

Caselaw

In *R v Hollinshead* [1985] 2 All ER 769, [1985] 3 WLR 159, where the defendants sold devices which, when fitted to an electricity meter, reversed the flow of current so that the meter recorded fewer units of electricity than were actually consumed. The difficulty with those facts is identifying a fraud by a particular person on a particular electricity company. The House of Lords held under the old law that the conduct was a conspiracy to defraud by the suppliers of the devices, despite the absence of a particular agreement with the end users to commit fraud. Before

> Fraud Act 2006, there was no appropriate substantive offence. The offence applied to articles whether they were specially made or adapted for use in fraud, or supplied with the intention that they be used to commit, or assist in the commission of fraud.

2.8.4. False licence is an 'article'

A false licence might be an article', as is used by bogus-brokers to assure investors that they are genuine. It must be remembered that 'forgery' is the process of making or adapting objects or documents with dishonest intention, whilst the crime of fraud is the crime of dishonesty against another including through the use of objects obtained through forgery. Therefore, copies, studio replicas, and reproductions are not forgeries though they may become forgeries through knowing and wilful misattributions.

2.8.5. Equipment attached to computer is an 'article'

Another type of 'article' for use in fraud would be the additional piece of equipment that a fraudster would attach to his computer, a small machine, with which he prints information and photos onto blank credit cards. Using another small machine the fraudster, who embosses the name and numbers into the card, is also using, an 'article' supplied in order to be used for fraud. The manufacturer of those machines and the supplier would be charged with inciting a crime.

2.8.6. Counterfeit credit card is an 'article'

Fraudsters can make their own credit cards with which they can obtain other identification documents and also use such equipment. Fraudsters may set themselves up as Internet servers where they can carry out passive information gathering techniques. A lot of important information can be passively harvested and subsequently used in a direct attack on an organisation. Information such as current service patching levels, internal network architecture layout and account details can be obtained. Such information leakage can be used to the detriment of an organisation.

2.8.7. Article-Telemarketing scheme is an 'article'

An article can be a telemarketing scheme in which mass marketing involves enticing victims by promising them large lottery or prize winnings in exchange for a relatively smaller service fee or tax, and once the fee is received, the promised funds are never delivered.

2.8.8. Domain Name System is 'article'

Fraudsters who are electronically skilled can (i) get access to internet Service registration; domain name systems. (ii) They can use search engines to retrieve distributed material relating to an organisation or their employees. (iii) They can access the information contained within each email delivery process. (iv) They can access the information about the way an organisation encodes and categorises the services that their online hosts provide; (v) Fraudsters can perform website analysis using information intentionally made public which may pose a risk to the organisation's security; (vi) Fraudsters study website error messages to a particular domain, searching for specific error messages generated by a website under development and use this information to gain a better understanding of the type of supplier of the web server technology.

> **Point to Note: Computer-related fraud**
>
> The 2001 International Convention on Cyber-crime includes in its pre-amble the conviction to pursue, as a matter of priority, a common criminal policy aimed at the protection of society against cybercrime, *inter alia*, by adopting appropriate legislation and fostering international co-operation. This Convention was deemed necessary in order to deter action directed against the confidentiality, integrity and availability of computer systems, networks and computer data as well as the misuse of such systems, networks and data by providing for the criminalisation of such conduct, as described in this Convention, and the adoption of powers sufficient for effectively combating such criminal offences, by facilitating their detection, investigation and prosecution at both the domestic and international levels and by providing arrangements for fast and reliable international co-operation; The Convention addresses computer related offences include computer-related forgery (Article 7) and computer-related fraud (Article 8).

2.8.9. Computer systems that generate 'articles'

There is a legitimate industry concerned with the security of computer systems that generates 'articles' (this includes any program or data held in electronic form) to test and/or audit hardware and software.

2.8.10. Dual use of 'articles'

Some articles will therefore have a dual use and prosecutors need to ascertain that the suspect has a criminal intent. If the article was supplied in the course or connection with fraud, then prosecutors should consider if their case is also an offence contrary to section 7 and / or section 6 of the Fraud Act 2006. An offence of making or supplying articles for use in frauds contrary to section 7 is punishable by a maximum of 10 years imprisonment and an offence of possession of articles for use in fraud contrary to section 6 is punishable by a maximum of 5 years imprisonment. Each case should be considered based on its own facts.

2.8.11. Elements to prove 'making or supplying articles for use in frauds'

Whilst the facts of each case will be different, the elements to prove the offence will be the same. Regarding dual use articles, consider the following factors: Does the institution, company or other body have in place robust and up to date contracts, terms and conditions or acceptable user polices? Are students, customers and others made aware of the Computer Misuse Act and what is lawful and unlawful? Do students, customers or others have to sign a declaration that they do not intend to contravene the Computer Misuse Act?

2.9.1. (FA 2006 s9) Section 9 -Participating in fraudulent business by sole trader

Fraud Act 2006, section 9 covers many frauds that are 'confidence' frauds, such as when someone sells a certain tea as a 'weight loss' substance or someone encourages people to buy a lottery ticket with a prize worth less than the shipping and handling charge required to obtain prize. Misrepresentation in soliciting prospective employees is another confidence fraud. Even in the year 1677, when fraudulent transactions pertaining to land and property could be carried out on unsuspecting people by a sharp businessman, such as a money lender, the

English Statute of Frauds 1677 meant that no action could be taken against an executor upon a special promise, or upon any agreement or contract for sale of lands, unless agreement was in writing and signed by the party to be charged therewith or some other person thereunto by him lawfully authorised.

Section 9 creates an offence of fraudulent business where a person 'outside the reach' of Companies Act 1985, s 458 is knowingly a party to the carrying on of a business with intent to defraud creditors of any person or for any other fraudulent purpose. This unusual drafting device is intended to apply the new fraud offence to people other than to a company, or other corporation to which s 458 Companies Act 1985 has been applied, but not to bodies specifically exempted from s 458 Companies Act 1985. Essentially the scope has been extended to sole traders and partnerships. Presumably, the fraud offence will be interpreted by the courts in a way identical to the Companies Act 1985 s 458 offence; notably, dishonesty as a necessary element of the offence.

The maximum penalty for the fraudulent business offence is 10 years' imprisonment. Fraud Act 2006 has raised the penalty for fraudulent trading to the same level. Today moneylenders who are not limited companies, but who may be in partnerships or may be carrying on a trade on their own, can still dupe people into signing contracts, a term of which would be to seize their property under certain circumstances. The new fraud offence is more akin to theft. Dishonestly obtaining services is analogous to dishonest appropriation of property. As the Law Commission put it, it can be committed by helping oneself to the service rather than dishonestly inducing another person to provide it. Previously, where a contract of insurance was bought over the internet by use of an illicit credit card, then, if the processing were entirely automated, no person would have been deceived, and there was no obvious offence committed. Such conduct is caught under the new fraud charge.

Under the old law, using a fake ticket to enter a football match would be a theft offence, by obtaining the gain by the display of a fake ticket and deceiving the person on the turnstile into believing the ticket was real. Anomalously, jumping over the same turnstile to watch the football is not an offence. The new law covers both those actions. Again, the ability for Fraud Act 2006 to keep pace with the changing methodology of crime is apparent. Using cloned satellite decoders to watch 'pay television' will be caught by the section.

2.9.2. (FA 2006 s9) Insurance frauds

Sole traders are renowned for committing insurance fraud when the going gets tough. There is at present no immunity for whistle blowers in the United Kingdom who report that a sole trader is attempting to commit an insurance fraud. Insurance fraud is colluded with in many sectors of industry such as the road accident repair sector and personal injury sector. There are no set rules for authorised agencies, which investigate insurance fraud but an ad-hoc set of individual provisions made by certain insurance companies. Were there an authorised agency in place, they could have a set list of information required for disclosure such as history of previous claims made by the insured; policy information relevant to the fraud under investigation; statement of proof of loss and policy payment records.

Sharing of information with an authorised agency would be most desirable. Such authorized agency would have automatic right to receive information. Immunity to anyone who reports suspected insurance fraud could be provided, if the information was not malicious. Such information received by this authorized agency would be protected under the Data

Protection Act and only after successful criminal prosecution may it be released.

2.9.3. (FA 2006 s9) Identity theft and sole traders

Identity theft is a much used method of fraud perpetuated by sole traders and this can be curbed by the fraud offence since there is no English legislation restricting access to personal information such as the USA's Federal Law 18 U.S.C. 1028 'The Identity Theft and Assumption Deterrence Act 1998', making identity theft a federal crime. There is no English privacy law.

2.9.4 (S9FA) Fraudulent uses of stolen identity

Identity theft is unassuming in its range of fraud because, by stealing an identity, a sole trader or partnership can use it for false advertising, false billing, forgery, embezzlement, false insurance claims, and internet securities fraud.

On the internet, equipped with such identity, it would be easy to reveal and to identify the name and address of the primary mail server, back-up mail server, its host or external provider such as 'blueyonder.co.uk'. Mining the internet further gives such fraudsters the multiple IP addresses and name aliases for one single service and digging into this would reveal aliases for the big servers such as Microsoft and then, by looking for weaknesses here, the sole trader can obtain a list of absolutely all the information of all named hosts, sub-zones and associated Internet Provider addresses. So, just one identity theft can lead to the identity theft of thousands, using the internet as an article that equips the fraudster.

2.9.5. (FA 2006 s9) Securities fraud by sole traders

Securities fraud may be instances of fraud by sole traders.
Example (i) - securities fraud by sole trader:
A broker, working with a group of employees as a self-employed or sole trader, commits fraud if he intentionally misleads an investor to his or her detriment.
Example (ii)-securities fraud by sole trader
An analyst, attached to such a broker, can be charged with fraud if he knowingly issues poor advice. If such a sole trader broker gives inside information to an investor that investor will be charged with fraud if they trade upon such inside information to which the rest of the public did not have access.
Example (iii) - Trafficking persons by sole traders
A set of sole traders whose abominable frauds are not yet fully appreciated, are those who deal in trafficked persons , those who organise trafficking of persons and supply brothels with trafficked persons. Trafficking of women and children is part of organised crime activity in which women and children are transported from Africa, South America, Asia, Middle East and Eastern Europe to Western Europe and North America to be used as prostitutes and for child pornography, slave labour, automobile couriers, body parts couriers, flora couriers, drugs couriers, arms couriers for gangs as part of transnational organised crime. Sole traders who commit fraud are also to be found posing as charities to extract money and goods from generous people. At another level, the status of 'charitable trust' is used as an artificial vehicle for tax avoidance.
Example (iv) - Sole trader who sells email addresses for fraud

Sole traders who sell email addresses are another such group. One internet company was sued by the New York Attorney General for selling of email addresses in what authorities estimate to be perhaps the biggest deliberate breach of internet privacy. The company, Gratis Internet, sold personal information obtained from millions of consumers despite a promise of confidentiality.

2.9.6. (FA 2006 s9) Sole Trader selling bogus products

Electronic signatures are possible today and with computerisation come the many hundreds of persons quite unaware that with a keystroke, they have just agreed to 12 months of Internet service or to a subscription of a magazine when they agree to have the free copy as advertised. Apart from export trade, Inland Revenue submission of Tax Returns and shopping on the internet, these not so obvious transactions are deemed to have been electronically signed. Since the Electronic Communications Act 2000 gives the electronic signature the same legal standing as a written signature (s2 (1)), this would mean that an unscrupulous person could set up an electronic business selling bogus products for which many have signed and therefore paid or made to pay. There are some 40,000 separate references in current English legislation to requirements that documents be in writing or signed. It facilitates the incorrigible sole trader who without conscience tricks the customer into an unworthy transaction.

2.9.7. (FA 2006 s9) Book-keeper to sole trader

Obtaining a pecuniary advantage by deception often applies to sole traders as in *R v Calender*. Anyone who makes the bookkeeping records for a sole trader and deliberately makes false entries, is committing the offence of false accounting and is guilty of being involved in a sole trader's dishonesty. If an employee of a sole trader corruptly gives or offers consideration for a favour in respect of the sole trader's affairs, this corruption is a fraud. To submit incorrect accounts and a certificate of

Fraud Investigation: Criminal Procedure and Investigation

disclosure, knowing them to be false, is a fraud where incorrect accounts are supported by fraudulent electronic invoices.

The UK needs an Authentication Protocol for all electronic documents used in evidence. There needs to be an Evidence Retention and Document Destruction Protocol agreed across European Member States, to keep standards of evidence alike. A document such as an email, an electronic invoice, or other business transaction, once sent, is preserved forever on a server somewhere but there is no protocol that servers must preserve all traffic or for how long, although a data retention law has just been passed.

A server outside the jurisdiction of the EU can do as it wishes and in fact, the Hotmail server informs all that it regularly destroys all its traffic records. AS for electronic invoices, Council Directive 2001/115/EC deals with business invoices within the EU, with the mandatory provisions of customer's VAT number, mandatory sequencing of invoicing, full name and address of buyer must to be preserved.

Even though all electronic invoices must be translated into the local language and kept for at least 4 years and up to 15 years, there is no provision made for relevant storage of such electronic transactions. For instance, in reality, if electronic invoices are stored in an accounting program, which updates itself automatically, the entire original document 'metadata' will be lost. Electronic documents can be altered or forged with a fraction of the effort it would take to do the same with hard-copy documents and cases would collapse. Even if forgery were to be the alternative offence, it would be nearly impossible to prove at what point it was forged or by whom and it would cost millions of pounds to gather such evidence in some cases.

2.9.8. (FA 2006 s9) Common frauds perpetrated by sole traders

Advance fee fraud is a common serious fraud perpetrated by a sole trader or a partnership of two or three persons. Bankruptcy fraud by a sole trader is still common. Embezzlement by trustee or employee is another. Fraudulent transfer of property in contemplation of bankruptcy is another. The making of a false declaration or statement under penalty of perjury is a fraud. The concealment or destruction of documents relating to the property or affairs of a debtor is a fraud. Here 'conceal' does not mean merely 'to secrete or hide away'. The defendant does not have to physically hide the property at all. 'Conceal' means to 'prevent the discovery of' the asset or 'to withhold knowledge of' the asset.

2.10. (FA 2006 s10) Section 10-Participating in fraudulent business carried on by a company

This section is significant in that the penalty for such frauds has increased from seven to ten years. Notable decisions show the culpability of directors of a limited company which extended to criminal liability *(DPP v Kent* and *Sussex Contractors Ltd and R v ICR Haulage Ltd.)*. In this case, Justice Stable held that the company is automatically held criminally responsible if an agent of the company acting in its business commits a crime. In 1993, in *R v Gomez,* the opposite decision was made. Then in *The Hellespont Ardent*, it was decided that there was no doubt that the question of attribution of knowledge to the company could not be answered by determining that the director or other officer was in breach of that duty and it could not be accepted that the company was fixed with that knowledge. Below is an instance of fraudulent trading:

> **Caselaw**
>
> *R v Freeman and Hodgkinson*
> A recent case of fraudulent trading is the case *R v Freeman and Hodgkinson*. The case concerned the failure and bankruptcy of the tank container manufacturer Universal Bulk Handling Ltd. This was a loss making business whose performance was fraudulently hidden by the two defendants. The company was formed in 1958, became a wholly owned subsidiary of Hadleigh plc in 1990. In 1999, it was discovered that there was a discrepancy of £11.5 million between what the accounts declared to be owing to the company and what in fact the company owed to both its suppliers and its customers. Hadleigh was placed into receivership. This is a case of fraudulent trading in order to trade out of its financial problems.

2.11.1. (FA 2006 s11) Section 11- Obtaining services dishonestly

Fraud Act 2006, section 11 makes it an offence for a person by a dishonest act to obtain services for which payment is expected, without paying for them. The offence carries five years' imprisonment; replaces obtaining services by deception under the Theft Act 1978, s 1; and is noticeably wider in that it applies to all dishonest obtaining of services, including those obtained by wholly automated processes. There is no need for a victim to be deceived into providing the services. Where payment is needed and a customer knows this, but still does not pay for the services and exhibits no intention of doing so, this offence is committed. For instance, if someone dishonestly uses payment cards or other false personal information to obtain services over the internet, this offence is committed.

The evidence required to secure a conviction is where the weakness of the law is. For business purposes, English law does not clearly state that an email can be classed as a business document. Business letters are not defined so that it is not clear whether it includes paper and electronic documents. The 2005 Civil Procedure Rules however introduced provisions for electronic disclosures by amending Practice Direction to CPR 31 in October 2005.

> **Caselaw**
>
> *R v Charles Forsyth* is a case in which where Charles Forsyth manufactured and marketed personal computers, which, after a time, were defective and left him running out of money. Forsyth obtained a US $1.5 million letter of credit dishonestly, claiming it was for bank overdraft purposes and claiming to have debtors in excess of $5 million. He also gave false information to secure a government grant.

2.11.2. (FA 2006 s11) Defences to criminal liability

It is important to understand the defences in order to avoid wrongful prosecution cases. There can be defences to the offence 'obtaining services dishonestly'. In *Younghusband v Luftig* [1949] 2 KB 354 the court said this about an unbroken line of authority: *"...that to commit an offence the defendant must have acted wilfully and falsely and that it is for the justices to decide whether he has done so, and, also that he does not commit an offence if he honestly believes that he was within his rights in describing himself as he did."*

The case came down to the question of whether the defendant was acting in good faith in describing himself as he did because he had an honest belief that he was entitled to do so. It is perfectly true. This is what the court said:

> *"He must of course have a reasonable ground for his belief. A person who has passed no examination and has received no qualification from a genuine teaching body, cannot adopt one of the titles mentioned in section 40 of the Act of 1858 and be heard to say that he believed he had such skill as would entitle him so to describe himself. We can sum up this part of the case by saying that there must be mens rea and the presence or absence of that state of mind must be tested on ordinary principles and in the light of common sense".*

It is clear that what the court meant in that passage was that the magistrate must apply ordinary principles and test the matter in the light of common sense and that, generally speaking, applying ordinary principles in the light of common sense, he would say that if a man had reasonable ground for believing what he said he believed, he was not acting honestly. There may be exceptions. A man may believe that which no other man of common sense would believe, but yet may honestly believe it. One of the matters which occurred to me, in addition to those mentioned by Justice Devlin, in the course of the argument, is that of the Bills of Exchange Act 1882, section 90, which states:

> *"A thing is deemed to be done in good faith, within the meaning of this Act, where it is in fact done honestly, whether it is done negligently or not".*

That section was inserted in the Bills of Exchange Act because, although that was the effect of the old cases, there came a series of cases, in which, if a man acted negligently, it was said that he could not pass a good title as he was not acting *bona fide*. Gross negligence or strong negligence is always evidence, very often the best evidence that a man is not acting negligently. If he has acted without any reasonable ground and says, "*I had not properly inquired, and did not think this or that*" that may be very good evidence that he is not acting honestly.

2.11.3. (FA 2006 s11) Defence of duress

The defence of duress may negate a particular intent specified by statute, as for instance, if an organised gang was making a person commit this offence by putting a gun to his head.

> **Caselaw**
>
> In R *v Steane*, the appellant, a British subject, was resident with his wife and children in Germany at the outbreak of war in 1939 and following threats and beatings, he made broadcasts for the German Broadcasting System. He was charged with 'doing an act likely to assist the enemy' and he swore that he never had any intention of assisting the Germans. Where the defence of duress is substantially raised, the burden of adducing evidence of such duress rests on the accused, but the ultimate burden of disproving that defence, to the satisfaction of the jury.

2.11.4. (FA 2006 s11) Defence of insanity

Insanity can mean exemption from criminal responsibility and the accused must prove that, because of a defect of reason, due to disease of the mind, he did not know the nature and quality of his act, or, if he did know this that he did not know that what he was doing is wrong. Since a balance has to be struck between the person's insanity and protection of the public, a fraud offender who faces trial and is considered insane, will enjoy a plea of 'not guilty due to insanity' entered on his behalf and consequently one of a range of orders can be imposed on the offender for his own and for public safety. Orders arise out of the Criminal Procedures (Insanity and Unfitness to Plead)

Act 1991(which amended the Criminal Procedure (Insanity) Act 1964. These orders are as follows:

(i) Hospital Order without time limit (mandatory only to murder so not applicable).
(ii) Hospital Order with time limit.
(iii) Guardianship Order.
(iv) Supervision and Treatment Order.
(v) Absolute Discharge.

If a person was insane at the time of the crime, he is considered fit to plead and will plead the defence of insanity, which if successful, will result in a special verdict of 'not guilty by reason of insanity'.

> **Caselaw**
>
> The case of *R v Peter Young* is a recent case in which the defendant pleaded insanity. A more recent case is the April 2006 report in which a couple were found guilty of masterminding the creation of the Trojan horse computer virus. This was an international espionage operation from their home in South London. The couple stole sensitive information from leading companies. Their charges consisted of aggravated fraud, unlawful computer access, virus insertion, installing tapping equipment, invasion of privacy, managing unlawful database and conspiracy.

2.12.1. (S12FA) Liability of company officers for offences by company

As to Fraud Act 2006, section 12(3), directors' fiduciary duties depend on the type of transaction involved. For example, tracking stock is a security whose dividend and liquidation rights, and therefore market performance, depend on individual businesses within a larger corporate enterprise. The director's obligation is to enhance the performance and value of the entire corporation. Internal transactions, even asset and funding allocation, become fraught with fiduciary significance when a subset of the shareholders may view them as prejudicial.

If the directors themselves are not proportionally invested in all the tracking stock, they theoretically lose the protection of the 'business judgement rule', should the law deem that they are personally interested in one or other side of the internal transactions. In transactions between business units, to the extent it is possible to ascertain an 'arm\s length' market standard, the entire fairness standard would be appropriate. Since more than two-thirds of global trade is carried out by multinational corporations, it is important that directors behave equitably. Since directors of a company are the 'directing mind and will' of the company, as per *R v McNamara*, they can be made liable for such offences as fraud. The case of *The Herald Free Enterprise* was one where directors were not found guilty of unlawful killing but in *R v J. F .Alford Transport Ltd.*, the transport manager and the managing director aided and abetted the falsification of tachograph records by lorry drivers employed by the company. These directors were found guilty.

2.12.2. (FA 2006 s12) Directors' Liability Insurance (DLO)

One unwanted aspect to this fraud offence is that it will spur companies to review their directors' and officers' liability insurance. It is because of insurance that much is not heard of fraud in the UK where insurance can be bought against a company being investigated, being defrauded, and a director defrauding or defrauded. There is no transparency in the insurance sector. In the issue of misuse of confidential information, the risk that companies may misuse information entrusted to them in one area in order to secure gains in another area can be insured against.

Companies may possibly have non- secure systems because they are insured against fraud and so the cost of fraud becomes added to cost to the cost of doing business, i.e; to the value only of the insurance premium. Guidelines by the FSA to the general insurance industry are *informal*. The risk is seen only as one of conflict of interest. There is a thriving market of intelligence companies in the city of London who sell their services as protection bodies to different firms with the remit of keeping the company's business secret and free from espionage. Yet espionage is their business. Companies in the city have contracts with such business intelligence firms, which are paid 'up-front', even before a fraud or breach in security occurs. Yet companies in the city use confidentiality agreements which are aimed at protecting sensitive information from being disclosed to anyone outside the discussions; maintain rights to a future patent or other form of intellectual property; stipulate what information or data can and cannot be disclosed to a third party and place a restriction on what the information can be used for. For example, details of a new technology could be released for use in a tender but not for producing the technology.

Yet despite such foolproof agreements, companies pay business intelligence companies to have access to all their information in order to protect it. Under the present accounting standards, there is no distinction made between traditional and finite risk agreements. Unless a complete understanding of a contract is in place, there should be no timely reimbursement of claims by the reinsurer.

> **Point to note: Aiding or abetting a fraud**
>
> Aiding a fraud means giving assistance to a fraudster. It is sufficient that that act be only a small amount of assistance. This can be in the acting as a look-out, or an employee who gives a password to a fraudster. Abetting involves the encouragement and support provided to a principal offender during the performance of the crime.

2.13.1. (FA 2006 s13) Section 13 Fraud Act –Evidence

Fraud Act 2006, section 13(1) (a) does not include, among such persons, lawyers from whom information was sought by any individual or company (see *Three Rivers District Council and others v Governor and Company of the Bank of England*). Section 13(3)(a) regarding the recovery or administration of any property could well be of a situation such as in *Healy v Brown and another*, the facts of which are that spouses executed mutual Wills in identical form and left the entirety of his or her estate to the surviving spouse. The property in dispute was 3 Phoenix Court and each Will stated that an interest in 3 Phoenix Court would be granted to the claimant, the wife's niece. The remainder of the estate was to be left to the husband's son by a first marriage. When the wife died, the husband transferred 3 Phoenix Court from his name to jointly his and his son's so that after he died the property became his son's. It was held that this constituted a fraud on his deceased wife and the court decided that 3 Phoenix Court was to be transferred to the claimant.

2.13.2. (FA 2006 s13) Related offence- conspiracy to defraud

Section 13 (4) states that 'related offence' means 'conspiracy to defraud'.

This common law offence of 'conspiracy to defraud' has been the bug-bear of the Fraud Act. There was worry that to eliminate this common law offence, which cannot sit well simultaneously with a statutory offence of Fraud, would make unworkable , the Criminal Justice Act 1993. Lord Goldsmith said, at the First Hearing in the House of Lords:

> *"The amendments look complex but they have a simple aim; that is, to ensure that our courts continue to have jurisdiction over frauds where the only element of the crime that takes place here is the actual gain or loss of property".*

2.13.3. (FA 2006 s13) S13- Defence of 'Evidence Obtained Unfairly'

One defence as to unfairly obtained evidence is as per section 78 of the Police and Criminal Evidence Act 1984. Section 78 gives the courts discretion to exclude from criminal trial, evidence which has been unfairly obtained. There are three main factors in the decisions under section 78 PACE and they are-bad faith on the part of the police; impropriety often in the form of breaches of PACE or its Codes of Practice, and the effect of such impropriety on the outcome of the case.

> **Points to Note: Relevance of evidence** It is firmly established in English law that the mere fact that evidence is obtained in an irregular fashion does not of itself prevent that evidence from being relevant and acceptable to a court. Non-compliance with PACE Code of Practice will not always result in evidence being rendered inadmissible as illustrated in *Basher v DPP* [1993] in which a failure to record a stop and search did not render the search unlawful.

> **Caselaw**
> ***R v Nadir* [1993] 4 All ER 513**
>
> A prejudicial evidence unfairness occurred in *R v Nadir [1993] 4 All ER 513*, at 517, Lord Taylor CJ explained that if a judge *"considers evidence the Crown wish to lead would have an adverse effect on the fairness of the trial, he can exclude it under section 78 of the Police and Criminal Evidence Act 1984..He also has a great discretion to exclude evidence which was preserved by section 82(3) of the 1984 Act which would allow the judge to exclude evidence he considers more prejudicial than probative".*

2.13.4. (FA 2006 s13) Evidence impropriety by entrapment

The fact that the evidence has been obtained by entrapment, or by an *agent provocateur*, or by a trick, does not, of itself, require the judge to exclude it.

If there is impropriety by the police, even though they did not act in bad faith, this will be a relevant factor in the exercise of the direction under section 78 PACE.

Fraud Investigation: Criminal Procedure and Investigation

> **Caselaw** *R v Alladice* **[1988]**, *R v Dunn* **[1990] and** *R v White* **[1991].** The impropriety may take the form of a breach of criminal or civil law or a failure to follow the procedures laid down by PACE and its Codes in relation to detention and questioning. Where there has been impropriety in the form of breaches of PACE or its Codes, the courts have deemed it relevant to consider the effect of the Police's conduct by taking notice of the extent to which the breaches were instrumental in obtaining the evidence, or whether the outcome of the case would have been any different if the evidence had been excluded as in these cases.

A person wishing to challenge the admissibility of evidence may first seek to establish a significant and substantial impropriety in the form of a breach of the Act or Codes. This can justify exclusion.

2.13. 5. (FA 2006 s13) Evidence that is 'privileged material' is a defence

The jurisdiction to restrain the use of privileged documents is based on the equitable jurisdiction to restrain breach of confidence. After a privileged document had been seen by the opposing party, the court might intervene by way of injunction if the circumstances warranted such intervention on equitable grounds. If the party in whose hands the document had come (or his solicitor) either had procured inspection of the document by fraud or on inspection, realized that he had been permitted to see the document only by reason of an obvious mistake, the court has power to intervene by the granting of an injunction. In such cases the court would ordinarily intervene, unless the case was one where the injunction could properly be refused on the general grounds affecting the grant of a discretionary remedy. So, in effect, privileged material may only formally come before the court by filing the relevant material at court and by election.

2.13.6. (S13FA) Evidence disclosure by POCA section 333 repealed

The existing offence of 'tipping off' in section 333 of POCA is repealed by paragraph 3, Proceeds of Crime Act 2002 (Amendment) Regulations 2007. Paragraph 4 of those regulations inserts a new section 333A into the Proceeds of Crime Act 2002 to create a new offence of 'tipping off' to cover the regulated sector.

2.13.7. Legal professional privilege upheld by Statutory Instrument

In December 2007, the Law Society of England and Wales was successful lobbying the government to uphold legal professional privilege and this resulted in a Statutory Instrument attached to the Proceeds of Crime Act. The government has stepped back from introducing a new absolute tipping off offence. In amending the Proceeds of Crime Act 2002 and the Terrorism Act 2000, the government had sought to remove the 'prejudice test'. This would have unnecessarily constrained lawyers in giving legal advice to clients. The Law Society persuaded the government to allow solicitors and others to discuss suspicious activity reports where this is unlikely to prejudice investigations. They successfully argued that the *'tipping off'* offence should apply only to regulated activities.

> **Point to Note: Tipping-off offence applies to solicitors**
>
> From 26 December 2007, the tipping off offence will no longer apply to solicitors. These regulations implement, in part, Directive 2005/60/EC of the European Parliament and of the Council of 26th October 2005 on the prevention of the use of the financial system for the purpose of money laundering and terrorist financing ("the Directive"). The regulations give effect to Chapter 3 of the Directive.

2.13.8.1. (FA 2006 s13) Evidence allowed if there is a Waiver of Privilege

Waiver may be *'express'* or *'implied'*. As with election, the essence of the question is to identify the stage at which the receiving party must be taken to have waived his privilege.

> **Caselaw**
>
> The case of *Pamplin v Express Newspapers Ltd* [1985] 2 All ER 185, [1985] 1 WLR 689 is one in which a document that might cause unfairness, was withdrawn.
>
> The judge said: *"In taxation, it will normally be a matter of express waiver only. It should always be possible to avoid having to get involved with implied waiver…A [receiving party] should not have imposed on him an unintended waiver unless fairness to both parties really does necessitate that result."*
>
> The way in which a receiving party would avoid having an unintended waiver imposed upon him is by withdrawing a document before that stage is reached.

2.13.8.2. (FA 2006 s13) Evidence that is non-privileged material is admissible

CPR s40.14 is not mandatory in that it merely provides that the court may put a receiving party to his election. Where the material for which disclosure is sought is not privileged, it is (theoretically) open to the court to order disclosure pursuant to Pt. 34 of the Civil Procedure Rules. In practice, however, most documents that are relevant to an assessment are privileged. In particular, solicitors' bills are privileged. Vice Chancellor Turner held in *Chant v Brown* (1862) 9 Hare 790, that this is on the ground that "*an attorney's bill of costs is, in truth, his history of the transaction in which he has been concerned*".

Mr. Justice Aldous appeared to have accepted a concession made by leading counsel that bills were privileged when, in *International Business Machines Corp v Phoenix International (Computers) Ltd* [1995] 1 All 412, he commented:

> "The reasonable solicitor would have been in no doubt that the legal bills were privileged documents."

Rimer .J also seems to have accepted this as being the correct position in *Dickinson*; he went on to say, however, that calculations made in relation to bills are not privileged. A 'client care letter' may be privileged depending on the nature of its contents and the context in which it is written—for general guidance see *Balabel v Air India* [1988] 2 All ER 246, [1988] 2 WLR 1036. A letter merely setting out the terms on which the solicitor will act is not privileged. Policies are not privileged, in that they must be disclosed.

2.13.8.3. Other laws that affect evidence- AML Regulations

There are conditions under which certain money laundering evidence will be admissible in court. Schedule 2 to the regulations makes amendments to the Proceeds of Crime Act 2002. Paragraph 2 of Schedule 1 inserts three new sections into the Terrorism Act 2000 to cover the requirements of Article 24 of the Directive. Section 21ZA provides a defence to the offences in sections 15 to 18 of the Terrorism Act 2000, if the person has made a disclosure to an authorised officer before becoming involved in a transaction or an arrangement and the person acts with the consent of the authorised officer. Paragraph 3(2) and paragraph 4 of Schedule 1 to the regulations amend sections 21A and 21B of the Terrorism Act 2000 respectively, in order to give full effect to the requirements of Article 22.1 of the Directive. Article 22.1 requires those covered by the Directive to make reports of knowledge and suspicions of money laundering and terrorist financing that have been *attempted* as well as *committed*. Paragraph 3(3) to (6) of Schedule 1 amends section 21A of the Terrorism Act 2000 to give effect to Article 23.2 of the Directive, which provides that Member States are not required to apply the reporting obligations to legal and other professionals when giving legal advice. To this effect, and after extensive lobbying by the legal profession, the United Kingdom has chosen not to apply obligations to solicitors.

2.13.8.4. Other laws that affect evidence- Criminal Justice Act 2003

Business documents are admissible under section 117 Criminal Justice Act 2003 and takes into account the modern business practice where a vast quantity of documents is created on a daily basis. As it would be impossible to require every person who had personal knowledge of the document's contents to testify in court, section 117(2) CJA 2003 makes business documents admissible as hearsay in criminal proceedings where the following conditions are satisfied *if:*

(i) the document was created or received in the course of a trade, business, profession or other occupation, or as the holder of a paid or unpaid office (see s117(2)(a)));

(ii) the person who supplied the information contained in the statement had or might have reasonably be expected to have had personal knowledge of the matters dealt with in the statement (se s117(2)(b));

(iii) each person, if any, through whom the information was supplied from the relevant person received the information in the course of a trade, business, profession or other occupation or as the holder of a paid or unpaid office (see s117(2)(c)).

In all, section 117 permits the reception into evidence of multi-hand hearsay which satisfies the requirements above. Business records, ledgers, invoices, hospital records, etc. will be admissible under s117(4), provided that documents satisfy the conditions laid down in s117(5).Section 117(7) incorporates a safeguard in relation to all documents that are sought to be admitted under s177. Section 117(7) provides that a court may make a direction to *exclude* a statement if the statement's reliability as evidence is doubtful in view of its contents; the source of the information contained in it and the way in which the document was acquired.

2.14. Fraud to facilitate terrorist financing through money laundering

Serious transnational organized criminals are always on the alert for prospective places to hide and to secure their ill-gotten proceeds. Offshore havens have long been the harbour of choice for these criminals, as well as for legitimate business-persons who evade taxes. Terrorists have traditionally relied upon two sources of funding: state and private sponsors. There are amendments to the Terrorism Act 2000 and the Proceeds of Crime Act 2002 which are consequential amendments. The relevant changes appear in paragraph 6 of Schedule 1 and paragraphs 2, 5, 6 and 8 of Schedule2 Statutory Instruments2007, Number 3398.

> **Point to Note: Off-shore banking facilitates money laundering for terrorist financing**
>
> Bermuda is one such offshore place where people launder money. The Bermuda Government in July 2008, announced a Bill to freeze companies' funds in crime investigations. Bermuda fails to comply with 29 international recommendations on anti-money laundering and Bahamas and Cayman Islands fail in 6 and 2 respectively.

2.15. Taxes Management Act and HMRC powers to force disclosure

Section 20, Taxes Management Act enables HMRC to serve a third-party information notice on an institution, such as a bank, without naming the taxpayer to whom the notice relates. To do this, it needs the permission of a special commissioner, who will only agree if the notice relates to a taxpayer whose identity is not known to HMRC or to a class of taxpayers whose individual identities are not so known; if there are reasonable grounds for believing that the individuals concerned may have failed to comply with any provision of TMA 1970; if any such failure is likely to lead to serious underpayment of tax; and the information requested is not readily available from another source. HMRC can serve notices under s 20(8A), to obtain disclosure of documents relating to an unidentified taxpayer or a class of unidentified taxpayers, and HMRC has the right to seek documents dating back more than six years, which is the limit for other notices served under section 20. Also, under the section 60 Serious Organised Crime and Police Act 2005 (SOCPA 2005) HMRC has powers to conduct its own investigations on tax fraud. HMRC can compel individuals to answer questions by issuing a disclosure notice, without seeking permission from the commissioners.

Under SOCPA 2005, HMRC can also compel banks to answer relevant questions. HMRC also has the power to execute a search warrant without a police officer being present if the disclosure notice is not complied with. Once disclosure is made, HMRC will also investigate to see if the funds in the account have not been diverted from a taxable source in the UK without having been fully declared for tax purposes.

2.16. Fraud Act criminalises a broad range of conduct

The Fraud Act 2006 simplifies a formerly complex area of the law and may help to avoid the use of technical defences which have no real merit. The breadth of the new fraud offence criminalizes a broader range of conduct, with the necessary result that a wider range of property may constitute the proceeds of crime. In the past, the anti-money laundering obligations of banks have focused primarily on the source of the customer's own funds.

2.17. Conclusion to Chapter Two

Overall, the Fraud Act gives a statutory definition of the criminal offence of fraud, defining it in three classes - fraud by false representation, fraud by failing to disclose information, and fraud by abuse of position. It provides that a person found guilty of fraud was liable to a fine or imprisonment for up to twelve months on summary conviction (six months in Northern Ireland), or a fine or imprisonment for up to ten years on conviction on indictment.

Further Reading for Chapter 2

www.anticorruptionforum.org.uk/acf/news/publications/newsletters/feb07/feb07.pdf

www.journalonline.co.uk/article/1004066.aspx

www.courtservice.gov.uk/judgmentsfiles/j2357/ingelheim-v-Dowelhurst.htm

http://www.lawreports.co.uk   www.opsi.gov.uk/ACTS/en2006/ukpgaen_20060035_en.pdf

www.jerseylegalinfo.je/publications/jerseylawreview/feb01/the_difficulties_binnington.aspx

www.evca.com/images/attachments/tmpl_14_art_97_att_1083.pdf

www.publications.parliament.uk/pa/cm200506/cmbills/166/en/06166x--.htm

linkinghub.elsevier.com/retrieve/pii/S1361372305702311

caselaw.lp.findlaw.com/cgi-bin/getcase.pl?court=2nd&navby=case&no=977029

www.publications.parliament.uk/pa/ld200506/ldbills/007/en/06007x--.htm

CHAPTER 3-
OTHER LEGISLATION THAT DEALS WITH FRAUD

3.1. Introduction

The Fraud Act does not cover all fraud offences but sits alongside many other statutes. Such statutes cover some specific frauds. Fraud offences not so covered are some theft offences, money laundering, cheating the revenue, forgery, and counterfeiting, false statements by company directors, fraudulent trading, and statutory tax offences. This chapter will list some of the alternate legislation that can be used instead of the Fraud Act and examine certain of these offences.

3.2. Fraud offences can be prosecuted using other statutes

Fraud offences can also be prosecuted under the Proceeds of Crime Act 2002 ("POCA") sections 340 and 333, relating to money laundering, failing to disclose , and tipping off, covered within sections 330 to 333 POCA; common law 'cheating the revenue'; section 1 Forgery and Counterfeiting Act 1981; section 52 Criminal Justice Act 1993- insider dealing; section 397 Financial Services and Markets Act 2000- misleading market practices; section 107 Copyright, Designs, and Patents Act 1988- intellectual property offences; section 92 Trade Marks Act 1994; sections 1-3 Computer Misuse Acts 1990; section 72(8) Value Added Tax Act 1994; conspiracy to defraud at common law; Serious Crimes Act 2007; Criminal Attempts Act; Aiders and Abettors Act; Insolvency Act; Companies Acts and Money Laundering Regulations.

> **Point to Note: Fraudulent trading can be prosecuted in other ways**
>
> Although the Fraud Act created a new offence of fraudulent trading by businesses not caught in the Companies Act legislation section 458 CA 1985, with a maximum penalty of ten years imprisonment, it does not carry a remedy as the Insolvency Act 1986, section 213 does.

3.3.1. Insolvency proceedings

There are freezing orders and search orders, bankruptcy proceedings, directors' disqualifications and insolvency proceedings available through the civil courts. When undertakings are broken, say, under the Insolvency Act, then the punishments often incurred become criminal matters.

> **Point to Note: Search Orders of computer and paper systems**
>
> A search order will allow premises to be searched in order to obtain certain documents. The Court places a heavy onus on the Applicant to provide accurate and compelling evidence before it will grant a search order and/or an injunction. In order to obtain the relevant Court order the evidence must to be properly presented. Once a Court has granted a search order the next stage is to have it served on the respondent and a full and proper search of the relevant premises within the terms of the order is made. A search order often provides for a clone to be taken of all computer systems and electronic storage equipment owned (wherever it may be kept) by the respondent. The next hurdle is reviewing the data

> (paper and electronic copy) obtained from the search in order to find the necessary evidence for litigation. Data needs to be filtered and it is essential that all the relevant documents are reviewed in a methodical manner.

Below is a table of *some* punishment of fraud offences under the Insolvency Act:

3.3.2. Criminal frauds can be punished by Insolvency Act.

Insolvency Act 1986	Prosecution	Punishment
s31	Bankrupt acting as receiver or manager	2 years in prison or fine or both
s6A(1)	False representation for purpose of obtaining members' or creditors approval of proposed voluntary arrangement	7 years in prison or fine or both
s51(5)	Un-discharged bankrupt acting as receiver	2 years in prison or fine or both
s89(4)	Director making statutory declaration of company's solvency without reasonable grounds for his opinion	2 years in prison or fin or both
s206(2)	Privity to fraud in anticipation to winding up	7 years or a fine or both
206(5)	Knowingly taking in pawn or pledge, or otherwise receiving company property	7 years or fine or both

Fraud Investigation: Criminal Procedure and Investigation

s208	Misconduct of company officer in course of winding up	7 years or fine or both
s209	Company officer or contributors destroying or falsifying, etc. company's books	7 years in prison or fine or both
s210	Company officer making material omission from statement relating to company's affairs	7 years in prison or fine or both
s216(4)	Contravening restrictions on reuse of name of company in insolvent liquidation	2 years or fine or both
s354(1)	Bankrupt failing to deliver property to or concealing property from official receiver or trustee	7 years or fine or both
s355(1)	Bankrupt failing to deliver books, papers and records to receiver	7 years or fine or both

Caselaw

***Re Diamond Commodities, Secretary of State for Business Enterprise and Regulatory Reform v Farndell*, Ch.D., 19 March 2008, Case No. 1547 of 2007**

Mr. Farndell sought to strike out a disqualification claim brought against him because of an allegation of fraud. Farndell's company Diamonds Commodities Ltd., incorporated in 1996, traded as an importer and exporter of nuts and had ceased trading in 2005, due to cash-flow difficulties. Diamonds Commodities had an invoice factoring agreement with HSBC Invoice Finance (UK) Ltd. which found major irregularities, including fictitious invoices, HSBC regarding the conduct and operation of the factoring facility. Because HSBC did not have strong documentation to bring before the court, the court decided to strike out the disqualification application. Such a claim must be well documented and substantiated and it was not. The court applied the standard of the balance of probabilities. As per *Re H (Minors) (Sexual Abuse Standard of Proof)* [1996] AC 563 at 586E and 587A, these being state as:

"The balance of probability standard means that a court is satisfied an event occurred if the court considered that on the evidence, the occurrence of the event was more likely than not. When assessing the probabilities the court will have in mind a factor to whatever extent is appropriate in the particular case, that the more serious the allegation the less likely it is that the event occurred and, hence, the stronger should be the evidence before the court concludes that the allegation is established on the balance of probabilities. Fraud is usually less likely than negligence...and...a balance of probability standard can accommodate one's instinctive feeling that even in civil proceedings, a court should be more sure before finding serious allegations proved than when deciding less serious matters."

3.3.3.1. Mareva Injunction – a civil action to freeze asset of fraud

Given the circumstances in which injunctive relief is usually sought within the context of complex, international commercial fraud cases, immediate action is generally required. In cases where the victim of fraud is dealing with a dishonest obligor with the propensity to transfer and conceal assets, the time taken to prepare and finalize a set of pleadings to ground a series of urgent *ex parte* asset-freezing applications to courts in what might be numerous foreign jurisdictions may well turn out to be time spent in vain. There is a risk that by the time a number of freezing orders are made, the subject property may no longer be in the location originally identified. The very fact that property gained by fraud s located within a foreign jurisdiction necessitates the retention of local counsel.

In complex international fraud cases, local counsel will need time to review and become familiar with what are generally voluminous and complex facts. Nevertheless, foreign jurisdictions may impose requirements that are difficult, if not impossible, to comply with. In such circumstances, and in cases where it is feared that the disposal or transfer of assets imposed with a constructive trust in favour of the plaintiff is imminent, other available methods of preserving wealth, such as a Mareva Injunction, must be considered. This involves placing a third-party guardian or holder of assets, such as a bank, on notice that those assets are imposed with a constructive trust in favour of someone other than the party who the guardian or holder has previously been led to believe is the true owner. In cases where a victim of fraud has information to the effect that targeted funds or assets are about to be transferred to another location where it might be impossible to gain access to them, an immediate and informal (or *de facto*) freeze of the assets may be effected by issuing a letter to the third-party asset holder in question, informing it of the true origin or beneficial ownership of the targeted funds or assets, and advising it of its potential accessory liability in the event of any transfer or disposal of the assets in question.

In situations where this informal procedure is used, sufficient proof should be provided to the third-party holder of assets to provide comfort that the conclusion being urged upon it as to the origin or provenance of the assets is in fact a reasonable one to be drawn in the circumstances. Such parties will be acutely aware of their liability to their customer in the event that any attempted transfer of such assets is blocked and it transpires that the basis for such blockage was non-existent or faulty. In issuing a Mareva letter, some evidence should be provided to support the conclusions urged and to provide sufficient justification to enable the third-party asset holder or guardian to refuse to relinquish control of the asset for the time being.

In many jurisdictions, exposing a bank or fiduciary holder of assets to actual knowledge of an apparent fraud on the part of a customer destroys the defence of good faith (or the defence implicit in the absence of knowledge of fraud) to a charge of money laundering. Permitting the transfer of assets or the withdrawal of funds in the face of actual knowledge of an apparent fraud linked to such wealth might expose officers and employees of the bank or other capital markets intermediary in question to criminal sanctions under money laundering prevention laws.

A *'Mareva by letter'* can invoke public law duties on the bank or fiduciary holder of wealth involved and civil liability may arise in that the true beneficial owner of the asset in question would be entitled to institute an action based on theories of *'knowing assistance in the dishonest breach of a constructive trust'* or *'knowing receipt of trust property.'*

The '*Mareva by letter*' represents a significant step in the fight against fraud. It can be an invaluable and effective pre-emptive asset preservation measure. It assists a victim of fraud in managing the risks of delay in time and considerable expense typically associated with an application to preserve assets through freezing or restraining orders. It potentially enables a victim of fraud likewise and perhaps more importantly, to avoid the necessity of posting asset-freezing indemnity bonds or security for costs, or to support cross-undertakings in damages. The '*Mareva by letter*' marks a milestone in the development of effective remedies in the context of loss occasioned by serious fraud.

3.3.3.2. Contract law may be used to deal with fraud

If a consumer suspects fraud, there is an alternative to police action through the 'Cancellation of Contracts Made in a Consumer's Home or Place of Work etc Regulations 2008'. These Regulations replace the 'Consumer Protection: (Cancellation of Contracts Concluded away from Business Premises) Regulations 1987', and take forward measures announced by the Government in its 'Response to the Public Consultation on Doorstep Selling and Cold Calling' in September 2006:

> *"To extend the cooling off period and the cancellation rights which currently apply to contracts made during unsolicited visits by traders to contracts made during solicited visits by traders; and require that a notice of the right to cancel the contract be prominently and clearly displayed in the same document where the contract is completed wholly or partly in writing."*

These Regulations apply widely and all traders, including builders, plumbers, carpenters etc, who respond to a solicited approach by a consumer, and who enter into a contract with the consumer (whether oral or written) in the consumer's home or place of work (or at the home of another individual) or on an excursion organised by the trader and away from the trader's business premises, are affected.

3.3.4. Consumer Credit Act 2006 can be used as a civil remedy against fraud

The Consumer Credit Act 2006 has been in force since 30 March 2006 and it has amended the Consumer Credit Act 1974, in order to protect consumers and create a fairer, more transparent and more competitive credit market. This Act repeals Section 127 (3) - (5) of the 1974 Act, giving the courts discretion over whether a regulated agreement is enforceable where key information has not been included in an agreement. Such missing information can be viewed as act of fraud by omission. The Consumer Credit Act 2006 introduces the concept of "unfair relationships" and replaces the little used "extortionate credit" test with a much broader-based test. For example, unfairness may be deemed to have arisen as a result of the way the product is marketed.

The Act establishes an alternative dispute resolution scheme by the Financial Ombudsman Service for disputes between consumers and consumer credit licence holders. High Net Worth borrowers are exempt from regulation because the 2006 Act provides a new definition of "individuals." It also established a consumer credit appeals tribunal. Post Contract Information provisions must be made by the credit provider and businesses must provide periodic statements of account to their customers. They must also provide arrears' notices and default notices, where applicable. Such a procedure gives the customer who s genuinely in difficulty, a chance to seek some form of agreement as to payments.

The fraudulent trader who has absconded with a loan of less than £25,000 would have been provided with an agreement containing a prescribed form of declaration which he must have signed to declare that the loan is for business purposes. Interest on default sums is restricted to simple interest. Failure of the credit provider to comply with the above requirements will impact on an agreement's enforceability.

3.4. Computer Misuse Act 1990

The word 'likely' is not defined in Computer Misuse Act but, in construing what is 'likely', look at the functionality of the article and at what thought the suspect gave to who would use it; whether for example the article was circulated to a closed and vetted list of IT security professionals or was posted openly. In the likelihood that an article has been used (or misused) to commit a criminal offence, the following points are to be considered.

(i) Has the article been developed primarily, deliberately and for the sole purpose of committing a CMA offence (i.e. unauthorised access to computer material)?

(ii) Is the article available on a wide scale commercial basis and sold through legitimate channels?

(iii) Is the article widely used for legitimate purposes?

(iv) Does the article have a substantial installation base?

(v) What was the context in which the article was used to commit the offence compared with its original intended purpose?

'Phishing' or collecting data on people and businesses to use in fraud is so prevalent in the United Kingdom that estimates of the number of phishing websites reveal that they are increasing in number by 15% a year.

> **Point to Note: Frauds needing information provided by victims**
>
> Internet-based schemes of tricking people into revealing confidential financial information, is the most risky fraud that taxpayers should be aware of. The HMRC warned people not to fall for predators posing as HMRC representatives who tell them they must reveal personal information to obtain whistle-blowing reward payments.

The Computer Misuse Act 1990 prohibits unauthorised access to data on computers and unauthorised modifications to computers' contents. Therefore, 'Phishing' by sending Trojan Horses (viruses) to people's computers, would fall under the Computer Misuse Act, but sending a spoof email linking to a website would not. In 'phishing', a false representation is made by sending a fake email. Email can be the 'article' in question. On 27th March 2006, the US government charged 4 persons in $1.2 million e-mail fraud scheme.

> **Points to Note: Viruses update as at November 2008**
>
> *Cross-site scripting*: Causes the browser to execute arbitrary client-side scripting code, hijacking the user's session and allowing the attacker to phish for account/financial information. *Injection flaws*: Improperly validated data passing through the interpreter can "confuse" it and open the way for malicious code to be injected into the interpreter. *Buffer overflows*: Mostly a C and C++ problem due to lack of memory, buffer overflows are similar to injection attacks; in this case, an attacker sends commands with too many characters and takes over the system, with full privileges. Insecure direct

> object reference: *Intentional or unintentional access to internal object handlers* leads to exposure of data. Information leakage and improper error handling: *Overly helpful error messages*: give too much information about a system—version, system type, error type, etc.—giving an attacker more knowledge to launch exploits. *Resource leak*: When programs leak memory, the operating system may terminate them for exceeding prescribed limits, affecting other programs on the computer. *Unintentional ignored expressions*: When expressions are ignored, code is unreachable and cannot perform needed action. For example, a bug discovered by a Coverity customer, in which a missing parenthesis kept a single routine from executing, turned out to be the worst exploit that company had seen in five years, according to Ben Chelf, founding CTO at Coverity. *Null pointer de-reference*: Invalid values assigned between operations lead to a hard crash, the most frequent cause of Windows' Blue Screen of Death. *Web services*: Malicious code can be injected into Web services entry points. Static analyzers include rule wizards and data APIs that perform cross-service analysis and identification of Web services entry points. *Custom cookies/hidden fields*: Attackers can view the underlying HTTP response payload by viewing the source code of a Web page or by using proxies to find hidden files and cookies.

The CMA, as amended by the Police and Justice Act 2006 will introduce Section 3A CMA an offence which penalises the making; supplying or obtaining of articles for use in offences contrary to sections 1 or 3 CMA. (Section 37 of the Police and Justice Act 2006); and increases the penalty for section 1 CMA (Section 35 of the Police and Justice Act 2006).

> **Point to Note: The Computer Misuse Act does not provide a definition of a computer.**
>
> This is because it was feared that any definition would soon become out of date due to the rapid with which technology develops. Definition is therefore left to the Courts who are expected to adopt the contemporary meaning of the word. In *DPP v McKeown, DPP v Jones* [1997] 2 Cr App R, 155, HL, at page 163, Lord Hoffman defined a computer as "*a device for storing, processing and retrieving information*".

There is jurisdiction to prosecute all CMA offences if there is "at least one significant link with the domestic jurisdiction" (England and Wales) in the circumstances of the case. In the case of *R v Waddon*, 6 April 2000, the Court of Appeal held that the content of American websites could come under British jurisdiction when downloaded in the United Kingdom. Section 1 CMA - unauthorised Access is amended by section 35 Police and Justice Act 2006 and Schedule 15 of the Serious Crime Act 2007. Sections 1 and 2 of the CMA must be read in conjunction with section 17 of the CMA, which is the interpretation section (*Attorney-General's Ref. (No 1 of 1991)* [1993] QB 94). The offence of unauthorised access requires proof of two *mens rea* elements.

There must be knowledge that the intended access was unauthorised; and there must have been an intention to obtain information about a program or data held in a computer – section 1(2) CMA. In the case of *R v Bow Street Magistrates Court and Allison (AP) Ex parte Government of the United States of America (Allison)* [2002] 2 AC 216, where the House of Lords considered whether an employee could commit an offence of securing "unauthorised access" to a computer it was held that the employee intentionally caused a computer to give her access to data which she knew she was not authorised to access.

3.5. The Police and Justice Act 2006 used to prosecute computer fraud

The Police and Justice Act 2006 amends the Computer Misuse Act 1990 and this will help in the prosecution of computer/internet frauds. On Jan 7th 2008, the CPS issued a DRAFT guidance document to assist prosecutors in understanding the amendments made to the 'Computer Misuse Act 1990' by the 'Police & Justice Act 2006'. This guidance is to assist Crown Prosecutors and Designated Caseworkers in the use of their discretion in making decisions in computer misuse cases.

> **Caselaw**
>
> In the case of *DPP v Bignell* [1998] 1 Cr App R8, two police officers, who were authorised to request information from the police national computer (PNC) for policing purposes only, requested a police computer operator to obtain information from the PNC which, unbeknown to the operator, was for their own personal use. His authority permitted him to access the data on the computer for the purpose of responding to requests made to him in proper form by police officers. No offence had been committed under section 1 of the CMA.

3.6. Prosecute malware-using Serious Crime Act 2007

Malware is no longer a prank but a form of cybercrime.

Section 3 CMA – Unauthorised Acts with Intent to Impair is amended by section 36 Police and Justice Act 2006 and Schedule 15 of the Serious Crime Act 2007. Every act relied upon to prove the section 3 CMA offence must have taken place after section 36 Police and Justice Act 2006 comes into force. Section 3 CMA should be considered in cases involving distributed denial of service attacks (DDoS), (1) as the term "act" includes a series of acts, (2) there is no need for any modification to have occurred and (3) the impairment can be temporary.

> **Caselaw**
>
> In the mail bombing case of *R v Lennon* [2006] EWCH 1201, 11 May 2006, the Divisional Court stated that, although the owner of a computer able to receive e-mails ordinarily consents to the receipt of e-mails, such consent did not extend to e-mails that had been sent not for the purpose of communicating with the owner but for the purpose of interrupting the operation of the system.

A person guilty of an offence contrary to section 3 is liable on summary conviction to imprisonment for a term not exceeding 12 months or to a fine not exceeding the statutory maximum or to both; or on conviction on indictment, to imprisonment for a term not exceeding ten years or to a fine or to both. Section 3A CMA – Making, supplying or obtaining articles-As inserted by section 37 Police and Justice Act 2006. Section 3A CMA covers making, supplying or obtaining articles for use in offences contrary to sections 1 or 3 CMA. Section 3A deals with those who produce, for example, malicious scripts or software designed to enable modification of television set top boxes. It does not criminalise possession per se unless an intent to use it to commit one of the other offences in section 1 or 3 CMA can be shown. Every act relied upon to prove the section 3A CMA offence must have taken place after section 37 Police and Justice Act 2006. A person guilty of an offence under this section is liable on summary conviction in England and Wales, to imprisonment for a term not exceeding 12 months or to a fine or to both; on conviction on indictment, to imprisonment for a term not exceeding two years or to fine or to both.

3.7. 1.Pension Scheme Frauds have the remedy of Govt. Compensation Scheme

In 1991 Robert Maxwell stole more than £400m from the Mirror Group Pension Scheme, which had about 32,000 members, to prop up his ailing businesses. From this scandal, far from the only one but the biggest and most notorious, came the Goode Report, followed by a still flowing torrent of legislation under the aegis of, mainly, the Department for Work and Pension and the Treasury, with two beneficial outcomes. There is protection for pension scheme members under three schemes.

(i) The Pension Protection Fund (a global pension scheme to absorb pension schemes in deficit whose employers became insolvent on or after 6 April 2005);

(ii) The Financial Assistance Scheme (which offers relief to pension scheme members, who lost some or all of their pension benefits because their pension schemes are in deficit and their employer became insolvent from 1 January 1997 and before 6 April 2005); and

(iii) The Fraud Compensation Scheme.

The precursor to the present scheme was established by the Pensions Act 1995, which, in ss 78 to 86. These provisions were repealed on 1 September 2005 and substantially re-enacted in ss 182 to 189 of the Pensions Act 2004, fleshed out by the Occupational Pension Schemes (Fraud Compensation Payments and Miscellaneous Amendments) Regulations 2005, SI 2005/2151. The 2005 Act replaced the Pensions Compensation Board with the Board of the Pension Protection Fund, whose functions, under s110 included holding, managing and applying (a) the Pension Protection Fund and (b) the Fraud Compensation Fund. The main compensation provisions apply to occupational pension scheme (with some exceptions, mainly public service schemes) are that compensation may be paid to the scheme's trustees, if the employer is insolvent, the assets of the scheme had been reduced, there were reasonable grounds for believing that the reduction was attributable to an offence and it was reasonable for the Compensation Board to pay an amount to the scheme's trustees.

3.7.2. Pension Fraud Compensation Rules

Under the original provisions, the amount of the compensation in a money purchase scheme was 90% of the amount of the money that had been lost. In the case of a final salary scheme the amount, by the time that the PCB was superseded, was an amount to bring the scheme's assets up 100% of its liabilities for pensioners and members within ten years of retirement and 90% in respect of the other members, in each case calculated on the minimum funding requirement (MFR) up to the value of the assets lost. Under the new provisions, the compensation in all cases is, broadly speaking 100% of the amount of money lost.

Section 182(1)(b) speaks of "an act or omission constituting a prescribed offence", which is defined in article 3 of SI 2005/2184, which reads as follows.

> *"Relevant offences: For the purpose of section 182(1)(b) (cases where fraud compensation payments can be made: reduction of scheme assets attributable to a prescribed offence), a prescribed offence is any offence involving dishonesty, and for these purposes dishonesty shall include an intent to defraud".*

This is a very broad definition, and it is not necessary that an offence is proved, to a criminal or any other standard of proof, as s182(1)(b) merely requires that the Board considers that there are reasonable grounds for believing that the reduction was attributable to an act or omission constituting a prescribed offence. The board is not required to report its findings. The PPF's annual report 2006/7 does not even contain the word "fraud" and the PPF's Strategic Plan 2006/7 to 2007/8 contains only three comments of interest about the fraud compensation fund.

Point to Note: Auditors of banks, insurance companies and charities have a duty to make reports to regulators.

The Pensions Act 1995 established important responsibilities for pension scheme auditors. The Auditing Practices Board has established principles and set standards for the profession through the Statement of Auditing Standards 620, "The Auditors right and duty to report to regulators in the financial sector". The principle determinant of the duty to report is whether a breach is likely to be of material significance to the regulator (level of materiality). The first case brought by the Occupational Pensions Regulatory Authority was 2002 case against Peter Lavender, (*R v Peter Lavender* [2002] unreported) a director of SSL

> Patient Transport Systems Ltd, who used the company's occupational pensions to prop up the failing company. Peter Lavender's defence was that he was not aware that the pension contributions were not being paid over to the pension scheme. He had instructed the bank to stop these direct debits. He was found guilty of fraudulent evasion.

3.7.3. Time span for receiving Pension Fraud Compensation

All pension fraud compensation cases are cleared within six months of completion of any external investigation. The number of formal complaints received about payment of compensation should be less than 0.5% of the total of members transferred to the Fund It has also been assumed that no substantial volume of fraud compensation claims will be received in the three years ending 31 March 2009. This assumption is informed by the low volume of cases processed by the former Pensions Compensation Board between 1997 and 2005. Offences for the purposes of the Fraud Compensation Scheme can include offences by any of the three main parties to a pension scheme, the employer, the trustees and the members and also third parties.

Fraud Investigation: Criminal Procedure and Investigation

> **Caselaw**
>
> In *Duckitt and ors v Ferrand and ors* ([2001] PLR 155, CA, the directors of the company, who were also the trustees of its pension scheme, procured the scheme to lend money to the company, which was not repaid, and members made complaints to the Pensions Ombudsman alleging mal-administration. In his determination the Ombudsman found for the complainants and said that he had no difficulty in finding that each of the loans was sought and made with the sole objective of keeping the Company trading. The course of action which Mr B and Mr D pursued in making the series of loans to the Company in admitted breach of trust establishes that they were recklessly indifferent to whether or not they were acting in the interests of the members of the Scheme so as to come within the meaning of fraud.

This *Duckitt* case was argued and decided, not on the question whether the trustees' conduct amounted to fraud, but on the question whether the Pensions Ombudsman had the power to make the appeal at all. This was part of a "war" between the Pensions Ombudsman and the Courts, in which the Court gained the upper hand and avoided dealing with the substantive issue. Fraud on the part of the trustees (in the context of clauses exonerating trustees' from liability and indemnifying them) was considered in *Armitage v Nurse* [1998] Ch 241, [1997] 2 All ER 705, at p 251 where Millett LJ said:

> "... *at the minimum an intention on the part of the trustee to pursue a particular course of action, either knowing that it is contrary to the interests of the beneficiaries or*

being recklessly indifferent whether it is contrary to their interests or not."

> ### Caselaw
>
> ### *R v Trustees of CW Cheyney* [2005] unreported
> This was a pension fund fraud, referred by the Occupational Pensions Regulatory Authority and accepted by the Serious Fraud Office.
>
> In 2005 the SFO published a statement of the Cheney case, in which the purchasers of the CW Cheney & Son Ltd removed the trustees of the company's pension scheme from office, appointed "puppet" trustees and extracted almost £2.2m from the scheme. The principal perpetrator, Kevin Sykes was sentenced on 7 October 2004 to six and a half years' imprisonment. Another SFO case involved a loan. Balfron Group Limited was sold to a company owned by the Stiedl Stiftung, a Liechtenstein trust. Mr. Bjorn Stiedl, a Danish businessman, was a director and Mr. Carsten Myrthue Iversen, a Danish lawyer, was company secretary and also the company's solicitor. The company's pension scheme of Balfron Group Limited, with assets of over £4.3m, made a loan agreement with a Virgin Islands company and pursuant to it lent over £2.1m, which were never repaid, and which were disbursed to various companies and persons associated with Mr Stiedl. Mr Stiedl and Mr Iversen were found him guilty of conspiracy to defraud on 13 June 2005. Today Iverson was sentenced to two years' imprisonment and ordered to pay £100,000 compensation to victims, with an additional 18 months imprisonment if he does not comply with the compensation order. Mr Stiedl was sentenced to four and a half years' imprisonment and agreed to pay compensation of over £2m.

3.8. Conclusion

The civil route for resolving business disputes remains the route taken in these times of rising fraud because the civil route includes more remedies for the victim and requires a lower standard of proof than by using the statutory criminal law for fraud.

> **Further Reading to Chapter Three**
>
> A.P. Carr, A.J. Turner, *Stone's Justice Manual, Volume 1 2008*, (LexisNexis, London 2008)
>
> Judge Abbas Mithani, *Mithani Directors' Disqualification*, (LexisNexis, London 2008)
>
> OECD, "Malware: A security threat to the internet community", 2008
>
> http://www.oecd.org/sti/security-privacy

CHAPTER 4- CONSPIRACY TO DEFRAUD, ATTEMPTED FRAUD, INCITEMENT TO FRAUD

4.1. Conspiracy to defraud

Conspiracy to defraud is one of the inchoate offences alongside incitement and attempt, but it is so widely used as a charge that it deserves a chapter of its own. The Criminal Justice Act 1993 makes provision for jurisdiction issues in relation to certain offences of dishonesty and blackmail. The SFO use the charge of 'conspiracy to defraud' in cases of 'misleading the markets' and 'insider trading'. 'Insider trading' is very difficult to prosecute and there are very few cases brought to trial in the United Kingdom. A conspiracy to defraud charge can also be brought as a private criminal prosecution as in the case of *Sears Group Properties Plc v Andrew Scrivener* [1998] in which Sears sued the group technical director for conspiracy to defraud the company between 1991 and 1997, alleging that Scrivener conspired with suppliers to overcharge on contracts for fitting out retail premises. The UK Fraud Act 2006 does not model the fraud offence on the offence of conspiracy to defraud which it considers too wide. However, the offence of conspiracy to defraud will remain as a common law fraud offence.

4.2. The new offence of fraud does not require proof of deception

This is an integral part of the Fraud Act 2006 offences. The concept of dishonesty in the fraud offence emphasises the act of the perpetrator and need not be proved to have caused the loss in question.

4.3. Positive misstatement fraud

Therefore, the offence of fraud can mean making a positive misstatement, or dishonestly making a false representation, or dishonestly failing to disclose information to another. In all cases, it is not necessary that any consequence comes from the fraud.

> **Point to Note: Passport fraud**
>
> Passport frauds are frauds by false representations. New measures to stop passport frauds are in place. From April 2008, all visa applicants over 5 years old will be required to supply biometric data before they are issued with visas to travel to the UK. Roll out is taking place on a country-by-country basis.

4.4. Conspiracy to defraud charge to be used in certain types of cases

The Attorney General's Guidance, issued 7th January 2007, states that the common law offence of conspiracy to defraud may be used in the following types of cases:

conduct that can more effectively be prosecuted as conspiracy to defraud. This includes cases where various types of criminality are found; and conduct that can only be prosecuted as conspiracy to defraud. This includes conduct which is not covered by any statutory provision, but which would amount to conspiracy to defraud.

4.5. Conspiracy to defraud charge

This offence is a major asset to investigators of complex fraud. The Fraud Act 2006 has greatly assisted the fraud investigator; however, some frauds are so involved that this offence is still the best choice. If the prosecutor feels that this is the best charge to be used in a case, he must now follow a certain procedure as laid down in the Attorney General's Guidelines. The prosecutor must set out the reason for using this charge and how this charge will add to the evidence likely to be called by the prosecution and defence and the justification for using the charge. The prosecutor must then provide the Attorney General with a record, which can be used during later deliberations as to the fate of the common law offence of conspiracy to defraud. In all, the use of the charge of conspiracy to defraud is subject to the general principles relating to all common law offences. Where a statutory alternative exists, there must be boundaries to common law offence usage because it breaches Article 7 of the European Convention on Human Rights 1950, which controls the growing use of common law offences outside their established bounds.

Fraud Investigation: Criminal Procedure and Investigation

> **Point to Note: whole authorities can commit fraud**
>
> The recently announced £19.8 million fine of Southern Water and the prosecution of Severn Trent acts as a warning that providing false or misleading information to industry regulators can have a high cost. Severn Trent was fined £19.8 imposed by Ofwat on Southern Water. It demonstrates a non-compliance with licence conditions. As an undertaker, Southern Water is obliged to provide Ofwat with accurate information about service levels, including information such as the number of complaints received, the number of customer calls and the level of billing of metered customers. Ofwat has found that Southern Water failed to provide reliable and accurate data in its June 2005 reports and deliberately manipulated the information that it did report in order to deceive Ofwat about its performance and avoid losing face with customers.

The charge of conspiracy to defraud is still much used today because in a conspiracy to defraud charge it is only necessary to prove the essentials of a charge. Tax evasion schemes, for example, are particularly likely to be caught by conspiracy to defraud charge. To bring complexity to the charge, conspiracy to defraud can occur over more than one territory. An agreement formed in one territorial area may be aimed at people in another area or other areas, or may reach into such areas in the course of its performance. This is an aspect of criminal conspiracy that has made it difficult to relate to the theory of territoriality, which has so much influence on common law rules concerning the administration of criminal justice.

4.7. The Criminal Justice Act 1993

CJA 1993 is a statute on procedure and it makes provision for such problems by making provision about the jurisdiction of courts in England and Wales in relation to certain offences of dishonesty and blackmail. T deals with two sets of offences which it calls Group A offences and Group B offences, as listed in section 1 of the Criminal Justice Act 1993:

"two groups of offences— (a) any offence mentioned in subsection (2) (a 'Group A offence'); and (b) any offence mentioned in subsection (3) (a 'Group B offence').

(2) **The Group A offences** are—

(a) an offence under any of the following provisions of the [1968 c. 60.] Theft Act 1968—

section 1 (theft);

section 15 (obtaining property by deception);

section 16 (obtaining pecuniary advantage by deception);

section 17 (false accounting);

section 19 (false statements by company directors, etc.);

section 20(2) (procuring execution of valuable security by deception);

section 21 (blackmail);

section 22 (handling stolen goods);

(b) an offence under either of the following provisions of the [1978 c. 31.] Theft Act 1978—

section 1 (obtaining services by deception);

section 2 (avoiding liability by deception);

(c) an offence under any of the following provisions of the [1981 c. 45.] Forgery and Counterfeiting Act 1981—

section 1 (forgery);

section 2 (copying a false instrument);

section 3 (using a false instrument);

section 4 (using a copy of a false instrument);

section 5 (offences which relate to money orders, share certificates, passports, etc.);

(d) the common law offence of cheating in relation to the public revenue.

(3) **The Group B offences** are—
(a) conspiracy to commit a Group A offence;
(b) conspiracy to defraud;
(c) attempting to commit a Group A offence;
(d) incitement to commit a Group A offence.

If persons conspire to defraud and that fraud is to be committed abroad, as long as they conspire in the UK, they can be charged with an offence, although they planned to commit the offence in other countries as per the Criminal Justice Act 1993, section 3, which states:

"(3) A person may be guilty of conspiracy to defraud if-

(a) a party to the agreement constituting the conspiracy, or a party's agent, did anything in England and Wales in relation to the agreement before its formation, or

(b) a party to it became a party in England and Wales (by joining it either in person or through an agent), or

(c) a party to it, or a party's agent, did or omitted anything in England and Wales in pursuance of it,

and the conspiracy would be triable in England and Wales but for the fraud which the parties to it had in view not being intended to take place in England and Wales."

Before the Criminal Justice Act 1993, they would be charged in the UK only if they conspired to defraud in the United Kingdom, even if the conspiracy to defraud occurred abroad.

> **Caselaw**
>
> The case of R *v ICR Haulage Ltd* [1944] 1 All ER 691, was one in which the appellant company and nine individuals were charged with conspiracy to defraud by overcharging. One of the nine individual defendants was the managing director of the company. The company was convicted and appealed and the appeal was dismissed. The offences created by the regulation are those of doing something with intent to deceive or of making a statement known to be false in a material particular. There was ample evidence on the facts as stated in the special case, that the company had conspired to defraud and had 0overcharged customers..

4.9. A one-man company can now be charged with conspiring to defraud

In *R v McDonnell* [1966] 1 All ER 193, McDonnell was charged with conspiring to defraud with a limited company of which he was a sole director. Now, the Fraud Act makes it possible statutorily, to charge a limited company with fraud.

4.10. 'Letters of Credit' can be made for deceit or conspiracy

Letters of Credit (see the glossary of accounting terms at front of this book) make for the tort of deceit or the tort of conspiracy when the buyer and seller collude to defraud a bank as in *Rafsanjan Pistachio Producers Cooperative v Bank Leumi (UK) plc [1992] 1 Lloyds Report 513* and in *Solo Industries UK Ltd v Canara Bank [2001] 1 WLR 1800, CA*. To be guilty of conspiracy to defraud, the defendant must be dishonest and must intend to defraud the proposed victim.

4.11. Example of a complex letter of credit case

Milton Kounnou (DOB 1/4/48), and his son, Stelios Kounnou, (DOB 16/8/77) purported to be metals suppliers. Their London-based companies were Simetal Ltd and Fimetco Ltd. These companies produced falsified shipping documents for presentation to banks in the Middle East against letters of credit opened on instructions of companies in Sharjah, United Arab Emirates, controlled by a Madhav Patel. His companies were Solo Industries and Zeeba Metals. Documentation (i.e bills of lading, invoices, certificates of origin and packing lists) was created throughout the period of September 1998 to March 1999. relating to cargoes of tin ingots, bismuth scrap, indium tin alloy, nickel scrap, and lead silver alloy totalling to about 450 metric tonnes. The stated shipping ports were in northern Europe (Helsingborg, Gothenburg, Thamesport and Hamburg). The declared destination was Dubai. But the consignments were either phantom shipments, or where there were shipments, they were low value metals such as scrap aluminium or lead ingots, disguised by the documentation as higher value cargoes. Patel's companies regularly opened letters of credit with Middle East banks; their frequent turnover generating sufficient funds to recycle back to his companies to settle the original debt. This achieved for Patel a positive reputation with the banks as being a businessman who settled debts punctually. Consequently banks became willing to extend more and more credit to him. The fraud snowballed. When the scheme collapsed in April 1999, the banks were owed around $200 million. Twenty banks in the Middle East were affected, principally the Arab Banking Corporation, Arab-African International Bank, Emirates Bank International, Gulf International Bank, Credit Agricole Indosuez and the Albarka Islamic Investment Bank.

The Kounnou-owned firms in London were the beneficiaries to the letters of credit. When they received payment, they would retain some of the money and transfer the remainder to companies controlled by Patel. The SFO opened its investigation in June 1999 in conjunction with the City of London Police Economic Crime Department after a complaint was received from Citibank in London. Milton Kounnou and Stelios Kounnou were charged in January 2002 with three counts of conspiracy (with Mahdav Patel) to defraud banks of funds. The Kounnous were also charged with fifteen counts of false accounting (i.e. producing falsified documents for accounting purposes).Madhav Patel's whereabouts are unknown. There is a warrant for his arrest issued by City of London Magistrates. Milton Kounnou pleaded guilty ahead of trial, to fifteen counts of false accounting and was sentenced to two years' imprisonment on each count; the sentence is to run concurrently. One count of conspiracy was withdrawn and two counts of conspiracy are to remain on the file. The SFO has decided to offer no evidence against Stelios Kounnou.

4.12.1. Attempt and incitement

Attempt and incitement, and also conspiracy to defraud are known as inchoate or incomplete offences. In each case, liability can be imposed on the defendant even though the completed offence is not committed. There are two justifications for such offences. The first is the common sense one of 'prevention is better than cure'. The second justification is that the suggesting, agreeing to commit or trying to commit a crime is a sign of the defendant's willingness that the crime should be committed and this shows culpability. This offence can be used provided that the indictment does not allege an inchoate and completed form of the same offence.

4.12.2. Intentionally encouraging or assisting crime

Since April 2008, Part 2 of the Serious Crime Act 2007, has repealed the common law offence of incitement. The offence of intentionally encouraging or assisting crime; and encouraging or assisting crime believing that an offence, or one or more offences will be committed. To assist another to commit a criminal offence is an offence.

4.13. Attempt

In the offence of attempt, the mental element is crucial. A plan to commit a fraud is formulated by a person. even on his own, it is an attempt to commit a crime. The essence of an attempt offence is that the substantive offence is not committed. Commonly, there are three different types of attempt.

(i) A thwarted attempt is an attempt where the defendant plans to commit a crime but just before he is able to do so, someone or something intervenes to prevent the defendant from committing the crime.

(ii) A failed attempt is one in which the defendant does everything he plans to do but his plan is ineffective.

(iii) An impossible attempt in one where the crime is in fact impossible.

An offence under section 1(1) of the Criminal Attempts Act 1981 is a trigger offence, if committed in respect of an offence under any of the following provisions of the Theft Act 1968:-section 1 (theft); section 8 (robbery); section 9 (burglary); section 15 (obtaining property by deception); and section 22 (handling stolen goods). Where the crime is a fraud, if a person commits an act, which is more than preparatory to the commission of a fraud, he can be charged with attempting to commit a crime. Any representation made with intention but which fails to deceive, would amount to the full offence of fraud by false representation, as per Fraud Act 2006, sections 1 and 2, even though no gain is actually made. If a person makes a representation, which he intends to be false, but because of his mistake, it is in fact true, he cannot be guilty of the offence of fraud as per section 2 (2) (a).

4.14. The 1981 Criminal Attempts Act

The correct approach in examining for an attempt offence is

"to look first at the natural meaning of the statutory words."

The line of demarcation between acts which are merely preparatory and acts which may amount to an attempt is not always clear or easy to recognize. There is no rule of thumb test. However, an accurate paraphrase of the statutory test is to ask whether the available evidence, if accepted, could show that a defendant has done an act, which shows that he has actually tried to commit the offence in question, or whether he is only ready, put himself in a position, or equipped himself to do so. The rule is that if the completed offence would be triable in England and Wales, an attempt to commit it will be so triable as per s.1 (1) and (4) of the Criminal Attempts 1981 Act.

4.15. Indictment for 'attempt' is the same as the full offence of fraud

An indictment for the statutory offence of an 'attempt' to commit a crime can be framed on the precedents for the full offence by inserting the words "attempted to" before the words charging the full offence. It is for the judge to rule whether there is any evidence capable of constituting an attempt, and for the jury to say whether they accept it as amounting to an attempt. There should therefore be a careful direction in every case as to the general principle as to what acts constitute attempts. As to sentencing for a criminal attempt offence, see the Criminal Attempts Act 1981, section 4.

4.16. Conclusion to Chapter Four

The offences of 'conspiracy to defraud', 'attempted crime' and 'assisting a fraud' can be said to be offences of encouraging crime. In conspiracy, an agreement between two persons is required but certain parties are excluded- spouses, young children and the intended victim. An attempted crime is an attempt under s1 (1) of the Criminal Attempts Act 1981. The Defendant is guilty of an 'attempt' when he has gone beyond the 'merely preparatory' stage. The essence of attempt is the defendant's intention.

Further reading to Chapter Four

V. Ahuja, "HSBC calls in police over 90 million Euro attempted fraud", Dow Jones Financial News Online, 14.8.2008.
http://www.efinancialnews.com/homepage/content/2350536154
Law Commission Report No 228 "Conspiracy To Defraud" (1994)
Webpage, Used Equipment Market Attempted Fraud Stories
www.usgyms.net/attempterfraud.htm

CHAPTER 5- COMMON FRAUDS, DETECTION AND PREVENTION

5.1.1. Introduction

The European Commission has studied the industry of cashless payment solutions and came to conclusion that purchases of flight tickets online as well as meals at restaurants are the most risky transactions. Having studied all the materials on fraud suits occurred between 2004 and 2007, purchase of flight tickets is less secured and, as a result, this kind of crime is the most common one. Online fraud is considered the easiest for criminals due to the relative simplicity of stealing an identity in the online world. Offline fraud cases include so-called skimming fraud in restaurants by waiters who use special devices, scimmers that read the necessary ID information from the plastic credit and debit cards when they are out of sight of the customer. The European Commission's Report stated that the most common kinds of fraud are airline ticket fraud, gaming and gambling frauds, online bank frauds, due to the increase of internet usage. Some types of frauds are set out below. However, more traditional frauds such as long-firm fraud, advance-fee frauds and mortgage frauds are still often the method of fraud used, although these are now completed by means of electronic format made available by open access to the world wide web. Electronic frauds are more difficult to investigate because there is no face-to-face contact between the perpetrator and the victim.

5.1. 2. Long-firm frauds

In a long firm fraud, the fraudster simply sets up in business as a wholesaler, and places orders with suppliers *with the intention of evading payment*. Initially payments are prompt in order to establish creditworthiness. Then larger orders are placed. When delivered, the goods are promptly sold. The aims and objectives of a long firm fraud are:

- to establish credibility with manufacturers and suppliers;
- to obtain as much goods as possible over a credit period extended for as long as possible;
- to finally make little or no payment to suppliers and creditors;
- to dispose of large amount of goods finally obtained with the minimum of delay; and abscond with the proceeds, avoiding identification and prosecution.

The fraud can be operated in a number of different ways. It may be a 'sole trader', but may be a limited company and one that has been purchased 'off the shelf' from a company formation agent or using the online method. The disadvantage to the fraudster of forming a new company, is that suppliers will be reluctant to supply on credit until a satisfactory trading period has elapsed. The company used in a long-firm fraud usually sells goods, or administration services and even financial services. Certain goods are preferred because they are not easily traceable – toys, toiletries, wines, spirits, fancy goods and confectionery, all have a quick turnover, and can be disposed of easily.

Premises are necessary in order to carry out this fraud. The size and type of premises will depend on the quantity and category of the goods or service to be handled. With goods that turn over very quickly such as beer, wines, or spirits, all that is needed is enough room to unload. In most cases, regardless of commodity, the goods do not stay on the premises very long and the premises are usually acquired on a short lease. The fraud is committed after lulling suppliers into a false sense of security, by prompt payments of the initial small orders, steadily increasing the value of such orders until the fraudster creates a very large order and absconds without payment. When references are required, fraudsters either nominate concerns controlled by themselves to provide references or quite simply prepare false references using modern desk top publishing methods and rented, or accommodation addresses. This is a long-firm fraud.

Other long-firm frauds are committed through bankruptcy offences. The Office of Fair Trading has never surveyed the number of persons going into business and then discontinuing legitimately in bankruptcy . The United Kingdom Directors' databases reveal that in the year 1999, there were 750,000 directors recorded as directing failed companies and of these 212,000 directors were involved in multiple failed companies, though there can be no assumption that a failed company is a fraudulent company, without a thorough study of the matter.

5.1.3 Advance fee fraud

Advance fee fraud or '419' fraud (named after the relevant section of the Nigerian Criminal Code) is a popular crime with the West African organised criminal networks. There are a myriad of schemes and scams - mail, faxed and telephone promises designed to facilitate victims parting with money. All involve requests to help move large sums of money with the promise of a substantial share of the cash in return. This type of fraud, originally known as the "Spanish Prisoner Letter", was carried out since at least the sixteenth century via ordinary postal mail. Such frauds have come to be associated in the public mind with Nigeria due to the massive proliferation of such confidence tricks from that country since the mid-eighties, although they are often also carried out in other countries, increasingly from European cities notably London and Amsterdam. Victim's individual monetary losses can range from the low thousands into multi-millions. True figures are often impossible to ascertain, because many victims, embarrassed by their naiveté and feeling personally humiliated, do not report the crime to the authorities. Others, having lost so much themselves, become "part of the gang" recruiting more victims from their own country of residence. There are reported cases of victims being unable to cope with the losses and committing suicide.

5.1.4. Mortgage frauds

The recent recession in the UK property market, has exposed a rise in mortgage fraud by organised criminals and the potential vulnerability of professionals to be exploited by organised crime syndicates.

How is the fraud perpetrated?

- A criminal syndicate will usually organise finance on a number of properties. The buy-to-let market is particularly vulnerable to mortgage fraud, whether through new build apartment complexes or large scale renovation projects.

- The nominated purchasers, who are taking out the mortgage, are likely to have no beneficial interest in the property and may even be fictitious.

- The value of the property is inflated and the mortgage will be taken out for the full inflated valuation.

- Often, mortgage payments are not met and the properties are allowed to deteriorate. The properties can also be used for other criminal or fraudulent activities such as drug production, unlicensed gambling and prostitution.

- When the bank seeks payment of the mortgage, the crime syndicate raises mortgages with another bank through further fictitious purchasers and effectively sells the property back to themselves, but at an even greater leveraged valuation.

- Because the second mortgage is inflated, the first mortgage is repaid together with the arrears, leaving a substantial profit. This may be repeated many times, until a bank finally forecloses on the property, only to find it in disrepair and worth significantly less than the current mortgage and its arrears.

Using the services of professionals

Organised criminals will generally involve at least one professional at the core of the fraud, to provide reassurance and direction to the other professionals instructed to act around the periphery. There is evidence that mortgage brokers and introducers have been used in this role in the past.

Mortgage lenders often rely on professionals to verify the legitimacy of a transaction and safeguard their interests. Lenders may not extensively verify the information they receive, especially in a rising market. They will subscribe to the CML Handbook and expect their solicitors or conveyancers to comply with their guidelines as a means of protecting their lending. Solicitors or licensed conveyancers are likely to be approached with packaged transactions and completed paper work. The lender will often have already received the loan applications, and granted the loan before they are instructed.

The solicitor or conveyancer will simply be required to transfer title to exchange and complete the transaction.

The solicitor or conveyancer will be encouraged to complete the Certificate of Title at the gross price and not the actual price paid for the property after allowances and discounts, while being discouraged from complying with obligations in the CML Handbook.

The Fraud Act 2006 makes mortgage fraud easy to prosecute. If a mortgage has been obtained by fraud, it is then the proceeds of crime. If solicitors complete a property transaction where the mortgage has been obtained by fraud, you risk committing a principal money laundering offence. Courts will assume a high level of legal knowledge and education, and be less willing to accept claims that a solicitor was unwittingly involved in a fraud if they have not applied appropriate due diligence to a transaction. For more information on how to protect against this type of fraud, the Council of Mortgage Lenders' Handbook is useful reading.

> **Caselaw**
>
> ***Pulvers v Chan*** **– [2007] EWHC 2406 (Ch)**
> Monies recovered after a mortgage fraud
> Mills & Reeve acted for the two partner firm of solicitors, Pulvers, against whom more than 20 mortgage fraud claims have been made. They in turn claimed against Mary West, a conveyancer employed by them, John Sinclair, the person behind the frauds, and others implicated in them. Pulvers had been acting for both borrower and lender in the transactions, with Mary West preparing and signing most of the certificates of title provided to the lenders before the loan monies were paid into Pulvers' account. In most of the cases, the lender eventually obtained a charge

but the property charged was not the entirety of the property which it had been represented would be secured. The judge found that that Mary West had known of the deception and that she had conspired with John Sinclair and the other defendants with an intent to injure the lenders. She was not liable as a recipient of trust moneys as she had not apparently received such moneys, but she was liable for dishonestly assisting a breach of trust. Where the lenders had paid money into Pulvers' client account, it had been held by the firm on trust for the relevant lender and it was vicariously liable to the lenders for the actions of Mary West even though she had been dishonest. Pulvers could claim equitable compensation from those defendants who had known recipients of trust moneys paid in breach of trust. The various defendants were also liable in conspiracy to the lenders and for dishonestly assisting a breach of trust.

Caselaw

R v. Asghar [1974] 1 WLR

Solicitor mortgage fraud- the defendant D, who was employed by a local authority to deal with mortgage applications, collaborated with the defendant A in submitting on behalf of third persons' mortgage applications, which to their knowledge contained untrue particulars about, inter alia, the applicants' financial status. When the local authority granted a mortgage, a cheque was sent to solicitors acting for both the local authority and the applicant. The solicitor would cash the cheque and pay the money to the applicant, who thereupon became the mortgagor. A was charged with five counts of obtaining property, namely, a cheque, by deception contrary to section 15 (1) of the Theft Act

> 1968. The defendant appealed on the grounds (i) that the prosecution had not established an intention on the defendants' part permanently to deprive the local authority of property either because the cheques would ultimately go back to, or become available to, the local authority, or, alternatively, because mortgage transactions involved loans which would be repaid by the mortgagor at a future date. *The appeal was dismissed because* it was the defendants' intention, dishonestly and by deception, to permanently deprive the local authority

SARs pertaining to mortgage loan fraud increased by 1,411 percent between 1997 and 2005. This report filing trend continues to the point where the FSA is taking action. But mortgage fraud is not a new phenomenon in the UK. There was a spike in mortgage frauds in the 1980s and 1990's. In 1991 the Law Society issued its 'Green Card Warning on Property Fraud', which was sent to every practising solicitor in England and Wales. This was guidance to conveyance solicitors on factors in a property transaction that might indicate a fraud was being perpetrated. It covered matters such as back to back sales, direct payments made by the buyer to the seller and sub sales. Since then the Law Society has revised its guidance from time to time and whilst the signs of mortgage fraud are listed as being 'not exhaustive' they are important to bear in mind when acting on a residential transaction. If the property market crashes, there will be an increase in litigation between the mortgage lenders and property professionals Property professionals must have in place practices to avoid litigation.

> **Point to Note: Proceeds of Crime Act used in mortgage frauds**
>
> The Proceeds of Crime Act 2002 created the Assets Recovery Agency and provided completely new powers to allow ARA (whose duties have now been taken over by the Serious Organised Crime Agency, "SOCA") to seek civil recovery of the proceeds of unlawful activity by an action in the High Court. This power has been taken over by SOCA since 2008. ARA and now SOCA, can also issue tax assessments where there are reasonable grounds to suspect that there is taxable income, gain or profit from criminal conduct. The Assets Recovery Agency (ARA) Financial Investigators secured the payment of £3.3 million from David Edward Dale from Bryncoch, Neath, a property developer who developed a portfolio of some 450 houses using fraudulent mortgages. The investigation into the activities of Mr. Dale covered the period from 1991 to 1999, during which he initially obtained at least 57 homes by unlawfully using the details of family and friends, before expanding his operation on a more commercial basis. He was convicted in September 2005 after pleading guilty to a range of counts of mortgage fraud. In July 2006 at the High Court in London, the Confiscation Order was reduced to £3.3 million, with the judges using their discretion as regards mortgages that were paid with legitimate funds. Mr. Dale was given 12 months to pay this amount.

5.1.5. Boiler room frauds

The term 'boiler room' in business refers to a busy centre of activity, often selling questionable goods by telephone. It typically refers to a room where salesmen work, selling stocks, and using unfair, dishonest sales tactics, sometimes selling penny stock or committing outright stock fraud. The term carries a negative connotation, and is often used to imply high-pressure sales tactics and sometimes, poor working conditions. A boiler room fraudster is usually a bogus stockbroker, often based overseas, who cold-calls investors and pressures them into buying worthless shares. Their favourite targets are middle-aged men with previous experience of buying shares, whose names they find on share registers. The most common victims of so-called boiler-room scams are experienced investors, who typically lose £20,000 each to the fraudsters. The fraudsters are usually well spoken and knowledgeable. They are also persistent. They might call their victim several times with offers of research, discounts on stocks in small overseas companies, or shares in a firm that is about to float. Boiler rooms make their money in one of two ways. They might simply take your money and walk away. Or they might sell you shares, but at vastly inflated prices and with exorbitant dealing charges.

> **Case Study of a Boiler-room fraud**
>
> In February, 2007, the Financial Services Authority (FSA) obtained interim injunctions against UK-based Chesteroak Ltd, and UK- based Bingen Investments Ltd(incorporated in Gibraltar), and Mr. Samuel Nathan Kahn because the FSA believed that they had been involved in assisting overseas boiler room activities in the UK without authorisation under the Financial Services & Markets Act 2000. The FSA also alleges that Bingen Investments Ltd was arranging investment deals and that Mr Kahn was knowingly involved in these regulated activities, also without authorisation. The FSA said both Chesteroak Ltd and Bingen Investments Ltd appeared to have been assisting a number of suspected boiler rooms based overseas who were approaching UK investors encouraging them to buy shares in UK companies. Because Chesteroak Ltd, Bingen Investments Ltd and Mr Kahn were not authorised by the FSA, investors may not claim compensation from the Financial Services Compensation Scheme or make a complaint to the Financial Ombudsman Service.

5.2. Technology frauds by Skimmers

Criminals can use certain equipment, known as skimmers, devices that can read the magnetised strip from a credit, or bank card to obtain account numbers, bank balances and verification codes. Skimming is a technique used by criminals to capture data from a bank card's magnetic strip by swiping the card through a device a device that resembles a mobile phone. The information from the magnetic strip is stored in the device until its memory fills up or until it is downloaded to a computer or transferred onto the magnetic strips of blank cards. After the data is copied onto a blank card, this card becomes a cloned card. The restaurant industry is particularly vulnerable to skimming. Skimming often relies on the cooperation of corruptible employees who can easily swipe cards without being seen.

5.3. Open Signals facilitate fraud

'Wardriving' or randomly searching for open internet signals to acquire free wireless internet service is another means of gaining identifying information for these frauds. Such signals can be used to gain access to the computers in companies that pay for the internet service and bypasses password security and secret codes. Fraudsters can gain such information in deleted emails also.

Criminals can also gain access to personal information through access-controlled internet services which require user authentication. The most common method of authentication is to associate a password with a user ID and because these passwords are often fixed and not often changed and a hacker can obtain a copy of the password encrypted file and run a commonly available tool named a reverse dictionary attack' to obtain the password. Information from cookies, which are stored by the internet service providers, can be stolen by hackers. There are data mining software tools that can give the fraudster the information he seeks.

5.4. Internet fraud- Pretexting

Pretexting is the means of gaining personal information by pretending to be a representative with a reliable company that the victim knows. There are websites where national insurance numbers can be purchased. This is mainly through the illegal accumulation of information held by banks, doctors, hospitals, credit reporting agencies, utility companies, and government agencies, video rental businesses, dentists, and the consolidation of such organisations. Lost and stolen government computers and data disks are a source for fraudsters. Deceased person's identities are a favourite means of identity fraud. The main facilitator of identity fraud, however, is the proliferation of computer technology which provides easy access to the information needed to commit many financial crimes remotely.

5.5.1. Identity fraud

Identity fraud has been qualified by many as the fastest growing crime of the 21st Century. However, its true scale is difficult to measure. Available statistics are inconsistent from one country to another and from one authority to another. Most data rely on consumer complaints but many victims do not report their case to the authorities.

Identity fraud has resulted in substantial economic losses for stakeholders, including victims, financial institutions, and even whole economies. In the UK, the Home Office estimates that ID fraud costs £1.7 billion to the UK economy and increased by 50% from the year 2002 to 2003. According to APACS, the UK payments association, online banking fraud had doubled in the first half of 206, compared with a year earlier. Identity fraud is a financial crime in which the suspect assumes the identity of the victim through the use of personal information and documents, and uses the new identity to commit fraud in various ways, leaving the person with the stolen identity to face the financial and legal responsibility for the suspect's crimes. It is a fast-growing white-collar crime. Identity fraud is committed after the theft of a piece of personal information which is then used to open new bank accounts, change postal address, rent property, establish services from utility companies, write fraudulent cheques, fraudulently transfer money, file for bankruptcy, obtain employment, establish a new identity or apply for a mortgage, car loan or mobile telephone. It can be facilitated by the internet where person web pages hold information and genealogical databases give criminals access to maiden names which are often used as passwords to bank accounts.

5.5.2. Beware relatives

Often identity frauds are committed by relatives of the victim, for example when parents with bad credit records use their children's names to obtain services and utilities. Relatives and close associates of relatives of the old and infirm can steal the identities of others for financial identity fraud purposes.

5.5.3. Associates can steal ID

Potential identity fraudsters are housekeepers, security personnel, gardeners, repairmen, contractors, decorators, landscapers, carers, babysitters, delivery people, furniture removers, mailmen, garbage collectors, utility meter readers, tutors, music teachers who give lessons in people's homes, friends, neighbours and your children's acquaintances. In the case of old persons, criminals know they there are usually the persons with most assets and less aware of fraud prevention precautions than others. Many such frauds take place among employees because employment information is more vulnerable as workplace expands to include remote locations, homes, cars, and hotel rooms, making it difficult for businesses to protect information such as electronic payroll and human resources data.

5.5.4. Birth Certificates and other personal documents

The most important issue with regard to identity fraud is the birth certificate which can be issues from every registrar of births in the country, these being dozens in number. This type of fraud can happen to anyone, regardless of age, gender, nationality, race or income level and the fraud can be sophisticated or low-level. It is a certainty that the more common the name, the easier the identity fraud. The primary element of the success of his crime is obtaining the personal information of a victim, primarily, the victim's name, date of birth, National Insurance Number, address, bank account number. There is much harm that can be done even two only one or two pieces of such information. For instance, if armed with the victim's name and date of birth, a birth certificate duplicate may be obtained and later used to obtain a driver's licence and credit card. Such credit card will usually have a different address from the victim' so that the statements are not sent to the victim and not until the harm has been done to some degree is the true holder of the identity sought.

> **Point to Note:**
>
> This fraud can be prevented is people do not carry about their NI numbers, birth certificate, passport and limit the number of credit cards they carry on their person; discard paper rubbish only after shredding; install locked letter-boxes and refuse to give personal; information out over the telephone.

The victim bears the responsibility of resolving identity fraud issues created by the criminal. The victim must first report the fraud to the police. The victim is accountable for correcting his own credit references with the credit reporting agencies. Traditionally, a thief steals an individual's actual identity, perhaps through stealing cheque books, personal bills, or details through open sources (internet, births & deaths registers etc). Such details may allow the thief to open bank accounts, gain credit cards, loans, social security benefits, or simply to take over the victim's existing accounts. The details may also be used to obtain genuine documents such as passports and driving licenses in that individual's name. If this is done, then the false identities are used to commit fraud.

The 2002 Cabinet Office Study, which covered the use of false identities and the theft of other people's identities, estimated that crime facilitated by identity fraud cost the UK £1.3 billion per annum. The Home Office Identity Fraud Steering Committee completed an exercise to update the Cabinet Office for the purpose of establishing trends in the cost of identity fraud. The latest estimate (http://www.identity-theft.org.uk/ID fraud table. pdf) is that identity fraud costs the UK economy £1.7 billion. The latest methods of ID theft involve: telephoning victims, pretending to be their bank, or other financial institution and asking them to confirm their personal details, passwords and security numbers.

5.5.7. Fraudulent uses of stolen ID

Identity theft is unassuming in its range of fraud because by stealing an identity a sole trader or partnership can use it for: false advertising, false billing, forgery, embezzlement false insurance claims, and internet securities fraud. On the internet, equipped with such identity, it would be easy to reveal and to identify the name and address of the primary mail server, back-up mail server, its host or external provider such as 'blueyonder.co.uk'. Mining the internet further gives such fraudsters the multiple IP addresses and name aliases for one single service and digging into this would reveal aliases for the big servers such as Microsoft and then looking for weaknesses here will give the sole trader a whole list of absolutely all the information of all named hosts, sub-zones and associated Internet Provider addresses. So just one identity theft can lead to the identity theft of thousands, using the internet as an article that equips the fraudster.

5.5.8. ID theft relating to deceased persons

Families must be extra vigilant when dealing with matters after the death of family members. Fraudsters look through the obituary pages to identify new names to use for ID fraud. They then build up identities by intercepting mail, obtaining copy birth certificates and using personal details on bills and other documents to open new accounts and defraud companies. It is vital that families ensure that all companies including banks, credit card and insurance companies are notified as soon as possible when someone passes away, to enable them to update their files and reduce the opportunities for fraudsters. Families must keep all personal details secure and shred personal documents. In recognition of the growing trend of ID Fraud involving deceased people's details, the government have recently agreed to provide death records to organisations like credit reference agencies on a much timelier basis. The most effective way of spotting such an identity fraud is to obtain a copy of the deceased's credit file. An executor can apply for another person's credit file, by contacting Equifax by post or telephone.

They will need to provide evidence of their status as an executor and proof of death. If it's thought that the identity of a deceased person is at risk, a relative or executor can also subscribe to the CIFAS Protective Registration service. A notice will be placed on the deceased's credit file informing lenders that there may be a risk of identity fraud.

> **Case Study: Use of ID theft method in the Darwin Insurance fraud**
>
> In the 2008 court case on the Darwin Insurance Fraud, the following story is told to set the scene for the way to stop frauds using deceased person's identities. Anne Darwin, 56, convinced insurance companies, a coroner and relatives that her husband had died in a canoe accident, Teesside Crown Court heard. On March 21, 2002, John Darwin, 57, pushed his canoe out to sea at Seaton Carew near Hartlepool then disappeared, living rough before fleeing to Panama, Central America.
>
> Darwin and his wife decided to go abroad, and he applied for a passport in the name of John Jones. Immigration authorities in Panama said they had no record of any movements involving a John Darwin or a John Jones using a British passport he had acquired by stealing a deceased person's identity.

5.5.9. Fraud against companies using stolen Ids

There are many ways in which attacks can be facilitated against companies through internal means. These include direct theft of Intellectual Property, passing on business information for personal gain to competitors, passing customer detail to third parties in order that attacks may be facilitated against that organisation. This is where there may be an employee of a financial institution passing customer account details to organised crime

5.6. Defective goods supplied abroad

Section 75 of the Consumer Credit Act 1974 now applies to overseas transactions as from August 2006. Section 75 provides for 'connected lender liability', which applies in certain circumstances to make a provider of credit (such as a credit card issuer) jointly and severally liable with the supplier to compensate the purchaser if the goods or services purchased with a credit card are defective. If the customer cannot obtain redress from the supplier for some reason, he or she may be able to obtain compensation from the card issuer. Finally, to illustrate how changes in other areas of law may become drivers of fraud as fraudsters are alert to ways to make fraudulent gains, three areas are used as illustrations- withdrawal of a pre-action admission; a stay of proceedings where a jurisdiction clause exists and the suspension of the retrospective effect of public access to court documents.

> **Point to Note: Loophole in criminal proceedings-withdrawal of admission**
>
> The recent Court of Appeal decision in *Stoke-on-Trent City Council v Walley* [2006] EWCA Civ 1137 has clarified when a claimant may contest the withdrawal of a pre-action admission notwithstanding the decision in *Sowerby v Charlton* [2006] 1 WLR 568 that pre-action admissions may be withdrawn without requiring the permission of the court or claimant. The Court of Appeal took the opportunity to give the following guidance on the procedure where pre-action admissions are later withdrawn: The correct approach for a claimant seeking to contest the withdrawal of a pre-action admission is to apply under Civil Procedure Rule 3.4(2) to strike out the defence on the grounds that it is an abuse of process of the court or is otherwise likely to obstruct the just disposal of proceedings. The claimant must show that the defendant has acted in bad faith by withdrawing his a dmission. In order for

> the claimant to show that a withdrawal of pre-action admission by the defendant is likely to obstruct the just disposal of the case, the claimant must show that the trial without the pre-action admission will be unfair because the claimant had agreed to the destruction of an item of real evidence, had agreed that an expert inspection which is no longer possible was not necessary or the witnesses have died or lost contact.

5.7. Internet frauds-Spamming

Sophisticated and extensive spamming frauds can be carried out to run a stock "pump and dump" scheme, whereby the criminals can send spam to tout thinly traded penny stocks, drive up their stock price, and reap profits by selling the stock at artificially inflated prices. They can use various illegal methods in order to maximize the amount of spam that evaded spam-blocking devices and trick recipients into opening, and acting on, the advertisements in the spam. Spamming can be done by using falsified "headers" in the email messages, using proxy computers to relay the spam, using falsely registered domain names to send the spam, making misrepresentations in the advertising content of some of the underlying email messages. Spam attackers have industrialised their methods. They use methods such as exploitation of vulnerable servers, mass registration of domain names, fast-flux hosting, data collection and data storage and analysis.

5.8. Internet fraud- Phishing

Phishing is the act of sending an email to a user, falsely claiming to be an established legitimate enterprise, in an attempt to defraud the user into surrendering private information that will be used for identity theft. Such an email directs the user to visit a website where they are asked to update personal information such as password, national insurance number and bank accounting details. The email may further suggest that the information is necessary to prevent the account from being suspended.

With this information the fraudster can do a number of things that include stealing the identity of the person who provided the information in the first place to undertaking attacks on that person's bank account. The email is sent to a large group of people, seeking out account users. This phishing fraud relies on the contents of the email request being adhered to by the account users and the details provided. It is worth noting that 5% of recipients respond to spam emails. As a result of a response, a new identity is created using the details provided and fraud is committed on the new identity.

The use of the phishing medium as a money laundering tool appears to be emerging, where volumes of compromised user data is sold to crime groups who aggregate the stolen funds into centralised false accounts by a principal organiser or "dump leader". The use of false employment websites, encouraging users to sign up and provide their banking facilities to forward money to other accounts for a 20% administration fee has also been revealed.

E-mails are created purporting to come from bank security departments were being circulated asking for username and password details in connection with Internet banking. The email invited account holders to click on a URL (Uniform Resource Locator), which generates a web page. Unsuspecting account holders account holders completed their user name and password on the web page. Unknowingly the account holder had linked into a web server run by a criminal enterprise. Once the user name and password have been obtained the criminal logs into the on line banking system of that account and transfers money from that account into another account from which he will be able to obtain the funds.

In order to facilitate the transfers a number of people are recruited who have accounts at the same bank as the target account. The recruitment involves advertisements on Internet forums and unsolicited emails offering jobs as 'money processors'. Respondents to the advertisements are in receipt of 7% commission of the monies that they handle. Once the stolen funds were received into the money processors' bank account, they were given instructions to withdraw the money in cash and then to use money transfer agents and send the money to criminal organisers.

5.9. Internet fraud-Nigerian or 419 frauds

1In one scenario, the defendants sent emails purporting to be from an individual suffering from terminal throat cancer needing assistance in distributing millions of pounds to charity. Most Nigerian or "419" frauds involve tales about payment of taxes, bribes to government officials, and legal fees and are often described in great detail with the promise that all expenses will be reimbursed as soon as the funds are spirited out of Nigeria. In actuality, the millions of dollars do not exist and the victim eventually ends up with nothing but loss. Once the victim stops sending money, the perpetrators have been known to use the personal information and cheques that they received to impersonate the victim, draining bank accounts and credit card balances until the victim's assets are taken in their entirety.

Whilst most law-abiding citizens would treat such an email as a laughable hoax, millions of dollars in losses are caused by these schemes annually. Some victims have been lured to Nigeria, where they have been imprisoned against their will, in addition to losing large sums of money.

5.10. Internet frauds- Bot-nets

Fraudsters may try to send their spam by utilizing a cybercrime tool known as a "bot-net," which is a network of "robot" computers that have been infected with malicious software code that in turn would instruct the infected computers to send spam. The criminal can earn profit when recipients respond to the spam and purchase the touted products and services. . There may be companies who want their stocks pumped by the scheme. Millions of pounds can be earned by such 'spammer' as a result of this type of illegal spamming activities. The types of products and services that are pitched may evolve over time, as can the types of illegal spamming techniques employed. Attackers are constantly investing in attack technology and their profits are reinvested to fund further fraud attempts.

> **Points to Note: Difficulties of discovering electronic crime**
>
> (i) Low visibility of attackers, their tools, techniques, organisation and communications.
>
> (ii) The end-to-end attack and response process.
>
> (iii) Victims have little knowledge of how compromises took place and are often unwilling to having computer infection.
>
> (iv) Victims are unwilling to admit to having disclosed information online.
>
> (v) Incident management is very time-consuming and requires specialist skills.
>
> (vi) E-Crime is not the core business of the bank, credit card issuer or merchant.

5.11. Internet Frauds- Internet Domain Names

The incidence of cyber-squatting is the fraudulent registration of trademarks as domain names. A recent battle between a coven of white witches and a property developer in Leicestershire, over the name "Highcross Quarters", has highlighted the issue of ownership of internet domain names. A domain name is an instrument of fraud depending on all the circumstances, including the similarity of a name to another, the intention of the defendant, and the type of trade involved. A domain name could be an instrument of fraud whether or not it would inherently lead to passing off.

> **Caselaw**
>
> Domain name instrument of fraud
>
> In the case of *Global Projects Management Ltd v Citigroup Inc and others* [2005] EWHC 2663 (Ch), [2005] All ER (D) 182 (Oct), it was held that the mere registration and maintenance in force of a domain name, which led people to believe that the holder of the domain name was linked with a person, had been enough to make the domain name a potential instrument of fraud, and amounted to passing off.

5.12. Cyber-squatting

Cyber-squatting is the abusive registration of trademarks as domain names. The availability of computer software to automatically register expired domain names and their "parking" on pay-per-click portal sites, the option to register names free of charge for a five-day trial period, the expansion of new registrars and the establishment of new generic top level domain names have created opportunities for fraud.

5.13. Internet frauds-Selling Pirated software online

Unwitting consumers at times are duped into purchasing pirated software online. This results in substantial lost revenue to the true developers of the software and can lead to consumers obtaining less desirable software than promised. Many online auctions offer pirated and counterfeit products. Such software products do not include proof of authenticity like original manuals and warranties, may have hand-written labels, and sellers may offer to make back-up copies, and this would suggests illegality. Compilations also may be pirated. And no trust mark from a known organization demonstrates that an online retailer is not reliable nor have a proven track record. If the seller does not give his address, this may be a sign that he is selling illegal software.

5.14. Online Bank frauds

Card skimming is the most prevalent bank card fraud. The European ATM Security Team (EAST) state that there were around 5,000 incidents of card skimming in 2007, totalling some 240 million Euros of reported losses. Card trapping attacks cost over 200 million Euros in 2007. See EAST website http://www.eas-team.eu.

Type of Crime	Definition
Card Skimming	The card details and PIN are captured at the ATM bank card machine (ATM) and used to produce counterfeit cards for subsequent fraudulent cash withdrawals. The customer sees a normal transaction and retains the card. Multiple cards are compromised in one attack at one ATM

Card Tapping	The card is physically captured at the ATM, and the PIN is compromised. Later the card is used to make fraudulent cash withdrawals. The customer loses the card. One card is lost in each attack.
Other card fraud	Includes transaction reversal fraud and cash trapping.

Table: Three types of bank fraud

To prevent online bank frauds, banks must implement robust and variable authentication; computer security; detect unusual behaviour and carry out consumer profiling.

The UK Banking industry estimates that online bank frauds are increasing but in relation to credit card fraud, it is only 11% of credit card fraud. E-banking frauds consist of Identity Theft by credentials and identities used to support carding, account takeover and loan fraud.

5.15. Internet Investment Frauds

The Internet serves as an excellent tool for investors, allowing them to inexpensively research investment opportunities. But the Internet is also an excellent tool for fraudsters. On Stock promoters who fail to tell investors that companies have paid them thousands pounds in exchange for touting their stock on the Internet are committing fraud. They lie about their own independence, lie about the companies they feature, and then take advantage of any quick spike in price to sell their shares for a fast and easy profit. The Internet allows individuals or companies to communicate with a large audience without spending a lot of time, effort, or money. Anyone can reach tens of thousands of people by building an Internet web site, posting a message on an online bulletin board, entering a discussion in a live "chat" room, or sending mass e-mails and so it is easy for fraudsters to make their messages look real and credible Hundreds of online investment newsletters have appeared on the Internet in recent years. Many offer investors seemingly unbiased information free of charge about featured companies or recommending "stock picks of the month." While legitimate online newsletters can help investors gather valuable information, some online newsletters are tools for fraud. Some companies pay the people who write online newsletters cash or securities to "tout" or recommend their stocks. While this isn't illegal, the newsletters should disclose who paid them, the amount, and the type of payment. Some online newsletters falsely claim to independently research the stocks they profile. Others spread false information or promote worthless stocks. The most notorious sometimes "scalp" the stocks they hype, driving up the price of the stock with their baseless recommendations and then selling their own holdings at high prices and high profits.

5.16. Passing off fraud- Misrepresentation about goods and services

The tort of passing off can also be used to protect a domain name. The key criterion for a successful passing off action is the presence of goodwill. The claimant must be able to demonstrate goodwill; there must be a misrepresentation about the goods or services offered by the defendant and actual or likely damage. The claimant must sustain actual or likely damage by proving a direct loss of sales; injurious association; injury through constant confusion; loss of licensing opportunity; dilution; or inferiority of the defendant's services or goods.

5.17. Fraud by Business Spread-Sheets

A relevant article used to commit financial fraud is the common spreadsheet. Most compliance officers and competent accountants have always known that a Spreadsheet has no "audit trail" and so is very difficult for reconciliation. For officers of a company, with a financial background, to deliberately set out only to use spreadsheets in their companies can be construed as using it for fraud. Spreadsheets have many weaknesses that do not satisfy requirements of compliance procedures and certainly not for the Sarbanes-Oxley Act 2002. Most public companies should not use spreadsheets as their main financial tool. The knowledge about spreadsheet weaknesses has been spread about in the accountancy community for over 20 years, long enough to be placed into some policy document or other. Officers who are gatekeepers of companies must maintain effective controls over the completeness, accuracy, validity and restricted access and review of information which some spreadsheets are not designed to perform; they are not audit tools but day-to-day management short-term tools. With no reviews of spreadsheet calculations, they are incorporated into financial statements, often causing millions of pounds of losses. They are a source of deficiencies, oversight, and errors that can cause a company to produce a restatement with all the adverse signals that that produces. Sabotage is easily carried out in spreadsheets because of a lack of audit trail and spreadsheets have only basic controls of password protection.

> **Point to Note: Be alert to spread-sheet manipulation for fraud**
>
> In March 2006 the Office of Government Commerce of the United Kingdom discovered spreadsheet error in a procurement programme and had to refuse a tender as a consequence.

5.18. Advance Fee frauds

An advance fee fraud occurs when the victim pays money to someone in anticipation of receiving something of greater value, such as a loan, contract, investment, or gift, and then receives little or nothing in return. The variety of advance fee frauds is limited only by the imagination of the criminals who offer them. They may involve the sale of products or services, the offering of investments, lottery winnings, "found money," or many other "opportunities." Criminals will offer to find financing arrangements for their clients who pay a "finder's fee" in advance. They require their clients to sign contracts in which they agree to pay the fee when they are introduced to the financing source. Victims often learn that they are ineligible for financing only after they have paid the "finder" according to the contract. Such agreements may be legal unless it can be shown that the "finder" never had the intention or the ability to provide financing for the victims.

5.19. Ponzi Fraud

A Ponzi fraud is essentially an investment fraud wherein the operator promises high financial returns or dividends that are not available through traditional investments. Instead of investing the victims' funds, the operator pays "dividends" to initial investors using the principle amounts "invested" by subsequent investors. The fraud is generally unravelled when the operator flees with all of the proceeds, or when a sufficient number of new investors cannot be found to allow the continued payment of "dividends".

This type of fraud is named after Charles Ponzi of Boston, Massachusetts, USA, who operated an extremely attractive investment scheme in which he guaranteed investors a 50 percent return on their investment in postal coupons.

Although he was able to pay his initial investors, the scheme dissolved when he was unable to pay investors who entered the scheme later.

5.20. Suspicious telephone calls leading to fraud

Across the financial services industry customers have received telephone calls from individuals claiming to be from a credit card company (such as Visa or MasterCard). The caller then persuades the customer to give information about their credit card, including the security code found on the back of the card. Neither banks nor credit card companies will call you a customer to ask for any security information about the customer's card.

5.21. Employee Fraud

Approximately £1.3 billion is spent by British organisations on employee expenses every year—about £500 per expense-claiming employee—as a result of lax managers and employee expense fraud. At least 15% of expense claims (about £800 million) do not conform to company policy. Other common forms include inventory manipulation, purchasing fraud, embezzlement and breaches of intellectual property law.

Signals of employee fraud include the following:

(i) A behavioural sign, such as an employee who seems to maintain a lifestyle outside his or her means, has sudden or persistent financial difficulties, or displays changes in emotional behaviour.

(ii) An employee who will not accept the help of an assistant or others in the company for his or her financial duties to the company (and may even refuse to take vacations). This is a very common sign that the employee is concealing fraud.

(iii) An employee who has a gripe with you or your company- such as being passed over for a promotion or denied a raise in salary.

(iv) A personal assistant who regularly "misplaces" or otherwise fails to provide you with itemized receipts for purchases he or she makes on your behalf.

Protective Measures against employee fraud should be seen as necessary expenses and treated as important policies. The following protective measures can be very useful, although they are not an exhaustive list.

(i) Establish written policies on theft and privacy and distribute them to all employees. The theft policy should have a zero-tolerance for theft by any employee, at any level in the company. The privacy policy should make it clear that the employees should have no expectation of privacy in the office, and that you have the right to search office computer records, office phone records, company-issued cell phone records, and the employee's office or workspace.

(ii) Ask all potential employees in interviews if they have ever stolen anything, from an employer or otherwise. These types of pre-screening questions can be surprisingly useful for weeding out potentially dishonest employees.

(iii) Perform background checks on all potential employees who will have financial duties. The background checks should include calls to former employers, and to people in addition to those that the potential employee offers as references. There are a number of reputable private investigation firms that can do background checks for you- from basic checks of relatively low-level employees to thorough checks for senior executives.

(iv) Make sure that there are dual controls for all bookkeeping and accounting functions. For example, one employee should handle receipts and payments, and a different employee should reconcile bank statements and be responsible for accounts receivable.

(iv) Limit physical access to chequebooks, credit cards, cash and other assets to authorized employees only.

(v) Engage independent auditors to audit internal documents regularly.

(vi) If the primary asset of your business is intellectual property, then require all employees to sign non-solicitation and proprietary information agreements at the beginning of their employment with you.

(vi) Consider purchasing fidelity insurance to protect your company from loss of money, securities or inventory resulting from crime and dishonest acts of employees.

(vii) Do not give a personal assistant access to unlimited amounts of credit. For example, consider giving him or her a credit card to use for your purchases that has a relatively low credit limit. In addition, if you have a personal assistant with access to your bank account or your credit cards monitor your statements regularly and require the assistant to provide you with itemized receipts at least once per month.

(viii) If you do suspect an employee of fraud or theft, consult with a solicitor and/or a reputable private investigation or security firm before you conduct an investigation. If you conduct the investigation unlawfully, you may find yourself with troubles worse than they may find those that you were investigating with troubles. By doing your homework on all potential employees and taking appropriate protective measures, you will improve the odds that your family business or you will not suffer from the highly unpleasant experience of employee fraud.

5.22. Benefit Fraud

Housing benefit and council tax benefit fraud are the most common types of fraud committed against the council and the most commonly detected. It is said that the average Local authority pays out about £181 million in benefits and that almost a million pounds of this is lost as a result of fraud every year. Local Authorities have in place a range of controls to prevent, detect and investigate benefit fraud. They also rely on the vigilance of the community to help us detect the fraudsters.

5.23. Frauds in Wills-Probate

The burden of proof is on the person seeking to have the will admitted to probate to demonstrate that the testator knew and approved of it. To demonstrate undue influence, the coercion must be sufficient to overpower the testator's own wishes. As testators cannot give direct evidence, the quality of evidence available from those who knew them is crucial.

The validity of the will itself may be challenged on the basis of one or more of the following- the testator's lack of testamentary capacity; lack of knowledge and approval of the contents of the will; and undue influence.

Undue influence is a species of fraud and requires proof that the testator was coerced into making a will in specific terms. For this to amount to undue influence, the coercion, whether by applying physical force or emotional pressure must be sufficient to overpower the testator's own wishes. This is notoriously hard to prove. Even if a will is valid, its provisions may be challenged after the testator's death on the ground that the will does not make reasonable financial provision for the claimant under the Inheritance (Provision for Family and Dependants) Act 1975. Post-death disputes over the provisions of wills have become an increasingly regular feature of the law reports and the press. A combination of sharp increases in real property values and a wider readiness to seek legal redress for perceived inheritance injustices has contributed to a heightened awareness of some long-available remedies.

> **Case Law**
>
> Often the legal and emotional issues are complex, as in *Cox-Johnson v Cox-Johnson and Others*, concerning the estate of Richard Cox- Johnson, dubbed the Rolling Stones' banker by the press, where personal e-mails and a secret video recording proved both newsworthy and of central legal significance.

5.24. Fraud by Exaggerating Personal Injury Claims

Those who exaggerate personal injury claims should be forced to forego the aspects of payouts to which they are entitled. An unsuccessful attempt was made in the recent case of *Churchill Car Insurance v Victor Kelly* to argue on appeal that a PI claim, which was partly tainted by fraud, should be disallowed altogether, on the basis that extreme cases of dishonesty were an abuse of the process of the court. The claim arose out of a road traffic accident in which liability was not in dispute.

5.25. Construction industry fraud

The construction industry is faced with a crime epidemic, with an estimated £400 million a year lost to fraud, theft and criminal damage. Some of the UK's stolen plant resurfaces as far away as Australia. Site security needs to be actively managed and an effective security strategy is essential.

5.26. Hedge Fund Frauds

In a recent New York case, Bear Stearns was ordered to pay US$125m plus interest to the estate of Manhattan Investment Fund ('MIF') because Bear Stearns ignored clear signs (and its suspicions) that MIF's manager was defrauding investors. Some cross- border frauds are facilitated by hedge funds. In general, the global hedge fund industry is intensely secretive. A recent survey of the industry revealed that the sector is rapidly expanding. It is estimated that there possibly may be 12000 hedge funds investing more than $7 trillion in the world's financial markets by 2008. Research has revealed that up to 1999, one could receive 30% returns, very lucrative indeed. Then most hedge funds tried to emulate the best and today, hedge funds' returns are less than 2%. in this $1000 billion industry. .The Chairman of the US Federal Reserve describes hedge funds as the shock absorbers of the financial markets. The corporate finance world is very complex and securitization is not normally a way for a company to obtain lower-cost financing through disintermediation. However, securitization does avoid the mark-up charged by an intermediary of funds and it enables a company to raise funds cheaply based on an allocation of risks that are assessed by parties having the most expertise. The difference between normal securitization and Enron's manipulation of SPEs is that Enron had high risk that stock prices could fall and that its asset values could fall. So, the structured transactions has dubious economic value whereas in most . securitization deals, the receivables are sold to SPEs with minimal recourse, so the SPE and its investor take the economic risks of collection and once the deal is closed nothing can happen to cause the risk allocation to be subsequently reversed.

5.27. Insolvency frauds

Liquidators may challenge transactions taking place shortly prior to formal insolvency. In brief, where a company on the verge of insolvency gives something away or sells something for less than its true value, that company's liquidator can seek to reverse the transaction because it was at an undervalue (subject to defences). The purpose is to conserve value in the debtor's estate by comparing inflow and outflow in monetary terms. Where a company on the verge of formal insolvency pays off a debt to a particular creditor, that company's liquidator can seek to recover the payment (subject to defences). The purpose is to prevent distortions of the *pari passu* distribution regime, whereby the insolvent company's estate should be divided among all creditors proportionally according to the amounts owed to each creditor by the insolvent company.

5.28. Other bank frauds

In a recent case decided at first instance in the Royal Court of Jersey the court had occasion to apply well-established principles of English law to resolve the common problem of which of two innocent parties must be made to suffer from the fraud of a third.

> **Caselaw**
>
> In *Izodia v Royal Bank of Scotland International Limited*, through an ingenious double deceit, the fraudster managed to appropriate £24.5 million from a bank account held by Izodia at the bank. The resulting litigation raised questions of mandate, actual authority, ratification and election, estoppel and the nature and extent of the banker's duty of care. The test for dishonest assistance is now essentially objective, namely whether defendants have a dishonest state of mind and their conduct falls below the normally accepted standard of honesty.

In general all bank frauds can be stopped if there were a global interoperable solution. Creating a fraud prevention culture has business advantages-an impact on profitability; customer confidence and regulatory compliance.

> **Points to Note**
>
> Bank Fraud Prevention Strategies
> Bank staff must be educated as to internal and external risks.
> Management must take ownership and there must be collective responsibility.
> Anti-Fraud Strategy must be supported by IT infrastructure.
> There needs to be private/public sector data sharing.
> Fraud Risk Management for banks:
> First line of defence- Responsibility
> Second Line of Defence – Oversight
> Third Line of Defence – Internal Audit

5.29. Technology frauds

The Fraud Act introduced a single statutory offence of fraud and created two new offences to stop technology fraud. To frustrate such frauds, controls need to be in place, controls such as procedures to frustrate attempts to over-ride controls, segregation of responsibilities, controls of reconciliation and journal entries – a key control, use of pre-numbered, sequential documents, review of audit logs, pre-employment screening, internal audits, authorisation limits for cheques, dual signatories for all cheques, regular back-up of data, surveillance, job rotations and a fraud procedure in place.

5.30. Tax Frauds

In the UK, there is tax avoidance and tax evasion. Tax avoidance occurs when a person lawfully escapes the tax laws by arranging their affairs in order to avoid tax. Tax avoidance is a class of civil non-compliance. It may be classed as tax mitigation as in *IRC v Duke of Westminster* [1936] AC1. It is legal deliberate tax minimisation. Today, taxpayers are not allowed complete freedom to manipulate the facts of their affairs in order to escape from taxation, even though no crime is alleged to have been committed.

> **Caselaw**
>
> In *MacNiven v Westmoreland Investments Ltd* [2001] UKHL 6, [2001] STC 237, the taxpayer manipulated his circumstances so as to provide a scheme in which a sum of money circulated and returned, in a preordained way, to the original lender so that an amount of interest could be paid and a tax advantage obtained. Lord Hoffman said that the word 'interest' is to be taken in the legal sense and not the commercial sense, and that there had been a genuine payment of legal interest, so that this was not illegal tax evasion.

Tax evasion is illegal. It is unlawful to fail to comply with the tax requirements of the country. It is criminal non-compliance which may result in imprisonment. To understand cross-border tax fraud, one needs to understand some cross-border tax issues. A person who makes profits can be taxed in one or more States with which the person is connected for direct tax purposes. Each State has its own tax rules but most States' direct tax rules have 3 common factors:-the territory in which the person resides (is a citizen, national or is domiciled); the location of the taxpayer's property and the location of the activities of the taxpayer.

An individual is connected to the UK for income tax purposes if the individual is resident in the UK. 'Resident in the UK' includes an individual who is permanently settled in the UK, or who is physically present in the UK for at least 6 months in ay period of tax assessment. A person resident in the UK is chargeable on that person's worldwide income, and not just on the profits arising in the UK.

The profits of a trade arising to a UK resident are chargeable to UK tax wherever the trade is carried on. In the case of capital profits, the Taxation of Chargeable Gains Act 1992 provides that an individual who I resident or ordinarily resident in the UK is taxable on chargeable gains made anywhere in the world provided that the individual is domiciled within the UK. An individual who is resident or ordinarily resident in the UK but who is NOT domiciled within the UK is taxable on chargeable capital gains made in the UK and also on assets situate outside the UK and which are remitted to the UK.

A company is resident in the UK for corporation tax if it is incorporated within the UK. A company not incorporated within the UK is nevertheless resident in the UK for corporation tax purposes if it s managed and controlled in the UK. A company which is resident in the UK is chargeable to corporation tax on all

Fraud Investigation: Criminal Procedure and Investigation

its profits wherever arising. A company resident in the UK, must pay tax in the UK on capital gains made anywhere in the world. The rules on connection to the UK need expert scrutiny. Most tax fraud cases are defended by argument that there is no 'trade' taking place. Cross Border tax evasion thrives on a combination of offshore financial services and the increasing sophistication of technology which can prevent government detecting taxable profits generated within their domestic economies.

Cyber-money enables some forms of tax evasion. Cybermoney can move around the world from computer to computer and in and out of smart cards anonymously without going through the banking system.

Steps in discovering cross-border frauds:

(i) Documents received or obtained by government.

(ii) Informants' testimony.

(iii) Statements by taxpayers and advisers.

(iv) Information from other domestic agencies.

Points to Note: Prevention of Credit Card Fraud

(i) Do not give out your credit card number(s) online unless the site is a secure and reputable site. Sometimes a tiny icon of a padlock appears to symbolize a higher level of security to transmit data. This icon is not a guarantee of a secure site, but might provide you some assurance.

(ii) Do not trust a site just because it claims to be secure.

(iii) Before using the site, check out the security/encryption software it uses.

(iv) Make sure you are purchasing merchandise from a reputable source.

(v) Do your homework on the individual or company to ensure that they are legitimate.

(vi) Try to obtain a physical address rather than merely a post office box and a phone number, call the seller to see if the number is correct and working.

(vii) Send them e-mail to see if they have an active e-mail address and be wary of sellers who use free e-mail services where a credit card wasn't required to open the account.

(viii) Consider not purchasing from sellers who won't provide you with this type of information.

(ix) Check out other web sites regarding this person/company.

(x) Do not judge a person/company by their web site.

(xi) Be cautious when responding to special offers (especially through unsolicited e-mail).

(xii) Be cautious when dealing with individuals/ companies from outside your own country.

(xiii) The safest way to purchase items via the Internet is by credit card because you can often dispute the charges if something is wrong.

(xiv) Make sure the transaction is secure when you electronically send your credit card numbers.

(xv) You should keep a list of all your credit cards and account information along with the card issuer's contact information. If anything looks suspicious or you lose your credit card(s) you should contact the card issuer immediately.

5.33. A fraud contingency plan for the 'Golden Hour'

This is called the "Golden Hour " after a fraud is discovered. This is the time to instigate the plan.

(i) Keep it confidential There will be a strong urge to tell other people, either to sound out suspicions or to share the responsibility for sorting out the problem. It is best to keep quiet and only tell other people on a 'need-to-know' basis. Most frauds, especially serious ones, are committed by people in a position of trust and they must not be tipped-off.

(ii) Fraud is headline gossip and the story will be the talk of the corporate corridors if confidentiality is breached. . Remember to secure emails and do not email your suspicions to colleagues.

(iii) Avoid confrontation. Fight or flight are the two human reactions to danger. Do not confront the person suspected of committing fraud. This might lead to their rapid destruction of any evidence.

(iv) The suspect is likely to talk to potential witnesses to encourage them to back up his story. He will hide any cash he has. Look for it.

(v) Do not pretend that the fraud has not occurred. Running away from suspicions will not help.

(vi) Fraud is often ignored because it is messy, there's often bad publicity, trades union involvement regarding the employees concerned, difficult conversations with regulators and worried shareholders, all on top of an already packed work schedule. In short, fraud is seen as too difficult a problem to deal with. However, the problem will only get bigger and lead to even bigger difficulties the longer it is ignored.

Take the following steps-

(vii) Refer to your *'Fraud Response Plan'*. Now is the time to activate it The incidence of fraud often arises when employees are having domestic problems coupled with an increased pressure at work to put in a good performance

(viii) Establish who is going to lead the investigation internally on the part of the company by pondering on questions such as-

(ix) Will the board delegate authority to a specific individual to lead the investigation?

(x) Should the Board even be informed? It will become necessary to refer the fraud upwards, depends on the level at which the fraud has been discovered and its potential size.
Know when to do so. This is a crucial point and particularly relevant for regional or national subsidiaries

(xi) Who will lead the internal company investigation? Who will sign-off the internal fraud investigation? At this stage audit and legal recourse may not be suitable. It may not be appropriate to ask the internal audit department or the external auditors as they may have a conflict of interest.

(xii) Appoint external investigators who are qualified to cover all the angles, including industry expertise and geographical coverage, especially if the investigation is likely to extend beyond the UK.

(xiii) Do not appoint the company's legal advisors. They may be experts in arbitration or commercial property, but not in fraud-related issues.

(xiv) Individuals' contact details must be easily available. The head of human resources or the head of IT must be at hand for the purpose of computer access and removal.

(xv) Establish the objective of the internal investigation. Once the internal investigation team is formed, the objectives of the investigation must be established. This may initially be simply to remove the employee, take civil action to recover the assets or initiate criminal proceedings.

(xvi) Contact government agencies. If the regulators need to be informed, it is better to contact them as soon as possible.

(xvii) Contact insurers. If the company has directors and officers (D & O) insurance it may need to inform the insurer at this point in order to ensure that the company is covered for investigation costs and legal fees.

(xviii) Make official announcement. If the company has shareholders, or other stakeholders, an official announcement to the market might be necessary.

(xix) Organise travel arrangements if necessary. Visa will have to be organised for investigations of foreign subsidiaries

(xx) Act quickly. Speed is of the essence in the immediate aftermath of a fraud being discovered. The goal is to act quickly in order to catch the fraudster and hopefully the money he or she has stolen. Deploying a package to a suspect's machine breaches ACPO Forensic Principle No.1. But initial search of machine can be regarded as intelligence gathering and once relevant machines identified, and then full ACPO Forensic Principles will apply. Evidence of such fraud will be in-desktop computer, mobile phone, CCTV, IE history, CD, USB stick, etc; Electronic documents and transactions, using remote scan; Emails, phone numbers, bank account numbers; Physical documents; Others involved in fraud; work colleagues and red flags such as high living. Do not alert the suspects. Search covertly. Time synchronise.

(xxi) Have a contingency fraud occurrence plan. A plan must be created for the first few hours, days and weeks of the investigation.

(xxii) Plan chronologically, the interview, suspension or dismissal of the suspect

(xxiii) Consider whether a civil court order is to freeze assets. At this point the police might have to be involved to seize papers in the suspect's home.
If the suspected fraudster is a bank signatory, the bank needs to be contacted.

(xxiv) A statement to explain the company's actions to staff must be prepared. A press statement should also be prepared. Have the right people in place for D-Day, such as lawyers, IT staff, HR professionals, trades union representatives and trained interviewers if appropriate.

(xxv) Witness statements, etc. If the fraud was brought to light by a whistleblower the team will need to consider any actions regarding how this witness should be treated.

(xxvi) Do not panic. It is vital that when a fraud comes to light the first reaction is not panic.

(xxvii) Stay in control. Speed of action and control are required for an effective investigation and recovery of funds. A pre-prepared *'Fraud Response Plan'* is essential.

5.34. Fraud Prevention- method against fraud- Confidentiality Agreement

A good employee will be prepared to sign a confidentiality agreement. This would state that he has a duty of confidentiality to the company and its clients and that information received in the course of employment will not be disclosed to persons outside the group and will not be used for an employee's own benefit or the benefit of others. If a company has a fraud ethics policy and reporting procedures in place, attempted frauds will be nipped in the bud, thus avoiding a scrupulous person from being forced to go to the police or to other authorities with the matter, as it will not arise if nipped in the bud.

Points to Note: Draft Model Policy on Fraud

Such a Policy would contain Headings such as:
- (i) Introduction and description of Types of Fraud.
- (ii) Values, Goals and Objectives.
- (iii) Responsibility of the Company Board.
- (iv) Rights and Responsibilities of Employees.
- (v) Rights and Responsibilities of Third Parties.
- (vi) Responsibilities of Legal Advisor.
- (vii) Responsibilities of the Auditor.
- (viii) Important Responsibilities of Others
- (ix) Investigations where the company is the victim.
- (x) Investigations where the company is the target.
- (xi) Investigations where the company is the Bystander.
- (xii) Conclusions.

5.36. Other preventive policies to combat fraud

Other policies and procedures that ought to be in place to prevent fraud are illustrated in the following table:

Title of Policy	Purpose and Effect
Pre-employment Screening	To verify the integrity of new employees, including part-time and agency staff.
Drugs Testing	A part of the pre-employment screening medical to ensure that new employees, part-time or agency staff are not addicted to narcotic drugs. The procedure may also be extended to annual medical examinations.
Probationary Reports	All new employees should be required to serve a three-month probationary period. This procedure leads to confirmation or termination of employment.
Temporary Staff	To identify the jobs in which temporary staff may *not* be employed. and the internal job rotation and transfer plans needed to cover absences in sensitive positions. Extends the pre-employment screening process to temporary and agency staff.
Job Descriptions and Contracts of Employment	To ensure that an employee's control responsibilities are incorporated as a central feature of their jobs, and particularly the requirement to comply with the Fraud Policy.
Special Agreements	Agreements on Confidentiality, assignment of patent and other intellectual property rights.

Consultancy	To ensure that the integrity of consultants is confirmed and that agreements protect the company.
Staff Handbook	To ensure that employees understand the company's goals, values, ethical standards and control standards.
Identification	To ensure that employees are provided with secure means of identification.
Training	To ensure that employees are trained in their control and other responsibilities.
Employee Expenses	To ensure that expenses are claimed accurately.
Annual Appraisals	To review each employee's performance and his or her competence with the Fraud Policy. Supervisors to discuss the Annual Declaration of Compliance during formal interviews.
Incentive	To ensure that incentive schemes cannot be abused o reward dishonesty.
Internal Reporting	To ensure that problems that come to notice in an employee's private life and which could have an impact on their job performance are reported to Audit and Legal departments.
Disciplinary	To ensure that employees suspected of poor performance or dishonesty, are dealt with fairly and in accordance with the law.

Exit Interviews	To ensure that employees, on termination of employment or transfer to another location, are interviewed, by other than their line managers, to make a closing Declaration of Compliance and to make recommendations for control improvements.
Termination	To ensure that all company property is returned on termination of employment and that employees are reminded of their confidentiality and other undertakings.
References	To ensure that references provided on past employees are accurate and do not mislead future employers. Specifically, if an employee has been dismissed for dishonesty, that fact should be reported openly and fairly.

5.37. Conclusion

Fraud costs the United Kingdom billions of pounds a year and it is synonymous with lying to secure financial benefit. Fraud threatens to blur the boundaries between what we see as right and wrong. The 2007 Fraud Review recommended the establishment of a National Fraud Strategic Authority within central government (but consisting of stakeholders drawn from the private and public sectors), and the establishment of a National Fraud Reporting Centre. It also recommended that a National Lead Police Force should be established, to act as a centre of excellence for other Fraud Squads and to assist with or direct the most complex fraud investigations. It is hoped that such implementations will combat the frauds as described in this chapter. Chapter 5 provides a wealth of examples of some of the many types of fraud today including identity theft, financial, auction, sweepstakes, and counterfeit payments, to name a few. Each one of these fraudulent schemes has caused people to lose millions of pounds. Of great concern is identity theft. Criminals have been known to steal social security or credit card numbers and to use this information as a basis for opening fraudulent accounts in the name of the persons whose identities were stolen, oftentimes without those victims being aware of it. Many bogus insurance claims are made each day, particularly related to trips and falls on the pavement.

This is a serious problem, which drains resources away from repairing and improving the highways themselves. There are many more schemes being devised by criminal minds.

Further reading for Chapter Five

P. Allonby, "Liar, liar", pg.28, Jane's Police Review, Jane's Info. Gp., Surrey, 8 August 2008

M. Clarke, "The control of insurance fraud: A Comparative View", British Journal of Criminology, Winter 1990; 30: 1 - 23.

European Commission, Special Eurobarometer: Consumer Protection in the European Market", September 2006, at http://ec.europa.eu/public_opinion/archives/ebs/ebs252_en.pdf

Identity theft Task Force, "Combating Identity Theft: A Strategic Plan", 23 April 2007 at
http://www.idtheft.gov

M. Levi, "Offender Organization and Victim Responses: Credit Card Fraud in International Perspective", Journal of Contemporary Criminal Justice, Nov. 1, 1998; 14(4): 368 - 383.

OECD, "OECD Anti-Spam Toolkit of Recommended Policies and Measures", 22 September 2006.

United Nations, "Results of the second meeting of the Intergovernmental Expert Group To Prepare a Study on Fraud and the Criminal Misuse and Falsification of Identity", Report of the Secretary-General, E/CN 15/2007/8, 2 April 2007,

J. K. Winn, "Couriers Without Luggage: Negotiable Instruments and Digital Signatures", 49 South Carolina L. Rev. 739 (1998)

CHAPTER 6- BRIBERY AND CORRUPTION IN CORPORATIONS, GOVERNMENT AND AUTHORITIES

6.1. Introduction

Research shows that there is a reduced propensity to invest in corruption-ridden countries, both on the side of foreign and domestic investors. This leads to reduced economic growth. Corruption tends to favour short-term capital movements (loans, speculative capital) over long-term investment, leading to monetary volatility and related economic instability. Corruption in a country further moves economic activity away from the formal sector towards the informal economy. This reduces government revenue and thereby the redistributive powers of the State and it makes it difficult to enforce consumer protection legislation. The effectiveness of public spending suffers from corruption as investment decisions are skewed in favour of such projects that can yield personal benefits for the decision-maker. The projects also become more expensive and the quality lower. Sectors that do not lend themselves readily to grand corruption, such as social services, are given less emphasis than some others are. On the revenue side, illegitimate exemptions, tax holidays, etc. make receipts decrease and worsens public services and infrastructure, reduces employment, and reduces growth. Other effects of corruption are a reduction in quality of law and order and more economic and social vulnerability of citizens. One increasingly well-documented aspect of corruption is the fact that it redistributes income and welfare to the detriment of the poor. The poor are more vulnerable than better-off people, and vulnerability is increased by the arbitrariness and lack of transparency that are important features of corrupt systems, not to speak of the costs of bribing officials in order to gain access to services. The poor are also the ones that cannot afford to shift from public to private services as a reaction to the scarcity and poor quality of services resulting from corruption in the public sector.

6.2. Bribery and Corruption

Throughout the world, bribery and corruption is classed as serious fraud, so much so, that there are many international conventions on Bribery and Corruption. Examples of bribery and corruption are active bribery, passive bribery, embezzlement, or misappropriation of public funds, trading in influence, illicit enrichment, and money laundering. If bribery is outlawed, companies worldwide will look for other means of exercising influence, whether legitimate or controversial.

> ### Case Study: Bribery for service
>
> Four people were found guilty at Reading Crown Court in a case of bribery for service contracts between a machinery maintenance firm and Mars, the confectionary company. The four convicted defendants are Barry Alexander Simpson and Roger Harper (both former co-owners of Iron firm Ltd, trading as Excel Engineering), Anthony "Tony" Frederick Welcher (a former employee of Mars UK Ltd) and his wife Georgina Welcher. Barry Simpson and Roger Harper owned and ran Excel Engineering from the early 1980's. Mars provided Excel Engineering with the bulk of its business. Tony Welcher was a middle manager at Mars responsible for maintenance of production lines. Welcher was able to deal with Excel Engineering over a number.

> of years without imposition of supervision or scrutiny Tony and Georgina Welcher purported to run a design consultancy business called GW Designs and claimed to have supplied computer aided design drawings to Excel Engineering and others. Georgina Welcher was also on the payroll of Excel Engineering as private secretary and chauffeur to Barry Simpson and Roger Harper. Tony Welcher's 88-year old mother was allegedly also employed by Excel Engineering - as a cleaner. In 2001, Excel Engineering was sold to new owners but thereafter the volume of business and income did not match past levels. It became apparent to the new owners that the company's success had been largely dependent on contracts from Mars in return for improper inducements. These bribes were usually in the form of regular cash payments, or in the form of gifts, to Tony Welcher and to others, including Georgina Welcher. Suspicions were reported by the new owners of Excel Engineering to Thames Valley Police and then referred to the SFO in summer 2002. Officers from the Thames Valley Police Economic Crime Unit worked in conjunction with the SFO investigation team

The OECD survey found that British companies are among the worst offenders for bribing foreign officials. *"Some 37 of the 55 companies which the World Bank publicly blacklists and has disbarred from participating in its contracts because of evidence of corruption are domiciled in Britain."*

However, if, for instance, the Home Office decides that a request does not concern a recognised crime in the requesting country but is merely a political incident, then the Home Office will refuse the request. This was made clear in the case of *R v Secretary of State for the Home Department, ex parte Fininvest Spa* . In this case the request concerned illicit payments to politicians, i.e., bribery. The Home Secretary took the view that the payments referred to were offences of bribery and corruption and not of false accounting nor of use of monies for criminal purposes. The Divisional Court upheld his decision, saying that it was for the requested state, the UK, to decide the nature of the offence and not the requesting state.

> **Caselaw:** *R v Secretary of State for the Home Department, ex parte Fininvest SpA and others,* 23 Oct. 1996
>
> The Italian prosecuting authorities sent a letter of request under the provisions of the European Convention on Mutual Assistance in Criminal Matters 1959 (implemented in the United Kingdom by the Criminal Justice (International Co-operation) Act 1990) to the Home Secretary requesting assistance in obtaining documents held by CMM, a company whose offices were in London. The documents were relevant to an investigation of a fraud in which the applicants, an Italian company and its present and previous presidents, were alleged to be involved. It was alleged that over 100bn lire had been removed from the company and used for criminal purposes, and a prosecution was already afoot against the third applicant for making illicit donations to a former Prime Minister and Leader of the Italian Socialist Party. The request was referred by the Home Secretary to the Serious Fraud Office under s 4(2A) of the 1990 Act. The Serious Fraud Office implemented the request by obtaining and executing a search warrant authorising entry to CMM's premises under s 2 of the Criminal Justice Act 1987. The applicants applied for judicial review of, inter alia, the Home Secretary's

decision to refer the request to the Serious Fraud Office, contending: (i) that the letter of request described the documents sought so widely that it could not properly be regarded as one for assistance in obtaining 'evidence' for the purposes of s 4 of the 1990 Act but was merely a fishing expedition; and (ii) that the Home Secretary should have considered whether or not the request concerned 'a political offence [or] an offence connected with a political offence' within the meaning of art 2(a) of the convention and, had he done so, he would have concluded that it did and refused assistance to the Italian authorities. The 1990 Act made provision for the obtaining of evidence in connection with a criminal investigation provided that the Home Secretary was satisfied that an investigation into a particular offence was being conducted and that there were reasonable grounds for suspecting that it had been committed. It followed that since the investigation for which the material was requested involved a wide-ranging international fraud, and the request was as precise and focused as it could sensibly be in the circumstances, the request could properly be said to be for the obtaining of evidence and not for the purposes of a fishing expedition *Rio Tinto Zinc Corp v Westinghouse Electric Corp* [1978] 1 All ER 434 and *Re State of Norway's Application (No 1)* [1989] 1 All ER 661 distinguished. The question whether an offence was 'political' for the purposes of art 2(a) of the convention had to be determined by the law of the requested state. However, although the Home Secretary was bound to consider art 2(a), he was not bound to reach a decision as to whether or not the offences were, or were connected with, political offences, since he could have decided that in any event he would not exercise his discretion under art 2(a) to refuse co-operation with the

> Italian authorities. Moreover, the making of illegal donations to a political party, although an offence committed in a political context, could not be regarded as political per se (ie political irrespective of motive or circumstance), since the offence was merely one against the ordinary law enacted for the proper ordering of the democratic process in Italy. Nor was it made political because the offender hoped to change government policy by buying political influence, or because the judiciary, by prosecuting him, hoped to clean up politics. The application would therefore be dismissed". *Application dismissed.*

In contrast, in the case of *R v Andrew Regan* (unreported) the media perceived this serious fraud prosecution to be politically motivated because Andrew Regan attempted to buy out the UK's Co-operative Wholesale Ltd., a business that is the Europe's largest mutual business and a company with a very long political and socialist history. The UK's Serious Fraud Office issued an international arrest warrant on the basis of theft by Mr Regan, rather than bribery and corruption, which, if pursued, would have been refused in line with Article 2 of the European Convention on Mutual Assistance and also in line with the UK's own decision in the *Fininvest* case, *R v Secretary of State for the Home Department, ex parte Fininvest SpA and others* [1997] 1 All ER 942.

6.3. Case of corruption that has been successfully prosecuted

> **Caselaw**
>
> *R v Terence Richmond* [1992], unreported
> The investigation was of the engineering industry and connected contracts.
> In *R v Terence Richmond* [1992], unreported, the Defendant pleaded guilty to charges of corruption arising out of contracts concerning the Channel Tunnel. He was sentenced to two years imprisonment suspended for two years and a confiscation order was made in relation to the profits he was shown to have made.

6.4 Case of bribery successfully prosecuted

> **Case Study: Bid rigging**
> X was an employee of a petroleum shipping company in the Bahamas. X was the repair and technical manager.
> The company opened a UK branch in the UK.
> The company had a ship management agreement with Esso Petroleum Company in relation to 11 UK registered ships.
> Esso used to invite bids for all aspects of ship refits. In one bid, 4 shipyards tendered.
> One of the 4 was K shipyard from Singapore.
> This is how the tendering process operated:
> There were refit contracts for 3 ships based in the UK. Tenders for the 3 ships were sought from a number of shipyards. Sealed bids were obtained from each shipyard. K's shipyard offered substantial discounts. X evaluated the bids and favoured K's bid.
> K's bid was accepted and this happened in 20 such bids. But K's discounts were unusual in timing and size. K was able to succeed in its bids because K was receiving confidential information from X about the rival bids and made payments to X of a total of £1.6 million for this information. X was charged with corruption contrary to Section 1 of the Prevention of Corruption Act 1906 and was sentenced to 3 years imprisonment.

6.5.1. The Public Bodies Corrupt Practices Act 1889

Section 1(1) of the 1889 Act makes it an offence for any person alone, or in conjunction with others, to corruptly solicit or receive, or agree to receive, for him/herself, or for any other person, any gift, loan, fee, reward, or advantage whatever as an inducement to, or reward for, or otherwise on account of any member, officer, or servant of a public body, doing or forbearing to do anything in respect of any matter or transaction whatsoever, actual or proposed, in which the public body is concerned. Section 1(2) of the 1889 Act creates a similar offence to that of section 1(1) above, in respect of anyone who corruptly gives promises or offers any gift, etc. The definition of a 'public body' is contained in section 7 of the 1889 Act (Archbold 31-134). This definition was amended and extended by section 4(2) of the Prevention of Corruption Act 1916 to apply to "local and public authorities of all descriptions". However, this definition does not include a government department or the Crown (*R v Naci Vedat Natji*, 2002 EWCA Crim 271), so corruption involving those persons should be charged under the 1906 Act. 'Corruptly' in the 1889 Act does not mean 'dishonestly' but means "purposely doing an act which the law forbids as tending to corrupt" (*Cooper v Slade 1851*). "Corrupt" has not been defined in law. Offences under the 1889 Act require the consent of the Attorney General, refer to Consents to Prosecute, elsewhere in the guidance (Crown Prosecution Service: Bribery and Corruption).

6.5. 2. The Prevention of Corruption Act 1906

The Prevention of Corruption Act 1906 makes it a crime to bribe any agent, an agent being anybody employed by or acting for another, whether in the public or private sector.

It is an offence for an agent to obtain a consideration as an inducement or reward for doing any act, or showing favour o disfavour to any person, in relation to his or her principal's affairs. It is a criminal offence for any person to give a consideration to an agent to induce him or her to do an act in relation to his or her principal's affairs. It is a criminal offence for any person or agent to knowingly falsify receipts, accounts or other documents with the intent to deceive the principal.

6.6. Prevention of Corruption Act 1916

If any person or agent of a person, holding or seeking to obtain a contract gives a gift to a public official, that gift shall be presumed to be corrupt unless the accused person can prove otherwise. This Act is soon to be repealed as soon as the anticipated new Statute is passed, perhaps in 2009.

6.7. Foreign Bribery

This is now covered by Part 12 of the Terrorism Crime and Security Act 2001. Part 12 extends the scope of the UK law on bribery to 'foreign' bribery. It does so by providing that he existing bribery offences are also offences if they are committed outside the UK or if they involve either foreign agents or principals having no connection to the UK, or holders of a foreign public office or officials of bodies or authorities which are the equivalent in the country concerned of those covered by the domestic offence. In all cases, the elements of the offence are unchanged. Part12 also allows for jurisdiction over UK nationals or bodies incorporated in the UK who commit one of the offences as now redefined, no matter where outside the UK the offence is committed.

6.8. Conclusion to Chapter Six

A general element without which corruption cannot be fought effectively is political commitment at high levels of government. Parliaments and parliamentarians are important factors in securing accountability and transparency in building national integrity systems and clear-cut rules regarding donation to political parties and individual candidates should be just as much part and parcel as combating corruption as steps towards controlling governments and the civil service. This is why we must ensure that the new ACPO Guidance on Police Corruption and the attached regulations and follow-up systems are internalised and gain a sufficient degree of personal significance and meaning for each and officer. A new bribery statute s expected in the year 2009. There are also other methods of tackling bibery and corruption using the common law, Criminal Justice Act 2004 and the Anti-terrorism, Crime and Security Act 2001.

> **Further reading for Chapter Six**
>
> B. Belbot, "Whistleblowing and lawyers", Journal of Contemporary Criminal Justice, Aug 1991; vol. 7: pp. 154 - 166.
>
> J. D. Calder, "New Corporate Security: The Autumn of Crime Control and the Spring of Fairness and Due Process", Journal of Contemporary Criminal Justice, Dec 1987; vol. 3: pp. 1 - 34.
>
> R. C. Cramer, "Is Corporate Crime Serious Crime? Criminal Justice and Corporate Crime Control", Journal of Contemporary Criminal Justice, Jun 1984; vol. 2: pp. 7 - 10.
>
> P. Green, "Disaster by Design: Corruption, Construction and Catastrophe", British Journal of Criminology, July 2005; 45: 528 - 546.

P. Green and T. Ward, *State Crime: Governments, Violence and Corruption.* (Pluto Press, London 2004)
G. W. Potter and L. K. Gaines, "Country Comfort: Vice and Corruption in Rural Settings", Journal of Contemporary Criminal Justice, Feb 1992; vol. 8: pp. 36 – 61

CHAPTER 7-
REGULATORY FRAUD- MONEY LAUNDERING, CARTELS AND OTHER CORPORATE FRAUD

7.1.1. Corporate frauds are sophisticated opportunistic frauds

Corporate fraud takes the form of sophisticated transactions, money laundering, employee frauds and executive frauds. Dimensions of managerial incentives that relate to incentives to commit fraud are incentive payoffs and stock price. Assuming that frauds will eventually be reversed via future accounting transactions or will be made public, managers only benefit from fraud to the extent that they can exercise options and sell stock before the fraud is reversed or revealed. Thus, incentives from vested or unrestricted sources, which offer short-term opportunities for profit, are more important in providing incentives to commit fraud. Even a small number of frauds can have large economic impact.

Executives who have been prosecuted for committing fraud face significantly greater potential payoffs (losses) from share price increases (decreases) compared to executives at regular firms, illustrating that managers at fraud firms face greater financial incentives to commit fraud. The stronger financial incentives stem primarily from unrestricted stock holdings. During fraud years, executives at fraud firms sell significantly more stock than control executives do. The ability to sell stock provides an incentive to commit fraud and fraudulent executives exercise significantly larger fractions of their vested options than executives in regular firms do do. Fraud firms face shocks that significantly reduce growth in earnings per share; their raw stock returns are essentially zero over the fraud period, and the first public news of the accounting problems leads to large negative excess returns. In principle, strong governance mechanisms could reduce the opportunity to commit fraud.

7.1.2.1. Money Laundering

Money laundering has been agreed as the processing of criminal proceeds in order to disguise their illegal origin. To stop money laundering is directly to stop future criminal activity from affecting legitimate economic activities. Jewellery stores, accountants, car dealerships, art galleries, video stores, horse racing, law firms, boat dealers, travel agents - what do these have in common? They have the common crime of being involved in money laundering. Money laundering has become a pervasive fraud, infecting not only financially-oriented firms (*bureaux de change*, international money transmitters, casinos) but also hotels, restaurants, vending machine operators and a host of retail businesses. Any business that deals with cash can be involved and its owner could become a money launderer. The persons aimed at are the people at the top of the pyramid of an unlawful activity who are insulated from the run of the mill operations of criminal activity. Money laundering is the act of concealing the proceeds of criminal activity in order to make them appear to have been legitimately obtained. Money laundering can also involve the unlawful movement of legitimate funds for the purpose of financing nefarious activity such as terrorism.

7.1.2.2. Money Laundering Legislation History

In this area, legislation changes as the criminality changes. The Second European Money Laundering Directive, upon which the UK's Proceeds of Crime Act 2002 (POCA 2002) and Money Laundering Regulations 2003 (SI 2003/2075) (the 2003 regulations) are based, was itself framed in an attempt to implement the 40 recommendations of the Financial Action Task Force (FATF), a multi-national standing body appointed by the Organisation for Economic Co-Operation and Development. The Regulations gave effect to EEC Council Directive 91/308 on prevention of the use of the financial system for the purpose of money laundering (OJ L166, 28.6.91), as amended by European Parliament and Council Directive 2001/97/EC (OJ L344, 28.12.2001).

Implemented in the UK in December 2007, the third European Directive (2004/0137) was officially approved on 7 June 2005 by the Council of Economic and Finance Ministers. The UK as a member of the EU was obliged to introduce domestic law in compliance with the Third Money Laundering Directive 2005/60/EC (the directive)—on the prevention of the use of the financial system for the purpose of money laundering and terrorist financing—by 15 December 2007, which it did. The third EU Directive on money laundering, in force in the UK since December 2007, already has many of its provisions in existing UK legislation, mainly the Proceeds of Crime Act 2002. For instance, the Proceeds of Crime Act 2002, Pt 7, makes a person guilty of an offence of money laundering if he enters into an arrangement which he knows or suspects facilitates the acquisition, retention, or control of criminal property.

7.1.2.3. Money laundering activity as per regulations

Only persons carrying on "relevant business" are affected. A relevant business includes (Regulation 2(2)): the regulated activity of:- accepting deposits; affecting or carrying out contracts of long-term insurance when carried on by a person

Fraud Investigation: Criminal Procedure and Investigation

who has received official authorisation pursuant to Article 4 or 51 of the Life Assurance Consolidation Directive; dealing in investments as principal or as agent; arranging deals in investments; managing investments; safeguarding and administering investments; sending dematerialised instructions; establishing (and taking other steps in relation to) collective investment schemes; advising on investments; or issuing electronic money; the activities of the National Savings Bank; any activity carried on for the purpose of raising money authorised to be raised under the National Loans Act 1968 under the auspices of the Director of Savings; the business of operating a bureau de change, transmitting money (or any representation of monetary value) by any means or cashing cheques which are made payable to customers; any of the activities in Annex 1 to the Banking Consolidation Directive (which activities are, for convenience, set out in Schedule 1 to these Regulations) when carried on by way of business, ignoring an activity falling within any of sub-paragraphs (a) to (d); estate agency work; operating a casino by way of business; the activities of a person appointed to act as an insolvency practitioner within the meaning of section 388 of the Insolvency Act 1986 or Article 3 of the Insolvency (Northern Ireland) Order 1989; the provision by way of business of advice about the tax affairs of another person by a body corporate or un-incorporate or, in the case of a sole practitioner, by an individual; the provision by way of business of accountancy services by a body corporate or un-incorporate or, in the case of a sole practitioner, by an individual; the provision by way of business of audit services by a person who is eligible for appointment as a company auditor under section 25 of the Companies Act 1989 or Article 28 of the Companies (Northern Ireland) Order 1990; the provision by way of business of legal services by a body corporate or un-incorporate or, in the case of a sole practitioner, by an individual and which involves participation in a financial or real property transaction (whether by assisting in the planning or execution of any such transaction or otherwise by acting for, or on behalf of, a client in any such transaction); the provision by way of business of services in relation to the formation, operation or management of a company or a trust; or the activity of dealing in goods of any description by way of business (including dealing as an auctioneer) whenever a transaction involves accepting a total cash payment of 15,000 euro or more.

7.1.2.4. Not money laundering activity

According to Regulation 2(3), the above does not apply to: the issue of withdraw-able share capital within the limit set by section 6 of the Industrial and Provident Societies Act 1965 by a society registered under that Act; the acceptance of deposits from the public within the limit set by section 7(3) of that Act by such a society; the issue of withdraw-able share capital within the limit set by section 6 of the Industrial and Provident Societies Act (Northern Ireland) 1969 by a society registered under that Act; the acceptance of deposits from the public within the limit set by section 7(3) of that Act by such a society; activities carried on by the Bank of England; any activity in respect of which an exemption order under section 38 of the 2000 Act has effect if it is carried on by a person who is for the time being specified in the order or falls within a class of persons so specified; any activity (other than one falling within sub-paragraph (f)) in respect of which a person was an exempted person for the purposes of section 45 of the Financial Services Act 1986 immediately before its repeal; the regulated activities of arranging deals in investments or advising on investments, in so far as the investment consists of rights under a regulated mortgage contract; the regulated activities of dealing in investments as agent, arranging deals in investments, managing investments or advising on investments, in so far as the investment consists of rights under, or any right to or interest in, a contract of insurance which is not a qualifying contract of insurance; or the Official Solicitor to the Supreme Court when acting as trustee in his official capacity.

7.1.2.5. Relevant business must comply

Persons carrying on a relevant business must comply with requirements relating to identification procedures, record-keeping procedures, and internal reporting procedures (Regulation 3(1) (a)). The identification procedures are detailed at Regulation 4; and the circumstances where it is not necessary to obtain evidence of any person's identity are detailed at Regulation 5. Particular provisions are made in relation to the identification of persons before they are allowed to use a casino's gaming facilities at Regulation 8.

7.1.2.6 Relevant businesses must have internal controls

The record-keeping procedures are at Regulation 6 and internal reporting procedures at Regulation 7. Persons carrying on a relevant business must establish such other procedures of internal control and communication as may be appropriate for the purposes of forestalling and preventing money laundering (Regulation 3(1)(b)); and take appropriate measures so that employees are made aware of the relevant provisions (i.e. the provisions of the Money Laundering Regulations 2003, SI 2003/3075, the Proceeds of Crime Act 2002 Pt 7 (ss 327–340), and the Terrorism Act 2000 ss 18, 21A (s 21A as added)), and are given training in how to recognise and deal with transactions which may be related to money laundering (Regulation 3(1)(c)).

7.1.2.7. It is an offence to not have procedures in place

Contravention of these provisions is an offence (Regulation 3(2)) and a person guilty of such an offence is liable: (1) on conviction on indictment, to imprisonment for a term not exceeding two years, to a fine, or to both;(2) on summary conviction, to a fine not exceeding the statutory maximum: see Regulation 3(2). The 'statutory maximum' is the prescribed sum within the meaning of the Magistrates' Courts Act 1980 s 32 (as amended): see the Interpretation Act 1978 s 5, Sch 1 (definition added by the Criminal Justice Act 1988 s 170(1), Sch 15 para 58).

7.1.2.8. Statutory inspection for money laundering offences

Provision is made in the Regulations for the registration and inspection of money service operators and high value dealers (Regulations 9 - 25). The meanings of 'money service operator' and 'high value dealer' are at Regulation 2(1). Supervisory authorities, which include *inter alia* the Financial Services Authority and the Bank of England, must disclose relevant information to the police if they know or suspect that someone has or may have been engaged in money laundering (Regulation 26).The Financial Services Authority has as one of its objectives the reduction of financial crime (see Financial Services and Markets Act 2000 s 2(2)) and the Authority may make rules in relation to the prevention and detection of money laundering (Financial Services and Markets Act 2000 Section s 146). There are also statutory provisions penalising

Fraud Investigation: Criminal Procedure and Investigation

those who assist in the retention of the proceeds of drug trafficking or criminal conduct and requiring banks and their employees to report suspicions or beliefs of money laundering to the police (Proceeds of Crime Act 2002 Pt 7). Anti-terrorism legislation has been enacted to prevent the retention or control of terrorist property, including money (Terrorism Act 2000). The prevailing consensus in early 2005 appeared to be that a breach of the reporting obligation under the Proceeds of Crime Act 2002 (PCA 2002), s 330 was a "thought crime". So if a defendant was subjectively or objectively suspicious about a transaction, a prosecution could be brought without any need to prove as part of the *actus reus* that the failure to report in fact related to criminal property or put another way that the relevant third party was in fact "engaged in money-laundering" actual knowledge or suspicion is not required under s 330 or s 331, nor, need it be proved that any money-laundering took place.

7.1.2.8. Proceeds of Crime Act

The general provisions of Proceeds of Crime Act (POCA) replaced and consolidated the old law contained in the Criminal Justice Act 1988, sections 93A to 93D, and the Drug Trafficking Act 1994. Section 327 prohibits concealing, disguising, converting or transferring criminal property. Section 328 prohibits acquisition, use or possession. Section 327 introduces a second mental element (in addition to the one required for criminal property; see above) in describing an offence where a person

> '... *enters into or becomes concerned in an arrangement which he knows or suspects facilitates (by whatever means) the acquisition, retention, use or control of criminal property by or on behalf of another person*'.

7.1.2.9. Part 7 of the Proceeds of Crime Act-definitions of money laundering

A person commits an offence by concealing, disguising, converting, or transferring criminal property (POCA s327). Criminal property is that which is had from criminal conduct. Criminal conduct is conduct which constitutes an offence in any part of the UK; or would constitute an offence in any part of the UK if it occurred there. No offence is committed if the person concerned makes a timely disclosure of the facts to the police, a customs officer or a person nominated for the purpose by the person's employer. It is also an offence to acquire, use, or have possession of criminal property. Criminal property is so termed if it constitutes a person's benefit from criminal conduct or it represents such a benefit (in whole or in part and whether directly or indirectly); and the alleged offender knows or suspects that it constitutes or represents such a benefit. The POCA offences under ss.328, 333,342 may be committed by anyone/in the course of any work. S.328 is the primary POCA offence which might be committed: entering into or becoming concerned in an arrangement which you know or suspect facilitates (by whatever means) the acquisition retention use or control of criminal property by another.

7.1.2.10. Money Laundering Regulations from December 2007

On 15 December 2007, the new UK Money Laundering Regulations came into force, replacing the Money Laundering Regulations 2003 and giving effect to the EU's Third Money Laundering Directive -the Directive on the Prevention of Money Laundering and Terrorist Financing. The EU's Third Money Laundering Directive was adopted in October 2005, under the UK's Presidency of the European Union. It seeks to implement the global money laundering standards produced by the Financial Action Task Force (FATF) in 2003. FATF is an inter-governmental body charged with the development and promotion of national and international policies to combat money laundering and terrorist financing. The FATF Money Laundering Standard consists of 40 Recommendations that seek to provide a complete set of counter-measures against money laundering, covering the criminal justice system and law enforcement, the financial system and its regulation, as well as international co-operation. In general, firms that are already subject to the requirements of the Money Laundering Regulations 2003 will not notice significant changes under the new Regulations.

7.1.2.11. Money Laundering Regulations 2008

HMRC has provided some general examples of indicators of suspicious activity in section 10.8 of MLR 8. On 1 August 2008, the revised money laundering regulations announced by the UK Economic means that all accountancy services providers (ASPs) not members of a HM Treasury approved accounting body, will be supervised directly by HMRC. ASPs need to submit their application by 30th September2008 if they wish to practice from 1st January 2009 onwards. Investigators of money laundering must check that licences are valid.

7.1.2.12. HMRC investigation of off-shore accounts

There is nothing new in HMRC's special interest in any offshore arrangements entered into by any taxpaying entity resident in the United Kingdom (UK). For years the very mention in accounts or documentation of opaque structures such as 'stiftung' or 'anstalt' was sufficient to merit fairly intense scrutiny by what was then a Somerset House specialist.

There is now extensive international co-operation between fiscal authorities, both inside and outside the European Union (EU), urged on by the wider membership of the Organisation for Economic Cooperation & Development (OECD). This international attack on tax evasion is also an attack on the offence of money laundering. Offshore Financial Centres (OFC's) which offer, in exchange for substantial revenues from those seeking anonymity, essentially tax-free havens with strong bank secrecy laws; state of the art telecommunications; no exchange controls; lax or non-existent regulation of banks and corporate entities (little or no auditing, no annual or other periodic reporting requirements); corporate structures that can be organized or acquired cheaply, quickly, and anonymously (including the ability to disguise the ownership of corporations or trusts through the use of nominee directors, bearer shares, and ready-for-hire trustees); predominant use of a major international currency (*e.g.,* U.S. dollars, Pounds Sterling, Euros); and no binding international agreements regarding cooperative law enforcement, are money launderers.

7.1.2.13. Caselaw on money laundering

Caselaw

The case of *R v Duff* [2002] *Manchester Crown Court,* made Jonathan Duff was convicted, was the first solicitor to be imprisoned for the offence of failing to report a suspicion of money laundering. This case has stripped away any last vestiges of complacency over money laundering in the solicitors' profession. For solicitors, the most disturbing aspect of the case is that Duff was not an intentional launderer of criminal funds. Instead, Duff's crime was an act of omission, namely a failure to report, which arose from a genuine misunderstanding of his own legal obligations. The 2007 Money Laundering regulations in force affect accountants providing 'privileged' services to clients in the same way as lawyers which means they do not have to report suspicions to SOCA. This is a very specific and limited change to the qualified accountants' duty to report knowledge or suspicion of money laundering.

Caselaw

Ali and others [2005] EWCA Crim 87, [2005] All ER (D) 16 (Jun) is one of the most significant decisions of the court in criminal law in 2005. It was thought that hundreds of appeals against money laundering convictions would be triggered by one of the most significant decisions in criminal law. Counsel for HM Customs and Excise said that if the court decided as it did, then this would trigger hundreds of appeals against conviction, all of which would have to be upheld. It would thus undermine the success of past law enforcement efforts against money launderers. In *Ali,* he court paid careful regard to the views of the legal academic community, and Hooper, in delivering the decision, declined to follow previous court authorities, explicitly adopting instead the critique of those authorities expressed by Professor Ormerod in his case note in the Criminal Law Review in April 2005 (but see rebuttable article in the 'The Criminal Lawyer', "Pepper v Hart revisited", January 2009).

Caselaw

The case of *Bowman v Fels* [2005] EWCA Civ 226, [2005] All ER (D) 115 (Mar) triggered new guidance to solicitors from the Law Society. Bowman v Fels, decided by the Court of Appeal on 8 March 2005, is extremely important for tax professional advisers, because it narrows the circumstances in which professional advisers are required to make a suspicious activity report (SAR) under the anti-money-laundering legislation set out in Part 7 of the Proceeds of Crime Act 2002 (POCA). Does the decision in Bowman v Fels impact on the obligation of a barrister and solicitor to make a SAR when representing a taxpayer who is seeking to make a voluntary disclosure to HM Revenue & Customs (HMRC) and make a civil settlement, taking advantage of the Hansard procedure? Although firms providing financial services have had procedures in place to prevent their services being used for money laundering for the past ten years (since MLR 1993), the inclusion of tax offences within the definition of money laundering has caused practitioners much anxiety. Out of fear of facing criminal proceedings themselves, some tax practices report anything remotely suspicious or 'wrong'. At the other end of the spectrum there are firms that refuse to believe that any of their (usually longstanding) clients could ever do anything which requires reporting. In between these extremes there is a third way. By adopting good practice management systems and coherent anti-money laundering policies, firms can be confident about when they do and do not need to report.

Fraud Investigation: Criminal Procedure and Investigation

Caselaw

The case of *Squirrell Ltd v National Westminster Bank Plc* [2005] EWHC 664 (Ch), [2005] 2 All ER 784) exemplifies the difficulties banks can face in their efforts to comply with the Proceeds of Crime Act 2002. In 2002, Squirrell Ltd opened a bank account with National Westminster Bank and began buying and selling mobile phones. In March 2005, the bank stopped operating the account and gave no reason for doing so. Squirrell claimed that the blocking of the account prevented it from carrying out its ordinary business and applied for an order that the account be "unfrozen" and the bank be made to explain its conduct. At the hearing, held before Mr Justice Laddie, HM Customs and Excise (HMCE) intervened and revealed that the bank had made an authorised disclosure pursuant to s 338 of the Proceeds of Crime Act 2002 (POCA 2002) regarding the operation of the account. HMCE successfully argued that the court could not make an order for payment out of the account, because to do so would contravene the POCA 2002 regime. The conduct of the bank was held to be "unimpeachable" and proceedings were stayed until the expiry of the "moratorium period". This decision provides a useful example of the difficulties facing banks in their efforts to comply with POCA 2002.

Caselaw

The money laundering case of *Gary Harper v The Director of the Assets Recovery Agency* (SPc 507) [2005] which was an assessment hearing where the Special Commissioners confirmed the assessments made on the facts. The Director of the Assets Recovery Agency in calculating the amount of discovery assessments had used a sound was sound methodology based on a proper approach to the assessment of undeclared income. It reflected an underlying principle that in all calculations of undisclosed chargeable income, only two things could happen to amounts identified as income, whatever their source: they were either spent or saved.

Caselaw

The Special Commissioner's decision in *Raja Munawar Khan v The Director of the Assets Recovery Agency*(SpC 503) [2006] is the second published judgment involving the Assets Recovery Agency (now SOCA) since its inception in 2002. The Special Commissioners had jurisdiction on appeal under the Proceeds of Crime Act 2002 s.320(1) to determine that an assessment by the Director of the Assets Recovery Agency under the Taxes Management Act 1970 s.29 was invalid on the grounds that the qualifying condition in section 317(1) of the 2002 Act was not satisfied.

Caselaw

The latest money laundering case is *K Ltd v National Westminster Bank plc [2006] EWCA Civ 1039*. In this case, the customer instructed the bank to transfer money received from a third party's offshore account in respect of a consignment of mobile telephones. For various reasons, these instructions aroused suspicion by the bank officer of money laundering and accordingly the bank made disclosure and sought consent to proceed with the transaction under the Proceeds of Crime Act 2002. In the meantime, the bank informed the customer that it was unable to comply or to discuss the matter further. The customer unsuccessfully sought an injunction against the bank, claiming that the bank had acted improperly. If a bank officer has suspicions that customer instructions may assist any use of criminal property, it would be a criminal offence under the Proceeds of Crime Act 2002 for the bank to carry out those instructions without the consent of SOCA. The bank's contractual obligation to fulfil customer instructions is therefore temporarily suspended on the grounds of illegality. During the period of suspension, contractual obligation can be neither a defence to the offence committed if the bank agrees to carry out instructions, nor a ca use of action for the customer if it refuses; and whether a bank officer is suspicious is a subjective fact, depending on a person's subjective response to a known set of facts. The Asset Recovery Agency (now taken over by SOCA) had obtained a 'without notice' freezing order over the defendant's house, alleging it had been purchased with proceeds of crime. In earlier proceedings involving the CPS, a judge had rejected such allegations and found the defendant to be the beneficial owner of the property. The injunction was permitted to remain in place in the public interest.

7.1.3.1. Vienna Narcotics Convention

Money laundering is a process whereby criminals conceal or disguise the proceeds of their crimes or convert those proceeds into goods and services. For purposes of the Vienna Narcotics Convention, money laundering is defined as:

> " (i) The conversion or transfer of property, knowing that such property is derived from any offence or offences established in accordance with subparagraph (a) of this paragraph. . ., for the purpose of concealing or disguising the illicit origin of the property or of assisting any person who is involved in the commission of such an offence or offences to evade the legal consequences of his actions; (ii) The concealment or disguise of the true nature, source, location, disposition, movement, rights with respect to, or ownership of property, knowing that such property is derived from an offence or offences established in accordance with subparagraph (a) of this paragraph . . . ."

Having defined the nature of the offenses, the VNC requires its signatories to enact legislation to "identify, trace, and freeze or seize proceeds, property, instrumentalities or any A new and more sinister form of money laundering, known as "reverse money laundering," involves the movement of legitimate money, unconnected with any prior criminal activity, through a series of transactions the ultimate purpose of which is to finance the commission of a crime or, worse yet, an act of terrorism, all without leaving a paper trail.

7.1.3.2. Organised crime

The size and sophistication of organized crime bears little resemblance to what one would infer from the characters in popular media portrayals but great resemblance to efficiently managed multinational corporations. The underground money laundering world are the so-called "Big Five" comprising the Colombian drug cartels, the Italian Mafia, the Russian Mafiya, the Chinese Triads, and the Japanese Yakuza, the Mexican drug cartels, Mediterranean/middle eastern drug gangs, terrorist groups, and Nigerian crime syndicates.

7.1.3.3. Extradition in money laundering cases

Extradition has not proved to be useful because extradition is a process of international cooperation that not only is anachronistic but also poses many legal hurdles. Any *obligation* of international extradition is regarded by national courts as subject to treaty. Such treaties are generally bilateral, making extradition from certain bank secrecy jurisdictions problematic. A definition of extradition is the surrender by one state or country to another of an individual accused or convicted of an offence outside its own territory and within the territorial jurisdiction of the other, which, being competent to try and punish him, demands the surrender. The crime in question must constitute an extraditable offence, *i.e.*, one for which extradition is proper. Even if Country B is a party to an extradition treaty, the underlying offense for which Country A seeks to prosecute must generally be characterized as an offence under the municipal laws of Country B.

7.1.3.4. Money laundering jurisdictions

When one associates these sorts of factors with particular jurisdictions, one would normally think of places like Antigua, the Bahamas, the Cayman Islands, Guernsey, the Netherlands Antilles, Costa Rica, Panama, and even more out of the way places like the Seychelles, Mauritius, and Vanuatu. However, more mainstream jurisdictions offer many of these benefits, *e.g.*, Liechtenstein, Austria, Luxembourg, Switzerland, as well as such places as Monaco, Gibraltar, and Madeira.

7.1.3.5. Asset forfeiture

For the global activity of money laundering, effective asset forfeiture regimes must be international in their sweep for fear that criminal enterprises might defeat municipal forfeiture laws by transferring their cash gains to another jurisdiction. Modern technology allows this to be done from the privacy of one's dwelling with the click of a mouse or the touch of a keyboard. The speed of global money transfers and the anonymity conferred by sophisticated encryption techniques greatly assist money launderers.

7.1.3.6. Social Impact of money laundering

Money laundering has devastating social consequences and is a threat to national security because money laundering provides the fuel for drug dealers, terrorists, arms dealers, and other criminals to operate and expand their criminal enterprises. In doing so, criminals manipulate financial systems in the United States and abroad. Unchecked, money laundering can erode the integrity of a nation's financial institutions. Due to the high integration of capital markets, money laundering can negatively affect national and global interest rates as launderers reinvest funds where their schemes are less likely to be detected rather than where rates of return are higher because of sound economic principles.

Other deleterious effects upon society have been expressed by the Office of the United Nations Secretary General, by economic studies performed by staff at the International Monetary Fund, and by recent scholarship.

Money laundering allows criminals to contaminate commerce with corruption, some even achieving economic power that can be used to subvert other segments of the economy. When past criminality remains undetected, it enables the criminal to enjoy the fruits of that criminality.

7.1.3.7. Front companies

Businesses that criminals have acquired legitimately or through extortion and violence conceal illegal flight capital - falsify international trade prices by overpricing imports and under-pricing exports. Then there are the underground bankers, international funds transmitters such as those involved in the notorious Colombian Black Market Peso Exchange and the money launderer *du jour*, Hawala.

7.1.3.8. Hawala financing

Tracing its ancient lineage to Asia, Hawala banks have evolved into a common method of money transmission throughout the Third World, including much of the Middle East. In contrast to modern banking operations, which operate more on the basis of negotiable instruments and government guaranties (*e.g.*, deposit insurance),

Hawala is a system dependent upon trust reposed in the middleman. One who wishes to send the money abroad takes it to the middleman, the Hawaladar, in exchange for some sort of receipt; the Hawaladar then notifies his contact in the desired destination country, another Hawaladar, and the latter will make the original amount of money, less a commission, available to a designated recipient (analogous to a "payee") at the other end. Even assuming that law enforcement could identify the funds in the correspondent account as derived from proceeds of a specific crime, the funds were taboo because the law regarded the foreign bank as the innocent owner.

7.1.3.9. Drug trafficking

Traffic in Narcotic Drugs and Psychotropic Substances, which was an

outgrowth of a late 1988 conference in Vienna and was intended to promote international cooperation in law enforcement efforts directed against "various aspects of illicit traffic in narcotic drugs and psychotropic substances having an international dimension. Notwithstanding accession to this treaty, many foreign nations have proved contumacious when it comes to complying with their legal obligations thereunder.

Determined to deprive persons engaged in illicit traffic of the proceeds of their criminal activities and thereby eliminate their main incentive for so doing, the signatories to the VNC have agreed to adhere to a legal structure contemplating enactment by each of them of comprehensive legislation authorizing confiscation of drug proceeds or instrumentalities used, intended to be used, or derived from proscribed narcotics trafficking activities.

Such property must be restrained or frozen even before entry of a domestic order of forfeiture. Each signatory shall then "confiscate" all forms of property, proceeds, or instrumentalities utilized in or derived from said offences by enactment of appropriate municipal laws, subject only to protection of innocent, bona fide third parties. This is so even if proceeds of the unlawful activity have been converted into other property nor intermingled with legitimate money or property, and forfeiture is also to be imposed upon after-acquired property derived from (or from income or other benefits arising from) any of the foregoing. No bank secrecy laws enacted by any signatory will excuse its failure to comply with these requirements. In order to prevent forfeitable property from being expatriated out of the reach of law enforcement, restraint and freezing of tainted assets should also be done for the benefit of any other signatory having jurisdiction over an offense established pursuant to the VNC. Specifically, with respect to any such offense, each signatory is to afford every other signatory "the widest measure of mutual legal assistance in investigations, prosecutions and judicial proceedings." This includes obtaining an order of confiscation for the other party's benefit with respect to forfeitable property within a signatory's jurisdiction, or, in the alternative, enforcing the other party's order of forfeiture with respect thereto. The same year that the VNC was negotiated, the Basle Committee on Banking Regulation and Supervisory Practices, a group formed under the auspices of the Bank for International Settlements in Basle, Switzerland and originally comprising bank regulators and central bank representatives of the Group of Ten countries, adopted its own Statement of international standards setting forth "the details of the agreed framework for measuring capital adequacy and the minimum standard to be achieved which the national supervisory authorities represented on the Committee intend to implement in their respective countries."

Prompted by concerns that adverse publicity flowing from the association (witting or unwitting, voluntary or involuntary) of banking organizations with criminal elements would erode public confidence in (and concomitantly the stability of) the banking system, these Basle "Principles" do not have the force of treaty or, indeed, any other legally binding character with respect to the member countries. They are directed at banking institutions within the member countries only. Nonetheless they introduced "KYC" (Know Your Customers), an essential part of banks' risk management practices, intended to discourage banks from doing business with a customer who prefers to remain anonymous and to encourage them, if it should come to their attention that funds on deposit are the proceeds of illicit activity, to refuse to continue serving that customer and possibly, in addition to closing the account, freezing the funds within.

7.1.3.10. Financial Action Task Force

The FATF is charged with analyzing and keeping abreast of money laundering trends and has improved on the Basle approach by promulgating a list of 40 recommendations that are updated regularly and that constitute a transnational framework for combating money laundering. Each of the twenty nine member nations furnishes information annually on the status of its domestic implementation of the 40 Recommendations and submits to on-site assessments by the FATF. This regime, like the Basle Statement of Principles, is not legally binding but operates instead by a process of peer pressure and moral suasion, which has proved to be reasonably efficacious in terms of inducing member states to enact implementing legislation. Furthermore, the FATF has supported the development of FATF-like bodies outside the European region, such as the Caribbean Financial Action Task Force and the Asia/Pacific Group on Money Laundering.

7.1.3.11. Vienna Narcotics Convention

One year after formation of the FATF, the Council of Europe adopted an anti-money laundering treaty which, by encompassing a wider array of illegal activities giving rise to money laundering than just narcotics trafficking (*i.e.,* arms trafficking, terrorist activities, and fraud), is slightly broader in scope than the Vienna Narcotics Convention. This multilateral treaty requires signatories to enact implementing legislation to criminalize the laundering of the proceeds of crime and to confiscate such proceeds, as well as instrumentalities and property the value of which corresponds to the proceeds and contemplates mutual legal assistance with respect to investigations, lifting of bank secrecy and freezing of assets.

The European Union itself, thorough its Council of Ministers issued its own Directive designed to achieve many of the same objectives. In addition to criminalizing money laundering without the limitation of a nexus to narcotics trafficking and encouraging multinational cooperation and coordination in investigative and enforcement efforts, the EU Directive takes a leaf from the Basle Commission's financial institution-oriented approach. An obvious shortcomings is the relatively high transaction reporting floor of €15,000. Another shortcoming is that the EU Directive does not mandate the criminalization of money laundering by domestic legislation. A third shortcoming is an exemption from KYC rules for bank-to-bank transfers, thereby facilitating money laundering using correspondent banking relationships with banks in bank secrecy havens or other jurisdictions with lax (or nonexistent) anti-money laundering laws. In addition to multilateral approaches, there are several bilateral treaties, creating regimes of mutual cooperation in the investigation and prosecution of transnational crime.

7.1.3.12. Mutual Legal Assistance Treaties

The Mutual Legal Assistance Treaties ("MLATs") create individual frameworks for bilateral cooperation not only in obtaining and preserving evidence but also in providing assistance to facilitate confiscation of criminal proceeds and instrumentalities. The weakness of these MLATs lies in drafting details. Rather than imposing obligations with some specificity, along the lines of the VNC, often key ingredients such as asset forfeiture and freeze orders are missing from individual MLAT recipes. Even the multilateral Inter-American species of MLAT suffers from these same defects.

Both the Vienna Narcotics Convention and the Strasbourg Convention fostered a trend toward tougher international law enforcement, as a number of European countries strengthened their laws with respect to confiscation of the proceeds of crime (principally drug trafficking), including Belgium, Luxembourg, the Netherlands, Switzerland, and the U.K.

Both the VNC and the Strasbourg Convention mandate that signatories implement procedures through domestic legislation for confiscation of property. Neither convention, however, distinguishes between two different approaches to confiscation -property or object confiscation and (B) value confiscation but contemplate that both models may be used, as do the majority of FATF member nations (with the express encouragement of the FATF itself). The distinction lies in the forfeiture to the state of the precise property in question versus the confiscation of a sum certain related to the value of said property.

7.1.3.13. Forfeiture of Title to property

Forfeiture of title to the precise property is so common with respect to *instrumentalities* of crime as to need no elaboration but raises interesting issues with respect to property representing *proceeds* of crime. Suppose, for example, that the criminal has, prior to arrest, already spent or otherwise alienated the proceeds. He then has enjoyed the benefits of the criminal conduct without having to worry about confiscation when caught, by no means an uncommon scenario in the criminal world. In this situation, the goal of effective deprivation of the fruits of criminal activity would clearly be frustrated. Another issue involves the treatment of innocent third party holders.

Neither the Vienna Narcotics Convention nor the Strasbourg Convention forbids the forfeiture of property in the hands of innocent third parties, though each addresses the rights of such individuals. For example, rights of third parties that are affected by a judicial decision of a signatory to the Strasbourg Convention are taken into account, and such decisions must be recognized unless the third parties did not have adequate opportunity to participate in the proceeding, the decision is incompatible with one already taken in the country requesting confiscation, or the decision is incompatible with the *ordre public* of the country receiving the request.

7.1.3.14. Innocent third parties

Many laws, as well as the United Nations' Model money laundering law, that endeavour to protect the rights of innocent third parties may be well motivated, but from an enforcement perspective they may at times make it too easy for a criminal to transfer proceeds offshore, through dummy corporations or nominees or otherwise, so that they are no longer, as a technical matter, susceptible to forfeiture. Where the actual proceeds of the criminal conduct have been transferred (or laundered) to another jurisdiction, but other assets traceable to the perpetrator remain within the reach of law enforcement, value confiscation becomes a highly useful tool. A value confiscation order can be simply a court order requiring the payment of a monetary amount equivalent in value to the proceeds of the crime. Indeed, some countries, like the U.K., have adopted value, confiscation as the default method.

7.1.3.15. Fines

Fines are subject to statutory ceilings that often have nothing to do with the value of the criminal proceeds; fines may also be influenced by prudential factors relating to the gravity of the offense and the perpetrator's financial condition, prior record, and miscellaneous personal circumstances. Value confiscation relates solely to the monetary value of the proceeds.

Both the VNC and the Strasbourg Convention give the confiscating state *carte blanche* with respect to disposition of the forfeiture proceeds. The state may simply keep the funds or it may earmark them, as some countries do, for use by law enforcement authorities in the fight against money laundering and other crimes. The possibility also exists for the state to share the forfeited proceeds with other states or with inter-governmental bodies dedicated to combating crime. Such sharing is, in fact, encouraged by certain international legislation. On an international level, the imprimatura of the two major conventions, of the FATF, and even of the U.N. General Assembly suggest that sharing of forfeited assets, whatever its potential moral shortcomings, has a firm legal foundation and is, moreover, regarded as an indispensable tool in the struggle against organized crime.

7.1.3.16. Effective enforcement

Effective enforcement of legal obligations is a problem. If anything could be used to characterize international anti-money laundering regulation it would be too much "carrot" and not enough "stick." Widely hailed as the most effective of the extant approaches, the FATF operates on the basis of moral persuasion . As the increase in volume of laundered funds demonstrates, passive regimes relying on the force of moral suasion have not stemmed the rising tide of money laundering. ICJ jurisdiction under the Strasbourg Convention is not mandatory but permissive. That treaty provides for dispute resolution in the first instance by settlement through negotiation or any other means of the parties' device, "including submission of the dispute to the European Commission on Crime Problems, to an arbitral tribunal whose decisions shall be binding upon the Parties, or to the International Court of Justice, *as agreed upon by the Parties concerned.*" Given VNC and Strasbourg Convention signatories' ability to avoid mandatory IC Jurisdiction, and in view of the dire macroeconomic consequences of money laundering and the use of laundered funds

7.1.3.17. Withdrawal from Treaties

The Vienna Narcotics Convention and the Strasbourg Convention could be amended to include explicit provisions for sanctions in the event of noncompliance with treaty obligations. There is evidence that targeted sanctions, such as the European Union blacklist of Serbian President Slobodan Milosevic and a variety of asset freezes, have achieved some measure of success. Furthermore, there are possibilities for increased multilateral cooperation in plugging those international trade loopholes that foster money laundering.

7.1.3.18. Hawala money

Hawala is a more difficult problem, in that criminalizing that activity outright would be not only an overbroad response to the danger posed but also constitutionally problematic. The simple solution, instead, is to mandate that all money transmission businesses be licensed and subjected to examination and supervision by state or federal regulators. Implementation of such a licensing requirement makes it easy both to monitor the flow of funds and to criminalize the conduct of any such business on an unlicensed basis. Once licensed, these businesses can readily be made subject to existing currency reporting and SAR requirements. Much of effective detection and deterrence of money laundering is based not on a lack of law enforcement tools but on their relative lack of efficacy. Confiscation represents the clearest and best technique, depriving the malefactors of their ill-gotten gains.

7.1.3.19. Electronic means of money laundering

In the past decade, there has been an increasing reliance on electronic means of transferring funds for personal and business purposes. One recent development has been the emergence of plastic cards with the capacity to store value electronically, which can be used for a range of retail transactions. With the advent of comprehensive anti-money laundering laws throughout the developed world, criminals are turning to alternative ways of moving funds across borders to circumvent reporting and detection systems. One identified risk is the misuse of prepaid stored value cards to keep the proceeds of crime and move them across borders without alerting law enforcement and financial intelligence units.

Another method of money laundering through the Internet would be to establish a company offering services payable through the Internet. The launderer then 'uses' those services and charges for them using credit or debit cards tied to accounts under his control (located perhaps in an offshore area) which contain criminal proceeds. The launderer's company then invoices the credit card company, which, in turn, forwards the payments for the service rendered. The launderer's company may then justify these income payments for a service rendered.

Fraud Investigation: Criminal Procedure and Investigation

> **Point to Note: A whole country committing money laundering offence**
>
> Large scale money laundering occurs when a whole country's black economy is laundered. As an example, take Latvia where money laundering occurs for the illegal sale of oil or natural gas. To launder the perceived 'black' money, a foreign company opens a subsidiary company in Latvia and opens then a shell corporation in an offshore zone, even Britain. The subsidiary orders a payment transfer from the shell corporation to the subsidiary's company account in a Latvian commercial bank. When the funds arrive, they are withdrawn in $. Dollars or Euros or £ currency and sent to the seller of the gas or oil.

7.1.3.20. Terrorist-related money laundering

Insufficient attention has been given to the terrorism-related threats posed by reverse money laundering and Hawala. While existing law does criminalize the transfer of money across the U.S. border with the intent to use it in aid of a criminal offense, purely internal money transmission for the same purpose is not unlawful. Electronic money is a retail payment product that is used predominantly for making small value payments. As an electronic means of payment, it is susceptible to the same risks of money laundering and terrorist financing as other retail payment products. In the absence of controls over the use of the product, there is a significant risk of money laundering taking place. The following factors will generally tend to increase the risk of electronic money products being used for money laundering or terrorist financing: the higher the value and frequency of transactions, and the higher the purse limit the greater the risk. The €15,000 threshold for occasional transaction is provided in the Regulations. Information sharing as to cross-border transactions may be the only way to fraud. Where there is a suspicion of money laundering or terrorist financing, the identity of the customer must be verified, irrespective of the transacted total.

7.2.1. A special case-Invoice Finance Companies & Money Laundering

Invoice finance companies offer a number of products to fund the working capital requirements of their clients; these generally fall into two categories - Factoring agreements and Invoice Discounting agreements. These can be operated on a Recourse or Non Recourse basis, and with or without disclosure of the assignment of the sales invoice to the client's customers, the debtors.

7.2.2. Factoring Agreements

Factoring is a contract between an invoice finance company and their client where revolving finance is provided against the value of the client's sales ledger that is sold to the invoice financier. The invoice finance company will manage the client's sales ledger and will normally provide the credit control and collection services. The client assigns all their invoices, as usually a whole turnover contract is used, after the goods or service has been delivered or performed. The invoice finance company will then typically advance up to 85% of the invoiced amount - the gross amount including VAT.

7.2.3. Invoice Discounting

Invoice discounting is a contract between the invoice finance company and their client where revolving finance is provided against the value of the client's sales ledger. The client will manage the sales ledger and will normally continue to provide the credit control and collection services. The client assigns the detail of all their invoices, as usually a whole turnover contract is used, after the goods or service have been delivered or performed.

7.2.4. The invoice finance company records and monitors

The company this on a bulk sales ledger basis rather than retaining the individual invoice detail. The invoice finance company will then typically advance up to 85% of the invoiced amount. The balance, less any charges, is then paid to the client once the debtor makes full payment to the invoice finance company. As the assignment is not usually disclosed the client undertakes the collection service under an agency agreement within the contract. The client is obligated to ensure that the payments from debtors are passed to the invoice finance company. The non-disclosure element has led to the frequent use of the colloquial title of Confidential Invoice Discounting being used to describe this product, but confidentiality only exists at the discretion of the invoice finance company (whilst they are prepared to operate the agency arrangement).

7.2.5. The use of invoice financing by criminals

As with any financial service activity, invoice finance products are susceptible to use by criminals to launder money. Both Factoring and Invoice Discounting products facilitate third party payments and may therefore be used by criminals for money laundering activity. The different invoice finance products available vary greatly and the degree of risk is directly related to the product offering.

7.2.6. The level of physical cash receipts directly received

This is extremely low, as the vast majority of debtors settle outstanding invoices by way of cheque or electronic payment methods. Therefore the susceptibility of the invoice finance sector at the traditional placement stage is very low. The risk within the invoice finance industry is at the layering and integration stages of money laundering.

7.2.7. Main Money Laundering Risks in Invoice Financing

The main money laundering risks within the invoice finance sector are payments against invoices where there is no actual movement of goods or services provided, or the value of goods is overstated to facilitate the laundering of funds. The level of risk will depend upon the nature of the product and the level of involvement by the finance company. Factoring should be considered to be a lower risk than invoice discounting, in view of the fact that direct contact is maintained with the debtor. Invoice discounting would represent an increased risk of money laundering due to the 'hands off' nature of the product.

7.2.8 Factors that increase risk of money laundering for invoice finance products

These factors are: cross border transactions; products with reduced paper trails; products where the invoice financier allows the client to collect the debt; confidential products; and bulk products.

> **Points to Note**
>
> Prevention of money laundering for invoice finance products
> 1. Individual items (invoices, customers, and cash) recorded and managed by the invoice financier.
> 2. Collections activity undertaken by the invoice financier. .
> 3. Regular ongoing due diligence and monitoring including on-site inspections and verification of balances.
> 4. Regular statistical monitoring.
> 5. Improve knowledge of the source of funds that are different to the usual credit risk checks.
> 6. Be aware that client errors could be one of the first indicators of the presence of money laundering.
> 7. Document short term breaches and establish controls.

7.2.9. Resistance to Money Launderers

There are a number of factors that make the invoice finance facility less attractive to the money launderer: - the high levels of contact between the financier and the client, in terms of physical audits and visits, and of statistical monitoring; and the sophisticated IT monitoring techniques used to detect issues with the quality of the underlying security, consisting of the quality of the goods and the customers (debtors). In the case of factoring, the item by item accounting and the regular direct contact with the debtors; the focus on the debtors in terms of creditworthiness and assessment of risk and the double scrutiny of payments, by the receiving bank and by the invoice financier.

7.2.10. Money laundering and reduced intervention

In general, the normally low to medium risk of money laundering will increase with the reduction of the levels of intervention by the financier and the increase in the size of foreign transactions through the account.

7.2.11. Enhanced due diligence

A risk-based approach is necessary to protect against charges of money laundering. This approach recognises that the reporting entity is in the best position to assess the risk of their customers, products and services and to allocate resources to counter those risks accordingly. Enhanced Due Diligence is appropriate in the following, but not exhaustive, list of situations where any party connected to the client is PEP and when the client is involved in a business that is considered to present a higher risk of money laundering. These are likely to include a client with any party associated with a country either on a residential or business activity basis that is deemed to have a relatively high risks of money laundering, or inadequate levels of supervision. Examples of these countries can be found listed within the country assessments made by the International Monetary Fund or the Financial Action Task Force. Another source of information can be found within the Transparency International Corruption Perception Indexes that are published on an annual basis. A client who carries a higher risk of money laundering by virtue of their business or occupation.

Examples of which could be a business with a high level of cash sales; a business with a high level of cross border sales, including Import-Export companies; a business selling small high value goods that are easily disposed of. These should be set out in the invoice finance company's risk-based approach.

It is likely they will include the following: - more frequent and detailed on-site inspections of the client's books and records, frequently called an 'Audit', with appropriate management oversight and action of any significant deficiencies; more frequent and extensive verification, usually by telephone contact with the debtor, of the validity of the sale and invoice values; greater management oversight of these facilities.

> **Points to Note: Merchant activity which is susceptible to money laundering**
>
> Betting and gaming offer a number of opportunities either with or without the collusion of the merchant. Funding of purses using cash presents a higher risk of money laundering.
>
> Multiple purses without verification of identity increase the risk.
>
> Allowances for refunds in cash for purchases made using electronic money will increase the risk. Non-verified third parties who use the product increase the risk.
>
> The technology adopted by the product may give rise to specific risks that should be assessed

7.2.12. Prevention of money laundering

An annual allowance for redemption of electronic money may reduce the risk by allowing funds to enter the system, but only allowing a relatively small amount (€1,000) to exit without verification.

> **Points to Note: Check for controls to:**
>
> (i) detect anomalies to normal transaction patterns;
>
> (ii) identify multiple purses held by a single individual or group of individuals, such as the holding of multiple accounts or the 'stockpiling' of pre-paid cards;
>
> (iii) look for indicators of accounts being opened with different issuers as well as attempts to pool funds from different sources;
>
> (iv) identify discrepancies between submitted and detected information between country of origin submitted information and the electronically-detected IP address;
>
> (v) deploy sufficient resources to address money laundering risks, including, where necessary, specialist expertise for the detection of suspicious activities; and
>
> (vi) restrict funding of electronic money products, to funds drawn on accounts held at credit and financial institutions in the UK, the EU or a comparable jurisdiction, and to
>
> (vii) restrict redemption of electronic money into accounts held at such institutions.

The Regulations state that for a business relationship and for occasional transactions (single or linked transactions of €15,000 or more, if not carried out as part of a business relationship) verification of identity must be carried out at the outset. This requirement includes verification of beneficial owners. Identity verified at the outset of the relationship with the customer. Where the customer is not physically present, "due diligence" needs to be balanced with the risk posed by the product itself. For electronic money products, provided the product is operated within the turnover limits, there is no due diligence required. MLR07 applies to all issuers of electronic money, regardless of whether they are regulated by the FSA or operate under a small electronic money issuers' waiver - small issuers are subject to HM Revenue and Customs' regulation in relation to AML compliance.

> **Point to Note: Loophole in the FSMA 2000 (Regulated Activities) (Amendment) Order**
>
> This amended the FSMA 2000 (Regulated Activities) Order 2001 to provide for the issuing of electronic money to be a regulated activity under FSMA. The loophole here is that some new money businesses are arranged so as not to involve "issuing of electronic money". One example of a new product is MOBILLCASH which is an "interactive" payment platform. It has been on the global market since 2006. They allow a person to access a merchant online and purchase a product and put the purchase as an addition to the person's mobile phone bill. Although it is 30% more expensive than if a credit card were used for the purchase, it has many users.

7.3.2. A situation to watch-the "Interactive payment platform

"MobillCash" as an example of an interactive electronic payment platform.

(i) The consumer online chooses Mobillcash as their preferred method of payment instead of a credit card choice.

(ii) Consumer receives a verification message on their mobile phone and responds

(iii) Mobillcash receives verification from consumer and processes the payment.

At present MobillCash can only be used to purchase online intangible goods. This means that it can be used to launder money into intangible goods and treated also as an expense deduction for tax purposes. MobillCash has had 1.7 million transactions from July 2006 to January 2008 with over 900 merchants signed up to use the facility. It operates globally. It has a 60-day payment procedure for which it charges 30% interest. It can be used for criminal fraud because there are no personal details entered online, only a mobile number and it needs the purchaser to press the button on that mobile phone to accept the transaction. *No bank account is required. No registration is required. Purchases can be from anyone of any age.*

There are no forms to fill in. Payment is made in seconds by pressing a button on the mobile phone. The target audience is people with no bank accounts including children. It can be used for online gambling. MobillCash plan to extend its business so that persons can register their credit cards with MobillCash which ties the credit card number with the phone SIM and allows purchases online.

7.3.3. Re-loadable purses

Those issuers that provide electronic money purses that can be recharged, whether card or purely server-based, are only required to undertake verification of identity procedures when the annual turnover limit of €2,500 is exceeded, or if the customer seeks to redeem more than the €1,000 annual allowance.

7.3.4. Purses send and receive payments

Where purses can both send and receive payments, such as for example in online account based products that enable person to person payments, the Euro 2,500 turnover limit is applied separately to sending and receiving transactions. In other words, the turnover limit is calculated separately for credit and debit transactions, and the verification requirement applied when either of the two is exceeded. The EU Regulation on Wire Transfers makes issuers verify the identity of customers seeking to undertake any single sending transaction that exceeds €1,000 in value, where verification has not already been undertaken.

7.3.5. Electronic money gift card products

Gift card products are susceptible to money laundering by buying many cards.

7.3.6. Maximum purse limit

A maximum purse limit should not exceed €1,000. Such cards should not allow for redemption of electronic money without verification of identity taking place, subject to a 150 *de minimus* allowance.

7.3.7. Transaction monitoring and/ or on-chip purse controls

These must be deployed that enable control of the systems and recognition of suspicious activity.

> **Points to Note: How to control money laundering**
>
> (i) Use transaction monitoring systems to detect anomalies.
>
> (ii) Implement systems to identify discrepancies between submitted and detected information.
>
> (iii) Implement systems to cross-reference submitted data against existing data for other accounts.
>
> (iv) Implement systems to interface with third party data sources to import information that may assist into detect fraud or money laundering.
>
> (v) Implement on-chip controls that impose purse rules.
>
> (vi) Implement on-chip controls to disable the card when a given pattern of activity is detected.

7.3.8. Suspicious Activity

If suspicious activity is detected by internal systems or procedures, the issuer must have particular regard to its obligations under POCA and the Terrorism Acts to report possible money laundering or terrorist financing.

7.3.9. Person to person systems

In person-to-person money transaction systems, the boundary between consumers and merchants is blurred if consumers register as merchants. In this case issuers should have systems in place that provide a means of detecting such activity. Issuers with such products must mitigate the greater risk of money laundering to which these products are exposed by implementing systems and controls that seek to identify transactions or patterns that fit money laundering typologies.

7.3.10. Second cardholder

Verification of identity for a second cardholder will mitigate the risk.

7.3.11. Electronic money issuer

Electronic money issuers should ensure that additional due diligence steps are undertaken if the risk posed by the product or customer increases, so as to pose a higher risk of money laundering or terrorist financing. Where payment from a funding institution is made electronically, it is usually not possible to verify the name of the account holder for the funding account.

7.3.12. Combating e-money fraud

E-Money fraud can be combated by the implementation of purse limits; usage controls, and systems to detect suspicious activity. Where electronic money is limited to small value payments, the use of this product is less attractive to would-be launderers. The electronic money products in commercial use today do provide the kind of privacy or anonymity that cash provides, but is limited in its utility.

> **Case Study: Checks & balances for a funding institution**
>
> Some issuers have developed a means of establishing control over a funding account using a process that is convenient and effective. A small random amount of money is credited to a customer's funding account and the customer is then required to discover the amount and to enter it on the issuer's website. By entering the correct value, the customer demonstrates access to the bank/card statement or accounting system of their bank or financial institution. This method, and its close variants, provides an acceptable means of confirming that the customer has access to the account, and therefore has control over it. It also provides a means of guarding against identity theft, contributing therefore to the verification of identity process.

7.3.13. Evidence of legitimate use

An account that is used to fund an electronic money purse over a period of time is likely to be used legitimately as the passage of time gives the rightful owner the opportunity to discover fraudulent use of the product and to block its use, which would in turn become evident to the issuer.

7.3.14. Due diligence

The Regulations require enhanced due diligence to be undertaken in all situations where the risk of money laundering is perceived to be high. These include instances where the customer is not physically present for identification purposes, as well as in respect of business relationships or occasional transactions with politically exposed persons (PEPs). Where electronic money purses are purchased or accounts opened in a non face to face environment, issuers should provide for additional means of due diligence to address the greater risk of money laundering or terrorist financing that is posed. The degree of enhanced due diligence required for PEP's will be proportionate to the risk posed by the product, as will the requirement for systems and processes to detect PEPs. Where electronic money transactions and cumulative turnover values are low, the risk posed by way of their use by PEPs for money laundering is also likely to be low. Issuers should therefore focus their resources, in a risk sensitive manner, on products and transactions where the risk of money laundering is high.

> **Point to Note: Transfer of funds regulation**
>
> European Regulation 1781/2006 on information on the payer accompanying transfers of funds (The Wire Transfer Regulation). Issuers are subject to the obligations of the Wire Transfer Regulation in their role as PSP of the payer, PSP of the payee and intermediary PSP.

7.4. Exemptions up to 1000 Euros

The Wire Transfer Regulation allows for the exemption of annual redemptions up to a cumulative total of €1,000. The PSP of the payee will not be able to distinguish transactions that legitimately do not include CIP from those that are merely incomplete. Issuers should attach CIP to the redemption transaction.

Case law

R (on the application of UMBS Online Ltd v Serious Organised Crime Agency & Revenue & Customs, 2007] All ER (D) 35 (May).

In The Attorney General for and on behalf of the *Republic of Zambia v Meer Care & Desai (a firm) and Others,* the High Court ruled that it would have little sympathy for solicitors who failed to adhere to money laundering regulations if allegations of dishonesty were subsequently made against them. The Attorney General for and on behalf of the *Republic of Zambia v Meer Care & Desai (a firm) and Others..* This was a claim against 20 defendants, including high-ranking Zambian government officials and English firms of solicitors. The claim arose from an alleged conspiracy to defraud the Zambian government of around $46m. The Zambian based defendants did not participate in the trial and it was left largely to the UK-based defendants, including the solicitors, to defend the conspiracy claims. After considering the evidence, the judge concluded that the Zambian defendants (who included the ex-President of Zambia and the head of the Secret Service) had all participated in a conspiracy to defraud the Zambian government and had breached their fiduciary duties. The judge considered the money laundering guidance issued throughout the period in question (i.e. 1995-2002). He emphasised that this guidance was meant to be read and that the court would have little sympathy with a solicitor subsequently confronted with a claim, who said he did not read those warnings. The court would carefully scrutinise a solicitor who maintained that although he was grossly negligent in not reading the warnings, he was not fraudulent. Smith J accepted that breach of the Solicitors

> Accounts Rules and money laundering regulations was not determinative of dishonesty, but he emphasised the importance of heeding the guidance provided. The judge held that failure to do so would expose a solicitor to allegations of gross negligence and would add to the evidence in deciding whether the solicitor was dishonest. Smith J concluded that the partner in D1 became a conspirator because he was aware that money was being improperly applied and chose not to question that activity. This was, the judge said, a classic case of blind eye dishonesty. This case shows the importance of adhering to money laundering guidance.

7.5.1. Criminal cartels

Cartel regulation in the UK operates on two levels, with the possibility of civil proceedings being brought against companies and criminal proceedings being brought against individuals. Full immunity from both types of action is potentially available under the OFT's leniency programme, and both companies and individuals are actively encouraged to contact the OFT if they suspect cartel activity. If found guilty of an infringement, companies face large fines and employees can face prison sentences with directors also subject to the possibility of being disqualified as a director for up to 15 years.

Under Enterprise Act section 188 an individual commits an offence if he dishonestly agrees with one or more other person(s) to make or implement, or to cause to be made or implemented, activities relating to at least two undertakings, operating on the same horizontal level in the market. The prohibited activities are price-fixing; the limitation of production or supply; market sharing; and bid rigging.

In 2008, four British Airways executives were charged with the criminal cartel offence found in the Enterprise Act 2002. This is the second UK criminal cartel offence prosecution. The first criminal cartel charge was against three former Dunlop employees in relation to a cartel for marine hoses. The marine hose executives were sentenced to between 30 and 36 months' imprisonment and one was required to pay £25,000 in costs. They were also all disqualified from acting as directors for between five and seven years. The Serious Fraud Office led the marine hose cartel offence prosecutions, which involved guilty pleas.

7.5.2. Risks of cartel offences

Cartels may exist in almost any industry. However, certain industry structures and commercial activities may increase the risk of cartel formation. These are:-customers that make regular, repetitive purchases by way of competitive tender; competitors that know each other well through social contact, trade associations, shifting employment or other legitimate activities; companies with immature corporate governance systems which fail to pay sufficient attention to compliance issues; price or margin increases in a depressed market; unexplained reluctance to compete on price and/or in particular areas and/or in respect of particular products. Other pointers to cartel activity are: unexplained reluctance to increase output; unexplained pricing or market share stability in a previously volatile market and regular unexplained parallel price increases.

Fraud Investigation: Criminal Procedure and Investigation

> **Points to Note**
>
> Actions to deter Criminal Cartels
>
> If a corporation or individual has identified a potential competition risk, the following checklist of actions is helpful:
>
> Establish whether the problem is an isolated matter or the 'tip of the iceberg'
>
> Does the agreement between competitors contravene the legal framework?
>
> Cease any contravening conduct and prevent repetition.
>
> Decide on new compliance procedures.
>
> Consider law enforcement leniency policy.
>
> Dealing with the OFT.
>
> Deal with money laundering regulation compliance issues.
>
> Devise a *mea culpa* strategy to deal with customer, supplier and competitor reactions and claims.

Price-fixing cartels which are covert agreements, informal or otherwise, to fix prices, share markets and rig bids for tenders. Price-fixing cartels cause the consumer to pay higher prices and have poorer quality products. The designer of products has reduced incentive to innovate and all parties have less choice. Also, the industry becomes less efficient.

7.5.3. 'Immunity from Prosecution' Procedure in Cartel Cases

Immunity from prosecution for accomplices was placed on a statutory footing on 1 April 2006 when SOCPA 2005, s 71 came into force. If a specified prosecution agency considers it is appropriate to offer suspects immunity from prosecution it must give them immunity notice. The only statutory recognition of criminal immunity before SOCPA 2005 can be found in the Enterprise Act 2002, s 190(4) which came into force on 20 June 2003, and which has yet to be tested by prosecution under that Act.

Immunity from prosecution for the cartel offence is granted in the form of a 'no-action letter' issued by the OFT, Enterprise Act section 190(4). To be granted a no-action letter and benefit from the immunity from prosecution conferred by the letter, an individual must fulfil, and continue to fulfil, five conditions. They must: admit participation in the criminal offence; provide the OFT with all the information available regarding the existence and activities of the cartel; maintain continuous and complete cooperation throughout the investigation and until the conclusion of any criminal proceedings; take no steps to coerce another undertaking to take part in the cartel; and refrain from further participation in the cartel from the time of its disclosure to the OFT.

Note that a UK director can to be extradited for conspiring to price-fix and obstructing the course of justice. Price-fixing falls within scope of conspiracy to defraud. The double criminality rule applies if offence is conducted abroad and in the UK. Note that extradition will rarely breach Article 8 of the Convention.

Caselaw

Norris v Government of the US [2007] EWHC 71 (Admin), [2007] All ER (D) 199 (Jan) is only the second instance in which the Divisional Court has confirmed that a British national should be extradited for white collar crimes pursuant to the controversial US/UK Treaty of Extradition 2003 (the Treaty) and the Extradition Act 2003 (EA 2003). However, in March 2008, the House of Lords disagreed with the US application for extradition of Norris.

If there is a legitimate means in which to transact business, a criminal mind will find a way to use it to their advantage. An illustration of this fact is the criminal scheme to use automatic teller machines (ATMs) to steal from legitimate users. In this scheme the criminal designs and affixes an ATM card reader to the facade of an actual ATM. An individual then comes to the machine, inserts his/her card, and uses the machine as normal. The card reader however, records the card information while the criminal retrieves the PIN number using binoculars or, in some cases, a video camera. Using technology available to all, the criminal then produces his/her own duplicate ATM card, uses the individual PIN, and withdraws money from the user's account.

7.5.4. Expenses frauds

One type of fraud that is prevalent in the business world is the fraudulent reporting of expense or travel. This crime represents one of the most abused business "re-entitlement" frauds and can often become a source of second income. The types of expense accounts that are most problematic are those based on reimbursement. The primary problem is not the reimbursement, but rather the lack of realistic expenditure controls on the employee. Often mileage is inflated because the company rarely checks mileage. The result is that the employee adds cash to his /her pockets over and above the truly deserved reimbursement. Employees can inflate hotel costs by staying in a cheap place and report expenses as if they stayed at the expensive hotel. Employees may forge documents to support their claims. Others may use hotel letterheads from a previous stay and reproduce the billing to be submitted for re-imbursement. Fraudulent submitted meal receipts are another common business fraud. Undated and hand-written receipts are accepted.

In one example, travel bookings were made by the General Manager on the internet; the itinerary and cost were printed and used as a basis for reimbursement. The General Manager then went back to the internet and changed the routing itinerary and travelled in another country for private purposes. As part of the Annual Performance Review, the General Manager received in writing a letter with his salary increase. He then told the Chief Finance Officer that he had further discussed his performance verbally with his boss and that the real salary increase should be x.

> **Case Study: Corporate fraud by diversion of assets**
>
> Another company fraud is when company assets are diverted, for example, when the General Manager has three computers, bought through travel expenses. Each travel expense contained an item called "cash withdrawal" for several hundred pounds without supporting evidence. Another example occurs when consultancy agreements are signed for thousands of pounds with little or no evidence of work done.

7.6.1. Fraudulent transactions in Companies

Some instances of fraudulent corporate transactions are as follows:

(i) Ghost employees-Private expenses from family members were claimed as business expenses.

(ii) Purchases made at inflated prices from other companies owned by same family.

(iii) In-collectable receivable amounts booked on a Balance Sheet Control Account.

(iv) Physical Inventory losses accounted for as "Goods in transit" by CFO.

(v) Communications fraud causes £25 BILLION losses to UK industry each year.

7.6.2. Evidence of corporate frauds

Evidence of such corporate frauds are electronic documents, emails, physical documents and the knowledge of individuals involved in the fraud and possibly, their work colleagues and associates. Evidence can be found in desktop computers, laptop computers, network traffic, network sharing, mobile phones, CCTV, swipe card entry, phone logs, emails, free hotmail, USB sticks, CDs, on-line storage, system logs, IE History, Home PC, fax or paper documents, zip files and encrypted files. All these can generate leads and direct the force of the investigation.

To capture such evidence needs searching out-of-hours whilst ensuring that all systems are synchronised to full legal standards. As an alternative to a full forensic imaging, there can be proxy log examination or remote scan of the suspect's PC. It depends on whether the suspect is computer literate, whether the suspect knows how to delete NTFS file system/Windows; whether the computer is password protected, whether the suspect uses MS Outlook and where the suspect normally stores business documents.

7.6.3. Insurance Cover

It is wise to remember that even when fraud is found to have been carried out by directors of a company, they sometimes have insurances called D & O policies to cover their legal defences. in both the US and UK over the last 25 years, expectations of directors, both executive and non-executive, have been transformed. Directorship now carries with it burdensome responsibilities and the increasing risk of personal accountability, not only in the civil courts, but also in criminal proceedings.

Directors can be interviewed by regulators, hounded by prosecutors and even extradited to jurisdictions where they may fear an unfair trial. Over the same period, there has been a growing recognition that, to encourage business leaders to take on these responsibilities, clarity and codification is needed; as is protection in the event that they are criticised by an aggrieved minority of members or by a regulatory or prosecuting authority. Particularly in common law countries, where proceedings are more common and where financial scandals have been prominently reported, many legislatures have relaxed the restrictions on companies indemnifying their directors and/or meeting the cost of D&O coverage.

7.6.4. Directors and Officers Insurance (D & O)

Just as it has become commonplace for professionals to be sued in the civil law jurisdictions of "old Europe" (and for professionals to insure, or even be required by law to insure, against that risk), so it has for claims to be pursued against directors and for D&O insurance to be taken out. The trend has spread as investment is increasingly made across borders and as multinational organisations acquire smaller entities and impose their corporate governance culture.

The exposure of directors to increased liabilities associated with listings, particularly on US Exchanges, has also led to increased demand for annual D&O and "long-tail" prospectus liability insurance products. Whilst the scope for potential liability has grown in most jurisdictions, the trend towards increased exposure has often been the result of a greater willingness to sue rather than a change in law. Most jurisdictions, for example, have long imposed on directors a duty to act with due skill and care, and in the best interests of the company, or required directors to have proper regard for the interests of creditors when faced with insolvency. What has changed is that legal rights are now being pursued and enforced more often and more vigorously than ever before.

The demand for D&O insurance will inevitably grow across Europe over the coming decade, particularly in those jurisdictions with a strong regulatory environment. It currently appears that this demand will be matched by the appetite to supply of UK-based insurers and reinsurers. The current softness and saturation of the UK market may explain this appetite just as much as the desire to write risks over a broader geographical canvas. At the same time, however, there is also widespread concern amongst UK underwriters that, in Central and Eastern Europe particularly, the writing of D&O cover is fraught with uncertainty. Chiefly, this uncertainty derives from the perceived unpredictability of local courts and from the different ways in which the concept of corporate governance is developing in different jurisdictions. In practical terms, a careful underwriter who is looking to diversify into other jurisdictions has two ways of containing his risk. The first is through the use of tight wordings, properly tailored to local legal requirements.

The second is through the underwriting process. This speaks volumes for the importance attached by insurers to getting their wordings right. However, in spite of the emphasis already placed on wordings by some insurers, D&O policies are often complex documents, especially when translated. In part, this is unavoidable as D&O is a sophisticated product.

However, it is also due to uncertainty as to how the policy will be interpreted in the local jurisdiction. There are some particularly vexed areas:

(i) Arbitration, which is often stipulated as the dispute resolution forum to avoid the unpredictability of local courts, is treated with suspicion in some jurisdictions.

(ii) The possibility that choice of law and jurisdiction clauses will not be enforceable.

(iii) Differences in the treatment of claims where an insured is accused of dishonest acts, which result in complex provisions dealing with such accusations.

(iv) Reluctance to cover the risk of claims brought by the company. Although "Insured v Insured" exclusions nearly always contain coverage "write backs" in relation to shareholder-derivative or liquidator actions, the concern remains that companies could try to claim against the directors as a way to recover from their insurers the consequences of the company's poor financial performance.

(v) Claims made cover, while now legal in most European jurisdictions, can be subject to complex rules, which may override express policy clauses. The claims made approach is sometimes not understood even by local brokers and difficulties in enforcement are not uncommon.

(vi) Unusual local laws, e.g. those requiring all onerous terms to be printed in a different font or countersigned by the insured directors.

Of course, policy wordings can only provide part of the protection necessary in an unfamiliar environment and reliance also needs to be placed on good underwriting process. Again, there are difficulties here for the underwriter, outlined below:

(vii) Are the prospective insured willing or able to provide full disclosure? Even where disclosure is given, it can be generalised and extensive questioning often produces little further detail.

(viii) What is the senior management's attitude to corporate governance? How can this be assessed when there is no prospect of meeting the Board?

(ix) Is there evidence that the Board is independent of the major shareholders of the company? Is the company well capitalised with acceptable debt leverage? Is the company's accounting system robust?

(x) What is the local business culture? Perhaps unconventional incentive payments, whilst illegal, are nevertheless common. Is unpredictable Government intervention a hazard? An underwriter may be able to contain his exposure by imposing tailored exclusions, but will these operate as intended or be disregarded by local courts?

(xi) Risk can be managed to some degree through reinsurance and by insisting on large co-insurance elements but in many respects this simply shifts the problem elsewhere.

7.6.5. Increasing demand for D & O Insurance

The picture then is of directors and officers across Europe feeling increasingly exposed to claims and, consequently, of an increasing demand for D&O coverage. Faced with a soft, saturated market in the UK and US (where there is now a high D&O take up even amongst SMEs), insurers have an appetite to meet this demand but (sometimes justified) limited confidence in their ability to assess and contain local risks. Significant progress has been made in developing wordings and processes that enable cost-effective cover to be marketed across multiple jurisdictions and the market for D&O will inevitably develop further over the next decade. When the claims volume rises and corporations with extensive regional operations start to hit major problems, only the insurers who have underwritten prudently and who have high calibre claims support will continue to thrive in that market.

7.7.1. Directors' duty to prevent fraud

The general duties owed by directors to their companies evolved through the interpretation of those duties by decisions of the English courts, that is, they were "common law" duties rather than being set out in statute. The Companies Act 2006 ("CA 06") has now introduced for the first time a statutory statement of directors' duties which will, when fully implemented, replace entirely those existing "common law" duties. Most of the provisions of CA 06 relative to duties and liabilities of directors came into force on 1 October 2007, but those dealing with conflicts of interest will not come into force until 1 October 2008.

7.7.2. Obligations of Company Directors in general

The Companies Act 1985 ("CA 85") also contained numerous provisions which imposed duties and obligations on directors of companies, and restrictions in respect of the manner in which they could behave in relation to their companies (often referred to as "fair dealing" provisions). CA 06 simply re-enacts many of these provisions without alteration, although some have been subject to significant changes. The most notable of these provisions are considered below. All references to sections of an Act in this note are to sections of CA 06 unless specifically stated otherwise. CA 06 does not contain a specific definition of the term "director". There is a general provision in section 250 which states that the expression "director" includes "any person occupying the position of director, by whatever name called", which includes a person who is treated by the board as such despite not having been validly appointed. The law also recognises the concept of "shadow directors" and many of the statutory provisions which apply to directors also apply to "shadow directors".

A shadow director is defined by section 251 as "a person (which may be an individual or a company) in accordance with whose directions or instructions the directors of the company are accustomed to act". A shadow director exerts control and may be held liable for his acts, particularly in cases of insolvency or where wrongful trading is alleged. A shadow director who exerts control but seeks to evade liability by not being appointed as a director will not be protected just because he has not been formally appointed.

7.7.3. General duties of Directors

Section 170 provides that the codified general duties of directors set out in sections 171-177 should be interpreted and applied in the same way as the common law rules and equitable principles which they replace, and regard should be had to the corresponding common law rules and equitable principles when interpreting and applying the statutory duties. Accordingly, courts will need to interpret and apply the general duties in a way that reflects the rules that they replace and it is thought that insofar as the newly codified duties do not encapsulate pre-existing duties, those duties will survive.

It therefore remains to be seen quite how different the new directors' duties regime will be from what went before.

The codified duties apply to all the directors of a company, including shadow directors and, in the case of the duties in sections 175 (duty to avoid conflicts of interests) and 176 (duty not to accept benefits from third parties), even former directors of the company. It should be noted that the law in this area is new and has not yet been the subject of interpretation by the courts. From 1 October 2007, four of the seven new codified provisions on directors' duties in CA 06 are in force:

7.7.4. Duty to act within powers (section 171 Companies Act)

Section 171 codifies the equitable rule that a director must act in accordance with the company's constitution and must only exercise his powers for their proper purpose. The section does not clarify aspects of the duty to exercise powers for proper purposes, such as how those purposes are to be ascertained, or the extent to which an improper purpose may taint a decision. Such matters will fall to be determined in accordance with previous case law, under which courts have approached the duty by first ascertaining the purpose for which the power was conferred, and then determining whether that was the director's substantial purpose when exercising the power.

The liability is strict: if the director's substantial purpose was not the purpose for which the power was conferred, it will not matter if he exercised the power in good faith or in the belief that it would promote the success of the company for the benefit of the members as a whole.

7.7.5.. Duty to promote the success of the company (section 172)

Section 172 replaces both a fiduciary duty which was usually summarised as being "to act in good faith in the best interests of the company", and also the statutory duty to consider the interests of the company's employees under section 309 of CA 85. Section 172 provides that a director must act in the way he considers, in good faith, would be most likely to promote the success of the company for the benefit of its members as a whole. In so doing, the director must have regard (among other matters) to: the likely consequences of any decision in the long term; the interests of the company's employees; the need to foster the company's business relationships with suppliers, customers and others; the impact of the company's operations on the community and the environment; the desirability of the company maintaining a reputation for high standards of business conduct; and the need to act fairly as between the members of the company.

Where the company's purposes consist of or include purposes other than the benefit of its members, the director must act in the way he considers, in good faith, would be most likely to achieve those purposes. The duty is subject to any enactment or rule of law requiring directors in certain circumstances to consider or act in the interests of the creditors of the company. Accordingly, the duty is displaced when the company is insolvent, and may be modified by an obligation to have regard to the interests of creditors as the company nears insolvency. It should be noted that: the duty will apply to all decisions made by a director, not merely formal decisions made by the whole board; "success" is not defined. It is thought that "success" in this context will usually mean "long-term increase in value" for commercial companies, and that what will promote the success of the company, and what constitutes such success, will be for the director's good faith judgment; the obligation to have regard to the listed factors is clearly subordinate to the overarching duty to promote the success of the company for the benefit of its members as a whole. However, the obligation to have regard to at least the listed factors, in carrying out the overarching duty, is mandatory; the list of factors is not exhaustive - directors should have regard to other matters relevant to the duty to promote the success of the company; and in having regard to the listed factors, the duty to exercise reasonable care, skill and diligence (section 174) will apply. In some cases, to satisfy the duty, it may be necessary to seek expert advice, for example in relation to impact on the community or environment.

7.7.6. Interests of present shareholders over future shareholders

Concerns have been raised about this section, including: whether directors should now give precedence to the interests of current members over future members. Historically, the fiduciary duty to act in the best interests of the company has been interpreted by identifying the company with its shareholders, both present and future and requiring directors to balance short-term and long-term interests. It is not clear that this will continue to be the case, but until the meaning of the section is more settled, directors may wish to seek professional advice in circumstances where the interests of the company's present members conflict with those of the company as a corporate body; how, or if, directors should document their compliance with the section.

The current prevailing view appears to be that it will be sufficient for board minutes to state that the directors have taken the factors set out in section 172 into account in carrying out their duty, and perhaps minute in more detail the consideration of any particularly relevant factor; and that, in conjunction with the new derivative action provisions in CA 06 (see paragraph 4 below), it will lead to a rise in class action style litigation from single-interest pressure groups which believe that a company has not given proper consideration to the issue in which they are interested However, this should prove difficult given the considerable procedural hurdles that members face in seeking to bring a derivative action. Notwithstanding this, for potentially controversial decisions, boards might want to seek the views of independent shareholders.

7.7.7. Duty to exercise independent judgment (section 173)

Section 173 also codifies the existing law. It provides that a director must exercise independent judgment. The duty will not be infringed by a director acting in accordance with an agreement entered into by the company that restricts the future exercise of the directors' discretion or in a way authorised by the company's constitution. It follows that any powers of delegation should be set out in the articles.

7.7.8. Duty to exercise reasonable care, skill and diligence (section 174)

Section 174 codifies the commonly accepted understanding of a director's duty of care, skill and diligence. Under section 174, a director must exercise the care, skill and diligence which would be exercised by a reasonably diligent person with both: the general knowledge, skill and experience that may reasonably be expected of a person carrying out the functions carried out by the director in relation to the company (the "objective" test); and the general knowledge, skill and experience that the director actually has (the "subjective" test).

So, at a minimum, a director must display the knowledge, skill and experience required by the objective test, but where a director has specialist knowledge, the higher subjective standard must be met. In applying the tests, regard must be had to the functions of the particular director, including his specific responsibilities and the circumstances of the company. The three further codified provisions on directors' duties in CA 06 will come into force on 1 October 2008 but may take longer.

7.7.9. Duty to avoid conflicts of interest (section 175)

From 1 October 2008 section 175 will replace the no-conflict rule applying to directors, under which a director must not, without the company's consent, place himself in a position where there is a conflict, or possible conflict, between the duties he owes the company and either his personal interests or other duties he owes to a third party. The duty applies, in particular, to the exploitation of property, information or opportunity, and whether or not the company could take advantage of the property, information or opportunity. Until 1 October 2008 the existing fiduciary duty continued to apply.

Where there are not sufficient independent directors, a conflict can be approved by the company's members (section 180(4)). The section does not apply to a conflict of interest arising in relation to a transaction or arrangement with the company, as that is covered by sections 177 and 182. The duty to avoid conflicts of interest will continue to apply after a person ceases to be a director as regards the exploitation of any property, information or opportunity of which he became aware when he was a director.

7.7.10. Duty not to accept benefits from third parties (section 176)

Section 176 codifies the equitable rule prohibiting the exploitation of the position of director for personal benefit. Until 1 October 2008 the equitable rule will apply. Under the section, a director must not accept any benefit (including a bribe) from a third party which is conferred because of his being a director or his doing or not doing anything as a director. Benefits conferred by the company, its holding company or subsidiaries, and benefits received from a person who provides the director's services to the company, are excluded. Benefits will also be excluded from the prohibition if their acceptance cannot reasonably be regarded as likely to give rise to any conflict of interest. This should exempt the acceptance of moderate and proportionate "corporate hospitality" by directors, but for the sake of clarity companies may wish to amend their constitutions (as envisaged and permitted by section 180(4)) to provide that where directors accept benefits under a specified value, they will not be in breach of their duty to the company.

The duty will continue to apply after a person ceases to be a director in relation to things done or omitted by him before he ceased to be a director – so that, as before, a director cannot simply resign and then accept an opportunity which he has diverted from the company itself.

7.7.11. Duty to declare interest in proposed transaction or arrangement with the company (section 177)

Section 177 will replace the equitable rule (in practice, already modified by the articles of most companies) that directors may not have an interest in a transaction with the company unless the interest has been authorised by the members. Until 1 October 2008 the equitable rule will continue to apply.

Under section 177, a director must declare to the other directors the nature and extent of any interest, direct or indirect, which he has or will have in a proposed transaction or arrangement with the company. The director need not be a party to the transaction for the duty to apply. An interest of another person in a contract with the company may require the director to make a disclosure under this duty, if the other person's interest amounts to a direct or indirect interest on the part of the director. The declaration must be made before the company enters into the transaction or arrangement. Where a declaration of interest proves to be, or becomes, inaccurate or incomplete, if the company has not yet entered into the transaction or arrangement a further declaration must be made, when the director becomes, or should reasonably have been, aware of the inaccuracy or incompleteness.

No declaration will be required: where the director is not aware of his interest or where the director is not aware of the transaction or arrangement, but directors will be treated as being aware of matters of which they ought reasonably to be aware; or if the interest cannot reasonably be regarded as likely to give rise to a conflict of interest, if the other directors are already aware of it, or if it concerns the terms of the director's service contract which have been (or are to be) considered at a board meeting or board committee; or where the company has only one director.

Section 177 only deals with proposed transactions or arrangements. Existing transactions and arrangements are covered by section 182, which provides that a director must declare the nature and extent of his direct or indirect interest in an existing transaction or arrangement entered into by the company, to the extent that the interest has not been declared under section 177.

7.7.12. Directors' interests in contracts

Subject to certain exceptions, a director may not be interested, directly or indirectly, in a contract with the company unless such an interest is permitted by the articles of association or by the shareholders in general meeting. At present, section 317 of CA 85 provides that it is the duty of a director who is in any way interested in a contract or proposed contract with the company to declare the nature of his interest at a full meeting of the directors of the company. Failure to disclose may result in a fine. From 1 October 2008 sections 177 (in respect of proposed contracts) and 182 (in respect of existing contracts) will replace section 317 of CA 85 (see paragraph 2.7 above).

7.7.13. Substantial transactions involving directors

Section 190 has replaced section 320 of CA 85 and provides that the approval of the company in general meeting is required if a director or connected person enters into a transaction to sell to or acquire from the company a substantial non-cash asset. Assets are deemed to be "substantial" where their value exceeds 10% of the company's asset value and is greater than £5,000, or where their value exceeds £100,000. If the required approval is not given, or the acquisition is not made conditional upon such approval being obtained, the transaction is voidable at the company's instance and the director or connected person is liable to account for any gain and indemnify the company for any loss or damage resulting from the transaction.

There are various statutory exceptions, for example the section does not apply to the acquisition of an asset as payment for loss of office or termination of employment, or to dealings in shares on a recognised investment exchange.

7.7.14. Director's contract of employment

If a director's service contract is for a fixed period of more than two years2, section 188 provides that it must first be approved by the shareholders in general meeting. If the approval is not obtained, the company can terminate the contract at any time by giving reasonable notice. This information may seem irrelevant but such knowledge can help the police to see breach of duties, liabilities, and criminal responsibility in the corporate area.

7.7.15. Restriction on loans to directors

A company may not make a loan to one of its directors unless the details of the loan have been disclosed and shareholder approval has been obtained via ordinary resolution (section 197). Companies can seek shareholder approval within a "reasonable time" of making a loan to a director.

Shareholder approval is not, however, required for: loans of up to £10, 000; or loans in connection with company business that do not exceed £50, 000; or loans to a director to defend proceedings (including a regulatory investigation) against himself brought in connection with his role for the company, on the basis that any such loan must repaid on conviction or if final judgement is given against the director.

If the company enters into a transaction in contravention of these provisions, it is voidable at the instance of the company and the director or connected person (or the director who authorised the loan) is liable to account to the company for any gain that he has made and to indemnify the company for any loss or damage resulting from the transaction. In contrast to the position under CA 85, there are no criminal sanctions for breach of the provisions.

7.7.16. Payments for loss of office

Section 217 provides that a company may not make any payment to a director as compensation for loss of office or as consideration for or in connection with his loss of office without the approval of the members in general meeting. "Loss of Office" now includes not only loss of the office of director but also the termination of any related employment; however, the bona fide settlement of a director's contractual or legal entitlement is exempted and does not require shareholder approval. The section is aimed at "golden parachute" arrangements which are wholly or partly "ex gratia" in nature.

7.7.17. Connected persons

The "connected persons" of a director for the purposes of the provisions summarised above are defined by section 252 and include: members of a director's family; companies with which the director is connected (because he controls the company or has at least a 20% equity interest in it); trusts set up for the benefit of the director or his connected persons; business partners of the director or his connected persons.

The definition of family members has been significantly extended by CA06 and now includes: spouse or civil (i.e., same-sex) partner; person (of either sex) with whom the director cohabits in an "enduring family relationship" and the infant children of such a person; and the directors' parents and children including adult children.

7.7.18. Breach of duty- Action by the company and derivative actions

The codified duties discussed above are owed to the company (section 170(1)). Only the company will be able to enforce them, although in certain circumstances shareholders may be able to bring a derivative action on the company's behalf.

Previously, the right to bring a derivative action was a rarely-used common law remedy, available only when the wrongdoing of the director in relation to the company was such as to constitute a "fraud on the minority". The circumstances in which derivative actions may be brought have been extended by CA 2006, and such actions are now expressly available for any breach of duty by a director, even if the director has not benefited personally from the breach. However, a member will face a number of procedural hurdles in bringing an action.

For example, a court must refuse permission for a claimant to bring a derivative claim where it is satisfied that either: a person acting in accordance with the general duty to promote the success of the company (under section 172) would not seek to continue the claim; or the act or omission giving rise to the cause of action has been authorised or ratified by the company (section 263(2)). In addition, section 263(3) prescribes factors that the court must particularly take into account when considering whether to give permission, which include: whether the member is acting in good faith in seeking to continue the claim; the importance that a person acting in accordance with the duty to promote the success of the company would attach to continuing the claim; whether the company has decided not to pursue the claim; and any evidence before the court as to the views of members of the company who have no personal interest (direct or indirect) in the matter.

Directors should also bear in mind the following deterrents to bringing a derivative claim: costs will usually be awarded against unsuccessful claimants; and even if a claim is successful, any damages will accrue to the company, not to the claimant. For these reasons, it may not necessarily be the case that the derivative action procedure will be used any more than the previous common law remedy.

7.7.19. Unfair prejudice

The ability of shareholders to bring an action in their own name, if they can show that the company's affairs have been conducted in a manner which is unfairly prejudicial to their own interests, is carried forward essentially unchanged from CA 1985 by section 944.Companies Act 2006. As before, such an action could be brought against directors as well as against the company and the court could make such an order against a director, for example for damages, as it sees fit depending upon the circumstances.

7.7.20. Remedies

Under section 178, the consequences of a breach or threatened breach of directors' duties are the same as they were for breach of the corresponding common law or equitable principles.

The remedy for a breach of section 174 (duty to exercise reasonable care, skill and diligence) will usually be damages. Remedies for breaches of other general duties may include: an injunction; setting aside of the transaction, restitution and account of profits; restoration of company property held by the director; damages; and/or termination of the director's service contract.

7.7.21. Relief from liability

Generally, a director of a limited liability company has no personal liability arising from the acts of the company itself. There are occasions, however, where, as a penalty for abusing his position, a director can incur both civil and criminal liability. For example, a director may be personally liable if: he or the company knowingly acts outside the powers given to them by the memorandum and articles; or the company becomes insolvent and the director has been involved in fraudulent or wrongful trading.

Although, in general terms, a director is not liable for a breach of duty by other directors of which he was ignorant or which occurred before he became a director, liability may arise if he has failed to supervise the activities of a guilty director in circumstances where his duty of care placed him under an obligation to do so or where, with a degree of common sense, he should have known that his action amounted to a participation in or sanction of the conduct which constituted the breach of duty.

For instance, a director who signs a cheque for an unauthorised loan may be liable, even though he had protested strongly against the making of the loan at the time.

As long as a transaction is within a company's objects as stated in its memorandum of association and is not one which a director is precluded by statute from undertaking, a company in general meeting may ratify it retrospectively even though it was outside the powers conferred on the directors by the articles. Under the provisions of section 35 of CA 85 (which remains the current law until 1 October 2008), such a transaction, if entered into by the directors with a third party acting in good faith, is enforceable against the company by that third party even if it is not within the company's objects as set out in its memorandum.

Certain breaches of duty cannot be ratified and these include: acts purporting to abrogate the rights of individual members or a class of shareholders; or acts which a company cannot lawfully do, either because the general law forbids them or they are ultra vires to the company; or acts which are fraudulent or dishonest.

Section 239 preserves the current law on ratification of acts of directors, but with a significant change. Any decision by a company to ratify conduct by a director amounting to negligence, default, breach of duty or breach of trust in relation to the company must be taken by a resolution of the shareholders without reliance upon votes in favour by the director or any connected person. A member "connected with" the director will include certain family members (section 252) and may include fellow directors (section 239(5) (d)). Ratification will bar the bringing of a derivative claim.

Even if the conduct has not been ratified, where a court is determining whether to permit a claimant to continue a derivative claim, it must consider whether the conduct could be, and is likely to be, ratified by the company. Section 1157 provides that where proceedings for negligence, default, breach of duty or breach of trust are brought against a director, the court may relieve him from liability if it considers both that: he has acted honestly and reasonably; and considering all the circumstances of the case, he ought fairly to be excused. A director may also apply to the court for relief where he has reason to expect that a claim may be made against him.

7.7.22. Insurance

Directors should give consideration to insuring against their potential liabilities. Whilst insurance cannot cover all liabilities a director may face (for example in relation to criminal penalties), it can limit a director's exposure. Section 233 permits a company to purchase insurance for its directors, and those of an associated company, against any liability attaching to them in connection with any negligence, default, breach of duty or breach of trust by them in relation to the company of which they are a director. If permitted by the articles, the company could take out and fund a directors' and officers' insurance policy (commonly known as "D&O" insurance).

These policies usually work on a "claims-made" basis, i.e. the insurer at the time the claim is made is obliged to provide cover, rather than the insurer at the time the act in respect of which the claim is being made was committed. D&O policies also tend to be offered on an aggregate basis whereby a single pot of money is available to cover all claims up to a certain limit over a specified period. Specific directors' liability insurance can also be obtained and the expenses may be met by the company if permitted under its articles of association. It could be said that the extension of companies' abilities to indemnify directors discussed below reduces the requirement for D&O insurance, as this is often provided principally for the peace of mind of the directors. Therefore, if this can be provided by way of an indemnity the need for insurance is reduced. However, D&O insurance may also be taken out to protect the company's balance sheet.

7.7.23. Indemnity

Sections 232 and 234 contain provisions in respect of the ability of companies to indemnify directors. The position is similar to that under CA 85. The basic prohibition - that a company cannot exempt a director from any liability attaching to him in connection with any negligence, default, breach of duty or breach of trust by him in relation to the company - still stands. However, a company may enter into a specific indemnity agreement with its directors in respect of liabilities to third parties (known as a "qualifying third party indemnity provision") or liabilities which they may incur as a result of acting as directors of a pension scheme of the company (a "qualifying pension scheme indemnity provision"), or may simply resolve to indemnify them against such liabilities as and when they occur, provided that: the liability incurred is not to the company itself or an associated company (i.e. within the same group of companies); it is not permissible to indemnify against a fine imposed as a result of criminal proceedings or by a regulatory authority; and it is not permissible to indemnify against any liability incurred in defending civil proceedings where judgment is given against the director. Companies may indemnify directors against the director's costs of defence proceedings as they are incurred, or costs incurred in an application for relief under section 1157, even if the action is brought by the company itself (subject to the director's liability to repay those costs in certain circumstances).

Funding provided for this purpose does not require shareholder approval under the provisions restricting loans to directors (sections 205 and 206 Companies Act 2006). The decision to indemnify directors can be taken by the board, subject to any restrictions in the company's articles of association. However, details of indemnities must be disclosed in the directors' annual report where they are for the benefit of one or more directors of the company.

7.7.24. Liability for corporate crimes

Potential liabilities extend across most of the criminal law. If a director, acting as such, commits a criminal offence, he may make the company liable to criminal penalties (and thereby be in breach of his statutory duty of care to the company).

Further, if a company commits an offence through the agency of some of its directors, or an employee, a director who has not directly participated in the offence may also become liable to penalties. In both cases the liability arises because the courts may see the directors as the company's "mind and will".

The mental processes of the directors (e.g. in forming a criminal intention) may be attributed to the company itself. In such cases the courts see the directors (or indeed, in some cases, officers or employees who are not directors) not as acting on the company's behalf, but as acting as the company itself.

There is no comprehensive statement of law on where the corporate "mind and will" is to be found. In criminal law, unlike the law of tort, an employer or principal does not have an almost automatic responsibility for the wrongful act of an employee or agent. The case law seems to suggest that the key is the degree of intention which has to be shown for an offence to be proved. Many regulatory statutes which create offences of a strict liability contain a formula along the following lines:

"Where an offence under this Act committed by a body corporate is proved to have been committed with the consent or connivance of, or to have been attributable to any neglect on the part of, any director, manager, secretary or similar officer ... he, as well as the body corporate, shall be guilty of the offence and shall be liable to be proceeded against and punished accordingly". A director is not necessarily guilty of a corporate offence if the relevant statute does not contain this formula. The position appears to be that offences of strict liability committed by a company cannot be made the vicarious responsibility of the directors unless the statute creating them so provides.

7.8. Conclusion to Chapter Seven

The introduction and strengthening of the regulatory, money laundering and corporate governance framework may have unintentionally increased the risk that the UK faces from fraud because the in-house resources that a corporation has available to prevent, detect and investigate fraud, the internal audit function, is so overstretched with the volume and complexity of financial auditing and reporting requirements, that it cannot deal effectively with the fraud risk. "*The excessive bank secrecy rules and a failure to exchange information on foreign tax evaders are relics of a different time and have no role to play in relations between democratic societies*", said the OECD Secretary-General Angel Gurra.

Further reading for Chapter Seven

M. Gill and G. Taylor, "Preventing Money Laundering or Obstructing Business? Financial Companies' Perspectives on 'Know Your Customer' Procedures", British Journal of Criminology, Jul 2004; 44: 582 - 594.

M. Levi, "Regulating money laundering: The death of bank secrecy in the UK", British Journal of Criminology, 1991; 31: 109 - 125.

CHAPTER 8-
ANALYSIS OF ORGANISED CRIME FOR CROSS -BORDER FRAUD

8.1.1. Organised crime in perspective

Today, organized crime is a transnational phenomenon and a cause for worldwide concern. Transnational crime groups may have profited more from globalization than legitimate businesses, which are subject to domestic and host country laws and regulations. Crime syndicates and networks, abetted by official corruption, blackmail, and intimidation, can use open markets and open societies to their full advantage.

Organised criminals are a structured group of three or more persons existing for a period of time and acting in concert with the aim of committing one or more serious crimes or offences in order to obtain, directly or indirectly, a financial or other material benefit. According to the UN Convention, a crime is transnational if it is committed in more than one state; if it is committed in one state but a substantial part of its preparation, planning, direction, or control takes place in another state; if it is committed in one state but involves an organized criminal group that engages in criminal activities in more than one state or if it is committed in one state but has substantial effects in another state.

8.1.2. Combating fraud by organized criminals by studying global gangs

To combat fraud perpetrated by organised criminals, UK police need to understand where organised criminal operate as well as what crimes are being committed elsewhere in the world. For example, the two leading organized crime

Fraud Investigation: Criminal Procedure and Investigation

problems in Cambodia are drug production/trafficking and human trafficking and in China, the gravest organized crime problems, are drug distribution, gambling and prostitution and violent crimes. A look at Hong Kong, which has been a British colony for more than 100 years before it returned to Chinese control in 1997 shows that Hong Kong has long been home to the secretive, ritualistic criminal organizations known as triads .Triad societies control private bus routes, fish markets, street markets, wholesale markets, entertainment centres, parking services, prostitution, illegal gambling, and extortion .

In China, corruption and a weak judiciary remain serious impediments to the effective prosecution of traffickers. In the Philippines, illegal drug business is controlled by predominantly Filipino- Chinese, or Chinese from China, Hong Kong, and Taiwan who are protected by local politicians.

In Taiwan, many influential gangsters are now chief executive officers of major business conglomerates, and they are heavily involved in the businesses of bid-rigging, waste disposal, construction, cable television networks, telecommunications, stock trading, and entertainment. This is the sort of intelligence that will help the police to prioritise resources and target the relevant areas for fraud.

8.1.3. Cross Border Electronic Fraud

The UK Fraud Act takes account of other jurisdictions in that UK businesses must comply with International Trade Law. The introduction of the United Nations Commission on International Trade Model Law on cross-border insolvency into English law will have a bearing on how cross-border insolvencies are conducted and may be seen as one area to scrutinise as a driver for fraud.

Other than the EU Insolvency Regulations (1346/2000), there is little statutory provision in the United Kingdom for an insolvency involving the United Kingdom and other countries but the introduction of the Cross-Border Insolvency Regulations 2006 enacts the UNCITRAL Model Law on Cross-Border Insolvency which supports international lending by making asset-recovery more streamlined and effective when a debtor operating across borders defaults.

Nine countries, including the US, have adopted this Model Law. The regulations apply where assistance is sought in the UK by a court in another state or by a representative of another state in connection with a foreign proceeding; where assistance is sought in connection with a proceeding under British insolvency law; where a debtor is subject to foreign proceeding and a proceeding under UK insolvency law at the same time; and where creditors or other interested parties in another state have an interest in starting or taking place in a proceeding under UK insolvency law.

8.2. Mapping technique used to detect fraud

Geographical mapping techniques have been applied to discover pockets of areas where this type of fraud is more prevalent. There are organised criminals who specialise in selling birth certificates. The UK government has published guidelines for the application of a law that makes it illegal to create or distribute so-called "hacking tools".

> **Point to Note**
>
> Almost every memo, spreadsheet, financial record, letter and report is created or processed by a computer.

Fraud Investigation: Criminal Procedure and Investigation

This measure is among amendments to the Computer Misuse Act included in the Police and Justice Act 2006.

8.3.1. Organised Crimes

The Home Office consultation document entitled 'New Powers against Organised and Financial Crime' established a civil prevention order to be used against individuals and organisations to prevent serious crime. The Home Office plans were to improve data-sharing within the public sector and between the private and public sectors so that financial crime may be more easily detected and prevented. The introduction of new offences of assisting and encouraging crime and proceeds of crime legislation are hoped o combat organised financial crime.

8.3.2. Defining organized crime

Law enforcement and politicians are not however the only players who have turned defining organized crime into an industry. Researchers who have accused these other individuals of manipulating our understanding of organized crime for organizational or personal gain are equally guilty. It has been argued that organized crime academic "experts" have spent a disproportionate amount of time advancing their own perspective by arguing the deficiency of competing definitions. Also the media has a particular fondness for anything relating to organized crime and works together or against the other interest groups to define, dramatize, and deliver to the public the various interpretations of the threats posed by organized crime.

Organised crime may be said to be economically motivated illicit activity undertaken by any group, association or other body consisting of two or more individuals, whether formally or informally organized, where the negative impact of said activity could be considered significant from an economic, social, violence generation, health and safety and/or environmental perspective. Without the notion of *duration* of criminal activity, without a requirement that there be an *organization,* without mention of the capacity to exert *violence and/or corruption,* organized crime is a significant criminal activity that involves at least two people where there is an economic motivation of some sort.

8.3.3. Fraud is part of organised crime

By this definition, most corporate crime, white collar crimes and financial frauds are not only *a part of* organized crime activities but rather they *are* themselves organized crime activities. Organized crime can also be defined as a unique *process* that makes organized crime activities different from and possibly more of a threat to society— warranting extra-ordinary enforcement and legislative capabilities. The definition of organized crime must have perceptions of "dangerousness". The criteria for dangerousness may be ethnically or commodity based. The term "organized crime" appears in criminal law literature since the 1920's. Much of the original stereotype regarding the nature of organized crime has been reinforced by biker gang hype and a preoccupation with drug trafficking to the exclusion of the vast array of other criminal commodities. Police, politicians and the mass media are true partners in the delivery to the public of the seriousness of these particular offences. Until recently, the subject of economic crime was of little interest to economists because it was viewed as a minor aberration that had little impact on the functioning of the economic system as a whole.

8.3.4. Contemporary organised crime

Today, it is accepted that organised crime increases the dangers of police corruption; spreads disrespect for the law among formerly law-abiding citizens. There have been studies of organised crime by criminologists who managed to gain direct access to the inner sanctum of so-called organized crime families. The mystery had been – if the organized crime group is not a business, what is it and why does it exist. The studies concluded that members of an organized crime group, when they engaged in economic pursuits, operated strictly as individuals or occasionally in small, ad hoc partnerships, engaged in a highly competitive criminal marketplace. The 'group' itself had quite a different role because illicit enterprises have no access to the formal economy and its institutions. So they do not use legal means such as dispute resolution, property right guarantees, and start-up capital. Therefore the crime "family" has a central role in the creation of the overall infrastructure necessary for their illegal success.

8.3.5. Illegal new goods and services

Organised crimes involve the production and/or distribution of new goods and services that happen to be illegal i.e., recreational drugs or illicit gambling, for example. The exchanges are multilateral, much like legitimate market transactions, involving (among others) producers, distributors, retailers and money-managers on the supply side and consumers on the demand side.

Since the transfers are voluntary, it is often difficult to define a "victim", unless it is some abstract construct like "society as a whole", a phrase that, by attempting to embrace all, ultimately includes nothing.

Although the total sums involved may be considerable, in themselves and in relation to the economy as a whole, provided the transaction remains voluntary, there are no definable losses to any individual from the act itself (though there may be from indirect consequences of the act).

The morality is accordingly debatable and the preferred policy response is therefore muddled. Since there is no really definable victim, in addition to standard forms of punishment, it has become popular to force the guilty party or parties to forfeit the gains.

Organised commercial crimes involve: the production of goods and services, which are, inherently legal, but whose methods of production and/or distribution are illegal. Since transfers occur within a normal business setting, exchanges are multilateral and, on the surface, voluntary. However there are inevitably involuntary elements as well. Fraud can be committed against workers, suppliers, financiers or customers. Because of the element of fraud, the morality should in principle be unambiguous- though in reality it is often difficult to differentiate fraud from simply sharp business practice.

8.4. May be an unlicensed operator to Fortune 500 company

Commercial organised crimes range from the domain of the unlicensed operator to the Fortune 500 Corporation falsifying cost data on a public sector contract, dipping into the company pension plan to finance a CEO's jet or deceiving customers with worthless product guarantees.

With the possible exception of drug trafficking no criminal act has achieved greater notoriety in recent years than corruption. Politicians (the major recipients) join with the international community to implement anti-foreign corruption legislation. The World Bank and IMF have joined the crusade—or led the crusade. Yet corruption remains a catch-all category in which several distinct acts are compounded and often confounded. In the analysis of economically-motivated crime, corruption should logically be seen not as a primary offence but as an instrument of that offence - either facilitating the conduct of the offence or helping to cover it up afterwards.

Corruption is far more commonly the domain of those seeking commercial advantage - it is used to subvert the normal mechanisms for achieving access to services or contracts, which are legal. It is an illicit payment for a legitimate good or service

8.5.1. Well educated organised criminals

Well educated and very used to the workings and vulnerabilities of bureaucracies with their fondness for paper work has meant that the types of crimes reflect these skills. Basically any and all fraudulent schemes are currently being carried out. Insurance and medical frauds, stock market manipulations, stolen cars, stolen fuel, and counterfeiting of all types (tokens, bank-drafts, cheques, and credit cards).

The advantage of organized crime is that it can be whatever one wants it to be a massive threat, a theatrical legacy, or petty criminals and hoodlum bikers. The lack of consensus around the term, the invisibility of much of the activity, and the natural links into the lives of the public for a large percentage of what are demand driven commodities, allows for a sense of personal relevance and fascination.

The complicity of the public through their support for many of these illegal goods and services mixes with evidence of the real, or in other instances exaggerated, violence initiated by some of these organized criminals to create an ambivalent and corruption-vulnerable environment. This milieu encourages distortion and manipulation. The mention of the words 'organized crime' has the power to draw the press, win votes, acquire law enforcement resources, and gain public support for various legislative or enforcement crackdowns. The arguments are often intertwined so that the actual 'organized crime' issues get lost.

8.5.2. Money laundering at the centre of organised crime

The Proceeds of Crime Act 2002 ("POCA") ss327-340 provide the framework for money laundering offences and for cross-border organised crime, sections 327 to 329 POCA are the relevant sections of POCA. There were amendments made by the Serious Crime and Police Act 2005 relating to POCA ss 327-329 which provide that a person does *not commit a money laundering offence under POCA ss327-329 if he knows or believes on reasonable grounds, that the relevant criminal conduct- was not, at the time it occurred, unlawful under the criminal law then applying in that country or territory and that it is not of a description prescribed by an order made by the Secretary of State.* This provides a bar to conviction.

POCA s 340(2) defines 'criminal conduct' as conduct which constitutes or would constitute an offence in any part of the United Kingdom if it occurred there. POCA s340(3) defines ' property as criminal property' if it constitutes a person's benefit from criminal conduct or it represents such a benefit and the alleged offender knows or suspects that it constitutes or represents such a benefit. POCA s 340(9) states that property is all property wherever situated and includes money; all forms of property, real or personal, heritable or moveable and things in action and other intangible or incorporeal property. POCA s 340(4) states that it is immaterial as to who carried out the conduct; who benefitted from it; or whether the conduct occurred before or after the passing of the Proceeds and Criminal Evidence Act.

8.6. Characteristics of organized crime

The characteristics of organized crime are on-going criminal activity; continuing conspiracy among the members of the group; structure greater than any single member and potential to use corruption and/or violence.

8.7. Organised gangs

Many organised gangs are concentrated in and around major urban centres, although some operate from smaller communities across the country. Organized crime groups can be found virtually everywhere there is profit to be made from criminal ventures. Multicultural organised gangs are increasingly evident as a reflection of the multi-ethnic demographics of their locality. Although cultural ties remain an influencing principle within the organized crime landscape, multi-ethnic groups may be based on the criminal capabilities of members rather than on their ethnic or cultural heritage.

Criminal groups target a wide range of professions with specialized skills in the legitimate economy, attempting to coerce or corrupt some individuals. For example, those within the commercial transport industry may be targeted to facilitate the movement of contraband. Other skills valued by criminal groups are those within the financial industry that facilitate money laundering or the concealment of proceeds of crime.

There are varying levels of criminal capabilities amongst organized gangs. The illicit drug market is dynamic and diverse, involving a wide range of drugs from domestic and foreign sources. These drugs are distributed across the country by criminal groups operating at all levels of capability and scope.

East European crime groups use both violence and corruption and use both from their earliest significant entry into UK and continue to use them. The evidence indicates that in contrast to some other criminal organizations, the East Europeans are very well educated and are often proficient in several languages. These factors plus a tradition of favour - giving and receiving and a need to work 'corrupt' deals as part of seemingly legitimate business has meant that the criminals have been very successful at penetrating 'systemically' into UK society. The types of East European criminal activity 'fits' with the profile of the criminal operators.

8.8. Criminal networks

In the 1980's organised crime was seen as a business, the common denominator in all three decades being human relations, producing networks, a system of ties between nodes for the provision of illicit goods and services, as well as the protection, regulation and extortion of those who engaged in the provision consumption of these goods and services. The main purpose of a network is internal pooling. The purpose of this pooling, through communication, can be a sense of belonging to the network, a pooling of standards, information or more tangible resources.

Criminal organizations can present themselves as businesses or networks; depending on whether we are looking mainly at these organizations' outside transactions or their relationships. There are certain characteristics, specific to of criminal networks that can be analyzed. Size is a fundamental characteristic of networks, in that it determines many other characteristics particularly the density of the networks.

8.9. People smuggling and contraband smuggling

There are smuggling groups which operate in smuggling people and contraband there are numerous criminal groups involved in a wide range of financial frauds. In many cases, these criminal groups operate across jurisdictions in order to access more victims and lessen the chances of detection. Criminal gangs continue to target personal and financial information.

8.10. Using Data from mail and garbage

Methods of obtaining this data range from mail or garbage theft to more sophisticated means such as modifying point-of-sale terminals (where payment cards are swiped to pay for goods), compromising corporate databases or through black market websites that sell stolen data. Payment card fraud, in which a single crime group can victimize hundreds of people, remains a serious financial threat.

8.11. Thinking outside the box

Law enforcement officials need to do more thinking "out of the box" in order to effectively combat the crime networks that are dominating transnational organized crime and furthering the fraud of money laundering in the UK.

On the premise that organized crime challenges the authority of the nation state, measures to correct this should be adopted by way of prevention of corruption of public officials, judges and legislation. There also needs to be allocation of resources to deal with the problem. International cooperation is vital because many criminal gangs often graduate to an international level or organized crime. Continuing with the present intelligence-led policing strategies is the key to the problem.

8.12. Proactive policing and surveillance methods are needed

Proactive policing, making use of surveillance methods, informants, and similar methods have characterized police efforts against organized crime in many countries for many years, adopting squad, task force and security service style deployments to deal with organized crime. The use of repentant gang members to give evidence and the use of witness protection programmes has characterized Italian police fight against organized crime, for instance, even though such methods have been criticized for mirroring the criminals. It is established from various research projects over the years that the only way to combat organized crime is to continue the enterprising methods of trading that goes on between the police and the criminals, even though the downside is the possibility of police corruption.

As well as this informal route, there is a technical route to combat organized crime by way of integrated intelligence analysis to map the organisations, events and activities in a network.

Such analysis enables police to chart and evaluate the power and vulnerability of individuals within a crime group and the UK already has such a system which supports enforcement and preventative action at the local and national level.

The bilateral and multilateral cooperation systems between countries is the third way to combat organized crime. In this respect, the United Nations has developed a systematic approach to organized crime through the development of clear goals and policies for prevention within international conventions.

8.13. Parallel Investigations to be considered

When dealing with cross-border organised crime, parallel investigations can cause problems in that although they are investigations of the same crime in different countries, they may not be simultaneous. Due process and proper standards of administration of justice takes longer in some countries than in others.

Even in one single country, different agencies may not be allowed to work together because of the laws of that country. For example, in the American case of *United States v Stringer*, 408 F. Supp. 2d 1083 (D. Or. 2006), the Oregon district court held that federal prosecutors may not work together with the Securities Exchange Commission ("SEC") in a single investigation, building their criminal case while hiding behind the SEC in order to sidestep the defendant's constitutional rights, although in this particular case the opinion was reversed when the Ninth Circuit Court of Appeals rejected the contention that parallel investigations may not merge or that a criminal prosecution may not be developed by means of a civil investigation (see *United States v Stringer*, 521 F. 3D 1189 (9th Cir. 2008)). The decision meant that while the government may not affirmatively mislead defendants to shield the existence of a criminal investigation, it is under no obligation to inform targets about a criminal investigation as long as the defendants are generally aware of the possibility of prosecution.

8.13. Conclusion to Chapter Eight

The cyber threat is rapidly increasing as the number of actors with the tools and abilities to use computers is rising. The country's vulnerability is escalating as the economy and critical infrastructures become increasingly reliant on interdependent computer networks and the World Wide Web. Large scale computer attacks on our critical infrastructure and economy would have potentially devastating results.

Cyber threats fall into two distinct categories- threats affecting national security that emerged with Internet technology, such as cyber terrorism, foreign-based computer intrusions and cyber theft of sensitive data; and traditional criminal activity facilitated by computers and the Internet, such as theft of intellectual property, online sexual exploitation of children, and Internet fraud. In both categories cyber attacks, intrusions, illicit file sharing, and illegal use of cyber tools are the basic instruments used by perpetrators. Domestic and foreign terrorist organizations, foreign intelligence actors, and criminal enterprises are increasingly using encryption technology to secure their communications and to exercise command and control over operations and people without fear of surveillance.

The rapid evolution of computer technology, coupled with ever-creative techniques used by foreign intelligence actors, terrorists, and criminals, requires investigators and professionals to have highly specialized computer-based skills.

Identify and neutralize the most significant individuals or groups conducting computer intrusions, the dissemination of malicious code, or other computer supported operations. Reduce the cyber intrusion threat by fully identifying the scope, objectives, methods, and operations of perpetrators, specifically targeting those affecting national security.

Develop a comprehensive list of cyber related targets for monitoring and protection. Increase the number of Cyber Action Teams available for rapid deployment to enhance operational response to cyber events that have a significant impact on the country's interests. Increase the breadth and depth of human sources that have first-hand knowledge of computer intrusions.

Identify and neutralize operations targeting intellectual property. Theft of intellectual property affects competitiveness and economic viability. Copyright industries and derivative businesses account for billions of pounds. Similarly, theft of trade secrets presents a serious economic and security threat.

Trade secrets represent some of the most valuable assets within the nation's corporate community, as much as 85 percent of a company's value, the loss of which would do irreparable or fatal damage. Yet unlike buildings or products, the "mobility" of trade secrets makes them one of the country's most vulnerable economic assets. Some intellectual property is so singular, or is so closely tied to national security research and development, that its loss to thieves or foreign intelligence services would cause incalculable harm. Coordinate with local, international, and industry partners to create and populate an intellectual property rights intelligence database. Increase the breadth and depth of human source coverage of computer-based intellectual property theft.

Organized criminal enterprises using the Internet for fraudulent activities present a significant and increasing criminal threat in the cyber arena. Typically, one or more components of the Internet is used to present fraudulent solicitations to prospective victims, conduct fraudulent transactions, or transmit the proceeds of fraud to financial institutions or others connected with the scheme. This crime problem is international and many schemes originate in the former communist countries of Eastern Europe. When Internet users — whether they are businesses or consumers — are crippled by Internet fraud schemes, the viability of e-commerce is compromised, adversely impacting the national economy. Efforts must be focussed on dismantling enterprises engaged in significant levels of fraudulent activity, especially those that are national and transnational.

Organised crime is a complex subject and some will say a 'chicken and egg' problem in that it is not certain as to the real amount of the so called 'organised' element, in which case, it is pointless setting up complex technical and electronic system to deal with gangs. It is not incorrect to consider whether orthodox policing methods are enough and these gangs are just opportunistically appearing as though they are 'organised' in a scientific way. Organised criminality can be studied simply by watching our known gangs and criminal families as the controversy in the criminology research points to. At worst, organized crime may be just exaggerated bullying, violence, theft, anti-social behaviour and apathy. It may be that drugs, people smuggling and corporate crime may be the real culprits, in which case resources need to be directed to corporate fraud.

Further reading

M. E. Beare and R.T. Naylor, "Major Issues Relating to Organized Crime: within the Context of Economic Relationships", Nathanson Centre for the Study of Organized Crime and Corruption, April 14, 1999.

A.A. Block and S. P. Griffin," Transnational Financial Crime: Crooked Lawyers, Tax Evasion, and Securities Fraud", Journal of Contemporary Criminal Justice, Nov 2002; vol. 18: pp. 381 - 393.

E. Brown, " Snitch: Informants, Co-operators and the Corruption of Justice", (Public Affairs, New York 2007).

D.L. Carter, "International Organized Crime: Emerging Trends in Entrepreneurial Crime" Journal of Contemporary Criminal Justice, Dec 1994.

J. Dubro, *Dragons of Crime*, (Octopus Publishing Group, Ontario 1992).

Jane's Intelligence Review, Special Report No. 10, "Mafiya: Organized crime in Russia", June 1996.

B. Liang and H. Lu, "Conducting Fieldwork in China: Observations on Collecting Primary Data Regarding Crime, Law, and the Criminal Justice System", Journal of Contemporary Criminal Justice, May 2006. J. McKenna, "Organized Crime in the Royal Colony of Hong Kong", Journal of Contemporary Criminal Justice, Nov 1996.

A. Nicaso and L. Lamothe, *Global Mafia*, (Macmillan, Canada, 1995).

N. L. Piquero and M. L. Benson, "White-Collar Crime and Criminal Careers: Specifying a Trajectory of Punctuated Situational Offending", Journal of Contemporary Criminal Justice, May 2004.

Transaction Periodicals Consortium "Best Practice in Intelligence Management with Respect to Chinese Organized Crime", Trends in Organized Crime, (Transaction Periodicals Consortium, New Jersey 1995).

CHAPTER 9- LEGAL AWARENESS

9.1. Introduction

The relevant aspects of law that affect the investigation and prosecution of a fraud case ought to be considered, especially the right to silence or the right not to incriminate oneself, privacy rights and the right to fair trial.

9.2 Self-incrimination

Research findings have long established that suspects are not always made truly aware of their rights, are often interviewed by very junior police officers and are rarely given a full copy of the Police and Criminal Evidence Act- Codes of Practice to read. (Section 37(1) of PACE), *"The Custody Officer shall determine whether he has before him sufficient evidence to charge a person with the offence for which he was arrested and may detain him at the police station for such period as necessary to enable him to do so".* The custody officer must make a subjective decision. If the suspect wishes to terminate a police interview by saying nothing, it must be terminated, thus forcing the officer to make a decision.

There have been no recent studies on how many suspects remains silent but n ACPO 1993 study showed that 5 % of suspects who received legal advice exercised their right to say nothing compared to 13% of those who did not have legal advice. This result was largely corroborated by research by the Royal Commission on Criminal Justice. The Police do deny the suspect legal advice for a certain time if they think fit and they can retain a suspect for a length of time without charge.

Fraud Investigation: Criminal Procedure and Investigation

The Police and Criminal Evidence Act Codes of Practice for the police to adhere to were issued under section 66 of the Police and Criminal Evidence Act 1984. The Codes cover the detention, treatment and questioning of suspects by police officers and include access to legal advice, time limits for detention and conditions in which suspects may be questioned. Breaches of the Codes may be taken into account if the court thinks that they are relevant to any question arising in the proceedings. Evidence obtained where breaches of the Codes of Practice have occurred may be excluded under the court's exclusionary discretion under s 78(1) of PACE, which states that

"In any proceedings the court may refuse to allow evidence on which the prosecution proposes to rely to be given if it appears to the court that, having regard to all the circumstances, including the circumstances in which the evidence was obtained, the admission of the evidence would have such an adverse effect on the fairness of the proceedings that the court ought not to admit it."

This could be seen as broader than the common law discretion to exclude and it encompasses a wider range of behaviour than that envisaged by section 76 PACE. Section 78 PACE has been used often by the Court. Provisions relating to the exclusion and admissibility of confessions obtained in circumstances of oppressive, inhuman or degrading treatment, or in circumstances which are likely to render them unreliable, may be found in section 76 of PACE. The Court's common law discretion to exclude evidence is preserved in section 82(3) of PACE. Section 82(3) states:

"Nothing in this Part of the Act shall prejudice any power of a court to exclude evidence (whether by preventing questions from being put or otherwise) at its discretion."

9.3. Confessions obtained unfairly

This section 82 PACE is designed to exclude confessions obtained by unfair or improper methods which would otherwise be admissible. A further step in causing the police to behave fairly during interrogation was provided by the tape recording of interviews. A Code of Practice issued under the duty placed on the Home Secretary under section 60(1) (b) PACE sets out the procedure for tape recording interviews with suspects. There must be a master tape which must be sealed in the presence of the suspect.

Tape recording has to be used when police interview a person cautioned of an indictable offence, including an offence triable either way, or where further questioning takes place following charging a suspect or informing him that he may be prosecuted, or where in such circumstances, the suspect is confronted with a written statement made by another person or the contents of an interview with another person. If the machine is switched off, then he should be cautioned again before resuming the interview as is the norm. It can be said that the enactment of PACE was intended to strengthen public confidence in the police and offer substantial protection to the suspect.

If the accused does confess in the absence of a solicitor, he may well argue that his solicitor would have advised silence if he had been present. If there is insufficient evidence to convict the solicitor present should advise the suspect to stay silence but this rarely occurs. Circumstances in which silence would be recommended include the case of the solicitor's client is distressed or confused at the time of the interview, or is suggestible, or under pressure from the police. At trial the defence can argue that silence was exercised on the basis of legal advice and that the jury should not draw an adverse inference, as the defendant was just following his solicitor's advice. If the silence is chosen on legal advice adverse inference should not be drawn from it.

In *R v Condron*, it was held that the giving of legal advice to remain silent did not of itself preclude the drawing of inferences. Other relevant authorities, such as *R v Hoare* and *R v Beckles* have confirmed that the genuine reliance by a defendant on his solicitor's advice to remain silent is not in itself enough to preclude adverse comment.

Considering the vulnerability of the suspect during questioning, the importance of access to legal advice and of the right to silence is clear. If the defendant is in alien surroundings and is subject to interrogation by experienced interrogators, then there is tremendous pressure on him to speak.

9.4. Derogation of the Right to Silence by the Serious Fraud Office and the BERR

The practical reality of modern UK law is that the right to silence is severely restricted by statutory and common-law exceptions as in Section 2 of the 1987 Criminal Justice Act. Statistics show that even where the right to silence does apply, it is rarely invoked. In 1992, in the case *R v Smith [1992] 95 Cr App R 191,* Lord Mustill said:

> "This expression (the right to silence) arouses strong but unfocused feelings. In truth, it does not denote any single right, but rather refers to a disparate group of immunities, which differ in nature, origin, incidence and importance, and also to the extent to which they have been encroached upon by statute."

Under various modern statutes, there is a duty to disclose information to the Inland Revenue, HM Customs and Excise and to a variety of inspectors who can compel answers on pain of contempt of court. In a Serious Fraud Office inquiry, the duty to answer questions may continue even when criminal proceedings have been commenced and until verdict. The ordinary requirement for a caution is over-ruled by the Criminal Justice Act 1987.

> **Caselaw**
>
> In *Kansal v UK* [2004], the ECHR found that the use at a subsequent trial of answers given under compulsion of the Official Receiver breached the fair trial provisions of the European Convention on Human Rights even though the trial took place before that Convention was incorporated into English law by the Human Rights Act 1998. Yash Pal Kansal ran a company which operated a chain of chemist shops. He went into receivership in 1988. He was subsequently charged with two offences of obtaining property by deception and at this trial, two transcripts were placed before the jury, transcripts of compulsory interviews with the Official Receiver. The House of Lords ruled that this was not against his human rights as the Human Rights Act 1998 could not be applied retrospectively and the case went to the ECHR where it was judged that there was an alleged violation of Article 6 because there had been an infringement of the right not to incriminate oneself and that the applicant had been deprived of a fair hearing. (The material at issue could have been obtained by the police within the intelligence process).

The right to silence or against self-incrimination is not the same as the right to be presumed innocent but both fall within the concept of the right to a fair trial. The principle of the presumption of innocence is that a person must not be convicted where there is reasonable doubt that he may not be guilty and tries to eliminate the risk of conviction based on factual error. The principle underlying the right to remain silent is of historical origin.

9.4.1. Legal Privilege

Many of the communications between the solicitor and the expert witness will be privileged. They are protected by legal professional privilege. They cannot be communicated to the court except with the consent of the party concerned. That means that a great deal of the communications between the expert witness and the lawyer cannot be given in evidence to the court. If questions were asked about it, then it would be the duty of the judge to protect the witness (and he would) by disallowing any questions which infringed the rule about legal professional privilege or the rule protecting information given in confidence, unless, of course, it was one of those rare cases which come before the courts from time to time where in spite of privilege or confidence the court does order a witness to give further evidence.

Subject to that qualification, it seems that an expert witness falls into the same position as a witness of fact. The court is entitled, in order to ascertain the truth, to have the actual facts which he has observed adduced before it and to have his independent opinion on those facts.

9.4.2. Legal Privilege in Documents

In 2006, the High Court held that legal advice privilege protects confidential communications passing between lawyers and clients, but does not protect preparatory materials, even if they are created for the purpose of enabling lawyers to advise. Such materials are protected only if they are subject to litigation privilege - that is, if the documents were created for the dominant purpose of gathering evidence to use in pending or contemplated legal proceedings or for giving legal advice in relation to such proceedings. If litigation is not pending or contemplated, preparatory materials will not be privileged and may need to be disclosed in subsequent litigation.

> ### Caselaw
>
> In *National Westminster Plc v Rabobank Nederland* [2006] EWHC 2332 (Comm) the court was asked to consider whether the defendant could claim privilege over two categories of document. The documents in question were: (i) two documents which were communications through the defendant's audit department, which had been disclosed in error and which the defendant sought to recover; and (ii) documents produced during the defendant's initial investigation into the events at the centre of the litigation. The judge confirmed the state of the law following *Three Rivers District Council v Bank of England* (No 5) [2003] QB 1556 and (No 6) [2005] 1 AC 610, in which it was held that legal advice privilege could be claimed only for confidential documents passing between the client and its legal advisers for the purpose of giving or obtaining legal advice or assistance. He therefore found that such privilege does not apply to the "sort of preparatory work which does not constitute communications between lawyer and client". The first category of document, in respect of which communication was through the defendant's audit department, could not be subject to legal advice privilege. Legal advice privilege does not extend beyond communications between lawyer and client. He also rejected the submission that the relevant individual from the audit department had been acting as the agent for the lawyers in collecting information, and that the individual was part of the "stream of information" between the lawyers and the client.

Preparatory documents which do not form communications (or draft communications) between lawyer and client are not protected by legal advice privilege, even if they were prepared for the purpose of taking legal advice.

Privileged documents are:

(i) Documents which will incriminate a party if they are disclosed and

(ii) those protected on the grounds of public policy, for example, documents the disclosure of which would be injurious to the public interest such as some government papers and diplomatic papers. This privilege arises where withholding disclosure or inspection of the documents concerned is necessary for the public functioning of the public service. In every case, the public interest in withholding disclosure or inspection should be balanced against the public interest in the administration of justice not being frustrated. In such a case, the privilege is not one that can be waived by a party and if necessary, the judge would insist that the document is not produced. In some cases, the privilege may require that the existence of the document should not be disclosed.

(iii) Public Interest Immunity is a third type of privileged documents.

The privilege may merely require that the documents be withheld from inspection. This privilege is known as Public Interest Immunity. A claim for Public Interest Immunity is usually made by a certificate or witness statement put forward by the political head of the public authority concerned, although the decision as to whether or not to uphold a Public Interest Immunity claim is for the court.

9.4.3.1. Legal Professional Privilege documents

These are classed as privileged whether or not litigation is pending. Communications between a party and his legal advisors are not to be disclosed when they are for the purpose of obtaining legal advice. This same privilege applies to communications between a solicitor employed by a party and the party itself and instructions to counsel. An example of this is the case of *R v Manchester Crown Co*urt. If substantial harm would be caused by disclosure, disclosure would not be allowed as in the case of *R v Chief Constable of West Midlands Police, ex parte Wiley.*

Such documents are privileged only when litigation is contemplated or pending. All communications between a party's lawyers and a third party, which came into existence with a view to litigation (even if that litigation has not yet been commenced), are privileged. The correspondence between a solicitor and an expert witness who has an advisory capacity, are privileged, as are "expert reports" obtained for this purpose. Such communications between the party itself and a third party, including another expert witness, are also privileged. The general rule is that where the dominant purpose of a document was to obtain assistance for a prospective legal action, the document will be privileged. Other privileged documents are "without prejudice" communications, the purpose of which documents is to enable the parties to negotiate without the risk that their proposals will weigh against them if negotiations fail.

Accordingly, letters offering settlement, or even suggested negotiations, are not to be disclosed, and if the negotiations result in a binding agreement between the parties, then the parties must rely on the documents concerned as evidence of the settlement.

However, if the document merely states "without prejudice" and it is not about settlement, then it is not privileged, notwithstanding it contains the words "without prejudice". The privilege of "without prejudice" documents can be waived but it must be waived by both parties to the negotiations. The principle behind legal professional privilege is the importance of a party of being able to consult its lawyers in confidence and in the knowledge that whatever a party tells its lawyers will not be revealed without its consent. Legal Professional Privilege can be over-ridden if a document came into existence in pursuance of fraud or crime.

In addition, if a privileged communication is in itself a material fact in proceedings, it will not be privileged. If privilege is waived by a party, then it is also lost, but the privilege is that of the party and not that of his legal advisor so that privilege can only be waived by the party itself.

Caselaw

R v (1) Chesterfield Justices (2) Chief Constable of Derbyshire, ex parte Bramley [1999] unreported

A search warrant could not be issued if there were reasonable grounds for believing that the material sought included items subject to legal professional privilege. Application was dismissed. The application was for judicial review of a decision of magistrates' sitting at Chesterfield on 7 January 1999 to issue search warrants in respect of two premises pursuant to s.26 Theft Act 1968. The police officers, purportedly acting in accordance with the warrants, seized documents subject to legal professional privilege. It was conceded before the hearing that the warrants should not have been issued because it had been made clear to the magistrates that the police had not been looking for stolen goods but were looking for documents as part of an investigation into an alleged fraud. It was also conceded that, the warrants having been obtained on an inappropriate basis, the searches and seizures were unlawful. A settlement had been agreed as to damages and the documents recovered. The applicant still sought a declaration that the entry, search and seizure

by the police officers at the two premises was unlawful. It was contended on behalf of the Chief Constable that if the warrants had been presented to the magistrates in the proper form, under s 8(1) Police and Criminal Evidence Act 1984 ('PACE'), the warrants would still have been issued and executed in the same way. The issue for the instant court was what in law and what in practice should be done where any question arose as to whether documents or information were truly subject to legal professional privilege. The court decided that if a constable making an application for a warrant did not volunteer information regarding legal privilege then the magistrate had to enquire if the material sought was subject to legal professional privilege. A warrant could not be issued if there were reasonable grounds for believing that the material sought included items subject to legal professional privilege. The criteria set out in
s 8 (1) PACE was directed to the state of mind of the magistrate when being asked to issue a warrant. The police officer was not required to be satisfied that there were reasonable grounds for believing that the material sought did not consist of or include items subject to legal professional privilege. A police officer, in executing a warrant must know its purpose and must not go further than that which was necessary to achieve that purpose, but he was not required to adopt a tunnel vision. An officer could not seize items subject to legal privilege, but only if he first had reasonable grounds for believing that the item in question was subject to legal privilege. Whether or not the constable had such grounds at the time of seizure was a question of fact to be decided in the context of any given case. A constable who had seized items under s. 8(2) PACE, which were later found to be outside the scope of the warrant and not covered by s.19 PACE, had no defence to an action for trespass to goods based on unjustified seizure. In order to defend the right to privacy the words of the statute should be strictly applied to.

9.4.3.2. Police Special Procedure Material

Material that is necessary to a case can be gained by a method the police call 'Special Procedure' by applying for a search warrant or a production order under Schedule 1 Police and Criminal Evidence Act 1984 and section 14 PACE describes what special procedure material is.

Special procedure material cannot include legal privilege material. If officers, using a search warrant, seize materials to be sifted at another location, any legal privilege material taken from the site named in the warrant, is not material that the police should have in their possession.

If however, legal privileged material is held in a computer on which are other documents for which a search warrant has been obtained, that computer can still be lawfully seized.

> **Caselaw - *R v Commissioners of Inland Revenue, ex parte H* [2002] EWHC 2164 (Admin).**
>
> A claim against HMRC was dismissed because the court decided that an Inland Revenue officer entering premises under the authority of a warrant issued pursuant to s.20C Taxes Management Act, found a computer, and had reasonable cause to believe that the data on that computer's hard disk might be required as evidence for the purpose of relevant proceedings. He was therefore entitled to seize and remove the computer even though it might contain irrelevant, non-incriminating material. The facts were that on 16 August 2001 the officers went to H's home in order to execute the warrant. H and his family were abroad. The officers made contact with H's father-on-law ('P'), who had the keys to H's house. P read the warrant and allowed the officers in. The officers seized and removed two computers for the purpose of imaging their hard disks. P signed an

> agreement authorising the imaging of the hard disks away from the house. Later that morning, H spoke to one of the officers on the telephone, in circumstances in which it was now alleged that he had ratified the imaging away from the house. By this application H contended that: (i) the officers, absent his agreement, were not authorised by s.20 TMA to copy the entirety of the hard disk in circumstances where, as was conceded to be the case here, the hard disks contained information that was irrelevant to any proceedings that might be being contemplated against H; (ii) P did not have H's authority to sign any agreement; (iii) H had not ratified or approved that agreement; (iv) in any event, the agreement was signed by P in circumstances where full and frank disclosure of its terms and effect had not been made; and (v) it was expressly provided by the agreement that the removal and imaging of the computer was not a search and removal for the purposes of s.20C(3) TMA.

9.5. 1. Confidentiality of Suspicious Activity Reports (SARS) and their makers' identity

The failure of the common law to recognise a right to privacy meant that the most important remedy people have against unlawful police surveillance is an action for breach of confidentiality which is why there is clear guidance on confidentiality as regards the Proceeds of Crimes Act 2002. The Proceeds of Crime Act 2002 requires banks and other businesses in the regulated sector to report knowledge or suspicion of money laundering to SOCA. These reports are commonly known as Suspicious Activity Reports (SARs).

Disclosure of SARs in certain circumstances might cause a real risk of serious prejudice to an important public interest.

Where disclosure is likely to be ordered in such a case, the prosecution has to carefully weigh the options as to whether it should proceed with the prosecution or withdraw proceedings. The personal safety of the reporter, and the interests of the disclosing institution, should disclosure become necessary, will be among a number of considerations taken into account on a case by case basis, but depending upon the circumstances of the case, may not be sufficient to prevent disclosure of the reporter's identity. Standard procedure to be followed by the police, other law enforcement agencies (LEAs) and the Serious Organised Crimes Agency(SOCA) in relation to the disclosure under the Criminal Procedure and Investigations Act 1996 (CPIA) of SARs, is as follows:-

The staged process should be for each item of unused material- Is it 'relevant'? Is it potentially 'sensitive' or non-sensitive? Does the 'disclosure test' apply? Is a 'PII application' necessary? (Chapter 13 tells how this fits into police fraud investigation management).

9.5.2. Relevant material

Under the statutory CPIA Code of Practice investigators must retain material which they obtain in the course of a criminal investigation and which may be relevant to the investigation. The content of the SAR will frequently be relevant to an investigation. Retained material which may be relevant to an investigation must be revealed to the prosecutor on a schedule of non-sensitive or sensitive material. The schedule of non-sensitive material will also be revealed to the defence.

9.5.3. Potentially sensitive material

Under paragraph 6.12 of the CPIA Code of Practice, in order to be 'sensitive', an item of unused material must pose a 'real risk of serious prejudice to an important public interest'. The risk must be real, not fanciful, and any consequent prejudice, serious. Examples of sensitive material may include, depending on the circumstances, material given in confidence. Whilst the SAR regime in itself is in the public domain, individual SARs are given in confidence on the grounds that, for example, in certain instances criminal offences attach to "tipping off" third parties as to their existence or contents.

Another example of material which may be sensitive is material relating to identity of persons supplying information to the police who may be in danger if their identities are revealed. Any specific item listed on either schedule can only be disclosed to the defence if it meets the disclosure test: 'there is something that might reasonably be considered capable of undermining the prosecution case against the accused or of assisting the case for him'. This means that items meeting the 'sensitive' test, but not meeting the 'disclosure' test; remain hidden and undisclosed to the defence. Items meeting the disclosure test will need a PII hearing.

PII Applications: The House of Lords judgement in the case of H&C, in February 2004, gives helpful guidance on potential PII applications and must be read and understood by all of those involved in the criminal prosecution process.

There is no duty to disclose material that is neutral or that is damaging to the defendant: *'if material does not weaken the prosecution case or strengthen that of the defendant there is no requirement to disclose it'*. In the majority of cases involving suspicious financial activity the relevant material (such as a bank statement) is adduced in evidence as a result of production orders. Any underlying SAR may tend to strengthen the prosecution case or be neutral, in which case there is no requirement to disclose it. It should not be assumed, however, that documents that indicate some suspicion can only damage a defendant's case, as the basis for suspicion could in some circumstances assist a defendant's case. SARs that are inconsistent with the subsequent evidence uncovered may well assist the defence. Note that PII not always necessary. It may be possible to disclose the SAR in a redacted form or by admissions (and thereby avoid the need for a PII application.) Each one will need to be considered on its own facts and checked carefully against the subsequent evidence. Therefore, where a SAR is regarded by an investigator as relevant to an investigation, the disclosure officer should consider, on a case by case basis, whether the SAR (or parts) is (are) sensitive (in the sense that its disclosure would give rise to a real risk of serious prejudice to an important public interest) and whether, accordingly, it should only be revealed to the prosecutor on a schedule of sensitive material. Careful consideration must also be given to disclosing items meeting the disclosure test: whether it (or parts) undermine(s) the prosecution case or assists the accused. In rare cases a PII application may be necessary.

9.6.1. Other legal developments- human rights issues

In most fraud cases with human rights issues, the issues are of fair trial, due process, and evidence obtained unfairly. In undercover operations care must be taken with regard to conversations with suspected offenders and there can be a fine line between conversation for the purpose of maintaining an undercover operation and questioning that will constitute an interview. One single question put to a suspected offender by an undercover investigator constitutes an interview (*R v Bryce*) and courts may exclude such evidence by undercover techniques when the accused's right to a fair trial is adversely affected. Recent developments are in the caselaw *R v Davis*,

Ellis, Gregory, Simms and Martin [2006] EWCA Crim. 19 May 2006 (anonymous witnesses do not necessarily lead to breach of Article 6); *Van Colle v Chief Constable Hertfordshire Constabulary* [2006] EWHC 360 (QB) (responsibility to protect prosecution witnesses from intimidation: Articles 2 and 8 engaged); and *R v Doherty* [2006] EWCA Crim. (25 October 2006) (intimidation of witness by D).

As to the use of informers, it is wise to remember the case of *R v Loosley, Attorney General's Reference No.3* [2002], a case of corruption of police dealing with informers, which states at para.60, *"controlled informers to undertake entrapment activities unsupervised carries great danger, not merely that they will try to improve their performances in court, but of oppression, extortion and corruption."*. Similar cases are *R v Dryden* [1995] All ER, *R v Bellman* [1989] and *Tsang Ping-nam v R* [1981] 1 WLR 1462.

9.6.2. Other legal developments- Abuse of Process allegations

At times, allegations have been made that there was improper consideration of criteria for prosecution. The case of *R v Adaway* [204] EWCA Crim 2831 was such a case and the Court of Appeal decided, in very strong terms, that a prosecution brought by a local authority, following a complaint to the Trading Standards Office, was oppressive and should not have been brought because it was an abuse of process to do so as it was clear that there was no evidence capable of meeting the authority's own prosecuting policy criteria. The Court of Appeal said:

> "*We have no information as to how much these proceedings have cost this local authority. We suspect that it must be many thousands of pounds. We cannot emphasize too*

> *strongly that before criminal proceedings are instituted by a local authority, acting in relation to a strict liability offence created by the Trade Descriptions Act 1968, they must consider with care the terms of their own prosecuting policy. If they fail to do so, or if they reach a conclusion which is wholly unsupported, as the conclusion to prosecute in this case was, by material establishing the criteria for prosecution, it is unlikely that the courts will be sympathetic, in the face of the other demands upon their time at Crown Court and at appellate level, to attempts to justify such prosecution*".

This is by no means an isolated case of manipulation or misuse of prosecution. There is the famous case from Stafford police who took a case to the House of Lords after they had prosecuted an Indian man for not wearing a seatbelt. Stafford police are in the league table as top of the police authorities where institutional racism still. exists. A similar case is *Abdul Ghafar v Chief Constable of West Midlands Police* [2000] C.A. 12th May 2000, in which the Indian man was awarded damages for wrongful imprisonment and the case was taken to the Court of Appeal.

9.6.3. Perjury by prosecution witnesses

Whether a case could be struck of as an abuse of process pending a summons against a prosecution witness for perjury is still unsettled. The case of *R v Newcastle –upon-Tyne Magistrates' Court, ex parte Still*, in 1996 is one case that raised this issue. In court, Justice Laws said:

> *"I understand that there is no authority directly upon the question whether the issue and maintenance of summonses charging perjury pending the trial of a criminal prosecution in which those receiving the summonses may be called to*

give evidence may constitute an abuse of the process of the court. It is enough for my purposes to consider the matter in relation only to the facts of the present case. It seems to me that few things could be more calculated to distort the process of Mr. Hedworth's trial than what has occurred here. These witnesses will go to the Crown Court with the threat of the summonses over their head…".

9.6.4. Adverse publicity can lead to a case being quashed as an abuse of process

The defence may apply to the courts for a stay of proceedings on the ground of abuse of process founded on prejudicial media publicity. There have been cases of the police tipping off of the media that a raid is to take place at a certain address and the newspapers splashing the incident on their front pages the following day. This can quash a case under the abuse of process doctrine. The courts to date advise the jury to disregard such publicity but this is no certain measure that an abuse of process will not be pleaded by the defendant or that the case will not go to the European Court of Human Rights.

> **Caselaw**
>
> ***Re Barot* [2007] Crim LR 741 : (2008) 1 Cr App R (S) 31 : Times, May 23, 2007**
> In keeping with the defendant's right to a fair trial, the lower court judge told the jury to disregard all newspaper publicity. This was upheld by the Court of Appeal and in their dicta, stated that newspaper editors and broadcasters should be trusted to fulfil their responsibilities under the strict liability rule and exercise "sensible judgment" about the publication of material that may interfere with the administration of justice. The media must also ensure

> that reporting does not constitute "serious misconduct" under the Costs in Criminal Cases (General) (Amendment) Regulations 2004, or else risk being ordered to pay substantial wasted costs if a trial has to be aborted or moved.
>
> Section 4(2) of the Contempt of Court Act 1981 states that a court may, where it appears necessary for avoiding a substantial risk of prejudice to the administration of justice in those proceedings (or in any other proceedings pending or imminent) order that the publication of any report of the proceedings, or any part of the *proceedings*, be postponed for such period as the court thinks necessary.

9.7. Police Conduct

To avoid cases being quashed and complaints and cases being brought against police with regard to their investigation of fraud cases, it is useful to remember that officers should support their colleagues in the execution of their lawful duties, and oppose any improper behaviour, reporting it where appropriate. Management of fraud investigations must comply with general police conduct which is regulated by the Police Act 1996, the Police Act 1997, the Police Reform Act 2002 and the Police and Justice Act 2006. Illegal police conduct can lead to suspension of the officer and this is regulated by the Police (Conduct) Regulations 2004.

Neither must officers consider unauthorized access to the Police National Computer or unauthorized modification of computer material as these are serious offences, both with six months imprisonment and/or fine. The offence of unauthorized modification of computer material covers a whole range of behaviour. It is not a widely known fact that the Data Protection Act (DPA) 1998 applies to the Police

National Computer and the DPA combined with Article 8 and Article 10 of the European Human Rights Convention has been seen to represent what is in fact a law of privacy, previously unrecognized in English law. Data held on police computers about suspected and convicted offenders is personal data as per the DPA. Similar paper records and personal data held on the PNC is personal data as per the DPA(see *R v Rees* [2000] LTL 20 October). Unauthorised disclosure carries a five year prison sentence.

9.8. The Regulation of Investigatory Powers Act 2000

The Act addresses the interception of communications and the covert acquisition of information about people. This ensures that activities of public authorities are subjected to a robust statutory framework which allows for proper independent control and monitoring. The main purpose of the Act is to control the use of surveillance and Covert Human Intelligence Sources operations by public authorities.

Police breach of this Act may exclude from trial any evidence gathered in breach of the Act; will give rise to a Police Conduct investigation and a damages claim by the person so intruded before the Investigatory Powers Tribunal. The Criminal Evidence (Witness Anonymity) Act 2008, is an Act to make provision for the making of orders for securing the anonymity of witnesses in criminal proceedings gained Royal Assent in July 2008. The Act creates a Witness Anonymity Order,

> *"A "witness anonymity order" is an order made by a court that requires such specified measures to be taken in relation to a witness in criminal proceedings as the court considers appropriate to ensure that the identity of the witness is not disclosed in or in connection with the proceedings. The*

kinds of measures that may be required to be taken in relation to a witness include measures for securing one or more of the following—

(a) that the witness's name and other identifying details may be—
- *(i) withheld;*
- *(ii) removed from materials disclosed to any party to the proceedings;*

(b) that the witness may use a pseudonym;
(c) that the witness is not asked questions of any specified description that might lead to the identification of the witness;
(d) that the witness is screened to any specified extent;
(e) that the witness's voice is subjected to modulation to any specified extent".

This Act follows the House of Lords judgment in *R v Davis* [2008] UKHL 36 handed down on 18 June 2008. This appeal concerned the use of anonymous witness evidence at trial, which is governed by the common law. The effect of the judgment is to restrict the courts' ability at common law to allow evidence to be given anonymously during criminal trials.

9.9. Police Powers

A development in relation to police powers is caselaw *Keegan v United Kingdom European Court of Human Rights*, 18 July 2006 (Strasbourg guidance on the search power: the importance of proportionality). Human rights principles are to be found in the Human Rights Act and are relevant to the delivery of public services. These principles comprise being treated with dignity and respect, fairness and involvement in personal decision-making, non-discrimination (in relation to other Convention rights), confidentiality of written and verbal communication, freedom of thought, conscience and religion and right to respect for one's private and family life and right to life.

Unlawfully obtained evidence, be it oral or in the form of a document, is an issue of fair trial.

9.9. Conclusion to Chapter Nine

The above are some of the current issues in the criminal prosecution of fraud. There are other issues such as the right to information, and police powers of entry and there will continue to be issues as the crime and prosecution of fraud becomes more sophisticated.

Further reading for Chapter Nine

A.L.T. Choo, *Abuse of process and judicial stays of criminal procedures*, OUP, Oxford 2008)

E. King, "Criminal law - financial regulation – fraud", New Law Journal N.L.J. (2008) Vol.158 No.7333 Pages 1128-1129

A. Reyes, *Cyber Crime Investigations: Bridging the Gaps Between Security Professionals, Law Enforcement, and Prosecutors* (Syngress Publishing, Massachusetts 2007).

P. Smith, *Punishment and Culture* (University of Chicago Press, US 2008).

E. Wilding, *Information Risk and Security: Preventing and Investigating Workplace Computer Crime*, (Gower, Aldershot 2006).

CHAPTER 10- INVESTIGATING AND PROSECUTING AUTHORITIES

10.1. Authorities that investigate and prosecute fraud

The United Kingdom has designated a number of competent authorities to investigate and prosecute fraud. Investigation and prosecution agencies include the following agencies responsible for the stated jurisdictions:

Area of the UK	Investigation & Prosecution Agencies
UK, being England, Wales and Northern Ireland as per the Interpretation Act	Serious Organised Crimes Agency Her Majesty's Revenue and Customs Serious Fraud Office Financial Services Authority Office of Fair Trading Department for Business, Enterprise & Regulatory Reform (BERR)
England and Wales	Crown Prosecution Service Revenue and Customs Prosecution Office
England and Wales	43 Regional Police Forces
Northern Ireland	Public Prosecution Service of Northern Ireland
Northern Ireland	1 Regional Police Force

Scotland	Crown Office and Procurator Fiscal Services
	Scottish Crime and Drug Enforcement Agency
Scotland	8 Regional Police Forces

10.2. Reasons for high risk of fraud in the UK

Because the UK is a major international centre for investment and private banking and has one of the largest commercial banking sectors in the world, it is at high risk of financial fraud. The UK insurance industry is the largest in Europe and third largest in the world. The UK is also one of the largest fund management markets in the world. The UK has a strong international orientation and attracts significant overseas funds .This includes international private wealth management, hedge funds and private equity. It must be remembered that the vast majority of business and financial dealings are undertaken honestly. It is only in a comparatively small number of instances that serious fraud occurs but when it does it can have serious effects to business confidence.

This is good reason for the specialist government agencies that investigate and prosecute the many types of fraud to be found in the UK markets. This chapter will explain how some of these agencies operate and how and when the Police take part in the various types of fraud investigations.

10.3.1. The Serious Fraud Office (SFO)

The UK has a specialist organisation for the investigation and prosecution of serious fraud. It is the Serious Fraud Office. The Serious Fraud Office (SFO) came into being on 6th April 1988. Before the SFO, many complex frauds were left uninvestigated and so were not prosecuted. The 1986 Fraud Trials Committee Report (the Roskill Report) had found that that the system for bringing frauds to trial was poor. The Report recommended that there should be an independent monitoring body (A Fraud Commission) to be responsible for studying the efficiency with which the fraud cases are conducted which should make an annual report. The Roskill Report recommended that the judge in a serious fraud trial should have power to order that a deposition be admissible in evidence at the trial where the witness is unavailable and this now occurs in certain cases.

The 1986 Roskill Report's recommendation to replace trial by jury in cases of complex fraud took the form of a 2007 Parliamentary Bill but was unsuccessful. The Roskill Report recommended that the prosecution or the defence should be entitled to apply to a High Court Judge if the case falls within the Guidelines for such a trial and that the defence should not be able to appeal against any subsequent conviction on the ground that the wrong tribunal was used.

Since 2008 the SFO is advocating and implementing a new plea-negotiation following the United States system. The SFO now sub-contracts its expertise to other countries in order to develop their law enforcement. The modern attitude of the SFO is that prevention of serious fraud is better than prosecution of serious fraud and to this effect; the SFO is in the course of developing such a framework. As from June 2008, the SFO is working with educationists and corporations to educate to prevent fraud. Fair resolution of fraud offences is in the public interest.

> **Point to Note: The Public Interest Test**
>
> The CPS and the Police have a Code which requires that the prosecution must ensure that fair and consistent decisions are made about commencing and continuing with a prosecution be in the public interest. Section 5.9 of the Code for the CPS identifies some common public interest factors in favour of the prosecution. These pubic interest factors include:
>
> (i) a conviction likely to result in a significant sentence;
> (ii) the offence was committed against a person serving the public;
> (iii) the defendant was in a position f authority or trust;
> (iv) there is evidence that the offence was pre-meditated.

Multi-national companies, wise to the implications of fraud prosecution are looking at which country they can be prosecuted in. Should a multi-national company be expected to be investigated by a leading jurisdiction such as the US FBI or the SFO, or by many different jurisdictions? In such circumstances, plea-negotiation is the best way of resolving the issues. To this effect, the EU is considering the creation of an EU Jurisdiction body which will decide which jurisdiction will take the lead in a fraud investigation.

> **Point to Note: Fraud (Trials without a Jury) Bill 2007**
>
> The Bill was intended to enable the Government to implement section 43 of the *Criminal Justice Act 2003*, which would allow cases involving serious and complex fraud to be tried by a judge acting alone without a jury in certain circumstances. The Bill sought to amend section 43 to require an application for a non-jury trial and any trial resulting from such an application to be heard by a High Court judge. The failed Bill was extended to England and Wales and Northern Ireland.

10.3.2. Criteria for SFO cases

The criteria for a case to be taken by the SFO are as follows:-

1. Cases where the monies at risk are at least £1 million, although the SFO does still investigate cases of less value if they are in the public interest. The Davie Report, appraising the SFO seven year performances to 1995, stated that this factor is simply an objective and recognisable signpost of seriousness and likely public concern, rather than the main indicator of suitability.

2. Cases likely to give rise to national publicity and widespread public concern and cases requiring highly specialised knowledge of stock exchange practices or regulated markets.

3. Cases with an international dimension and cases where legal, accountancy and investigative skills need to be brought together.

4. Cases which are complex and in which the use of 'Section 2, Criminal Justice Act 1987' powers may be appropriate.

10.3.3. The Police and the SFO

The SFO conducts its investigations in conjunction with the Police. The Police have its own constitutional structure, command structure and accountability to their own Chief Police Officers. But they are also full members of the integrated multi-disciplinary SFO investigating teams.

Police skills compliment those of the SFO lawyers, accountants, financial investigators and other specialists. Since 1996, there has been in place a formal Memorandum of Understanding between the SFO and Police Forces. The SFO also works alongside government departments, regulators, the Crown Prosecution Service and foreign authorities, depending on the case in hand.

10.3.4. When a case is referred to the Serious Fraud Office

When a case is referred to the SFO, due consideration is given to the role of the regulatory authorities, the FSA, the OFT, the BERR. If the Director of the SFO decides that the Public Interest is better served by appropriate action taken by the regulators, the case may then be referred to them. During the course of, and at the end of the case, conduct which is not criminal but nevertheless casts doubt on the fitness of an individual or corporation to act in financial matters may be referred to the relevant regulatory body. Borderline conduct will also be referred. The SFO has an armoury of legislation with which to investigate and prosecute serious fraud including the European Arrest Warrant, Extradition laws, the and Criminal

Justice Act 1987- Section 2 Notices and it will soon have soon the European Evidence Warrant.

10.3.5. The powers of the 1987 Criminal Justice Act

Section 2 of the Criminal Justice Act 1987 contains provisions where, not police, but lawyers and accountants in the SFO question suspects after giving written notice that they must answer questions about an investigation at a specified time and place or immediately.

This power to question is a delegated power from the Director of the Serious Fraud Office. In serious fraud cases, the directors of companies, solicitors, and accountants must answer section 2 Notices. Section 2 Notices can be used to question solicitors about their clients. Without a Section 2 Notice, a solicitor who so cooperates would be in breach of client confidentiality. Section 2 of the Criminal Justice Act 1987 gives the Director of the SFO powers to require individuals to furnish information, answer questions and produce documents.

The powers conferred by Section 2 can only be used for the purposes of an investigation by the SFO or a request made by the Attorney General of the Isle of Man, Jersey or Guernsey. It is a criminal offence to fail without reasonable excuse to comply with a notice under Section 2 or to make a statement which is false or misleading.

> **Caselaw**
>
> *R v Michael Ward* [1996] Unreported
> Michael Ward, former Chairman and CEO of European Leisure plc, was convicted of causing the falsification of a document and making a false statement contrary to Section 2 Criminal Justice Act 1987. This conviction followed an earlier Office of Fair Trading investigation which led to three men's convictions for conspiracy to defraud.

Where the section 2 Notice is directed at a person under investigation, an answer given to SFO investigators may not be given in evidence against that person at subsequent criminal proceedings unless that information given was false or inconsistent. Section 2(2) CJA 1987 is used by lawyers and accountants of the SFO to question individuals.

Section 2(3) gives these lawyers and accountants the power to requisition documents. Sections 2 (4) to 2(7) gives the Director of the SFO powers of search and seizure and he can sub-contract this power to a firm of accountants. Section 2 (11) allows the Director of the SFO to sub-contract this power to a competent investigator, other than a constable.

Section 2A was added to the CJA 1987 (by the recent Criminal Justice and Immigration Act 2008) and allows the Director of the SFO to use the section 2 powers set out 'for the purpose of enabling him to determine whether to start an investigation. Section 2A was brought into force in July 2008. It should be noted that it represents an extension to the SFO's powers in cases of suspected corruption in that the section 2 powers are now available before an investigation has been formally opened, whereas in relation to cases of other serious fraud section 2 powers may only be used after the

Director has concluded that 'the affairs of any person' should be investigated.

> ### Caselaw
>
> *Re Arrows (no.4)* 1994] 3 All ER 814.
>
> The liquidators refused to hand over to the SFO their transcript of an insolvency investigation but the House of Lords decided that a criminal court judge and not the Companies Court Judge has the right to decide on a Section 2 request *Re Arrows (no.4)* 1994] 3 All ER 814.
>
> The issue that the House of Lords had to decide was whether the liquidators on receipt of a Section 2 Notice should be required to supply to the SFO copies of the transcript of an examination conducted by them under S 236(1) (a) Insolvency Act of a director of Arrows charged with various offences. The HL held that if a Court directs that its officers shall not produce documents, this must provide a reasonable excuse to those officers for failure to do so, but it was an improper exercise of the discretion of the Companies Court judge as this was a matter for a criminal court judge to decide on, under S78 PACE, to exclude any evidence which would have such an adverse effect on the fairness of the proceedings that the Court ought not to admit it.

10.3.6. Mutual Assistance in cross- border frauds

The 1959 European Convention on Mutual Assistance in Criminal Matters ensures that countries afford to each other the widest measure of mutual assistance in proceedings in respect of offences, the punishment of which, at the time of the request for assistance, falls within the jurisdiction of the judicial authorities of the requesting country.

10.3.7. Reservations to the Convention on Mutual Assistance in Criminal Matters

The UK has made some reservations to the Convention on Mutual Assistance in Criminal Matters. These are:-

1. The reservation of the right to refuse to assist if the person concerned has already been convicted or acquitted of an offence based on the relevant conduct in the United Kingdom or in a third State.

2. The right not to take evidence or gather other material in the face of a privilege and absence of compellability; or if it is against the public interest; if it affects the Crown; if it affects the country's security; if it affects UK public order; or in the case of double jeopardy.

> **Point to Note**
>
> The Double Jeopardy Rule has been quashed in the Criminal Justice Act 2003(s 36(3)A of the Criminal Justice Act 1988, as inserted by the Criminal Justice Act 2003). The legal principle which prevents people being tried for the same crime twice, the double jeopardy rule, has been scrapped in England and Wales . The Court of Appeal can now quash an acquittal and order a retrial when "new and compelling" evidence is produced. The ban on "double jeopardy", which has existed for around 800 years, took effect in March 2005

10.3.8. Freezing the suspected proceeds of crime

The UK Crime (International Co-operation) Act 2003 allows overseas freezing orders to be given effect regardless of the nature of the authority making the order in a participating country. This is more useful than the instrument previously used, Clause 19 of the Mutual Assistance Convention, which allowed for seizure of evidence only if a court or authority makes the request for assistance.

Part I of the 2003 Act deals with Mutual Legal Assistance generally and with freezing orders in relation to property and evidence. The Act extends the range of circumstances in which mutual assistance may be requested and makes such assistance quicker, more flexible, and more effective. The provisions apply to relations among EU Member States, with respect to both incoming and outgoing requests. Interpol may now make requests for assistance.

Section 14 of the Crime (International Co-operation) Act 2003 enables the territorial authority, (i.e. the Lord Advocate), to be able to arrange for evidence to be received in connection with overseas criminal proceedings and administrative proceedings if the territorial authority is satisfied that an offence under the law of the requesting state has been committed or there are reasonable grounds for suspecting the same and proceedings have been instituted in that country or an investigation carried on there.

Section 16 of the Act allows the SFO to apply for and execute a search warrant or a production order in response to an overseas request in identical circumstances as would be possible in relation to a domestic case.

Section 19 states that any evidence seized under section 16 or section 17 is to be sent directly to the overseas authority making the request and not to the central authority. However, if such evidence is seized by a police constable, it is immune from direct transmission.

Section 20 deals with Overseas Freezing Orders (OFO). Such an order must be made by a criminal court or by a prosecuting authority and the OFO must relate to criminal proceedings instituted in a criminal investigation-taking place in the participating country in respect of a listed offence with a prison term of at least 3 years.

Section 31 allows the court to hear witnesses or experts by telephone.

Sections 32 to 46 are particularly relevant to fraud cases. It allows countries in the EU to provide information about bank accounts at the request of other countries. Section 42 deals with unlawful disclosure of information by financial institutions and makes this a criminal offence.

10.3.9. Description of a freezing order

A freezing injunction or order prohibits any dealing with monies held in a bank account. The fact that the dealing is beneficial to all concerned will not stop its being a contempt of court. Freezing injunctions are used in both the criminal and the civil cases. Their purpose is to ensure that a defendant cannot hide his assets with effect of when a judgment is eventually given against him. Before a freezing injunction is applied for, work undertaken will include discrete internal investigations, money laundering enquiries, property and mortgage fraud investigations, asset tracing, and initiatives to tackle intellectual property theft, investigating serious and organised criminal activity and identifying proceeds of crime.

Freezing injunctions try to achieve their aim by prohibiting the defendant from moving his assets. The courts' standard forms provide that he must not "dispose of or deal with or diminish the value of his assets." It is contempt of court for a defendant to ignore the injunction. It is a contempt of court for a third party deliberately to assist the defendant to act in breach of the terms of an injunction.

As a result, if a bank is informed that a freezing injunction has been granted against one of its customers, it must stop all withdrawals from the customer's accounts, except withdrawals expressly allowed by the terms of the injunction. If a bank *negligently* allows the defendant to withdraw funds from his accounts, it will not have any liability, whether in contempt of court or directly to the party that obtained the injunction. If the bank knew of the injunction, and its conduct was deliberate, the bank can be fined and for contempt of court and individuals concerned can be imprisoned.

10.3.11. SFO new strategy of plea bargaining

The SFO has taken the lead of the United States prosecutors and the SFO are now willing to negotiate in order to save time and money. Much of the success of US criminal fraud investigations is a result of the prosecutor's authority to negotiate plea agreements. All defendants may negotiate to exchange their expensive procedural rights and a long prison sentence for the 'certainty and ease of conviction' and a lesser sentence.

Faced with the risk of a long prison sentence, many defendants can trade information for a lesser term because prosecutors have an incentive to forego long prison sentences, using a combination of statutory penalties and Sentencing Guidelines. Prosecutorial power is stringent and most effective in the pre and post trial stages of a criminal matter. Such plea bargaining as is planned by the SFO will move the UK adversarial legal system closer to the European inquisitorial system and will rely more on investigation rather than trial. The investigative European legal system centres on a thorough investigation, on assembling and screening facts.

> **Case Study**
>
> Although sophisticated mechanisms are often used to hide the proceeds of criminal activity, sometimes cash is simply hidden in socks, old handbags, ladies' tights, toilet rolls, ladies' bras and even wigs. In one case, £400,000 was so discovered. In some cases, a covert search is necessary. A covert search of a company's premises over the course of a weekend, including a search of the accounts office and that of the financial controller, uncovered evidence of stolen company funds without arousing the suspect's suspicion and enabled injunctive proceedings to prevent dissipation to be pursued the following day.

10.4.1. How the Financial Services Authority (FSA) investigates and prosecutes fraud

The Financial Services and Markets Act 2000 (FSMA) which created the Financial Services Authority (FSA) also created 36 criminal offences, which the FSA has the responsibility to investigate. The FSMA gives the FSA information gathering powers. Section 165 FSMA enables the FSA to require an authorised person to provide information and documents of a specified description within a specified period of time and at a specified place. Investigators are empowered by sections 167 and 168 of FSMA and authorised persons to be investigated must be notified under section 170. Sections 176 and 177 enable a Magistrate to issue a search warrant. The objective of the FSA regulations is to ensure the efficiency of the financial markets and to maintain and sustain investor confidence in the financial markets.

As a regulator, the FSA has extensive powers. It can, for example, compel information from witnesses (although statements obtained by compulsion cannot be used against their maker).

10.4.2. FSA Objectives

The FSA's Objectives are:

(i) To make financial crime more costly for criminals.

(ii) To deter abuse of the UK financial system.

(iii) To achieve an industry perception of money well spent.

(iv) To raise consumer awareness of financial crime issues.

(v) To contribute to an effective national fight against financial crime.

(vi) To have a balanced approach to money laundering and other fraud.

10.4.3. FSA powers to prosecute

The FSA has power to prosecute a number of offences relating to the conduct of financial services activity.

(a) Offences relating to the conduct of making misleading statements (section 397 Financial Services and Markets Act 2000),

(b) Insider dealing. Apart from the FSMA, the FSA can also use the Criminal Justice Act 1993 to prosecute insider dealing. Insider dealing fraud is especially enabled by information technology and with the expansion of financial trading, both geographically and technologically. Insider dealing is the use of sensitive or privileged information that has not yet been released to the public in order to take advantage of the market. It includes the misuse of information to avoid a loss or to make a profit.

(c) Breaches of regulations relating to money laundering.

> **Point to Note: Who prosecutes insider dealing?**
>
> Apart from the FSA, the Crown Prosecution Service (CPS) and the BERR can also prosecute insider dealing under the Criminal Justice Act 1993, part v, which implements the European Community Directive on insider dealing, Dir 89/592 [1989] OJ L 334/30).

10.4.4. Impact on fraud enforcement of the Regulatory Enforcement & Sanctions Act

The Regulatory Enforcement and Sanctions Act 2008 seeks to implement the recommendations of the 2005 Hampton Report ("Reducing Administrative Burdens: effective inspection and enforcement") and the 2006 Macrory Review ("Regulatory Justice: Making Sanctions Effective"), and is intended to deliver a more effective, risk-based and proportionate enforcement system. It will apply to a broad range of regulators, including the FSA.

10.4.5. Proposed Local Better Regulation Office to deter fraud

Part 1 of the Act establishes the Local Better Regulation Office, the objective of which is to promote better communications between local and national regulators. Part 2 is intended to confer new enforcement powers (an "extended sanctioning toolkit") on regulators in relation to relevant offences, including a wide range of criminal offences.

The following criminal offences now carry sanctions:

(i)   breaches of the general prohibition;

(ii) breaches of the financial promotion restriction and

(iii) breaches of money laundering regulations;

(iv) insider dealing and

(v)   misleading statements and practices.

The new sanctions are intended to reduce the burden on the criminal courts, and will be used in combination with each other and existing sanctions available to regulators.

10.4.6. Powers of FSA extended sanctions toolkit

The FSA has an 'extended sanctioning toolkit' and this includes:

(i)   power to issue fixed monetary penalties;

(ii) power to impose discretionary requirements (for example, variable monetary penalties);

(iii) steps to be taken to ensure that the incident of non-compliance will not continue or recur;

(iv) steps to be taken to restore matters to how they would have been had the non-compliance not occurred); and

(v)   power to issue notices for the cessation of activities which constitute an offence and give rise to a "significant risk of serious harm to human health, the environment or the financial interests of consumers".

The FSA already has the power to accept enforcement undertakings, i.e., promises made by the non-compliant person to the regulator to take specific actions related to the non-compliance. The new and extended powers are intended to provide a quick and cost-effective way for regulators to address non-compliance.

10.4.7. FSA has no power to accept certain enforcement undertakings

The FSA does not have the power to accept enforcement undertakings from non-compliant firms. The FSA may currently only formally request undertakings under the Unfair Terms in Consumer Contracts Regulations 1999. The FSA does not have the power to suspend the activities of approved persons under FSMA.

10.4.8. FSA pursues Insider Dealing Fraud with Police assistance

The FSA, concerned at the failure of the London hedge fund community to stamp out insider trading and other market abuses, plans to provide a template on how to prevent market abuse.

In assessing the priority of FSA requests for assistance in its cases, Police must consider the seriousness of the offences being investigated.

10.4.9. FSA cannot use covert investigation methods of the police

The FSA does not itself have any authority to deploy more covert forms of investigation such as interception of telephones etc, which could make it easier for it to mount proactive investigations. If it wishes to use such powers, it must request assistance from other criminal investigating agencies such as the Police or the Serious and Organised Crime Agency. This is key evidence in prosecuting insider dealing.

> **Point to Note**
>
> The FSA announced in March 2008, that from March 2009, firms will have to record all telephone conversations and electronic communications relating to client orders and the conclusion of transactions in the equity, bond, and derivatives markets.

10.4.10. Sentence for insider dealing conviction

The maximum sentence of imprisonment for insider dealing or other forms of market misconduct in the UK was seven years. Since the Fraud Act 2006, in force since January 2007, this is now a ten year sentence, if indicted as a fraud offence. To date, the longest sentence passed for an insider dealing offence is of four years imprisonment (the case of *Asif Butt*). In the past, the judiciary has not viewed market misconduct offences as particularly serious.

> **Case- law**
>
> Insider dealing landmark case-*R v Asif Butt and others* [2005]
>
> Five men were convicted of conspiracy to insider dealing. They had used illicitly obtained information to win money via spread betting. Asif Butt had abused his position of trust by divulging highly sensitive information and along with four others, had placed bets relating to 19 companies between 1998 and 2002.

10.4.11. FSA prosecutes the fraud of market abuse

The FSA investigates and prosecutes market abuse. It investigates and prosecutes companies whose conduct amounts to market abuse and can impose multi million pound fines on companies. There were major changes in FSA Enforcement in 2007 when they introduced a new Enforcement Handbook, a move towards Principles-based regulation rather than a risk-based regulatory regime.

10.5.1. How the Office of Fair Trading (OFT) investigates and prosecutes fraud

The UK Enterprise Act 2002 (EnA 2002) created a criminal offence for cartel activity and power to investigate and prosecute cartels is with the OFT and the SFO. The Enterprise Act implemented the EU Market Abuse Directive 2003/6/EC, and repealed the Traded Securities (Disclosure) Obligations 1994 and made for a widened Part VI of the Financial Services and Markets Act 2000.

The decision to prosecute a cartel rests with the Director of the SFO.

There is a Memorandum of Understanding between the OFT and the Director of the SFO. Section 190 (4) EnA makes provision for immunity from prosecution of an offence in certain cases. This is to encourage individuals who may be involved in a cartel to whistle-blow in exchange for leniency. Immunity from prosecution for a cartel offence takes the form of a no-action letter to that person or company from the OFT. The OFT policies are published, under statutory duty, in the form of guidance Although the EnA has been in force since 2004, it was not until June 2008 that the OFT had its first criminal conviction.

> **Case Study: Criminal Cartel**
>
> David Brammar was the Managing Director at Dunlop Oil and Marine Ltd. and Bryan Allison was Dunlop's Sales Director. Dunlop Oil and Marine Limited, is a manufacturer of marine hose based in Grimsby. The two men had dishonestly participating in a cartel to allocate markets and customers, restrict supplies, fix prices and rig bids for the supply of marine hose and ancillary equipment in the UK (Marine hose is used by the oil and defence industries for transporting oil between tankers and storage facilities). In May 2007, the OFT executed search warrants at Dunlop and elsewhere and discovered evidence of a criminal cartel, which they duly prosecuted successfully.

The OFT today is actively protecting the UK consumer. Recent reports tell of the OFT investigation into claims that diet pills and diet products actually do help users to lose weight. Global DM Licensing sent mailings to UK consumers, under the name The AccuSlim Centre, claiming that the Accu-Slim Bead was a 'fat burning acupuncture without needles, diets, exercise, or effort'. It was claimed that by placing one Accu-Slim Bead behind the ear each day users could eat as much as they liked and still lose 'at least 30 pounds in the next 30 days' as the bead stimulated the acupressure points that trigger 'automatic weight loss. Such misleading claims included those for the Accu-Slim Bead, marketed as 'a safe and proven method to lose excess weight once..., without the slightest chance of failure' .The OFT contacted Global DM Licensing to express concerns over the potentially misleading claims being made, and requested evidence to support the claims. The company could not provide satisfactory proof of the claims made in the mailing and were unable to demonstrate with scientific evidence that its claims were true. OFT gained assurance from the company that it would stop sending Accu-Slim Bead mailings to UK consumers.

10.6.1. The Department of Trade and Industry (BERR) investigates company frauds

The BERR is a government body that investigates limited companies, partnerships, and directors of companies. Under the Companies Act, the BERR can compel accountants, actuaries, auditors, lawyers, and bankers to give assistance in connection with a company under investigation. The BERR refers many cases to the SFO after such a section 447 Companies Act enquiry.

> **Caselaw**
>
> *R v Philippe Roux* [1998] Unreported.
> Making a misleading statement contrary to S47 (1) Financial Services Act 1986.
> Roux was a CEO of Norton Ltd which proposed a rights issue to raise money. He put forward his own company Manstorm Ltd, whose sole director was his mother, as a sub-underwriter in respect of a Rights Issue. Manstorm Ltd proceeded to pledge to purchase 89% of Norton shares to a value of £ 1.75 million. When the underwriter called for proof that Manstorm Ltd could afford to pay this £1.75 million, Roux got one of Norton's legal advisors to write a comfort letter, a sort of gentleman's non-legal guarantee, on the solicitor's company notepaper, falsely stating that Manstorm Ltd did have the £1.75 million. So the rights issue proceeded but did not entice investors enough to take on even the 11% of remaining shares. The rights issue collapsed and the underwriters called on the sub-underwriter, Manstorm Ltd. to pay up on the insurance. But Manstorm Ltd was only a penny-poor off-the –shelf one-man company with no money to speak of. The BERR called in the Metropolitan Police who referred the case to the SFO. Roux was fined £10,000 and disqualified from acting as a company director for 5 years.

The BERR have the right to investigate, because, in a free market, all those who deal with companies whether as investors, suppliers, or consumers should be protected from unscrupulous or fraudulent practices. The Secretary of State has powers of investigation where fraud or other misconduct is suspected; shareholders have been denied reasonable information; and in the public interest.

> **Points to Note: Directors Duties in preventing fraud**
>
> Companies Act 2006 relating to directors' conflicts of interests will be implemented on 1 October 2008:
> Section 175 - Duty to avoid conflicts of interest;
> Section 176 - Duty to not accept benefits from third parties;
> Section 177 - Duty to declare interest in proposed transaction or arrangement;
> Sections 182-187 - Chapter 3 of Part 10 - Declaration of interest in existing transaction or arrangement.

The origins of the general duties of directors are based on common law rules and in certain equitable principles, now replaced by statutory duties in Companies Act 2006. Directors' general duties do not allow a director to escape any other obligation he has, including obligations under section 214(4) of the Insolvency Act 1986.

> **Point to Note: The Companies (Audit, Investigations and Community Enterprise) Act 2004**
>
> This Act closed a loophole concerning the indemnification of directors by third parties. It used to be the practice in some groups that one group company would indemnify the director of another group company and this circumvents the rule that the company could not indemnify its own directors. However, the Companies Act 2006 permits all companies to indemnify directors against third-party claims, subject to requirements.

10.6.2. Conflict of interest between the SFO, the Police and the BERR

The purpose of a BERR investigation is totally different to the purpose of a SFO or a Police fraud investigation. There are statutory constraints on the amount of information that the BERR can hand over to the Police or the SFO. After a BERR investigation, its report is made public and can be used by victims of fraud in a civil court in respect of damages.

10.7.1. Local Authorities' Model Code of Conduct to stop Civil Servant fraud

Since 1 October 2007, Local Authorities have had a new Model Code of Conduct which includes measures to stop fraud. The new Model Code of Conduct applies to all of the authorities covered by the individual existing Codes and listed in the Local Government Act 2000, e.g. Local Authorities, Parish Councils and Police Authorities. Under the new procedures in the Local Government and Public Involvement in Health Act

2007, a Local Authority is able to make provision for enabling a Standards Committee where it considers that the action it could take is insufficient, to refer a case to the Adjudication Panel for a decision by the Panel on the action that should be taken. The Panel can apply stronger penalties than Standards Committees.

If an Ethical Standards Officer ("ESO") of the Standards Board concludes that the Code of Conduct has been breached, he may decide to refer the case to the Adjudication Panel or the local Standards Committee for determination. Members must not prevent anyone obtaining information to which they are entitled by law, e.g. under the Freedom of Information Act 2000.

10.7.2. Conduct complaints and the Standards Committee

Under the new Code, anyone can make an allegation of improper conduct but members are no longer under any obligation to do so. Under the new procedure, an allegation is initiated by the making of a written allegation to a Standards Committee that a member has failed to comply with the Code. On receipt of such allegation, a Standards Committee must refer the allegation to the Monitoring Officer; refer the allegation to the Standards Board; and decide no action should be taken and give written reasons.

Where an allegation is referred to the Standards Board, the Standards Board must either "refer it to an Ethical Standards Officer for investigation; decide to take no action giving written reasons; or refer the allegation back to the Standards Committee. Members must make impartial decisions. It is necessary to look beyond pecuniary or personal interests when considering the bias test. Members must not be biased or appear to be biased.

10.7.3. Criminal Conviction of Local Authority Members

The Code now also applies to Members at any time where their behaviour has led to a criminal conviction. In such cases only certain provisions of the Code will have effect. These are the provisions dealing with intimidation of complainants in relation to alleged breaches of the Code; conduct giving rise to disrepute; and improper use of a Member's position to bestow an advantage or disadvantage on any person.

10.7.4. Criminal conviction for fraud breaches LA Members' Code

There is a breach of the Code only if the action has subsequently resulted in a criminal conviction. Members must now declare that they have a personal interest, and the nature of that interest, before the matter is discussed or as soon as it becomes apparent to them except in limited circumstances. There is a new exemption to the rule on declaring a personal interest to the meeting but this exemption only applies where the interest arises solely from membership of, or a position of control or management on any other body to which the member was appointed or nominated by the authority; and any other body exercising functions of a public nature (for example another local authority.

In these circumstances, provided the member does not have a prejudicial interest, they only need to declare their interest when they speak on the matter.

10.7.5. Any gift over £25 in value to a LA member must be declared

Members need not declare a personal interest relating to a gift or hospitality of at least £25 if the interest was registered more than three years before the meeting. Members are not required to disclose sensitive information not included in the register of interests.

A member, who has made an executive decision in relation to a personal interest, must ensure that any written decision records the existence and nature of that interest. Members must register any gifts or hospitality worth £25 or over that they receive in connection with their official duties as a member, and the source of the gift or hospitality. They must register the gift or hospitality and its source within 28 days of receiving it. After three years have passed since registration of the gift or hospitality in the register of interests, the obligation to disclose that interest to any relevant meeting ceases. Members must not use, or attempt to use, their position improperly to the advantage or disadvantage of themselves or anyone else.

10.7.6. LA Members' Interests may be a conflict of interest

Members have a personal interest in any business of their authority where it relates to or is likely to affect an interest that they must register and an interest that is not on the register, but where the well-being or financial position of the member, their family, or people with whom they have a close association, is likely to be affected by the business of their authority more than it would affect the majority of inhabitants of the ward or electoral division affected by the decision and inhabitants of the authority's area.

The categories of interests include:

(i) Membership or position of control or management in any other bodies to which the member has been appointed or nominated by the authority.

(ii) Any bodies exercising functions of a public nature (e.g. government agencies) or directed to charitable purposes, or whose principal purposes include the influence of public opinion or policy, including any political party or trade union; job(s) or business (es).

The name of an employer or people who have appointed the member to work for them.

(iv) The name of any person who has made a payment to the member in respect of their election, or expenses they have incurred in carrying out their duties.

(iv) The name of any person, company or other body which has a place of business or land in the authority's area, and in which the member has a shareholding of more than £25,000 (nominal value) or of more than 1/100th of the share capital of the company.

(v) Any contracts between the authority and the member,

(vi) The member's firm (if a partner) or a company (if they are a paid director or if they have a shareholding as described above) including any lease, licence from the authority and any contracts for goods, services or works. Where the contract relates to use of land or a property, the land must be identified on the register.

(vii) Any gift or hospitality over the value of £25 and the source of a gift or hospitality.

(viii) Any land and property in the authority's area in which the member has a beneficial interest (or a licence to occupy for more than 28 days).

Members have a personal interest in a matter if that matter affects the well-being or financial position of members,

members of their family, or people with whom they have a close association, more than it would affect the majority of people in the ward or electoral division affected by the decision, or in the authority's area or constituency. This includes the members and their jobs and businesses; the members and their employers, firms they are a partner of, and companies they are a director of; any person or body who has appointed the member, members of their family or close associates, to any position; and corporate bodies in which the member or they have a shareholding worth more than £25,000.

According to Standards Board, a 'member of your family' should be given a very wide meaning. It includes a partner (someone you are married to, your civil partner, or someone you live with, in a similar capacity), a parent, a parent-in-law, a son or daughter, a stepson or stepdaughter, the child of a partner, a brother or sister, a brother or sister of your partner, a grandparent, a grandchild, an uncle or aunt, a nephew or niece, and the partners of any of these people.

A person with whom you have a close association is someone that you are in either regular or irregular contact with over a period of time who is more than an acquaintance. It is someone a reasonable member of the public might think you would be prepared to favour or disadvantage when discussing a matter that affects them. It may be a friend, a colleague, a business associate or someone whom you know through general social contacts.

10.7.7 Personal Interest

A 'personal interest' will also be a 'prejudicial interest' in a matter if all of the following conditions are met:-

(i) The matter does not fall within one of the exempt categories of decisions.

(ii) The matter affects financial interests or relates to a licensing or regulatory matter or a member of the public, who knows the relevant facts, would reasonably think the personal interest is so significant that it is likely to prejudice the member's judgement of the public interest.

10.7.8. 'Prejudicial interest' categories

Paragraph 10(2) (c) of the Code states that a member will not have a prejudicial interest if the matter relates to any of the following functions of their authority:

Housing: if they hold a tenancy or lease with the authority, as long as the matter does not relate to the member's particular tenancy or lease.

School meals or school transport and travelling expenses: if the member is a parent or guardian of a child in full-time education or a parent governor, unless it relates particularly to the school the member's child attends.

Statutory sick pay: if the member is receiving this, or entitled to it.

An allowance, payment or indemnity for members: Any ceremonial honour given to members.

Setting council tax or a precept: Members will only have a prejudicial interest in a matter if it falls into one of the following categories:

(i) The matter affects the member's financial position or the financial position of any person or body through whom the member has a personal interest; and the matter relates to an approval, consent, licence, permission or registration that affects the member of any person or body with which the member has a personal interest.

(ii) The interest must be so significant that it is likely to prejudice judgement of the public interest. If a member of the public with knowledge of the relevant facts would reasonably conclude that the interest is so significant that the member's judgement of the public interest might be prejudiced, then the member has a prejudicial interest.

The Local Government Act 2000 enables Ethical Standards Officers to refer allegations that a member has breached the Code of Conduct to monitoring officers. An Ethical Standards Officer may refer an allegation at any point before they complete an investigation into the allegation. Ethical Standards Officers can refer completed investigation reports to monitoring officers for Standards Committees.

10.8.1. Her Majesty's Revenue and Customs

The Board of Inland Revenue was formed in 1849 and in 1909 this became the Board of Customs & Excise. In 2005 Customs and Excise merged with Inland Revenue to form the new HM Revenue and Customs (HMRC).

10.8.2. Powers of HMRC

The Customs and Excise Management Act 1979, Police and Criminal Evidence Act 1984 (Application to Customs and Excise) Order 1985 SI 1985/ 1800, Article 5, and the Value Added Tax Act 1994 gave Customs powers to obtain information, to enter and search premises, and to investigate Value Added Tax offences. Since 2008, Her Majesty's Revenue and Customs (HMRC) has enjoyed additional powers. HMRC already have considerable powers with respect to investigation of persons and companies in the pursuit of tax evasion and taxes undeclared. Now income tax evasion, evasion of direct taxation, evasion of indirect taxation are all criminal offences. The new powers effectively bring the powers of HMRC with regard to income tax, close to all police powers and tone down some of the powers HMRC already have with regard to VAT in line with police powers and codes of practice.

10.8.3. Issues of Fair trial

There is not in place any policy of accountability or transparency with regard to HMRC's investigative processes. Accountability reports must include such items:

1. How many times have search warrants been sought every year.
2. How many times the investigations entailed the seizure of computers.
3. How many persons voluntarily attended at police stations?
4. How many arrests were made elsewhere than at police station and the reasonable availability of other means for carrying out HMRC's duties. Omissions that would otherwise constitute an offence would likely result in loss of, or serious damage to, property and businesses and will be litigated in the courts.

HMRC should only proceed without a written authorization from a senior official for acts or omissions that would otherwise constitute an offence and that would likely result in loss of or serious damage to property, or for directing another person to commit an act or omission that would otherwise constitute an offence, under very limited circumstances. He or she must believe, on reasonable grounds, that the grounds for obtaining an authorization exist, but it is not feasible under the circumstances to obtain the authorization, and that the act or omission is necessary to prevent the imminent loss or destruction of evidence of an indictable offence. This leads to the issue of computerised evidence.

10.8.4. Electronic or Computer Evidence

Discovery today involves significantly more digital content to sift than ever before, resulting in a costly and time-consuming start to litigation or regulatory investigation. In fact, one of the most common complaints from corporations today is that the cost of discovery is simply too high, making compliance with regulatory rules and litigation requests extraordinarily challenging and at times even crippling.

The impact of e-mail is staggering. According to a recent study published by The National Law Journal, corporations are projected this year to spend one billion pounds for electronic discovery services, and many billions of pounds to manage e-mail. Who is going to pay for the billions of pounds cost of sifting through a myriad of companies' computers to ascertain whether there is evidence of tax evasion? It would cost such companies a fortune to defend themselves by duplicating the same electronic investigation that HMRC will have made in order to defend themselves crippling many companies and bankrupting many people, thus creating no future tax collections from these defendants.

10.8.5. Metadata – issues of computer evidence

Metadata is information about, and contained within, a document. It describes how, when and by whom the document was created, accessed, modified, and formatted. Metadata is frequently not viewable in the document without special effort. It is easily altered and destroyed inadvertently, and much or all of it is not reproduced if the document is imaged or printed. Like other electronic information, if relevant, its destruction could subject a party to sanctions.

There is no policy booklet which the HMRC holds that instructs on the retrieval or storage of digital evidence and the sharing of this evidence with defence lawyers. The handling of metadata in litigation and the handling of other types of electronically stored information is not clarified.

10.8.6. HMRC investigation of fraud

HMRC might decide to investigate on obtaining a suspicious activity report (SAR) , which is a piece of information which alerts law enforcement that certain customer activity is in some way suspicious and might indicate money laundering or terrorist financing and thus non-payment of taxes. SARs are sent by members of the regulated sector to Serious Organised Crime Agency and are subsequently passed to law enforcement agencies (LEAs) for action. A recent government report on SARS states that systematic information maintained by Law Enforcement Authorities (LEA) on their use of SARs is limited and often of poor quality and there is not much feedback information as to its usefulness as regards prosecutions, for example. The report makes 15 recommendations for action and one recommendation states:- *"Recommendation 8 (critical). Because of associated efficiency gains for users of SARs, database cross-checks between Elmer and relevant national databases (e.g. PNC, JARD) should be automated, such that database hits are highlighted when looking at a SAR or series of SARs on Elmer; this should be handled by NCIS/SOCA, perhaps in conjunction with the Police Information Technology Organisation (PITO)."* Once there is such an investigation of a person, that person's police records are searched.

There is no accountability by the HMRC in this respect. Citizens do not know that SARs are sent electronically (via internet or fax) or in hard copy to SOCA and once received, SARs are input into Elmer, the SARs database, and may undergo cursory analysis and SARs and other forms of criminal intelligence are sent to LEAs for action. SARs are occasionally sent to the law enforcement or equivalent sections of a number of other organisations, including the British Transport Police, Department of Trade and Industry, Ministry of Defence Police, and the Serious Fraud Office and HMRC.

SARs may also be sent to national financial intelligence units in foreign jurisdictions, usually at their behest. National LEAs include HMRC and HMRC also has other broader sources of information at their disposal. Evidence gathering is where investigation begins, and may be through various court orders.

10.8.7. HMRC takes on the role of Police

Training of HMRC investigators is needed because they take on the role of the police. The aim of these modernisations is to prosecute tax evaders. Such alleged tax evaders are defendants in this criminal process and will have cases quashed because newly trained HMRC officers' reports in the same vein as Police Reports but effective discovery requiring that the recipient of discovered information be able to understand it. HMRC are not trained to write police reports. There is a time limitation for customs offences and this is within 20 years of the commission of the offence.

10.8.8. HMRC Reports by non-police reporters

On reading a typical police report, lawyers must look for the report of the first officers on the "crime scene". What descriptions did the arriving officers give of the conditions of the scene- this includes the position of moveable objects and alleged victims? What did the first officers on the scene do upon their arrival, e.g., where did they go, what did they do to secure the scene? Did police also arrive at the scene? Did they conduct a further investigation? What did they observe? What did they look for? Did the HMRC or police take measurements and or make diagrams of the scene? How many diagrams or sketches? Of what? Did the officers talk with witnesses? Who? When? Where? Were the witness statements recorded, e.g., written, tape-recorded, and paraphrased into the report? What did the witnesses say? Were photographs taken? Who? When? Of what? How many? Were samples, e.g., fingerprints, trace evidence, collected? Who collected what and from where? How was the collected evidence transported to the crime lab or other repository? Is there a log reflecting each item collected?

Did a criminal expert or forensic expert subsequently examine the items collected at the scene? Does any portion of a sample collected for testing remain for analysis by a defence expert? So HMRC will now have to learn to write police reports in order to give the defence a fair trial.

10.8.9. Tax & VAT Frauds

Frauds fought by HMRC are-carousel frauds, repayment frauds, phoenix frauds, VAT evasion, smuggling, oil frauds, and money laundering.

10.8.10. 'Fraudulent evasion of duty' fraud.

Fraudulent evasion of VAT is a criminal offence under Value Added Taxes Act 1994, s 72(1). A person commits this offence if he is knowingly concerned in, or has a view to taking steps of fraudulent evasion of VAT by himself or another.

Fraud Investigation: Criminal Procedure and Investigation

Caselaw

R v Goodwin and Unstead [1997] STC 22, CA.
Fraudulent evasion of VAT .
Anabolic steroids were goods which were integrated into the economy of the Community and therefore liable to VAT. Appeal against conviction was dismissed. On 4 December 1997 at the Crown Court in Durham the appellants pleaded guilty, following a ruling by the trial judge, to being knowingly concerned in the fraudulent evasion of value added tax (VAT) contrary to s.39(1) Value Added Tax Act 1983. Carlo Citrone was sentenced to 18 months' imprisonment suspended for two years, prosecution costs of £20,000 and an order was made that the anabolic steroids be forfeited and destroyed. John Citrone was sentenced to 15 months' imprisonment, suspended for two years, prosecution costs of £20,000 and an order was made that the drugs be forfeited and destroyed. The Crown's case was that the appellants were selling both within the UK and abroad anabolic steroids to such a volume as to render them liable to register for payment of VAT. The appellants were not licensed to supply the steroids under the Medicines Act 1968. The appellants sought to quash the indictment on the basis of judgments of the European Court of Justice (the ECJ) that demonstrated that; (i) VAT was not chargeable on the unlawful supply of anabolic steroid drugs and that consequently the indictment did not disclose an offence known to law and/or; (ii) the question of whether or not such supply was chargeable to VAT should have been referred to the ECJ for a ruling. But anabolic steroids were within the narrow category of goods which were integrated into the economy of the Community and could be lawfully and openly offered for sale. Where there was a legitimate trade and an illicit trade each had to be taxed equally in order not to confer a fiscal privilege on the criminal. The court declined to refer the case to the ECJ. Appeal dismissed.

Fraudulent evasion can include obtaining a VAT repayment or refund, and deliberate non-payment when payment is due as in *R v Dealey,* CA Crim Div [1997] STC 217. HMRC also investigates money laundering.

10.8.11. HMRC Powers to seize and detain

HMRC officers have the power under Police and Criminal Evidence Act 1984 (Application to Customs & Excise) Order 1985, SI 1985/1800, Article 5, and under Criminal Justice and Police Act 2001, Part 2, and Customs and Excise Management Act 1979 and Value Added Tax Act 2994, to seize and retain anything found on the premises, notwithstanding that the thing is not evidence of a customs offence. *This power is beyond police powers.* HMRC can use a Writ of Assistance, not available to the Police, to enter any building or place at any time, day, or night, to search for, seize, detain, and remove anything liable for forfeiture.

Since 15th February 2008, HMRC is able to intercept phone calls, emails and letters, as well as bug residential premises and private vehicles. These additional powers were granted to HMRC in the Serious Crime Act 2007, which did not come into force until the relevant statutory instrument was issued on 15th February 2008. HMRC does not need to seek authorisation for any of its surveillance activities.

All HMRC surveillance is to be conducted in compliance with the Regulation of Investigatory Powers Act 2000 and is subject to checks by the Office of Surveillance Commissioners and the Interception of Communication Commissioners Office.

10.8.12 The Chilcot Report 2008-Privy Council Review of Intercept as Evidence

The report's objective was to set out a regime which would allow the use of intercepted material in court. The report concludes that it would be possible to provide for the use of intercept as evidence in criminal trials in England and Wales by developing a robust legal model, based in statute and compatible with the ECHR, starting from the PII Plus model (a legal model allowing the evidential use of intercept, developed within Government in 2006-07).

The intercepting agency shall decide whether a prosecution involving its intercepted material shall proceed. Intercepted material originating from the intelligence agencies shall not be disclosed beyond cleared judges, prosecutors, or special (defence) advocates, except in a form agreed by the originator. Material intercepted through the use of sensitive signals intelligence techniques shall not be disclosed unless the Secretary of State is satisfied that disclosure will not put the capability and techniques at risk.

No intelligence or law enforcement agency shall be required to retain raw intercepted material for significantly more or less time than needed for operational purposes. Law enforcement agencies shall be able to use interception to provide strategic intelligence on criminal enterprises, and retain the intelligence sometimes for a number of years, regardless of the progress of specific Criminal cases. Anything so provided to law enforcement agencies shall be subject to the same disclosure obligations as other intelligence intercept. Because of the particular risks involved in introducing intercept as evidence in civil proceedings, the report recommends that any change to the current legal regime for interception in the civil courts only be considered following successful change in criminal proceedings (see http://www.official-documents.gov.uk/document/cm73/7324/7324.pdf. for the full Chilcot report).

10.8.13. Obstructing an HMRC Officer

The Regulatory Impact Assessment for VAT amends the VAT Act to clarify that the power for HM Revenue and Customs officers to inspect goods for VAT purposes includes the power to mark the goods or their packaging and to record any information relating to the goods by electronic means.

10.8.14. Carousel fraud

Carousel fraud is the term used to describe the VAT-free import of goods from another EU State and their sale from one business to another within the UK, followed by re-export. VAT is charged on the business-to-business sale but is not handed over to HMRC, as the business selling the goods disappears. The business purchasing the goods will in the meantime have reclaimed the VAT it has paid. To remove the opportunity for this type of fraud, which typically has involved portable high-value electronic goods and is estimated to have cost HMRC between £1.12 and £1.9bn in 2004/5, the VAT rules have been changed so that in some circumstances it is no longer the seller, but the buyer who has to account to HMRC for any VAT.

Charities purchasing over £5,000 worth of mobile phones or computer chips are responsible for accounting to HMRC for VAT on the supply from 1 June 2007. Mobile handsets (including Black-Berries), pay as you go mobile phones, 3G data cards and 'wifi' cards all fall within the scope of the VAT reverse charge, although mobile phones and Black-Berries purchased with an airtime contract are excluded. Computer chips are only subject to the reverse charge where they are not sold as part of an assembled item, and items such as laptops, PCs and computer servers are not within the remit of the reverse charge.

Where over £5,000 worth of goods subject to the reverse charge are supplied, the supplier will request the purchaser's VAT registration number and may make other enquiries to establish the customer's *bona fides*. Invoices for goods subject to this reverse charge will specify that the customer must account to HMRC for VAT on the purchase, and may detail the amount of VAT that should be paid. VAT must then be accounted for, but the purchaser can recover any input tax on the same VAT return, subject to the usual rules.

> **Point to Note: Carousel fraud**
>
> The EU estimates more money is lost to missing trader intra-community (MTIC) or carousel fraud each year than the £34.2bn spent on the Common Agricultural Policy (*The Guardian*, 17 March 2007). the abolition of tax duties between member states, an objective of the Sixth Council Directive of 17 May 1977 (77/388/EEC), which acknowledged that member states should be able to take limited special measures derogating from the Directive to avoid fraud.
>
> There are 3 elements to a carousel fraud. A business would import small high value goods from a business in the European Union. The supply of goods was VAT exempt. When the UK business sold the goods on, it charged VAT. It then disappeared, having failed to account for the VAT. The goods would be sold through a chain of companies with VAT ostensibly being charged. The goods would then be exported back to the original European Union country and would be zero-rated. However, VAT would be claimed back, ostensibly to recoup the VAT paid on the purchase

> of goods by the exporting company. The fraudulent money would then be fed back up the chain of transactions. In order to create a distance between the import and export companies, one or more buffer companies would be used as intermediaries. These companies would have immaculate VAT records and would trade normally. The latest carousel fraud case is *R v Said Mubarak Ahmed and others* [2008] EWCA 1386.

10.8.15. VAT fraud by purported charities

Many fraudulent evasion of VAT are carried out by persons who purport to be charities. Now HMRC has overhauled its VAT Rules to combat this fraud. Charities purchasing goods subject to the reverse charge that will be used for both business and non-business purposes, must account for VAT to HMRC on the entire purchase. Following this, the value of the goods should be apportioned between business and non-business use and the necessary restriction applied to the deduction of the input tax on the VAT return. In 2008, HM Revenue and Customs implemented a new clearances system. This follows the 2006 Review of Links with Large Business, and precedes the removal of the current four Finance Act restrictions in April 2008 to extend its clearance service to more businesses. During the pilot, clearance applications are accepted from businesses and their advisors where there is a demonstrable material uncertainty about the tax consequences of transactions that are commercially significant to their business. This relates to transactions that were covered under Code of Practice 10 and VAT Notice 700/6. Statutory clearances and charities continue to follow the existing arrangements. HMRC new extended service begins April 2008.

10.9.1. Massive frauds on the Department of Social Security (DSS)

DSS frauds are so large that there is a whole structure dedicated to investigating and prosecuting this type of fraud.

10.10.1. Home Office: Police Anti- Corruption Strategies
Police corruption is an issue dealt with by the Home Office.

> *"Corruption undermines everything the law enforcement community works towards. It impoverishes whole communities, and threatens the safety and security of the many for the benefit of a very few"* – Interpol Secretary General.

10.10.2. ACPO Guidelines on anti-corruption in the police service

In 2000, ACPO published its anti-corruption policy-

"This policy is a key part of the Association of Chief Police Officers Corruption Prevention Strategy. It is considered best practise for all police forces to have such a policy so that all their staff can have confidence in the reporting mechanisms available to them. This policy aims to create a climate where staff feels a genuine obligation to openness and transparency when reporting breaches of professional standards. Their motivation arising from a desire to maintain the integrity of the Police Service and with knowledge that such action will be universally acknowledged as right. This Policy is the first step towards this aspiration."

ACPO Corruption Prevention Guidelines:

(i) Section 2 provides background information.

(ii) Section 3 outlines the principles upon which this policy document is based.

(iii) Section 4 sets out the range of mechanisms for Professional Standards Reporting

(iv) Section 5 outlines the ways in which support will be provided to those who make professional standards reports and documents the key responsibilities of staff involved in the process.

Breaches of professional standards include criminal activity, unethical behaviour, breaches of the 'Codes of Conduct', malpractice and dishonesty.

The ACPO Guidelines on corruption may be used by police staff to: support to other strands of the force Corruption Prevention Strategy and to make professional standards reports and complements.

However the Corruption Guidelines do not over-ride

(i) Grievance Procedure

(ii) Complaints & Discipline procedures (Police (Discipline) Regulations 1985 and Police (Conduct) Regulations 1999)

(iii) Civil Staff Inefficiency and Misconduct Procedures.

(iv) Unsatisfactory performance procedures (Police (Efficiency) Regulations 1999

(v) Codes of Practice for acceptance of gifts and hospitality.

(vi) Public Interest Disclosure Act 1998.

10.10.3. Multiple Methods of Reporting Corruption

The ACPO policy provides for a number of different methods through which breaches of professional standards can be reported both openly and confidentially. It is vital that immediate and positive feedback is given to an individual who makes a professional standards report. In promulgating this policy the term 'doing the right thing' will be used. When open reports have been made i.e. the identity of the individual and the fact of the report is known to his or her colleagues, appropriate support must be given to the individual from the outset of the case and must continue until the issue is fully resolved. This includes pro-active management support and action, staff association and trade union involvement and advice on access to professional personnel support services. Visible, active, and supportive leadership must be demonstrated by line managers when dealing with an individual who has made an open professional standards report.

10.10.4. Information and Intelligence relating to Corruption

When an open professional standards report is made all documentation referring to it will carry a protective marking which limits access to it to those people who have a legitimate need to see it. Details of any professional standards report will be held within a designated unit under appropriate security. In confidential cases knowledge of the identity of the person who has made the report will be kept to a minimum based upon strict need to know criteria.

10.10.5. Public Interest Disclosure Act 1998

Whistle-blowing by employees is protected by the Public Interest Disclosure Act 1998. The Act applies to 'workers' which includes members of the police support staff. Although police officers are specifically excluded, officers who make professional standards reports in good faith will be fully supported in accordance with the spirit of this legislation. The types of disclosures which individuals are encouraged to report under the Public Interest Disclosure Act includes information relating to a criminal offence; the breach of a legal obligation; a miscarriage of justice; a danger to the health and safety of an individual; damage to the environment; deliberate covering up of information in respect of any of the above matters. The scope of this Act goes further than the Professional Standards Reporting Policy e.g. it specifically includes health and safety issues. Individuals who are protected by the provisions of the Act can complain to an Employment Tribunal if they have been subjected to a detriment as a result of making a protected disclosure. The remedies available to a tribunal include reinstatement, re-employment, and compensation.

10.11. Government Anti-Corruption Procedure

In 2001, a new disclosure regime was introduced as part of the Political Parties Elections and Referendum Act 2000 (PPERA) to give transparency to and to regulate the funding and expenditure of political parties. It has been only partially successful in reducing the exposure of the UK political system to corrupt practice. The "loans for peerages" affair, which broke in March 2006, has reinforced cynicism in the regime.

> **Case Study: 'Cash for Peerage' inquiry**
>
> In March 2006, a number of men who had been nominated for peerages were rejected by the House of Lords Appointments Commission. It was reported that they had all provided funding to the Labour Party during the previous year for the election campaign. Such funds had allegedly not been disclosed under the PPERA rules on the basis that they were 'commercial' loans. Questions have been raised about these loans and a number of loans to the Conservative Party. Crimes may have been committed if there had been deception in concealing the true nature of donations or loans and/or if loans or donations were offered in return for peerage nominations or vice versa which would have been in breach of the Honours (Prevention of Abuses) Act 1925.

10.12. Conclusion to Chapter Ten

Major corruption is facilitated by money-laundering. People who acquire money corruptly need to hide it away safely, disguised as legitimate funds. When such money is traced, often to a safe haven country, mechanisms are needed to confiscate and return it. The UK Money Laundering Regulations 2007 are now in force. The UK is a wealthy country and the different agencies discussed above all together help to fight the many kinds of fraud.

Further reading for Chapter Ten

The following websites have many relevant documents:
Association of Chief Police Officers
http://www.acpo.police.uk/
Association of Police Authorities
http://www.apa.police.uk/apa
Crown Prosecution Service
http://www.cps.gov.uk/
http://www.cps.gov.uk/about/index.html
Department of Trade and Industry
http://www.BERR.gov/
Financial Services Authority
http://www.fsa.gov.uk/
Her Majesty's Revenue and Customs
http://www.businesslink.gov.uk/
Insolvency Service
http://www.insolvency.gov.uk/
National Policing Improvement Agency
http://www.npia.police.uk/
Office of Fair Trading
http://www.oft.gov.uk/
Serious Fraud Office
http://www.sfo.gov.uk/
Serious Organised Crime Agency
http://www.soca.gov.uk/
The Home Office
http://www.homeoffice.gov.uk/

CHAPTER 11- ANALYSIS OF THEFT ACTS 1968 AND 1978

11.1.1. Introduction

A very important point to put across to all Police officers is that the Fraud Act 2006, in force since 15th January 2007, is not retrospective. Financial fraud takes time, years and years in some cases, of step-by-step planning and progressing to the big fraud (apart from opportunist frauds. Therefore fraud can be prosecuted now in respect of matters from up to 25 years ago, in tax cases, for instance. So all statutes matter, especially the Theft Acts (1968 and 1978) the Fraud Act (2006), and old and new Companies Acts (1985 and 2006).

Keep your old copies of the Theft Acts- they will be useful for years to come. The Fraud Act 2006 provides some transition provisions as set out in Schedule 2. Under Section 3 (1) of Schedule 2 the old Theft Acts offences will continue to apply for any offences partly committed before 15 January 2007. Section 3 (2) of Schedule 2 defines "partly committed" as when a relevant event occurred before 15 January 2007, and another relevant event occurred on or after 15 January 2007. Section 3 (3) of Schedule 2 defines a relevant event for the purposes of the Fraud Act as

> *"... any act, omission or other event (including any result of one or more acts or omissions) proof of which is required for conviction of the offence."*

When reviewing cases in which it is uncertain when a relevant event occurred and it may have happened before, on or after 15 January 2007 prosecutors should request that police obtain as much information as possible to assist in identifying the date on which any relevant events occurred. This should be possible in the vast majority of fraud cases. In cases when the uncertainty as to the date cannot be rectified it is proper practice to put alternative counts on the indictment under the 2006 Act and the previous legislation.

> **Caselaw**
>
> In *R v Bellman* [1989] A.C. 836 the House of Lords considered whether mutually inconsistent and destructive counts can appear on an indictment. Their Lordships held that where there is prima facie evidence that a defendant has committed either crime A or crime B then both crimes may be charged and left to the jury, even though proof of crime A will establish that D cannot have committed crime B and vice versa. Where it is clear that D has committed crime A or crime B but there is no evidence to say when the crime has been committed then neither crime can be left to the jury. In cases where alternative counts have been placed on the indictment, prosecuting advocates should be reminded of *R v Bellman*.

The repeals and revocations made by the Fraud Act 2006 are to be found in Schedule 3 of the Fraud Act. The old law comprised a disordered list of offences whose common core was 'dishonestly obtaining something by deception'. The main difference lay in the 'something' that had to be obtained.

11.1.2. Repealed sections of the Theft Acts

The repealed sections are Theft Act 1968, sections 15, 15(A), 15B, 16, 20(2), 24A (3), and 24A (4). The repealed sections of the Theft Act 1978 are sections 1,2,4(2)(a) and 5(1). Section 15 of the Theft Act 1968 covers obtaining property by deception; and section 15A covered a money transfer. Theft Act 1968 Section 15A & 15B-obtaining a money transfer by deception- is repealed. Section 15A offence was only secured when the defendant dishonestly obtained a money transfer by deception, provable by the reciprocal debiting and crediting of bank accounts. Deception generally required a false representation by the defendant which fooled the victim. It was two-sided. Section 15(4) Theft Act 1968 defined what could be a deception: - words, conduct, silence, fact or law and present intentions. In the repealed s15 Theft Act 1968, the defendant must obtain property belonging to another by deception, dishonestly, with intent permanently to deprive. To understand the reasoning behind the repeals made by the Fraud Act 2006, one needs to understand the old deception offences. Section 15(1) read: "A person who by any deception dishonestly obtains property belonging to another, with the intention of permanently depriving the other of it…" committed the offence.

The *actus reus* involved obtaining property belonging to another by deception. It covered obtaining ownership, possession or control of the property but unless 'property' was actually obtained, no offence was committed. Due to the wide interpretation of 'appropriation' in theft, most cases of obtaining property by deception, apart from some minor exceptions, would also be theft.

The *mens rea* required dishonesty, an intention permanently to deprive and deliberation or subjective recklessness in respect of the deception, i.e. essentially knowing that the representation was false or might be and that the victim would or might be taken in by it. Repealed section 16 Theft Act 1968 covered obtaining property by a pecuniary advantage. Repealed section 20(2) Theft Act 1968 covered obtaining property by the execution of a valuable security.

'Pecuniary advantage' is narrowly defined and so allowed a person to borrow money by way of overdraft; or to take out insurance or annuity or better terms therefore or to win money by betting. 'Pecuniary advantage' means obtaining more money than one ought to have obtained. It can refer to situations where one should have paid for something, but did not. Before the repeal, a *causal nexus* must be proved, i.e. was the crime a direct result of the deception? Was the deception that which caused the gain? The term deception in Section 16, Theft Act 1968 has the same meaning as in section 15 of the 1968 Theft Act 1968.

This section 16 has been repealed because it is *not* now necessary to prove deception in such a fraud and the only element present should be dishonesty. However, the Fraud Act has not repealed the offence of *attempted* deception, i.e. the offence of attempting to obtain property by deception. The new fraud offences are 'obtaining services dishonestly', 'possessing articles for use in fraud' and 'participating in a fraudulent business.' The deception offences have been repealed and replaced with dishonestly offences of fraud.

11.1.3. Repealed Theft Act 1968, section 25(5) - going equipped for stealing

The Fraud Act schedule 1 amends section 25 Theft Act 1968, by deleting reference to 'cheating.' The offence of 'going equipped', making section 25 Theft Act 1968 extend to 'going equipped for burglary and theft'. Everything which fell within section 25(1) Theft Act 1968 in respect of going equipped to cheat is accommodated by the new provision in Section 6(1) Fraud Act 2006. Section 6(1) Fraud Act covers a person's disguise, a false charity collection box, a false charity sponsor form, a stolen cheque-book and counterfeit goods intended to be sold as genuine goods.

11.1.4. Obtaining conviction under Theft Act 1968 s15, 15A, 15B, 16, 20(2)

The difficulty in securing conviction was that 'obtaining' could be of ownership, possession or control. Dishonesty does not mean mistake. This section needed the intention to 'permanently deprive' and this is repealed The Fraud Act 2006 replaces the deception offences as listed in Schedule Fraud Act 2006, with a general offence of fraud and adds a further offence of dishonestly obtaining services. The Fraud Act eliminates this condition, especially in the areas of intellectual property, when art objects are stolen for copying purposes and then returned. Clauses 6 and 7 of the Fraud Act allow prosecutions of individuals involved at the many stages of production and supply of counterfeit artworks.

> **Caselaw**
>
> In *R v Preddy* [1996] 3 All ER 481 the defendant had practiced mortgage fraud, securing the grant of a mortgage advance by giving false details of identity, income, etc. on his mortgage application form. The deception caused the mortgage lender to instruct its banker to transfer the advance monies electronically direct from the lender's bank account to the defendant's bank account. *The decision was that the defendant did not contravene section 15* Theft Act 1968 because he did not obtain any property which *belonged to another*. The credit balance in the lender's account was cancelled or extinguished when its bank transferred this money to the defendant's bank. The defendant did not obtain the lender's credit balance. He obtained a new and different credit balance which, being a debt which his bank owed to him from the moment of its creation, never ever belonged to anyone but the defendant. Now this loophole has disappeared with the Fraud Act 2006.

11.1.5. 1. Repealed sections of the Theft Act 1978

The Theft Act 1978 came about in order to correct some deficiencies in the Theft Act 1968, as were highlighted by cases such as R *v Greenberg [1972]* and *DPP v Ray [1973]*.

Even after the Theft Act 1978, it was found that this was not enough to catch all dishonest transactions by automated means, as in the case *R v Dhjillan [1996]*. The Theft Act 1978 supplemented the earlier deception offences in English law contained in sections 15 and 16 of the Theft Act 1968 by reforming some aspects of those offences and adding new provisions. Sections 1 and 2 were repealed on 15th January 2007 with the implementation of the Fraud Act 2006. Repealed section 1 of the Theft Act 1978 covered obtaining services. Repealed section 5(1) Theft Act 1978, stated that there must be a deception which had the same meaning as in section 15(4) of the Theft Act 1968, i.e. any deception (whether deliberate or reckless) by words or conduct as to fact, or as to law, including a deception as to the present intentions of the person using the deception or any other person. This deception must be the cause of the obtaining. The defendant must have obtained a service as defined in s1 (2), i.e. the victim must confer a benefit on the defendant (or another). The 'services' must be non-gratuitous, i.e. the benefits must be provided by the victim of the deception in the expectation that they are to be paid for at commercial rates. It must have been conferred by the doing, causing, or permitting of some act and a failure to act which conferred a benefit was not sufficient.

Thus, a person who employed a lawyer or accountant without ever intending to pay might have committed an offence under s1 Theft Act 1978. But a person who lied to a neighbour to secure the loan of a power drill did not commit an offence because the benefit was not obtained on the understanding that it has been or will be paid for. Note that the also repealed Theft (Amendment) Act 1996 provided that a loan amounted to a service.

11.1.5.2. Repealed section 2 of the Theft Act 1978 - evasion of a liability to pay

Section 2 provided that subject to an enforceable liability, where a person by any deception, dishonestly secured the remission of the whole or part of any existing liability to make a payment, whether his own liability or another's; or with intent to make permanent default in whole or in part on any existing liability to make a payment, or with intent to let another do so, dishonestly, induced the creditor or any person claiming payment on behalf of the creditor to wait for payment (whether or not the due date for payment is deferred) or to forgo payment; or dishonestly obtained any exemption from or abatement of liability to make a payment; he was guilty of an offence.

This repealed s.2 Theft Act 1978 consisted of three offences all involving dishonestly obtaining services by deception. These were: (1) securing the remission in whole or in part of any existing liability to pay ;(2) inducing the victim to wait for or forego payment; and(3) obtaining an exemption from or abatement of a liability to pay.

In (1) the defendant would have had to be under a liability to make a payment and by then practising a deception, he got the creditor to agree either to extinguish his liability altogether or to reduce it.

In (2) the defendant would have firstly incurred a liability to pay and then used a deception to cause the creditor to wait for payment or to forget it altogether. The offence required the defendant to intend never to pay, so that, if he only intended to put off payment to ease the immediate financial pressure, he could not commit the offence.

In (3), this offence is committed when the defendant used the deception at the outset to affect a prospective liability not yet incurred, such as when the defendant, before starting his journey, told the taxi driver a false sob story so that the driver agreed to carry the defendant free of charge. The defendant here obtained an exemption from liability to pay. Another example was if the defendant had falsely claimed to be an OAP, so to secure half-price admission to a football match, making him obtain an 'abatement of liability' to pay because of the deception. The deception came first and prevented him from incurring the liability he should have occurred. This section.2 Theft Act 1978 offence is now treated as a fraud offence and deception need not be proved.

> **Caselaw**
>
> *R v Ray* [1974] AC 370 House of Lords
> An example of a case of evading liability by deception would have been dining in a restaurant and leaving without paying, as in *Ray* [1974] AC 370 House of Lords. The House of Lords then ruled that Ray had had a pecuniary advantage because he had not paid for the restaurant meal, and had deceived by the implied representation of being an honest customer who was going to pay.

Repealed Section 2(1) Theft Act 1978 was divided into three parts, all of which required that a deception caused the obtaining, and that there was a liability to pay which was legally enforceable. Under repealed s2(1)(c) Theft Act 1978, for there to have been an offence of avoiding incurring a debt there must have been dishonesty and a deception which obtained exemption from or abatement of liability to make a payment.

Both repealed sections 2(1) (a) and (b) Theft Act 1978 required an "existing" liability to pay and did not cover situations where the point of the deception was to prevent a liability from arising in the future.

All three parts of the repealed section 2(1) Theft Act 1978 required proof that the creditor is deceived into releasing the defendant from the obligation to pay in some way. Repealed section 2(1) (a) Theft Act 1978 covered the deception which dishonestly secured the remission of the whole or part of an existing liability to make a payment. Unlike the other two subsections, this required that the victim knew that a liability existed and knew how much he or she was remitting. It did not cover situations where the defendant tricked the victim into believing that no money was owing .If A borrowed £50 from B and, when repayment was due, claimed that a change of circumstances made it impossible for him to repay some or all of the money and this deception persuaded B to forgive the loan, or to accept £10 in full satisfaction, then the offence was committed.

Repealed section 2(1) (a) required an existing liability to make payment but, it did not require that the creditor knew that he or she was "letting the defendant off". The section was also concerned with dishonestly inducing a creditor to wait for payment.

Repealed section.2(3)Theft Act 1978, an amendment to Theft Act 1968 , is a particular instance of "wait for payment" because of the general principle that accepting a cheque (even a worthless cheque) as the means of payment, meant that, until the creditor received notice that the cheque had been dishonoured, he or she stopped seeking payment.

Repealed section 2(3)Theft Act 1978 provided that a person induced to take a cheque or other security for money by way of conditional satisfaction of an existing liability was to be treated not as being paid but as being induced to wait for payment.

11.2.1. Theft Act 1978 section 3 is still in force

Theft Act 1978, Section 3, 'making off without payment', still in force and provides:

(i) Subject to subsection (3) below, a person who, knowing that payment on the spot for any goods supplied or service done is required or expected from him, dishonestly makes off without having paid as required or expected and with intent to avoid payment of the amount due shall be guilty of an offence.

(ii) For purposes of this section 'payment on the spot' includes payment at the time of collecting goods on which work has been done or in respect of which service has been provided.

(iii) Subsection (1) above shall not apply where the supply of the goods or the doing of the service is contrary to law, or where the service done is such that payment is not legally enforceable.

(iv) Any person may arrest without warrant anyone who is, or whom he, with reasonable cause, suspects to be, committing or attempting to commit an offence under this section.

Section 3 Theft Act 1978 is intended to protect legitimate business concerns and applies where goods are supplied or a service is performed on the basis that payment will be made there and then. This includes a restaurant where the meal is supplied on the understanding that the bill will be paid before the diner leaves and the passenger in a taxi who runs off without paying the fare at the end of the journey, and the motorist who fills up with petrol at a garage and drives off when the attendant is distracted For these purposes, it must be proved that the defendant knew that payment on the spot was required or expected, and made off dishonestly with intent to avoid payment of the amount due.

Section 3 Theft Act 1978 is intended to avoid any problems from the application of civil law principles. For example, the Sale of Goods Act determines when the ownership of goods passes. If the goods are being ascertained as part of the contract, title will pass when the goods are identified or measured. In a restaurant, this will probably occur when the food is cooked and plated. In a garage, it will occur when the fuel is measured as it passes through the pump into the car's tank.

To be a theft, the goods must belong to another when the appropriation occurs. Similarly, if ownership passed before an intention to avoid payment was formed, running off might be a breach of civil law but it was not a crime. This became too common an event and so the law had to be clarified to enable convictions to be obtained despite civil law niceties. Theft Act 1978- section 4(2) (a) is repealed.

11.2.2. Theft Acts sections still in force

Theft Act 1978 sections 3 has *not* been repealed.

What must be remembered is that the section 3 Theft Act 1978 offence- 'making off without payment', has not been repealed.

Examples of s3 Theft Act 1968 offence were – obtaining a taxi ride, a haircut, a massage, a house survey, or property repairs and a loan when one has no intention to pay. Other examples include obtaining a university education by falsely claiming to have entrance qualifications.

Also section 2 Theft Act (Amendment) 1996- the offence of 'retaining a wrongful credit' has *not* been repealed.

11.2.3. Theft Act 1968-section 24 A (3) & (4) - 'dishonestly retaining a wrongful credit' is NOT repealed.

The Fraud Act 2006 states that nothing in paragraph 6 of Schedule 1 affects the operation of section 24 of the Theft Act in relation to goods obtained in the circumstances described in section 15(1) Theft Act 1968 where the 'obtaining' is the result of a deception made before the commencement of that paragraph. As to dishonestly retaining a wrongful credit, nothing in paragraph 7 of Schedule 1 affects the operation of section 24A(7) and (8) of the Theft Act 1968 in relation to credits falling within section 24A(3) or (4) of that Act and made *before* the commencement of that paragraph.

11.3. Comparison of some aspects of the Fraud Act with the Theft Acts

For the offence of fraud by false representation to be fulfilled, the only physical conduct required is the making of a representation. Nothing needs to result from the making of the representation. The Defendant does not need to obtain anything as a consequence of the representation and there is no need for anyone to be fooled or taken in by the representation or even to be aware of it. No communication of the representation is required. But in the old deception offences, criminal deception in the Theft Act 1968, sections 1 to 7, the precedent for the meaning of deception was derived from the 1903 case *Re London and Globe Finance Corporation*, in which the court said that to deceive is to induce a man to believe that a thing is true which is false, and which the person practising the deceit knows or believes to be false. And so the defence against credit card frauds and fraud at a bank machine used to be that deceit can be practiced only on a human mind.

The obtaining was argued by the defendant to be too remote from deception.

11.4. The limitations upon the meaning of 'property' for the purposes of theft by section 4 Theft Act 1968 was not applicable to deception

Mortgage frauds could have been prosecuted under section 1 of the 1978 Act (obtaining services by deception), section 15A of the 1968 Act (obtaining a money transfer by deception) or, if payment was made by cheque, section 20(2) of the 1968 Act (procuring the execution of a valuable security by deception), but not under section 15 of the 1968 Act (obtaining property by deception). Now they can simply be treated as a fraud. Most of the offences created by the Theft Acts involve dishonesty as a specific ingredient. The offences created by sections 17 (false accounting), 19 (false statements by company directors, etc., 21 (blackmail) and 22 (handling stolen goods) of the 1968 Act, and sections are "Group A" offences within Part I of the Criminal Justice Act 1993.

11.5. 1.Maximum sentence for the fraud offence

Mortgage frauds could have been prosecuted under the since repealed section 1 of the 1978 Act (obtaining services by deception), since repealed section 15A of the 1968 Act (obtaining a money transfer by deception) or, if payment was made by cheque, since repealed section 20(2) of the 1968 Act (procuring the execution of a valuable security by deception), but not under since repealed section 15 of the 1968 Act (obtaining property by deception). Now they can simply be treated as a fraud. Most of the offences created by the Theft Acts involve dishonesty as a specific ingredient. The offences created by sections 17 (false accounting), 19 (false statements by company directors, etc., 21 (blackmail) and 22 (handling stolen goods) of the 1968 Act, and sections are "Group A" offences within Part I of the Criminal Justice Act 1993.

Mortgage frauds are being committed on a grand scale and real estate has long been the preferred choice and one of the oldest known ways to transfer proceeds illegally between parties.

Tax fraud schemes are closely linked to mortgage frauds. In 2006, the OECD surveyed 18 countries to look at the widespread illegal practices within the real state sector. The extent of property fraud remains unclear and none of the countries investigated were able to report official statistics even though property transaction figures are readily available. Mortgage frauds use many methods including manipulating transaction prices, using false identities, not declaring transactions and gains, and using corporations to disguise the identity of those benefitting.

As an example, an individual might use cash gained from illegal activities to buy a plot of land, the price of the plot undeclared to sellers. He builds an apartment block and the undeclared gains are ploughed into other construction projects in a further chain of undeclared or under-invoiced deals involving other parties. To further obscure the transactions, the original sellers might also conduct their dealings via "straw men" to disguise ownership. The buyers might try to avoid taxation by reporting artificial losses to offset the gains from the undervalued sale. Ways of hiding ownership include the use of off-shore companies or complicated ownership structures to make acquisitions or to acquire properties overseas without reporting the transactions. There is also the fraud of "property flipping" which occurs where property changes hands rapidly in a chain of buying and selling, much like the stock exchange fraud of "churning" a stock to increase its price. Mortgage fraud can occur through the use of off-shore financial institutions. A bank account is opened in a tax haven country. A loan to finance the acquisition of real estate s made by the offshore bank through its correspondent in the country where the purchase is made. The loan is guaranteed by deposits abroad. The criminal uses illegal funds under the guise of a loan and may even be able to declare and deduct the interest on the loan against any taxable income.

If caught, they usually claim that they were negligent in completing the tax return. However, a civil standard of proof applies on a challenge to an assessment of penalty for such negligent submission of income tax returns, as per *Commissioners of Revenue and Customs v Khawaja*, Chancery Division, The Times, 20 October 2008.

11.4.2. Maximum sentences under Theft Acts

The maximum terms of imprisonment for indictable offences under the Theft Acts are as follows:

Theft Act offences	Sentence
Robbery , assault with intent to rob, aggravated burglary;	Life
Burglary of a dwelling, blackmail, handling stolen property	14 years
Burglary other than of a dwelling, obtaining property by deception, obtaining a money transfer by deception, retaining a wrongful credit;	10 years
Theft, false accounting, suppression of documents and procuring the execution of a valuable security by deception;	7 years

Removal of articles from places open to the public, abstraction of electricity, obtaining a pecuniary advantage by deception, obtaining services by deception, evasion of liability by deception	5 years
Going equipped to steal, making off without payment;	3 years
Aggravated vehicle taking	2 years
Taking a conveyance without authority (increased, from a day to be appointed, by the Criminal Justice Act 2003, s.281 (4)-(6)).	6 months

11.5. Summary of all sections of Theft Act 1968 repeals

THEFT ACT 1968	Quote
Section 15 Obtaining property by deception	A person who by any deception dishonestly obtains property belonging to another, with the intention of permanently depriving the other of it, shall on conviction on indictment be liable to imprisonment for a term not exceeding ten years......

Section 15 A Obtaining a money transfer by deception	A person is guilty of an offence if by any deception he dishonestly obtains a money transfer for himself or another. A money transfer occurs when a debit is made to one account; a credit is made to another and the credit results from the debit or the debit results from the credit. References to a debit or credit are to a credit of an amount of money and to a debit of an amount of money. It is immaterial whether the amount credited is the same as the amount debited; whether the money transfer is effected on presentment of a cheque or by another method; whether any delay occurs in the process by which the money transfer is effected; whether any intermediate credits or debits are made in the course of the money transfer; whether either of the accounts is overdrawn before or after the money transfer is effected. A person guilty of an offence under this section shall be liable on conviction on indictment to imprisonment for a term not exceeding ten years.

Section 15 B Interpretation of Section 15 A.	The following provisions have effect for the interpretation of section 15A of this Act. Deception has the same meaning as in section 15 of this Act. Account means an account kept with a bank or a person carrying on a business if in the course of the business money received by way of deposit is lent to others or any other activity of the business is financed, wholly or to any material extent, out of the capital of or the interest on money received by way of deposit. Deposit here has the same meaning as in section 35 Banking Act 1987 (fraudulent inducement to make a deposit). All the activities which a person carries on by way of business shall be regarded as a single business carried on by him. Money includes money expressed in a currency other than sterling or in the European currency unit.
Section 16 Obtaining pecuniary advantage by deception.	A person who by any deception dishonestly obtains for himself or another any pecuniary advantage shall on conviction on indictment be liable to imprisonment for a term not exceeding five years. The cases in which a pecuniary advantage within the meaning of this section is to be regarded as obtained for a person are cases where he is allowed to borrow by way of overdraft, or to take out any policy of insurance or annuity contract, or obtains an improvement of the terms on which he is allowed to do so; or he is given the opportunity to earn remuneration or greater remuneration in an office or employment, or to win money by betting.

Section 20 (2) Suppression, etc. of documents.	A person who dishonestly, with a view to gain for himself or another or with intent to cause loss to another, by any deception procures the execution of a valuable security shall on conviction on indictment be liable to imprisonment for a term not exceeding seven years and this subsection shall apply in relation to the making, acceptance, endorsement, alteration, cancellation or destruction in whole or in part of a valuable security, and in relation to the signing or sealing of any paper or other material in order that it may be made or converted into , or used or dealt with as, a valuable security, as if that were the execution of a valuable security.
Section 24 A (3) Dishonestly retaining a wrongful credit.	
Section 23 A (4) Dishonestly retaining a wrongful credit.	

11.6. Summary of all sections of Theft Act 1978 repeals

Section 1 Obtaining services by deception.	A person who by any deception dishonestly obtains services from another shall be guilty of an offence. It is an obtaining of services where the other is induced to confer a benefit by doing some act, or causing or permitting some act to be done, on the understanding that the benefit has been or will be paid for. It is an obtaining of services where the other is induced to make a loan, or to cause or permit a loan to be made, on the understanding that any payment (whether by way of interest or otherwise) will be or has been made in respect of the loan.

Fraud Investigation: Criminal Procedure and Investigation

Section 2 Evasion of liability by deception.	A person shall be guilty of an offence where by any deception, he dishonestly secures the remission in whole or in part of any existing liability to make a payment, whether his own liability or another's; or with intent to make permanent default in whole or part on any existing liability to make a payment or with intent to let another do so, dishonestly induces the creditor or any person claiming payment on behalf of the creditor to wait for payment (whether or not the due payment date for payment is deferred) or to forgo payment; or dishonestly obtains any exemption from or abatement of liability to make a payment. Liability here means legally enforceable liability. A person induced to take in payment a cheque or other security for money by way of conditional satisfaction of a pre-existing liability is to be treated not as being paid but as being induced to wait for payment.
Section 4 (2) (a) Sentence not exceeding 5 years-repealed	Punishments. A person convicted on indictment shall be liable for an offence of making off without payment, to imprisonment for a term not exceeding 5 years.
Section 5 (1) Deception has same meaning as in s15 Theft Act 1968.	Deception means any deception (whether deliberate or reckless) by words or conduct as to fact or as to law, including a deception as to the present intentions of the person using the deception or any other person. As to company officers who are guilty of obtaining services by deception or evasion of liability by deception, section 18 Theft Act 1968 applies. –Repealed.

11.7. The fraud offences not covered by the Fraud Act 2006

Offences Not Covered by Fraud Act 2006	Quote
S1 Theft Act 1968 Basic definition of 'theft'.	A person is guilty of theft if he dishonestly appropriates property belonging to another with the intention of permanently depriving the other of it and thief and steal shall be construed accordingly....
S2 Theft Act 1968 Definition of 'dishonesty'.	A person's appropriation of property belonging to another is not to be regarded as dishonest if he appropriates the property in the belief that he has in law the right to deprive the other of it, on behalf of himself or of a third person; if he appropriates the property in the belief that he would have the other's consent if the other knew of the appropriation and the circumstances of it; or if he appropriates the property in the belief that the person to whom the property belongs cannot be discovered by taking reasonable steps.

| S3 Theft Act 1968 Definition of 'appropriates'. | Any assumption by a person of the rights of an owner amounts to an 'appropriation' and this includes, where he has come by the property (innocently or not) without stealing it, any later assumption of a right to it by keeping or dealing with it as owner. Where property or a right or interest in property is or purports to be transferred for value to a person acting in good faith, no later assumption by him of rights which he believed himself to be acquiring shall by reason of any defect in the transferor's title, amount to theft of the property. |

S4 Theft Act 1968 Definition of 'property'.	Property includes money and all other property, real or personal, including things in action and other intangible assets. A person cannot steal land, or things forming part of land and severed from it by him or by his directions, except in the following cases-when he is a trustee or personal representative, or is authorised by power of attorney, or as a liquidator of a company, or otherwise, to sell or dispose of land belonging to another, and he appropriates the land or anything forming part of it by dealing with it in breach of the confidence reposed in him; or when he is not in possession of the land and appropriates anything forming part of the land by severing it or causing it to be severed, or after it has been severed; or when, being in possession of the land under a tenancy, he appropriates the whole or part of any fixture or structure let to be used with the land. Land does not include incorporeal hereditaments. 'Tenancy' means a tenancy for years or any less period and includes an agreement for such a tenancy, but a person who after the end of a tenancy remains in possession as statutory tenant or otherwise is to be treated as having possession under the tenancy and 'let' shall be construed accordingly. A person who picks mushrooms growing wild on any land, or who picks flowers, fruit or foliage from a plant growing wild on any land, does not (although not in possession of the land) steal what he picks, unless he does it for reward or for sale or other commercial purpose.

| | Wild creatures, tamed or untamed, shall be regarded as property, but a person cannot steal a wild creature not tamed nor ordinarily kept in captivity, or the carcass of any such creature, unless either it has been reduced into possession by or on behalf of another person and possession of it has not since been lost or abandoned, or another person is in course of reducing it into possession. |

S5 Theft Act 1968 Meaning of 'belonging to another'.	Property shall be regarded as belonging to any person having possession or control of it, or having in it any proprietary right or interest (not being an equitable interest arising only from an agreement to transfer or grant an interest). Where property is subject to a trust, the person to whom it belongs shall be regarded as including any person having a right to enforce the trust, and an intention to defeat the trust shall be regarded accordingly as an intention to deprive of the property any person having that right. Where a person receives property from or on account of another, and is under an obligation to the other to retain and deal with that property or its proceeds in a particular way, the property or proceeds shall be regarded (as against him) as belonging to the other. Where a person gets property by another's mistake, and is under an obligation to make restoration (in whole or in part) of the property or its proceeds or of the value thereof, then to the extent of that obligation the property or proceeds shall be regarded (as against him) as belonging to the person entitled to restoration, and an intention not to make restoration shall be regarded accordingly as an intention to deprive that person of the property or proceeds. Property of a corporation sole shall be regarded as belonging to the corporation notwithstanding.

S6 Theft Act 1968 'With the intention of permanently depriving the other of it'.	A person appropriating property belonging to another without meaning the other permanently to lose the thing itself is nevertheless to be regarded as having the intention of permanently depriving the other of it if his intention is to treat the thing as his own to dispose of regardless of the other's rights, and a borrowing or lending of it may amount to so treating it if, but only if, the borrowing or lending is for a period and in circumstances making it equivalent to an outright taking or disposal…….
S7 Theft Act 1968 Sentence for 'theft'.	A person guilty of theft shall on conviction on indictment be liable to imprisonment for a term not exceeding seven years.
S8 Theft Act 1968 Sentence for 'robbery'.	A person guilty of robbery if he steals, and immediately before or at the time of doing so, and in order to do so, he uses force on any person or puts or seeks to put any person in fear of being then and there subjected to force, shall on conviction on indictment be liable to imprisonment for life.

S9 Theft Act 1968 Sentence for 'burglary'.	A person is guilty of burglary if he enters any building or part of a building as a trespasser and with intent to commit any offence of stealing anything in the building or part of the building; of inflicting on any person therein any grievous bodily harm or raping any person therein and of doing unlawful damage to the building or anything therein, and on conviction on indictment he is liable to imprisonment for a maximum of 14 years where the offence was committed in respect of a building and 10 years in any other case.
S10 Theft Act 1968 Sentence for 'aggravated burglary'.	A person who commits any burglary and at the time had with him any firearm, imitation firearm, any weapon of offence, shall on conviction on indictment be liable to imprisonment for life.
S11 Theft Act 1968 Sentence for 'removal of articles from places open to the public'.	Removal of articles from places open to the public carries a prison sentence not exceeding 5 years.
S12 theft Act 1968 Sentence for taking motor vehicle or other conveyance without authority.	Liable on summary conviction to a fine not exceeding Level 5 on the standard scale, to maximum of 6 months imprisonment or to both.

S12A Theft Act 1968 Aggravated vehicle taking	On conviction on indictment, liable to imprisonment for a term not exceeding 2 years or 14 years if an accident causes a death.
S13 Theft Act 1968 Sentence for 'abstracting electricity'.	A person who dishonestly uses without due authority, or dishonestly causes to be wasted or diverted, any electricity shall on conviction on indictment be liable to imprisonment for a term not exceeding 5 years.
S14 Theft Act 1968 Extension to thefts from mails outside England and Wales, and robbery, etc. on such a theft.	Liable to be prosecuted, tried and punished in the UK, without proof that the offence was committed there.
S17 Theft Act 1968 False Accounting.	Where a person dishonestly with a view to a gain for himself or another or with intent to cause loss to another- destroys, defaces, conceals or falsifies any account or any record or documents made or required for any accounting purpose; or in furnishing information for any purpose produces or makes use of any account, or any such record or document as aforesaid, which to his knowledge is or may be misleading, false or deceptive in a material particular, he shall, on conviction on indictment, be liable to imprisonment for a term not exceeding 7 years.

S18 Theft Act 1968 Liability of company officers for certain offences by company.	Liable to be proceeded against and punished accordingly.
S19 Theft Act 1968 False statements by company directors, etc.	Liable to 7 years imprisonment.
S21 Theft Act 1968 Blackmail	Liable to 14 years imprisonment.
S22 Theft Act 1968 Handling stolen goods	Liable to up to 14 years' imprisonment.
S23 Theft Act 1968 Advertising rewards for return of goods stolen or lost.	Liable to a fine not exceeding Level 3 on the standard scale.
S24 Theft Act 1968 Offences relating to stolen goods.	Treated as fraud with maximum 10 years imprisonment.

S24A (1),(2), (5)to (12) Dishonestly retaining a wrongful credit.	Imprisonment for a term not exceeding 10 years.
S25 Theft Act 1968 Going equipped for stealing.	Imprisonment for a term not exceeding 3 years.
S26 Theft Act 1968 Search for stolen goods.	Grant for warrant to search and seize the same.
S27 Theft Act 1968 Evidence and procedure on charge of theft or handling stolen goods.	On the trial of 2 or more persons indicted for jointly handling any stolen goods, the persons so charged may be tried together and the jury may find any of the accused guilty if the jury is satisfied that he handled all or any of the stolen goods, whether or not he did so jointly with the other accused or any of them.

S30 Theft Act 1968 Spouses or civil partners can bring proceedings against each other for theft.	A person shall have the same right to bring proceedings against that person's wife or husband for any offence as if they were not married and give evidence for the prosecution at every stage of the proceedings. No such proceedings are allowed for any stealing or damaging property belonging at the time to that person's wife or husband or civil partner. But if a person is jointly charged with his wife or civil partner for stealing, proceedings can go ahead.
S31 Theft Act 1968 Effect on civil proceedings and rights.	A person shall not be excused by reason that to do so may incriminate that person or the spouse or civil partner of that person of an offence under the Theft Act 1968 from answering any questions put to that person in proceedings for the recovery or administration of any property, for the execution of any trust or for an account of any property or dealings with property or from complying with any order made in any such proceedings. But any such statements made shall not be admissible in evidence against that person or against the spouse or civil partner of that person.
S32 Theft Act 1968 Effect on existing law and construction of references to offences.	Common law offences of larceny, robbery, burglary receiving stolen property, obtaining property by threats, extortion by colour of office or franchise, false accounting by public officers, concealment of treasure troves, are banished. Common law offences of cheating and relating to the public revenue are still offences.

S33 Theft Act 1968	Act does not extend to Scotland.
S34 Theft Act 1968 Interpretation of 'gain' and 'losses.	Gain and loss mean gain and loss only in money or other property. 'Gain' includes a gain by keeping what one has, as well as a gain by getting what one has not. 'Loss' includes a loss by not getting what one might get, as well as a loss by parting with what one has.
S3 Theft Act 1978 Making off without payment.	Amended by SOCPA 2005 Schedule 7. Punishment by a prison sentence not exceeding 2 years.
S4 Theft Act 1978 Punishments.	All Theft Act 1978 offences carry a summary conviction punishable by 6 months or a fine of £1000.

11.8. Conclusion to Chapter 11

The 1968 Theft Act is based on "a fundamental reconsideration of the principles underlying this branch of the law" (Criminal Law Revision Committee: 8th Report, Cmnd. 2977). The 1978 Act was intended to remedy perceived defects in the 1968 legislation and there is an overlap between offences. The various offences created by the Theft Acts are not mutually exclusive. Now, however, the Fraud Act removes the complexity in some sections of the Theft Acts and has a maximum sentence of ten years and is simpler to administrate.

Further reading for Chapter Twelve

Legislation can be accessed from the Government website
http://www.opsi.gov.uk/legislation/about_legislation.htm
Theft Act 1968
Theft Act 1978
Fraud Act 2006

CHAPTER 12- INVESTIGATION OF ELECTRONIC FRAUD

12.1. Introduction

This is a very important chapter in a fraud law book. It covers the operations of a fraud investigation. It is to be remembered that a fraud investigation will aim to find information as well as evidence and the distinction between the two is important.

Evidence is information set out in a way that a court will admit as being capable of proving a fact. This becomes a vital point when information obtained in one case is used for the purposes of another case or if evidence in one case is to be used as evidence for another case or evidence in one case is used as information in another case. It must be borne in mind that the Criminal Procedure and Investigations Act 1996 regulate material used by the defendant and the prosecution.

There are statutory powers conferred on public bodies charged with the investigation and prosecution of crime and the regulation of markets. There is the power to require a person to answer questions on oath in the Criminal Justice Act 1987, s2(2);Companies Act 1985, s434; Insolvency Act 1986 ss236 and 366; Financial Services Act 1986 ss94 and 105;and Banking Act 1987 s39.

The power to search premises is found in PACE ss 8 and 9; Proceeds of Crime Act 2002 ss 352 to 354; Criminal Justice Act 1987 s 2(4); Taxes Management Act 1970 s 20(1)(c) and Customs and Excise Management Act s 118C(3).

The power to require production of documents or other material is found in PACE s 9; Proceeds of Crime Act 2002 ss 345-351; Criminal Justice Act 1987 s2(3); Taxes Management

Act 1970 s 20BA; Customs and Excise Management Act s118D.

12.2.1. Interviewing

We all undertake interviews. Some are more important and extensive than others. But they all require intellectual and inter-personal skills. Doctors must interview patients, as well as undertake tests. Lawyers must interview clients, to discover their instructions and, like the police, they must also interview witnesses. Unless that is done well the case may be lost. After the miscarriages of justice brought to light in the 1970s, such as the murder of Maxwell Confait in 1972 and subsequent government inquiries, the Police and Criminal Evidence Act 1984 (PACE 1984) was introduced to transform procedures for obtaining evidence.

12.2.2. Interview techniques

The government has also encouraged practical research that has produced interviewing techniques to improve the quality and quantity of information obtained from interviewees, e.g. interview recall can be improved by using a technique known as the "cognitive interview". This approach uses psychological research on how we perceive, store and retrieve information, to enable the witness to give as full and accurate an account of the event as possible. Similarly "conversation management" techniques develop rapport between interviewer and interviewee, which improves the standard of information generated from the interview. Police officers, and others such as government fraud investigators, are trained in these techniques and regularly use them in interviews. These models reduce the likelihood of wrongful confessions, and do not involve oppressive or coercive techniques. The aim is to obtain more information about the disputed incident which can be checked using forensic science.

12.2.3. Credibility

Should evidence which is obtained using these techniques be accorded greater credibility than information which is obtained from an interview conducted in a different manner? If so, a judge, statute or code, might identify a range of criteria to be considered, e.g. were leading questions avoided, was the interviewee assured that s/he was free to tell everything s/he considered relevant about the incident? Were directed questions left to the end, to clarify ambiguities?

12.2.4. Actions consistent with professional practice

The Court of Appeal disagreed. It was inappropriate to find the doctor negligent when his actions had been consistent with professional practice. The trial judge should not have taken the *Bolitho v City and Hackney Health Authority* route to declare professional standards inadequate, without giving counsel and the expert witnesses a chance to explain why doctors interview in that manner.

The Court of Appeal was also surprised at the agreed professional practice of not asking any specific, closed, questions, and ordered a retrial. The doctor knew about the serious consequences of A's shunt.

So this could be seen as a distinctive case, where normal professional practice should not apply. There is a case for doctors adopting approaches consistent with those developed for interviewing vulnerable witnesses (see 'Achieving Best Evidence in Criminal Proceedings: Guidance for Vulnerable and Intimidated Witnesses, Including Children', Home Office Communication Directorate, January 2002), where closed questions are considered appropriate, at the end of an interview, to minimise confusion.

12.2.5. Ethical interviewing

The lack of intra-professional understanding has led interview researchers and practitioners to consider adopting a statement of the principles of ethical interviewing (see *www.port.ac.uk/iii2/*). The statement proposed that "obtaining a confession should not be the primary goal when interviewing someone suspected of committing a crime or other wrong"; and suggests seeking a confession might lead to oppressive interviews where reliability should be challenged.

This is a controversial proposal in today's world in that interviewing should aim to make confession easier.

12.3.1. Investigating electronic fraud

The Internet, computer networks, and automated data systems present an enormous new opportunity for fraudulent activity. Computers and other electronic devices are being used increasingly to commit, enable, or support frauds perpetrated against persons and organizations. Whether the fraud involves attacks against computer systems, the information they contain, or more traditional frauds electronic evidence increasingly is involved and there is an overwhelming volume of investigations and prosecutions that involve electronic evidence.

Practices, procedures, and decision-making processes for investigating electronic fraud need to be prepared by technical working groups of practitioners and subject matter experts who are knowledgeable about electronic fraud. Such guides address the investigation process from the fraud scene first responder, the laboratory then to the courtroom.

Such guides address

(i) Fraud scene investigations by first responders.//
(ii) Examination of digital evidence.//
(iii) Investigative uses of technology.//
(iv) Investigating electronic technology frauds.//
(v) Creating a digital evidence forensic unit and//
(vi) Courtroom presentation of digital evidence.

Due to the rapidly changing nature of electronic and computer technologies and of electronic fraud, updates of the information contained within the guides are necessary.

12.3.2. Electronic Fraud Scene

Each of the individuals in this team needs to be experienced in the intricacies involved with electronic evidence in relation to recognition, documentation, collection, and packaging. Define the scope and breadth of the work. Each guide must focus on a different aspect of the discipline.

The law enforcement response to electronic evidence requires that officers, investigators, forensic examiners, and managers all play a role. Officers may encounter electronic devices during their day-to-day duties. Investigators may direct the collection of electronic evidence, or may perform the collection themselves. Forensic examiners may provide assistance at fraud scenes and will perform examinations on the evidence. Managers have the responsibility of ensuring that personnel under their direction are adequately trained and equipped to properly handle electronic evidence. Each responder must understand the fragile nature of electronic evidence and the principles and procedures associated with its collection and preservation. Actions that have the potential to alter, damage, or destroy original evidence may be closely scrutinised by the courts.

12.3.4.1. Power of Seizure under the Police and Criminal Evidence Act

PACE provides many powers for the seizure of property.

Section 20 provisions apply to powers exercised under a section 8 warrant for indictable offences; powers exercised under section 18 following arrest for an indictable offence; powers under Schedule 1 for special procedure material; powers exercised under section 19 when officers are lawfully on the premises and powers under Schedule 4 Police Reform Act 2002 and exercised by investigating officers. Also PACE Code B, paragraph 7.6 reinforces the power to require electronically stored information to be produced in a visible and legible form that can be taken away or reproduced.

Section 21 PACE makes provision for the supplying of copies of records of seizure to certain people after property has been seized. Section 22 of PACE makes provision for the retention of seized property. Information gained as a result of a lawful search may be passed on to other individuals and organisations for purposes of investigation and prosecution.

It must not be used for private purposes (See Code of Conduct for Police Officers). Part 2 of the Criminal Justice and Police Act 2001 provides the police with specific powers to "seize and sift" under strict conditions and subject to a number of rigid procedural safeguards. One such safeguard is the specific application of Code B of PACE.

This power is rarely used because it is necessary to show that it is essential to do so. If at any time after seizure legal privilege material is discovered, section 54 PACE imposes a general duty on the officer in possession of the property to ensure that the item is returned as soon as reasonably practicable after the seizure.

Where a person exercises a power of seizure by sections 50 or 51, that person will be under a duty, on doing so, to give the occupier or person from whom property is seized, a written notice. That notice will specify what has been seized and the grounds on which the powers have been exercised, the effect of the safeguards and the rights to apply to a judicial authority for the return of the property, the name and address of the person to whom notice of an application to a judge and an application to be allowed to attend the initial examination should be sent.

12.3.4.2. Procedures

Procedures to promote electronic fraud scene investigation must be in place. Managers should determine who will provide particular levels of services and how these services will be funded. Personnel should be provided with initial and ongoing technical training. Certain cases will demand a higher level of expertise, training, or equipment, and managers should have a plan in place regarding how to respond to these cases.

12.3.5. The Nature of Electronic Evidence

Electronic evidence is information and data of investigative value that is stored on or transmitted by an electronic device. As such, electronic evidence is latent evidence in the same sense that fingerprints or DNA (deoxyribonucleic acid) evidence is latent. In its natural state, we cannot "see" what is contained in the physical object that holds our evidence.

Equipment and software are required to make the evidence visible. Witness statements may be required to explain the examination process and any process limitations. Electronic evidence is, by its very nature, fragile. It can be altered, damaged, or destroyed by improper handling or improper examination. For this reason, special precautions should be taken to document, collect, preserve, and examine this type of evidence. Failure to do so may render it unusable or lead to an inaccurate conclusion.

12.3.6. The Forensic Process

The nature of electronic evidence is such that it poses special challenges for its admissibility in court. To meet these challenges, follow proper forensic procedures. These procedures include, but are not limited to, four phases: collection, examination, analysis, and reporting.

The collection phase involves the search for, recognition of, collection of, and documentation of electronic evidence. The collection phase can involve real-time and stored information that may be lost unless precautions are taken at the scene. The examination process helps to make the evidence visible and explain its origin and significance. This process should accomplish several things. First, it should document the content and state of the evidence in its totality. Such documentation allows all parties to discover what is contained in the evidence. Included in this process is the search for information that may be hidden or obscured. Once all the information is visible, the process of data reduction can begin, thereby separating the "wheat" from the "chaff." Given the tremendous amount of information that can be stored on computer storage media, this part of the examination is critical.

Analysis differs from examination in that it looks at the product of the examination for its significance and probative value to the case. Examination is a technical review that is the province of the forensic practitioner, while analysis is performed by the investigative team.

A written report that outlines the examination process and the pertinent data recovered completes an examination. Examination notes must be preserved for discovery or evidence purposes. An examiner may need to testify about not only the conduct of the examination but also the validity of the procedure and his or her qualifications to conduct the examination. When dealing with electronic evidence, general forensic and procedural principles should be applied:

(i) Actions taken to secure and collect electronic evidence should not change that evidence.

(ii) Persons conducting examination of electronic evidence should be trained for the purpose.

(iii) Activity relating to the seizure, examination, storage, or transfer of electronic evidence should be fully documented, preserved, and available for review.

Without having the necessary skills and training, no responder should attempt to explore the contents or recover data from a computer (e.g., do not touch the keyboard or click the mouse) or other electronic device other than to record what is visible on its display.

12.3.7. Electronic Evidence

Electronic evidence is information and data of investigative value that is stored on or transmitted by an electronic device. Such evidence is acquired when data or physical items are collected and stored for examination purposes.

Electronic evidence:-is often latent in the same sense as fingerprints or DNA evidence; can transcend borders with ease and speed; is fragile and can be easily altered, damaged, or destroyed and is sometimes time-sensitive.

12.3.8. Electronic Evidence handled at the fraud scene

Precautions must be taken in the collection, preservation, and examination of electronic evidence. Handling electronic evidence at the fraud scene normally consists of the following steps:

(i) Recognition and identification of the evidence.

(ii) Documentation of the fraud scene.

(iii) Collection and preservation of the evidence.

(iv) Packaging and transportation of the evidence.

The necessary legal authority to search for and seize the suspected evidence will have been obtained beforehand. The fraud scene will have been secured and documented (photographically and/or by sketch or notes). Fraud scene protective equipment (gloves, etc.) should be used as necessary. The improper access of data stored in electronic device may violate provisions of certain laws, including the Human Rights Act 1998. Because of the fragile nature of electronic evidence, examination should be done only by appropriate personnel.

12.3.9. .How to handle Electronic Evidence

It is recommended that investigative plans be developed in compliance with policy and laws.

12.3.10. Electronic Devices: Types and Potential Evidence

Electronic evidence can be found in many of the new types of electronic devices available to consumers. Many electronic devices contain memory that requires continuous power to maintain the information, such as a battery or AC power.

Data can be easily lost by unplugging the power source or allowing the battery to discharge. After determining the mode of collection, collect and store the power supply adaptor or cable, if present, with the recovered device.

12.4. 1. Computer Systems

A computer system typically consists of a main base unit, sometimes called a central processing unit (CPU), data storage devices, a monitor, keyboard, and mouse. It may be a standalone or it may be connected to a network. There are many types of computer systems such as laptops, desktops, tower systems, modular rack-mounted systems, minicomputers, and mainframe computers. Additional components include modems, printers, scanners, docking stations, and external data storage devices. For example, a desktop is a computer system consisting of a case, motherboard, CPU, and data storage, with an external keyboard and mouse.

12.4.2. Primary Uses

For all types of computing functions and information storage, including word processing, calculations, communications, and graphics.

12.4.3. Potential Evidence

Evidence is most commonly found in files that are stored on hard drives and storage devices and media.

12.4.4. User-Created Files

User-created files may contain important evidence of criminal activity such as address books and database files that may prove criminal association, still or moving pictures that may be evidence of fraudulent activity, and communications between criminals such as by e-mail or letters. For example, a drug deal lists may often be found in spreadsheets.

12.4.5. User-Protected Files

Users have the opportunity to hide evidence in a variety of forms. For example, they may encrypt or password-protect data that are important to them. They may also hide files on a hard disk or within other files or deliberately hide incriminating evidence files under an innocuous name. Evidence can also be found in files and other data areas created as a routine function of the computer's operating system. In many cases, the user is not aware that data are being written to these areas. Passwords, Internet activity, and temporary backup files are examples of data that can often be recovered and examined. There are components of files that may have evidentiary value including the date and time of creation, modification, deletion, access, user name or identification, and file attributes. Even turning the system on can modify some of this information.

12.4.6. Computer-Created Files

Computer created files are -Backup files; Log files; Configuration files; Printer spool files; Cookies; Swap files; Hidden files; System files; History files and Temporary files.

12.4.7. Other Data Areas

Other data areas are the Port; Replicator; Docking Station and Server. These take the form of Bad clusters; Computer date, time, and password; Deleted files; Free space; Hidden partitions; Lost clusters; Metadata; Other partitions; Reserved areas; Slack space; Software registration information; System areas and unallocated space.

12.4.8. Central Processing Units (CPUs)

CPU's are components of computers. Often called the "chip" the CPU is a microprocessor located inside the computer. The microprocessor is located in the main computer box on a printed circuit board with other electronic components. Its primary uses forms all arithmetic and logical functions in the computer. CPU's control the operation of the computer. The device itself may be evidence of component theft, counterfeiting, or remarking.

12.4.9. Memory

Memory is the removable circuit board inside the computer. Information stored here is usually not retained when the computer is powered down. It stores user's programs and data while computer is in operation. The device itself may be evidence of component theft, counterfeiting, or remarking.

Access Control Devices are smart cards, dongles, and biometric scanners.

A smart card is a small handheld device that contains a microprocessor that is capable of storing a monetary value, encryption key or authentication information (password), digital certificate, or other information. A dongle is a small device that plugs into a computer port that contains types of information similar to information on a smart card. A biometric scanner is a device connected to a computer system that recognizes physical characteristics of an individual (e.g., fingerprint, voice, and retina).

12.4.10. Processor

This provides access control to computers or programs or functions as an encryption key. Its potential evidence value is the identification/authentication information of the card and the user, level of access, configurations, permissions, and the device itself.

12.4.11. Answering Machines

This is an electronic device that is part of a telephone or connected between a telephone and the landline connection. Some models use a magnetic tape or tapes, while others use an electronic (digital) recording system. It records voice messages from callers when the called party is unavailable or chooses not to answer a telephone call. It usually plays a message from the called party before recording the message. Since batteries have a limited life, data could be lost if they fail. Therefore, appropriate personnel (e.g., evidence custodian, lab chief, and forensic examiner) should be informed that a device powered by batteries is in need of immediate attention. Answering machines can store voice messages and, in some cases, time and date information about when the message was left. They may also contain other voice recordings

12.4.12. Digital Camera

A Camera is a digital recording device for images and video, with related storage media and conversion hardware capable of transferring images and video to computer media.

12.4.13. USB Dongles Parallel

Digital cameras capture images and/or video in a digital format that is easily transferred to computer storage media for viewing and/or editing.

12.4.14. Potential Evidence

Potential evidence takes the form of images; Time and date stamp; Removable cartridges; Video and Sound.

12.4.15. Handheld Devices

A personal digital assistant (PDA) is a small device that can include computing, telephone/fax, paging, networking, and other features. It is typically used as a personal organiser. A handheld computer approaches the full functionality of a desktop computer system. Some do not contain disk drives, but may contain PC card slots that can hold a modem, hard drive, or other device. They usually include the ability to synchronize their data with other computer systems, most commonly by a connection in a cradle. If a cradle is present, attempt to locate the associated handheld device.

Handheld computing, storage, and communication devices are capable of storage of information. Since batteries have a limited life, data could be lost if they fail. Therefore, appropriate personnel (e.g., evidence custodian, Lab chief, forensic examiner) should be informed that a device powered by batteries is in need of immediate attention.

12.4.16. Hard Drive

This is a sealed box containing rigid platters (disks) coated with a substance capable of storing data magnetically. It can be encountered in the case of a PC as well as externally in a standalone case. It is used for the storage of information such as computer programs, text, pictures, video and multimedia files.

12.4.17. Memory Card

A memory card is a removable electronic storage device, which does not lose the information when power is removed from the card. It may even be possible to recover erased images from memory cards. Memory cards can store hundreds of images in a credit card size module. It is used in a variety of devices, including computers, digital cameras, and PDAs. Examples are memory sticks, smart cards, flash memory, and flash cards. A memory card provides additional, removable methods of storing and transporting information.

12.4.18 Modems

A modem, internal and external (analog, DSL, ISDN, cable), wireless modem, PC card. A modem is used to facilitate electronic communication by allowing the computer to access other computers and/or networks via a telephone line, wireless, or other communications medium. The device itself is potential evidence. Network card components are indicative of a computer network. They consist of Network cards and associated cables. Network cards also can be wireless. A LAN/NIC card is used to connect computers. Cards allow for the exchange of information and resource sharing. Potential Evidence is in the device itself.

12.4.19. Routers, Hubs, and Switches

These electronic devices are used in networked computer systems. Routers, switches, and hubs provide a means of connecting different computers or networks. They can frequently be recognized by the presence of multiple cable connections.

12.4.20 Servers

A server is a computer that provides some service for other computers connected to it via a network. Any computer, including a laptop, can be configured as a server. A Server provides shared resources such as e-mail, file storage, Web page services, and print services for a network.

12.4.21. Network Cables and Connectors

Network cables can be different colours, thickness, and shapes and have different connectors, depending on the components they are connected to. Connects components of a computer network. The devices themselves are primary evidence.

12.4.22. Pagers

A handheld, portable electronic device that can contain volatile evidence (telephone numbers, voice mail, e-mail). Cell phones and personal digital assistants also can be used as paging devices. Primary Uses are for sending and receiving electronic messages, numeric (phone numbers, etc.) and alphanumeric (text, often including e-mail). Since batteries have a limited life, data could be lost if they fail. Therefore, appropriate personnel (e.g., evidence custodian, lab chief, and forensic examiner) should be informed that a device powered by batteries is in need of immediate attention. Potential evidence is found in address information, text messages, e-mail, voice messages and telephone numbers.

12.4.23. Printers

One of a variety of printing systems, including thermal, laser, inkjet, and impact, connected to the computer via a cable (serial, parallel, universal serial bus (USB), firewire) or accessed via an infrared port. Some printers contain a memory buffer, allowing them to receive and store multiple page documents while they are printing. Some models may also contain a hard drive. Primary Uses are to print text, images, etc., from the computer to paper. Printers may maintain usage logs, time and date information, and, if attached to a network, they may store network identity information. In addition, unique characteristics may allow for identification of a printer.

12.4.24. Removable Storage Devices and Media

Media used to store electrical, magnetic, or digital information (e.g., floppy disks, CDs, DVDs, cartridges, tape). Primary Uses include store of computer programs, text, pictures, video, multimedia files, etc. New types of storage devices and media come on the market frequently; these are a few examples of how they appear.

12.4.25. Scanners

An optical device connected to a computer, which passes a document past a scanning device (or vice versa) and sends it to the computer as a file. Converts documents, pictures, etc., to electronic files, which can then be viewed, manipulated, or transmitted on a computer. The device itself may be evidence. Having the capability to scan may help prove illegal activity (e.g., child pornography, cheque fraud, counterfeiting, and identity theft). In addition, imperfections such as marks on the glass may allow for unique identification of a scanner used to process documents.

12.4.26. Miscellaneous Electronic Items

There are many additional types of electronic equipment that are too numerous to be listed that might be found at a fraud scene. However, there are many non-traditional devices that can be an excellent source of investigative information and/or evidence. Examples are credit card skimmers, cell phone cloning equipment, caller ID boxes, audio recorders, and Web TV. Fax machines, copiers, and multifunction machines may behave internal storage devices and may contain information of evidentiary value. The search of this type of evidence may require a search warrant.

12.4.27. Copiers

Some copiers maintain user access records and history of copies made. Copiers with the scan once/print many feature allow documents to be scanned once into memory, and then printed later. Potential evidence takes the form of documents; user usage log and time and date stamp.

12.4.28. Credit Card Skimmers

Credit card skimmers are used to read information contained on the magnetic stripe on plastic cards. Potential evidence **is** information contained on the tracks of the magnetic stripe includes card expiration date; user's address; credit card numbers and user's name.

12.4.29. Digital Watches

There are several types of digital watches available that can function as pagers that store digital messages. They may store additional information such as address books, appointment calendars, e-mail, and notes. Some also have the capability of synchronizing information with computers. Potential evidence lies in address books; notes; appointment calendars and phone numbers.

12.4.30. Facsimile Machines

Facsimile (fax) machines can store pre-programmed phone numbers band a history of transmitted and received documents. In addition, some contain memory allowing multiple-page faxes to be scanned in and sent at a later time as well as allowing incoming faxes to be held in memory and printed later. Some may store hundreds of pages of incoming and/or outgoing faxes.

Potential Evidence: documents; phone numbers; Film cartridge; Send/receive log.

12.4.31. Global Positioning Systems (GPS)

Global Positioning Systems can provide information on previous travel via destination information, way points, and routes. Some automatically store the previous destinations and include travel logs. Potential evidence may be found in the home; way point coordinates; previous destinations; way point name; and travel logs.

12.5.1. Investigative Tools and Equipment

Special tools and equipment may be required to collect electronic evidence. Experience has shown that advances in technology may dictate changes in the tools and equipment required. There should be access to the tools and equipment necessary to document, disconnect, remove, package, and transport electronic evidence. Preparations should be made to acquire the equipment required to collect electronic evidence.

The needed tools and equipment are dictated by each aspect of the process: documentation, collection, packaging, and transportation.

12.5.2. Tool Kit

There should be general fraud scene processing tools (e.g., cameras, notepads, sketchpads, evidence forms, fraud scene tape, and markers).

Additional items that may be useful at an electronic fraud scene:

Documentation Tools

Cable tags; Indelible felt tip markers; Stick-on labels.

Disassembly and Removal Tools

A variety of nonmagnetic sizes and types of: Flat-blade and Philips-type screwdrivers, Hex-nut drivers, Needle-nose pliers, Secure-bit drivers, Small tweezers, specialized screwdrivers (manufacturer-specific, e.g., Compaq, Macintosh), Standard pliers, Star-type nut drivers, Wire cutters.

Package and Transport Supplies

Antistatic bags, antistatic bubble wrap, cable ties, evidence bags, and evidence tape; packing materials (avoiding materials that can produce static electricity such as styrofoam or styrofoam peanuts); packing tape; and sturdy boxes of various sizes.

Other Items

Items that should also be included within a police fraud department's tool kit are: gloves; hand truck; large rubber bands; list of contact telephone numbers for assistance; magnifying glass; printer paper; seizure disk; small flashlight; and unused floppy diskettes.

12.6. Securing and Evaluating the Scene

The first responder should take steps to ensure the safety of all persons at the scene and to protect the integrity of all evidence, both traditional and electronic. All activities should be in compliance with departmental policy and laws. After securing the scene and all persons on the scene, the first responder should visually identify potential evidence, both conventional (physical) and electronic, and determine if perishable evidence exists. The first responder should evaluate the scene and formulate a search plan. Follow jurisdictional policy for securing the fraud scene. This would include ensuring that all persons are removed from the immediate area from which evidence is to be collected. At this point in the investigation do not alter the condition of any electronic devices: ***If it is off, leave it off. If it is on, leave it on.*** Protect perishable data physically and electronically. Perishable data may be found on pagers, caller ID boxes, electronic organizers, cell phones, and other similar devices. The first responder should always keep in mind that any device containing perishable data should be immediately secured, documented, and/or photographed. Identify telephone lines attached to devices such as modems and caller ID boxes. Document, disconnect, and label each telephone line from the wall rather than the device, when possible. There may also be other communications lines present for LAN/Ethernet connections. Consult appropriate personnel/agency in these cases. Keyboards, the computer mouse, diskettes, CDs, or other components may have latent fingerprints or other physical evidence that should be preserved. Chemicals used in processing latent prints can damage equipment and data. Therefore, latent prints should be collected after electronic evidence recovery is complete.

12.7. Conduct preliminary interviews

Separate and identify all persons (witnesses, subjects, or others) at the scene and record their location at time of entry. Consistent with departmental policy and applicable law, obtain from these individuals information such as Owners and/or users of electronic devices found at the scene, as well as passwords (see below), user names, and Internet service provider. Any passwords required to access the system, software, or data. (An individual may have multiple passwords, e.g., BIOS, system login, network or ISP, application files, encryption pass phrase, e-mail, access token, scheduler, or contact list.)

12.8.1. Documenting the Scene

Documentation of the scene creates a permanent historical record of the scene. Documentation is an ongoing process throughout the investigation. It is important to accurately record the location and condition of computers, storage media, other electronic devices, and conventional evidence. Documentation of the scene should be created and maintained in compliance with departmental policy and laws. The scene should be documented in detail.

12.8.2. Initial documentation of the physical scene:

Observe and document the physical scene, such as the position of the mouse and the location of components relative to each other (e.g., a mouse on the left side of the computer may indicate a left-handed user).Document the condition and location of the computer system, including power status of the computer (on, off, or in sleep mode). Most computers have status lights that indicate the computer is on. Likewise, if fan noise is heard, the system is probably on. Furthermore, if the computer system is warm, that may also indicate that it is on or was recently turned off.

Identify and document related electronic components that will not be collected.

Photograph the entire scene to create a visual record as noted by the first responder. The complete room should be recorded with 360 degrees of coverage, when possible.

Photograph the front of the computer as well as the monitor screen and other components. Also take written notes on what appears on the monitor screen. Active programs may require videotaping or more extensive documentation of monitor screen activity. Movement of a computer system while the system is running may cause changes to system data. Therefore, the system should not be moved until it has been safely powered down.

Additional documentation of the system will be performed during the collection phase.

12.9.1. Evidence Collection

The search for and collection of evidence at an electronic fraud scene may require a search warrant. Computer evidence, like all other evidence, must be handled carefully and in a manner that preserves its evidentiary value. This relates not just to the physical integrity of an item or device, but also to the electronic data it contains. Certain types of computer evidence, therefore, require special collection, packaging, and transportation. Consideration should be given to protect data that may be susceptible to damage or alteration from electromagnetic fields such as those generated by static electricity, magnets, radio transmitters, and other devices.

Electronic evidence should be collected according to departmental guidelines. In the absence of departmental guidelines outlining procedures for electronic evidence collection, the following procedures are suggested. Prior to collection of evidence, it is assumed that locating and documenting has been done. Recognize that other types of evidence such as trace, biological, or latent prints may exist. Follow police protocol regarding evidence collection. Destructive techniques (e.g., use of fingerprint processing chemicals) should be postponed until after electronic evidence recovery is done.

> **Points to Note: Search warrants**
>
> Applications as per SOCPA s8.
>
> Access to excluded or special procedure material are in SOCPA s9 and Schedule 1.
>
> A search warrant issued by a judge can be an 'all purpose' warrant, as provided for in SOCPA, s113 (10) to (14).
>
> Safeguards for obtaining search warrants are in ss 15 and 16 SOCPA and PACE Code B, s2.
>
> An officer of the rank of inspector or above may direct a designated investigating officer not to wear a uniform for the purpose of a specific operation. As per SOCPA, s 122(2).
>
> A contravention of pace or the codes or any other illegal or unfair conduct may result in the evidence which was thereby obtained being ruled inadmissible. This is the effect of s 78 PACE which provides that the court may exclude evidence on which the prosecution proposes to rely on , *'having regard to all the circumstances, including the circumstances in which the evidence was obtained, the admission of the evidence would have such an adverse effect on the fairness of the proceedings that the court ought not to admit it'.*

12.9.2. Non-electronic Evidence

Recovery of non-electronic evidence can be crucial in the investigation of electronic fraud. Proper care should be taken to ensure that such evidence is recovered and preserved. Items relevant to subsequent examination of electronic evidence may exist in other forms (e.g., written passwords and other handwritten notes, blank pads of paper with indented writing, hardware and software manuals, calendars, literature, text or graphical computer printouts, and photographs) and should be secured and preserved for future analysis. These items frequently are in close proximity to the computer or related hardware items. All evidence should be identified, secured, and preserved in compliance with police guidelines.

12.9.3. Stand-Alone and Laptop Computer Evidence

Multiple computers may indicate a computer network. Likewise, computers located at businesses are often networked. In these situations, specialized knowledge about the system is required to effectively recover evidence and reduce your potential for civil liability. *When a computer network is encountered, contact the forensic computer expert in your department or outside consultant identified by your department for assistance.* A "stand-alone" personal computer is a computer not connected to a network or other computer. Standalones may be desktop machines or laptops. Laptops incorporate a computer, monitor, keyboard, and mouse into a single portable unit. Laptops differ from other computers in that they can be powered by electricity or a battery source. Therefore, they require the removal of the battery in addition to stand-alone power-down procedures. If the computer is on, document existing conditions and call your expert or consultant. If an expert or consultant is not available, continue with the following procedure:

After securing the scene, read all steps below before taking any action (or evidentiary data may be altered). Record in notes all actions you take and any changes that you observe in the monitor, computer, printer, or other peripherals that result from your actions. Observe the monitor and determine if it is on, off, or in sleep mode. Then decide which of the following situations applies and follow the steps for that situation.

Situation (i)

Monitor is on and work product and/or desktop is visible.

Photograph screen and record information displayed.

Situation (ii)

Monitor is off.

(a) Make a note of "off" status.
(b) Turn the monitor on, then determine the monitor status Regardless of the power state of the computer (on, off, or sleep mode), remove the power source cable from the computer—NOT from the wall outlet. If dealing with a laptop, in addition to removing the power cord, remove the battery pack. The battery is removed to prevent any power to the system. Some laptops have a second battery in the multipurpose bay instead of a floppy drive or CD drive. Check for this possibility and remove that battery as well.
(c) Check for outside connectivity (e.g., telephone modem, cable, ISDN, DSL). If a telephone connection is present, attempt to identify the telephone number.

(d) To avoid damage to potential evidence, remove any floppy disks that are present, package the disk separately, and label the package. If available, insert either a seizure disk or a blank floppy disk. Do NOT remove CDs or touch the CD drive.

(e) Place tape over all the drive slots and over the power connector.

(f) Record make, model, and serial numbers.

(g) Photograph and diagram the connections of the computer and the corresponding cables.

(h) Label all connectors and cable ends (including connections to peripheral devices) to allow for exact reassembly at a later time.

(i) Label unused connection ports as "unused." Identify laptop computer docking stations in an effort to identify other storage media.

(j) Record or log evidence according to departmental procedures.

(k) If transport is required, package the components as fragile cargo.

Situation (iii)

> **Monitor is on and screen is blank or screen saver is visible.**
>
> (a) Move the mouse slightly (without pushing buttons). The screen should change and show work product or request a password.
> (b) If mouse movement does not cause a change in the screen, DO NOT perform any other keystrokes or mouse operations.
> (c) Photograph the screen and record the information displayed.
> (d) Proceed to step c.

12.9.4. Evidence from computers in a complex environment

Business environments frequently have multiple computers connected to each other, to a central server, or both. Securing and processing a fraud scene where the computer systems are networked poses special problems, as improper shutdown may destroy data. This can result in loss of evidence and potential severe civil liability. When investigating criminal activity in a known business environment, the presence of a computer network should be planned for in advance, if possible, and appropriate expert assistance obtained. It should be noted that computer networks can also be found in a home environment and the same concerns exist. It is important that computer networks be recognized and identified, so that expert assistance can be obtained if one is encountered.

Indications that a computer network may be present include: the presence of multiple computer systems; the presence of cables and connectors, such as those depicted in the pictures at left, running between computers or central devices such as hubs; information provided by informants or individuals at the scene; the presence of network components.

12.9.5. Peripheral Evidence

The electronic devices such as the ones in the list below may contain potential evidence associated with criminal activity. Unless an emergency exists, the device should not be operated. Should it be necessary to access information from the device, all actions associated with the manipulation of the device should be documented to preserve the authenticity of the information. Many of the items listed below may contain data that could be lost if not handled properly.

Examples of other electronic devices (including computer peripherals):Audio recorders; Answering machines; Cables; Caller ID devices; Cellular telephones; Chips. (When components such as chips are found in quantity, it may be indicative of chip theft.); Copy machines; Databank/Organizer digital; Digital cameras (still and video); Dongle or other hardware protection devices (keys) for software; Drive duplicators; External drives; Fax machines; Flash memory cards; Floppies, diskettes; CD–ROMs; GPS devices; Pagers; Palm Pilots/electronic organizers; PCMCIA cards; Printers (if active, allow to complete printing); Removable media; Scanners (film, flatbed, watches, etc.); Smart cards/secure ID tokens; Telephones (including speed diallers, etc.);VCRs; and Wireless access point.

When seizing removable media, ensure that you take the associated device that created the media (e.g., tape drive and cartridge drive).

12.10. 1. Packaging, Transportation, and Storage

Actions taken should not add, modify, or destroy data stored on a computer or other media. Computers are fragile electronic instruments that are sensitive to temperature, humidity, physical shock, static electricity, and magnetic sources. Therefore, special precautions should be taken when packaging, transporting, and storing electronic evidence. To maintain chain of custody of electronic evidence, document its packaging, transportation, and storage. Ensure that proper procedures are followed for packaging, transporting, and storing electronic evidence to avoid alteration, loss, physical damage, or destruction of data.

12.10.2. Packaging procedure

(i) Ensure that all collected electronic evidence is properly documented, labelled, and inventoried before packaging.

(ii) Pay special attention to latent or trace evidence and take actions to preserve it.

(iii) Pack magnetic media in antistatic packaging (paper or antistatic plastic bags). Avoid using materials that can produce static electricity, such as standard plastic bags.

(iv) Avoid folding, bending, or scratching computer media such as diskettes, CD–ROMs, and tapes.

(v) Ensure that all containers used to hold evidence are properly labelled.

If multiple computer systems are collected, label each system so that it can be reassembled as found (e.g., System A–

mouse, keyboard, monitor, main base unit; System B–mouse, keyboard, monitor, main base unit).

12.10.3. Transportation procedure

Keep electronic evidence away from magnetic sources. Radio transmitters, speaker magnets, and heated seats are examples of items that can damage electronic evidence.

Avoid storing electronic evidence in vehicles for prolonged periods of time. Conditions of excessive heat, cold, or humidity can damage electronic evidence. Ensure that computers and other components that are not packaged in containers are secured in the vehicle to avoid shock and excessive vibrations. For example, computers may be placed on the vehicle floor and monitors placed on the seat with the screen down and secured by a seat belt. Maintain the chain of custody on all evidence transported.

12.10.4. Storage procedure

Ensure that evidence is inventoried in accordance with departmental policies. Store evidence in a secure area away from temperature and humidity extremes. Protect it from magnetic sources, moisture, dust, and other harmful particles or contaminants. Be aware that potential evidence such as dates, times, and systems configurations may be lost as a result of prolonged storage. Since batteries have a limited life, data could be lost if they fail. Therefore, appropriate personnel (e.g., evidence custodian, lab chief, and forensic examiner) should be informed that a device powered by batteries is in need of immediate attention.

12.11.1. Forensic Examination by Fraud Type

The following outline should help officers/investigators identify the common findings of a forensic examination as they relate to specific fraud categories. This outline will also help define the scope of the examination to be performed.

12.11.2. Auction Fraud (Online)

Account data regarding online auction sites.- Accounting/bookkeeping software and associated data files; address books; calendar; chat logs; customer information/credit card data; databases; digital camera software; email/notes/letters; financial/asset records; image files; internet activity logs; internet browser history/cache files; online financial institution access software; records/documents of "testimonials"; telephone records.

12.11.3. Computer Intrusion

These are address books; configuration files; e-mail/notes/letters; executable programs; internet activity logs; internet protocol (IP) address and user name; internet relay chat (IRC) logs; source code; and text files (user names and passwords).

12.11.4. Economic Fraud (Including Online Fraud, Counterfeiting)

These are address books; calendar; cheque, currency, and money order images; credit card skimmers; customer information/credit card data; databases; email/notes/letters; false financial transaction forms; false identification; financial/asset records; images of signatures; internet activity logs; online financial institution access software.

12.11.5. Extortion

Extortion by using date and time stamps; e-mail/notes/letters; history log; internet activity logs; temporary Internet files; user names.

12.11.6. Identity Theft

Using hardware and software tools; backdrops; credit card generators; credit card reader/writer; digital cameras; scanners; identification templates; birth certificates; cheque cards; digital photo images for photo identification; driver's license; electronic signatures; fictitious vehicle registrations; proof of motor insurance documents; scanned signatures; social security cards; internet activity related to ID theft; e-mails and newsgroup postings; erased documents; online orders; online trading information; system files and file slack; World Wide Web activity at forgery sites; negotiable instruments; business cheques; cashier's cheques; counterfeit money; credit card numbers; fictitious court documents; fictitious gift certificates; fictitious loan documents; fictitious sales receipts; money orders; personal cheques; shares transfer documents; traveller's cheques; vehicle transfer documentation.

12.11.7. Software Piracy

Software piracy can be perpetrated using chat logs; e-mail/notes/letters; image files of software certificates; internet activity logs; serial numbers; software cracking information and utilities; user-created directory and file names that classify copyrighted software.

12.11.8. Telecommunications Fraud

Telecommunications fraud can be perpetrated by using cloning software; customer database/records; electronic Serial Number (ESN)/Mobile Identification Number (MIN) pair records; e-mail/notes/letters; financial/asset records; "How to phreak" manuals; internet activity; telephone records.

At a physical scene, look for duplication and packaging material. The following information, when available, should be documented to assist in the forensic examination: - case summary; internet protocol addresses (es); keyword lists; nicknames; passwords; points of contact and supporting documents.

> **Further Reading on Electronic Fraud Investigation**
>
> D. Blacharski, *Network Security in a Mixed Environment,* (IDG Books, California 1998).
>
> E. Casey, Digital *Evidence and Computer Fraud: Forensic Science, Computers and the Internet,* (Academic Press, San Diego 2000)
>
> F. B. Cohen, A *Short Course on Computer Viruses,* (John Wiley & Sons, New Jersey 1994).
>
> D.E. Denning, *Information Warfare and Security,* (Addison-Wesley, Boston 1999).
>
> J. Guisnel, *Cyberwars: Espionage on the Internet,* (Plenum Press, New York 1997).
>
> National White Collar Fraud Centre, *Using the Internet as an*
> *Investigative Tool, First Edition,* (National White Collar Fraud Centre, Virginia 1999).
>
> E.S. Raymond, The *New Hacker's Dictionary, Third Edition.* (MIT Press, London 1998).

K.S.Rosenblatt, *High-Technology Fraud: Investigating Cases Involving Computers,* (KSK
Publications, California 1996).
M.Wolff, How *You Can Access the Facts and Cover Your Tracks Using the Internet and Online Service,* (Wolff New Media, LLC, New York 1996).

CHAPTER 13-
POLICE FRAUD INVESTIGATIONS-
POLICIES AND MANAGEMENT

13.1. Introduction

This single chapter has been provided by Jeneth Williams.

Fraud investigation is managed differently in many police forces from other serious and organised crime. Frequently the crime is left to a constable or investigator to be investigated with only a supervisory overview. This chapter is written as though the management support is available as even if there is only one investigator the roles and processes are still relevant. Other organisations should have similar processes as the considerations are those you would expect to see for any major investigation.

13.2. Follow the evidence

Whatever the management of the investigation the objectives for the investigation should remain the same: a search for the truth and the conviction of the offenders through a fair and just investigation. This should be achieved by gathering all the evidence available, pursuing all reasonable lines of enquiry and assessing the facts to establish what has happened and to identify the perpetrators and successfully prosecute them. The investigation must be conducted within the principles of the Human Rights Act and take cognisance of CPIA rules.

13.3. Computerised solutions

Due to the nature of economic crime it is unlikely that an investigator will have a system such as Holmes 2 to help with the management of the investigation as this is resource intensive and not best suited to the fraud investigation. There are several computerised solutions available to assist, the majority of which are based around a scanning system with the addition of a file build programme for the management of statements and exhibits. The end result is a computerised file with hyperlinks to relevant exhibits, statements and documents this allows the case to be delivered in local courts with basic IT. When building the case it is helpful for the investigator to recognise that the majority of serious fraud cases do end in a trial and creative thinking on the part of the investigator is required to provide the evidence in as simple and understandable style as possible for a jury.

13.4. Presentation of Evidence

Fraud can be complex with offending often difficult to understand. This give the opportunity to the defence to exploit the complexity and confusion, so the simpler the presentation of the evidence to the jury the higher the chance of a conviction. Consider the use of charts and I2 associations to keep the basic facts clear – that Suspect A stole from Victim B utilising this method (trick). Repetition of these simple facts is allowed regardless of any objections from the defence.

Case Study: Property Fraud

X an auction house proprietor who was also director of several companies was profiting by selling houses on behalf of financial institutions for their bottom price to one of his companies before the open auction occurred. The houses were then sold through another auction house at their true value with X keeping the profit.

> Y wants to sell a house that has been re-possessed
>
> Y puts a bottom value of £100 K on the sale and employs X auction house to complete the sale
>
> X knows the property would in an open auction probably achieve £150 – 175 K, but sells the property to Company Z (he is a director of this company) prior to the auction for £100K
>
> X then auctions the property through another auction house and the property sells for £150K with X pocketing the £50K
>
> The defence tried to confuse the jury by introducing lots of associates and co-directors and the myriad of companies involved. By clear charting we were able to demonstrate the offenders association with and indeed control of these companies and that his auction house was at the heart of the fraud. The chart was continually used by the prosecution as a rebuttal. The defence would explain how a certain transaction occurred and why their client was not involved. The prosecution would then put up the chart and point to the company involved show the defendant's involvement with that firm and then link this back to the auction houses showing each transaction clearly linked to the defendant. The defendant was convicted of fraud by abuse of position.
>
> The defendant was in a position in which he was expected to safeguard, or not act against, the financial interests of another person and he dishonestly abused the position to make financial gain for himself.

13.5. Initial Assessment

When a report of fraud is received it is important to spend some time assessing the complaint. The initial assessment should consist of a check against the force acceptance criteria, if a crime has actually been committed and if so which offence. Frequently frauds reported to the police are not crimes but are bad debts, which should be pursued through the civil courts. As stated in Chapter 2 some frauds reported to the police can and should be investigated by other agencies. Having established that it is a crime and that it fits the force acceptance criteria then the crime should be recorded and then the allegation further assessed as below.

13.6. Investigative assessment

The investigative assessment is an important step in managing the investigation. Its purpose is to review the allegation and the information that is available to identify what offences have been committed and by whom. The best resource to do this work is an experienced fraud investigator who can bring skills and knowledge to the role and will recognise anomalies in the allegation and also opportunities for investigation. The assessment process involves checking the evidence available in the allegation and asking a number of questions. Intelligence sources should also be researched to identify any similar cases nationally with the suspects and also any previous offending or intelligence held. It must be remembered at this stage there will be an allegation but it is unlikely that a detailed statement will have been taken.

A format should be established for the assessment process to ensure that the same criteria is applied to each assessment and thus be able to justify the decision making process with transparency. The victims of many frauds will object if the police fail to investigate their offence.

> **Points to Note: Basis for an assessment**
>
> What happened?
> What offences have been committed?
> Who has committed the offences and what is their individual involvement?
> What is the offender profile? (Intelligence?)
> How many victims are there?
> What is the victim profile?
> What is the total loss to the victims and victim impact?
> Are there any known assets? (Compensation / Confiscation)
> Are there any political / public interest issues indicated in the complaint?
> Are there any community / economic implications?
> Does the offending fit in the National Intelligence Model - Level 2 or 3 serious and complex?
> Is there any evidence of involvement of serious crime groups?
> Does the offending involve corruption or abuse of position?
> Are there clear lines of enquiry?

13.7. Identify all possible scenes

Without establishing these facts an investigation cannot be directed and decisions made in relation to whether the police investigate are difficult to justify. It is important at this stage to identify any possible scenes - such as in the event of a 'long firm fraud' (see chapter 5) – as there may be forensic opportunities, which will be available for a limited time. I decision on whether to investigate may be taken quickly in order to action any search and forensic recovery where time is of the essence.

13.8. Acceptance of Investigation

The process of accepting an investigation will differ from force to force an organisation to organisation. Some forces and organisations utilise the National Intelligence Model process within the tasking and co-ordinating process for economic crimes and other forces deal with economic crime separately to other serious crime. One of the key measures of acceptance must be having the resources available to investigate. There is no point accepting an investigation if there is insufficient resources to conduct the enquiries. A good assessment will identify the likely enquiries and an experienced investigator can estimate the likely time span and lines of enquiry for the investigation. The use of the tasking and co-ordinating model assists where there are insufficient resources. The resourcing can be raised as an issue for the unit and the reprioritising of current work or a request for additional resources can be addressed here within a clear decision making body.

13.10. Investigation Policy

The investigation policy should be set by the supervising officer usually the head of the unit who will identify the parameters of the investigation - which offences will be investigated and which offenders will be pursued - based on the assessment document.

> **Points to Note: Policy Strategy**
>
> The policy should also set out the strategy in relation to the following:
> Financial Investigation
> Setting Investigation Parameters
> Witness Strategy
> Victim Strategy
> Suspect Strategy
> Search and Seizure Strategy
> Decision Making and Recording
> Human Rights
> Disclosure

The policy in relation to disclosure should be documented. Disclosure needs to be managed as invariably there are large numbers of documents and other evidence in a fraud case. The policy should be set as to how this will be controlled. Many forces and other agencies have a computerised solution, which involves scanning the material and managing it electronically. This can be beneficial as all stages of the process can also be done electronically. The rules in relation to disclosure are contained in the CPS Disclosure Manual which is a practical guide covering the provisions of the Criminal Procedures and Investigations Act 1996, the Code of practice and the Attorney General's Guidelines. There is a duty on the investigation to retain any material relevant to the investigation and through the CPS or prosecutor to reveal this to the defence if it affects or undermines the prosecution case or assists the defence as stated in the defence statement.

13.11. Case material

Material that is classed as sensitive should also be retained but will not be revealed to the defence. This material can be excluded by an order from the case judge following a PII (Public Interest Immunity) Hearing.

Sensitive material is classed as

(i) Material revealing police techniques

(ii) Material given in confidence

(iii) Confidential internal police communications

(iv) Confidential internal police information or intelligence

> **Point to Note: sensitive documents**
>
> Article 9 of the ECHR deals with sensitive documents which are defined as documents, classified as top secret, secret or confidential in accordance with the rules of the institution concerned, which protect essential interests of the European Union or of one or more of its member states in the areas of public security, defence and military matters.

If following a PII hearing the material is not excluded a risk assessment as to any repercussions for individuals or organisations should be conducted and a decision as to whether proceed with the case made in view of the likely outcomes should the material be revealed to the defence. Material excluded as a result of a PII hearing may at a later stage become so relevant that continued exclusion is not in the public interest and at this point a risk assessment as above should be conducted.

13.12. Financial Investigation

At this early stage consideration in the investigation should be given to the movement of the proceeds of the identified criminality and the utilisation of the powers within the Proceeds of Crime Act 2002. Financial benefit is the motivation behind most frauds and following the money trail can identify assets and offenders with clear irrefutable evidential links. In particular the offence of money laundering should be considered and a possible future confiscation of assets.

Compensation for the victims can be achieved through the confiscation process and it is important to make this clear to the victims so there is no civil redress being pursued alongside the criminal investigation.

Other powers that can be used within the Proceeds of Crime Act are the restraint powers whereby identified assets can be restrained until after the trial, and if convicted, can be restrained until the conclusion of the confiscation proceedings. Assigning an accredited Financial Investigator to assist in the investigator would be considered good practice if the investigator did not have this accreditation. An accredited financial investigator acts under the Proceeds of Crime Act 2002, as amended by the Serious Crimes Act 2007 section 76- additional powers to seize property to which restraint orders apply.

13.13. Setting Investigation Parameters

It is also important at this stage to speak to the prosecuting agency and identify a caseworker for the investigation. In some cases for the police and the SFO this will involve using a prosecutor based at the CPS Casework Directorate (London, Birmingham and York). The early involvement of the prosecutor can ensure that there is agreement with the policy and can also be useful to agree other parameters of the investigation such as the number of witness statements that are required. This is particularly helpful when there a large number of victims and taking detailed statements from them all would be unnecessary and time consuming. It is often acceptable to have detailed statements from a small number of victims and records of the other victims' details and their loss. This is only applicable if the same modus operandi of the offenders has been used in each case. The offences to be investigated should be the offences for which the investigation will be least complicated using the fewest resources but which is supported by the evidence and will meet the objectives of the investigation.

> **Case study: Limiting the Investigation**
>
> Three companies were set up to trade among themselves and to borrow money from the banks to finance non-existent goods. A number of offences where committed including factoring fraud and fraudulent trading. The decision was made to only investigate the factoring fraud as all the offenders were implicated in the offence and the evidence was readily available. The investigation into the factoring offence also covered the majority of the losses as the main losers where the finance companies who had lent money against false invoices. The investigation, by limiting it like this, would be concluded in 6 months (at least 12 months earlier than if we also investigated the fraudulent trading) and the penalties for the offenders were commensurate with the investigation. All three offenders were given custodial sentences and given lifetime bans from holding directorships.

13.14. The Witness Strategy

As part of the investigation policy a witness strategy will be set. This will identify the victims who will have detailed statements taken from them and those from whom basic details will be taken. If it is not possible to make the decisions at this time then some criteria should be drawn up to apply against a first account from the witness.

> **Points to Note: Example of witness strategy**
>
> An example of such a criteria could be
> The age of the witness
> Current mental state (some people are badly effected by being a victim of an offence with financial loss)
> Significant gain / loss (some witnesses can be gainers in particular early victims of a pyramid fraud)
> Has the witness had significant personal contact with an offender?

13.15. Is the witness in any way implicated in the offending?

Each witness should also be identified in relation to their status –

(i) Vulnerable

(ii) Intimidated

(iii) Key and significant

If a witness fits into any of these categories then there is a requirement to video record their testimony – provided they consent. The first 2 categories also are entitled to access special measures when giving evidence.

13.16. The Victim Strategy

A documented strategy for dealing with the victims of the offending should also be considered to document how the investigator will comply with the Victim's Charter.

Note that this is only applicable to a recorded crime so may not be relevant to other agencies.

The strategy should cover:

(i) Completing a Victim Personal Statement (this explains to the court the effect the offending has had on the victim and is often appropriate in cases of fraud against individuals).

(ii) Setting clear timescales for how often contact should be made with the victim(s) to ensure they are informed of progress.

(iii) Consideration of Special Measures in the court proceedings (if these are appropriate).

(iv) Providing the details of the witness service to the victim in the event of the case going to trial to ensure the victim is familiar with the court environs and what will happen on the day.

13.17. The Suspect Strategy

The suspect strategy should also be agreed at the Investigation Policy stage. The strategy will consider all the known suspects and their involvement in the crime. If any suspect is not going to be pursued then this should be documented. If not all suspects are known then a method of identifying the suspects should be agreed. Before any suspect is investigated the details of the suspect, and their involvement, should be considered by the unit supervisor and a decision made as to whether they will be pursued.

The suspect strategy should contain the following:

(i) Method for identifying suspects.

(ii) Forensic opportunities with each suspect (with fraud this may involve using a forensic accountant to look at the personal finances of the suspect).

(iii) Arrest timelines and disclosure policy. (This is important for fraud cases as there are often a large number of paper exhibits, which, need to be disclosed to the suspect and if this is done following arrest it may affect the custody time limits. The decision relating to disclosure of information to the defendant prior to interview needs to be considered carefully and should only be done with a legal representative and should be recorded.)

(iv) Interview arrangements and Bail and charging procedures

13.18. The Search and Seizure Strategy

As part of the investigation policy a search and seizure strategy should be agreed. All searches should be approved and items to be taken from each premise agreed and linked to the investigation strategy – relevant to the investigation. Clarity is required about what evidence the teams are looking for and the search should not be a 'see what we find when we get there' process. Consideration should be given for how the search teams will deal with any legal privilege material issues should the search result in their seizure. Fraud investigators regularly use the 'Docman' system for the search and seizure process as it provides a system for recording items seized and the relevant information in relation to where the items were. This system has stood the test in court on many occasions and the use of the system or a similar system should be considered.

Forensic recovery is part of the search strategy both in relation to the deployment of Crime Scene Investigators for recovery of physical evidence but also to the requirement for forensic recovery of particular items identified as of evidential importance to the enquiry.

The supervisor should set out in the search strategy the paperwork to be completed and the power under which the search is conducted – PACE or warrant. The use of S50 / 51 powers under the Criminal Justice and Police Act 2001 should be considered and applied where appropriate and the service of the written notices be recorded. Part of the search strategy should include a risk assessment for each premise to cover risks to the investigators, occupants and risks relating to the premises and likely contents.

13.19. Decision Making and Recording

Each investigation should have a documented decision log which identifies the key decisions, the information that they are based on and the justification for the decision. The decisions in relation to the parameters of the investigation should be clear as this is the area most likely to come into question as there will be offences not investigated and therefore victims who will feel that they have not received a proper level of service. There is also the possibility that the decisions made at this stage of the enquiry will be questioned during any trial or if the prosecution should fail.

It is important at this stage to document the offences and offenders that will be investigated and the reasons for this and also to document any decisions taken not to follow a line of enquiry or pursue a suspect.

The strategies mentioned above will all have a link to the decision log as the basis of each strategy should link to a decision in relation to management of the investigation.

The style of recording the decisions made is usually a personal preference but as a minimum should contain the time and date the decision was made, the information on which the decision is based, – what is known at the time, what the decision is - exactly and clearly, and the justification / reason for that decision. The decision should clearly be attributed to the person making it and where it is a decision on policy and it has been made by someone other than the supervisory officer it should be countersigned by this person to show they agree with the decision. Where there is disagreement with the decision made this should be recorded again with the reasons why.

> **Case study: Supervision**
>
> When reviewing the evidence and policy file of a case involving three defendants a supervisory officer, who felt the evidence linking one of the offenders was tenuous, requested that the prosecution of that defendant ceased. This was then discussed at a case conference with the prosecutor who disagreed and the prosecution continued. The defendant was acquitted and made an official complaint against the investigator. The decision log reflected the fact that the supervisor had requested that the prosecution cease and the fact that the prosecutor felt there was sufficient evidence to continue. The complaint against the investigator was dropped and complainant referred to the prosecuting agency.

13.20. Human Rights Act 1998

The Human Rights Act has relevance to the decision-making and management of all investigations. The act covers many areas; the most relevant to the investigator are:

Article 2 Right to life;
Article 5 Liberty and Security;
Article 6 Right to a Fair Trial and
Article 8 Respect for Private and Family Life.

All actions and decisions should comply with the principles of the Human Rights Act and these should underpin all investigations:

(i) Justification (legality) – That there are reasonable grounds to suspect that the person under investigation has some knowledge of or involvement in the offending.

(ii) Necessity – that the methods used are necessary and alternative methods have been considered and the proposed action is the most suitable to achieve the objective.

(iii) Proportionality – the activities must be proportionate to the matter being investigated. There must also be consideration of the balance between the intrusiveness and what will be achieved. It should be shown that the decision making has been accountable and that less intrusive methods have been considered and rejected and the reasons why.

(iv) Collateral Intrusion – This refers to the level of intrusion into the private lives of the suspect and others not under suspicion the method adopted will have. It is not sufficient to use the phrase collateral intrusion will be minimal without clear explanation of what collateral intrusion there will be and how this will be minimised. It must also be shown to be proportionate to the offence under investigation. This aspect should be monitored throughout the activity. Community issues should also be taken into account when accepting collateral intrusion will occur particularly in sensitive areas.

(v) Authority – that any actions taken had the correct authorities and legal requirements have been met.

13.21. Conclusion

The investigative policy should provide the direction required for the investigation and should be reviewed on a regular basis to take into account any change in circumstances. Should any changes to policy be required these should be documented in the decision log and agreed with the person in charge of the investigation.

CHAPTER 14-
THE SERIOUS FRAUD OFFICE INVESTIGATION PROCEDURE

14.1. Introduction

The Serious Fraud Office plays a key part in the maintenance of confidence in the financial institutions of the United Kingdom and its combined expertise of lawyers, accountants, the police and other agencies is designed to ensure that where serious criminal fraud offences are suspected, they will be investigated and, if the evidence is available, prosecuted, notwithstanding their complexity.

14.2. How conflicts of interest is dealt with by the SFO

A conflict of interest can exist where SFO staff and contractors ("all staff") have personal or professional interests which may conflict with the interests or the work of the SFO. Whether or not the staff member is tempted to act against the interests of the SFO, a conflict of interest will exist if it could appear to an external observer that they may do so. This section refers only to conflicts of interest which may occur in the vetting, acceptance, investigation and prosecution of cases. For further information concerning non-operational conflicts you should consult the Staff Guide, or the Head of Resources and Planning.

SFO policy is that staff should avoid placing themselves in a position where their personal interests may conflict with those of the SFO. Where any risk of a conflict arises, the staff member should declare it to the Case Controller or Head of Division. Staff may accept offers of hospitality from, for example, Counsels' Chambers or firms of accountants, which allow staff to meet others involved in the criminal justice process informally. However consideration should always be given as to whether a potential conflict of interest may arise. Factors to take into account include the nature and value of the hospitality; and the relationship between the SFO and the hospitality host. Gifts of more than nominal value should be reported to the Case Controller or Head of Division. When allocated a case to work on, all staff should satisfy themselves that there is no potential conflict of interest between themselves and their duties to the SFO.

14.3. Reporting Conflicts of Interest at the SFO

Actual or potential conflicts on casework should be reported immediately to the case controller and the head of division in writing. Conflicts in vetting or acceptance of cases should be reported immediately in writing to the appropriate assistant or deputy director or to the director. It is particularly important to make a report as soon as the conflict becomes apparent and before there is any active involvement in the case. The case controller and the head of division (or the appropriate assistant or deputy director) will decide the extent of any necessary restrictions and record the decision in the case policy file, or at the vetting stage, in the vetting file. Special care is needed in the treatment of information that: the SFO wishes to receive from third parties; or is generated by the SFO (in whatever form).

The SFO will be under obligations of confidence in relation to this information. This restricts how the information may be used or disclosed. The law on confidentiality does not prevent the proper use of confidential information by the SFO for the purpose of preventing and detecting crime. Disclosure for some other purpose must be through a gateway such as s3 Criminal Justice Act 1987 ("CJA 87") ("section 3 gateway").

The section 3 gateway permits the SFO to disclose information:

3. to any government department; or
4. for a prosecution in England or elsewhere; or
5. to specified regulatory bodies in England or elsewhere.

The procedure for such disclosure appears at 'Procedure for making a request to HMRC'. Some laws makes it an offence to disclose information. They include: Official Secrets Act 1911 -1989; Data Protection Act 1998; Regulation of Investigatory Powers Act 2000; Financial Services and Markets Act 2000; and the Companies Act 1985 and 2006. This may mean in some instances that the SFO cannot disclose information to other parties. Care should therefore be taken concerning the use of information which has been supplied on confidential terms.

Members of the public may approach the SFO with information in the expectation that this information will be kept confidential. Members of the public, whether potential witnesses or not, should never be assured that complete confidentiality can always be guaranteed. The SFO may, for example, be required to disclose the information under the provisions of the unused material disclosure rules when the information undermines the prosecution case or assists the defence case. If the information is sensitive it may be appropriate to make a Public Interest Immunity application to the court to protect that information. Some information provided by the public may have to be disclosed under the provisions of the Data Protection Act 1998 ("DPA") or the Freedom of Information Act 2000 ("FOIA"). Most SFO casework information is confidential and members of the public will not be entitled to receive it. It is clearly in the public interest that this information is not given out as it may undermine the SFO's ability to undertake its primary duty; to investigate and prosecute serious fraud. However, there are exceptions to this general policy. Members of the public will be able to access SFO information in certain circumstances:

Under the DPA an individual, including a defendant, suspect or witness, is entitled to request and receive details of any personal information held on them by the SFO. There are exceptions to this right, for example when disclosure would prejudice the prevention or detection of crime, the apprehension or prosecution of offenders or prejudice the administration of justice (s31 DPA). Under the FOIA any member of the public has a right of access to information held by the SFO. To facilitate the SFO duties to provide information, a publication scheme has been published on the SFO web page which sets out the information available to the public. Some SFO information is exempt from disclosure. This will be mainly in relation to SFO case investigation and prosecution material which it is not in the public interest to disclose (s30 & s31 FOIA).

Any member of the SFO who receives a request for information under the DPA and FOIA must bring this to the attention of the SFO Information Officer immediately. The SFO is required to deal with requests for information under strict time limits. Further information about public requests for information can be found in the Freedom of Information Act and Data Protection Act topics. Sometimes an SFO investigation is so sensitive that special provisions should be adopted as the publication of any details, speculation, or the fact that an investigation is being undertaken would cause significant damage to the SFO prospect of obtaining vital evidence. In such circumstances all witnesses who are interviewed in connection with the case should be given a reasoned explanation as to why the information should be treated in confidence and why it would be wrong to pass it on. The witness should be asked to sign (or give on tape) a confidentiality undertaking in the following terms. Case Controllers may be required to make affidavits should the Director need to apply for an injunction to prevent disclosure or publication. Evidence of all decisions and actions taken to ensure security must be readily available.

A solicitor should not be required to sign an undertaking to ensure that information imparted at interview is not disclosed. Any decision by a solicitor to release confidential information provided to his client falls within a solicitor's duty to act only on his client's express instructions. In the event that a conflict of interest arises between a solicitor and the SFO concerning disclosure of confidential information, official guidance should be sought from the Law Society rather than seeking judicial review. Personal information relating to staff is confidential. Certain personal information will be held by the Personnel Unit or line managers for reasons of staff appraisal and sickness assessment purposes. This information is held in confidence subject to the exemptions contained within the DPA.

14.4. Official Secrets Act 1989 and SFO investigations

Under the Official Secrets Act 1989 ("OSA 89"), it is an offence for a civil servant to disclose, without lawful authority, information damaging to the national interest in a number of specified categories: security and intelligence; defence; international relations; foreign confidences; information which might lead to the commission of crime; information relating the interception of communications or warrants issued under the Security Services Act 1989: fail to take reasonable care to prevent the unauthorised disclosure of a document or article protected by the Act; retain such a document or article contrary to official duty; disclose information which it would be reasonable to expect might be used to obtain access to information covered by the Act. S1 Official Secrets Act 1911 protects information useful to an enemy. SFO staff should remember that these legal requirements still apply after they have left the Civil Service.

14.5. Confidentiality of Market Sensitive Information

Confidentiality issues arise in relation to inside information about companies whose securities are listed, particularly up to the stage at which an SFO/BERR investigation is announced or otherwise becomes public. It is not possible to consider every circumstance or eventuality that might arise. Therefore when considering particular situations SFO staff should use common sense, paying particular attention to the possibility that confidential activity may become public knowledge and the way in which official acknowledgement is given to actions which have hitherto been confidential.

14.6. Inside Information

"Inside Information" for the purposes sections 56 and 57 Criminal Justice Act 1993 ("CJA 93") means information which: relates to particular securities or to a particular issuer of securities or to particular issuers of securities and not to securities generally or to issuers of securities generally; is specific or precise; has not been made public; and if it were made public would be likely to have a significant effect on the price of any securities.

For the purposes of this Part, securities are "price-affected securities" in relation to inside information and inside information is "price-sensitive information" in relation to securities if and only if the information would, if made public, be likely to have a significant effect on the price (i.e. value) of the security. All enquiries from the press should be directed to the Press and Information Office's staff are not authorised to speak to the press unless it has been arranged with the Press and Information Office. S3 CJA 87 sets out those authorities the SFO may disclose information to and the circumstances in which the information may pass. When providing information under this section the written authority of the Director is required. When considering s3 disclosure of information you should have regard to the Court of Appeal judgment in *Kent Pharmaceuticals and Ors v The Director of the SFO and Ors [2004] EWCA (Civ) 1494* concerning whether the SFO should give advance notice to the owner of the information of its intention to use the statutory gateway. The Court gave guidance as to when an opportunity to make representations should be given. The Director of SFO should decide on notification of disclosure on a case-by-case basis. As general rule notification of impending disclosure should be given in sufficient time to enable the document owner to raise any objection e.g. because of commercial sensitivity. It will sometimes be inappropriate to notify because the documents are simply being passed to another investigating/prosecuting authority or are required for an investigation which may be hampered if the owner is aware. Sometimes it may be inappropriate or impracticable to give notice of proposed disclosure or, within sufficient time to allow a response e.g. where the documents are required urgently elsewhere or where to do so would hamper investigations. In such circumstances if no notice was given prior to disclosure, the Director must consider whether to do so after disclosure has taken place. The SFO should not allow itself to be drawn into satellite litigation.

When you are providing background information to the Director you should ensure that you specifically address the issue of whether advance notice may be required. This will ensure that the Director is properly informed when exercising his discretion as to whether disclosure should take place and, if so, the procedure that should be adopted. S3 (4) CJA 87 also allows the Director to enter into an agreement for the supply of information to or by him. S3 (5) CJA 87 and the Data Protection Act 1998 entitles SFO staff members authorised by the Director to disclose information to any government department. Many authorities with which the SFO has regular dealing with will have corresponding information gateways allowing for disclosure of information to the SFO.

14.7. Obtaining Confidential Information from HMRC

With effect from 18th April 2005 the services of the Inland Revenue and HM Customs & Excise were integrated to form Her Majesty's Revenue & Customs "HMRC"). The information gateways in place prior to the formation of HMRC remain in place for the moment. S1 7(2) Anti-Terrorism, Crime & Security Act 2001 ("ATCSA") provides for the disclosure of confidential revenue information by HMRC for any of the following purposes: - any criminal investigation whatever which is being or may be carried out in the UK or elsewhere; any criminal proceedings whatever which have been or may be initiated in UK or elsewhere; initiating or bringing to an end any such investigation or proceedings; facilitating the determination of the above. The SFO is thus no longer limited to requests and constraints under s3 (1) CJA 1987.

14.8. Disclosure overseas

Only the Secretary of State (Home Office) may direct that revenue information may be disclosed overseas. The SFO cannot share information obtained from HMRC without their consent. There may in due course be some blanket "directions", e.g. for EU countries; but meanwhile specific case by cases consent (or even a formal Order) will be needed. The preconditions are in s1 8(3) ATCSA.

14.9. Supporting Documents

A Code has been published and the SFO is bound by it. Please read it carefully alongside the individual Memoranda of Understanding (MOUs) the SFO signed with both revenue departments prior to their integration. The SFO signed separate MOUs with Customs and Inland Revenue. These MOUs remain in effect following the integration of the departments and set out the practical basis on which disclosure will be made and the procedure for making requests. A list of SFO staff allowed to authorise requests is maintained by the Policy Division.

14.10. Procedure for making a request to HMRC

Written requests must be authorised by a member of staff from the list of authorised staff. Requests must be on the appropriate form, which can be found as the last page of the Memorandum of Understanding for each Revenue Department.

The form can be completed by any investigator.

A request can relate to more than one legal person.

Give brief details of the SFO investigation ("nature of enquiry").

Case Controllers must be satisfied that the disclosure requested will be for one of the permitted purposes; necessary for the prevention or detection of crime (Art 8 HRA); proportionate to the purpose for which it is requested (i.e. reflects the nature of the crime and the needs of the investigation). The request must indicate the protective marking appropriate to the sensitivity of the information requested or provided.

14.11. Confidentiality & Information Gateways

Special care is needed in the treatment of information that: the SFO wishes to receive from third parties; or is generated by the SFO (in whatever form). The SFO will be under obligations of confidence in relation to this information. This restricts how the information may be used or disclosed. The law on confidentiality does not prevent the proper use of confidential information by the SFO for the purpose of preventing and detecting crime. Disclosure for some other purpose must be through a gateway such as s3 Criminal Justice Act 1987 ("CJA 87") ("s3 gateway"). The s3 gateway permits the SFO to disclose information: to any government department; or for a prosecution in England or elsewhere; or to specified regulatory bodies in England or elsewhere. The procedure for such disclosure appears at 'Procedure for making a request to HMRC'. Some laws make it an offence to disclose information. They include: Official Secrets Act 1911 -1989; Data Protection Act 1998; Regulation of Investigatory Powers Act 2000; Financial Services and Markets Act 2000; and the Companies Act 1985. This may mean in some instances that the SFO cannot disclose information to other parties. Care should therefore be taken concerning the use of information which has been supplied on confidential terms. However, there are exceptions to this general policy. Members of the public will be able to access SFO information in certain circumstances: Under the DPA an individual, including a defendant, suspect or witness, is entitled to request and receive details of any personal information held on them by the SFO. There is s to this right, for example when disclosure would prejudice the prevention or detection of crime, the apprehension or prosecution of offenders or prejudice the administration of justice (s31 DPA). Under the FOIA any member of the public has a right of access to information held by the SFO. To facilitate the SFO duties to provide information, a publication scheme has been published on the SFO web page which sets out the information available to the public. Some SFO information is exempt from disclosure. This will be mainly in relation to SFO case investigation and prosecution material which it is not in the public interest to disclose (s30 & s31 FOIA). Any member of the SFO who receives a request for information under the DPA and FOIA must bring this to the attention of the SFO Information Officer immediately. The SFO is required to deal with requests for information under strict time limits.

14.12. Members of the public and SFO confidentiality

Sometimes an SFO investigation is so sensitive that special provisions should be adopted as the publication of any details, speculation, or the fact that an investigation is being undertaken would cause significant damage to the SFO prospect of obtaining vital evidence. In such circumstances all witnesses who are interviewed in connection with the case should be given a reasoned explanation as to why the information should be treated in confidence and why it would be wrong

Fraud Investigation: Criminal Procedure and Investigation

to pass it on. The witness should be asked to sign (or give on tape) a confidentiality undertaking in the following terms. "I have been told that premature disclosure of any information given to or by me in connection with this case may severely prejudice the investigations being conducted by the SFO. I undertake to keep all information, including the fact that the SFO is conducting the investigation, confidential until such time as I am advised this is no longer necessary. I undertake not to discuss the investigation with anyone other than my own legal adviser and to make my legal adviser aware of this undertaking." Case Controllers may be required to make affidavits should the Director need to apply for an injunction to prevent disclosure or publication. Evidence of all decisions and actions taken to ensure security must be readily available.

14.13. Solicitors and SFO confidentiality

A solicitor should not be required to sign an undertaking to ensure that information imparted at interview is not disclosed. Any decision by a solicitor to release confidential information provided to his client falls within a solicitor's duty to act only on his client's express instructions. In the event that a conflict of interest arises between a solicitor and the SFO concerning disclosure of confidential information, official guidance should be sought from the Law Society rather than seeking judicial review.

14.14. Confidentiality of SFO Staff Personal Information

Personal information relating to staff is confidential. Certain personal information will be held by the Personnel Unit or line managers for reasons of staff appraisal and sickness assessment purposes. This information is held in confidence.

14.15. Official Secrets Acts 1989 and 1911

Under the Official Secrets Act 1989 ("OSA 89"), it is an offence for a civil servant to disclose, without lawful authority, information damaging to the national interest in a number of specified categories: security and intelligence; defence; international relations; foreign confidences; information which might lead to the commission of crime; information relating the interception of communications or warrants issued under the Security Services Act 1989; fail to take reasonable care to prevent the unauthorised disclosure of a document or article protected by the Act; retain such a document or article contrary to official duty; disclose information which it would be reasonable to expect might be used to obtain access to information covered by the Act. Section 1 of the Official Secrets Act 1911 protects information useful to an enemy. SFO staff should remember that these legal requirements still apply after they have left the Civil Service.

14.16. Attorney General's Disclosure Guidelines

Disclosure of Information in Criminal Proceedings, as per this Attorney General's Guidelines, is applicable to serious fraud cases as well as to cases investigated by the police.

1. Every accused person has a right to a fair trial, a right long embodied in our law and guaranteed under Article 6 of the European Convention on Human Rights. A fair trial is the proper object and expectation of all participants in the trial process. Fair disclosure to an accused is an inseparable part of a fair trial.

2. The scheme set out in the Criminal Procedure and Investigations Act 1996 (the Act) is designed to ensure that there is fair disclosure of material which may be relevant to an investigation and which does not form

Fraud Investigation: Criminal Procedure and Investigation

part of the prosecution case. Disclosure under the Act should assist the accused in the timely preparation and presentation of their case and assist the court to focus on all the relevant issues in the trial. Disclosure which does not meet these objectives risks preventing a fair trial taking place.3.

3. Fairness does, however, recognise that there are other interests that need to be protected, including those of victims and witnesses who might otherwise be exposed to harm. The scheme of the Act protects those interests. It should also ensure that material is not disclosed which overburdens the participants in the trial process, diverts attention from the relevant issues, leads to unjustifiable delay, and is wasteful of resources.

4. These guidelines build upon the existing law to help to ensure that the legislation is operated more effectively. In some areas guidance is given which goes beyond the requirements of the legislation, where experience has suggested that such guidance is desirable.

5. Investigators and disclosure officers must be fair and objective and must work together with prosecutors to ensure that disclosure obligations are met. A failure to take action leading to proper disclosure may result in a wrongful conviction. It may alternatively lead to a successful abuse of process argument or an acquittal against the weight of the evidence.

6. In discharging their obligations under the statute, code, common law and any operational instructions, investigators should always err on the side of recording and retaining material where they have any doubt as to whether it may be relevant.

7. An individual must not be appointed as disclosure officer, or continue in that role, if that is likely to result in a conflict of interest, for instance, if the disclosure officer is the victim of the alleged crime which is the subject of criminal proceedings. The advice of a more senior officer must always be sought if there is doubt as to whether a conflict of interest precludes an individual acting as the disclosure officer. If thereafter the doubt remains, the advice of a prosecutor should be sought.

8. Disclosure officers, or their deputies, must inspect, view or listen to all material that has been retained by the investigator, and the disclosure officer must provide a personal declaration to the effect that this task has been done. The obligation does not apply, however, in the circumstances set out in paragraph 9 below.

9. In some cases, out of an abundance of caution, investigators seize large volumes of material which may not, because of its source, general nature or other reasons, seem likely ever to be relevant. In such circumstances, the investigator may consider that it is not an appropriate use of resources to examine such large volumes of material seized on a precautionary basis. If such material is not examined by the investigator or disclosure officer, and it is not intended to examine it, but the material is nevertheless retained, its existence should be made known to the accused in general terms at the primary stage and permission granted for its inspection by him or his legal advisers. A section 9 statement will be completed by the investigating officer or disclosure officer describing the material by general category and justifying it not having been examined. This statement will itself be listed as unused material and automatically disclosed to the defence.

10. In meeting the obligations in paragraph 6.9 and 8.1 of the Code, it is crucial that descriptions by disclosure officers in non-sensitive schedules are detailed, clear and accurate. The descriptions may require a summary of the contents of the retained material to assist the prosecutor to make an informed decision on disclosure. The same applies to sensitive schedules, to the extent possible without compromising the confidentiality of the information.

11. Disclosure officers must specifically draw material to the attention of the prosecutor for consideration where they have any doubt as to whether it might undermine the prosecution case or might reasonably be expected to assist the defence disclosed by the accused.

12. Disclosure officers must seek the advice and assistance of prosecutors when in doubt as to their responsibility, and must deal expeditiously with requests by the prosecutor for further information on material which may lead to disclosure.

13. Prosecutors must do all that they can to facilitate proper disclosure, as part of their general and personal professional responsibility to act fairly and impartially, in the interests of justice. Prosecutors must also be alert to the need to provide advice to disclosure officers on disclosure issues and to advise on disclosure procedure generally.

14. Prosecutors must review schedules prepared by disclosure officers thoroughly and must be alert to the possibility that material may exist which has not been revealed to them. If no schedules have been provided, or there are apparent omissions from the schedules, or documents or other items are insufficiently described

or are unclear, the prosecutor must at once take action to obtain properly completed schedules. If, following this, prosecutors remain dissatisfied with the quality or content of the schedules they must raise the matter with a senior officer, and if necessary, persist, with a view to resolving the matter satisfactorily.

15. Where prosecutors have reason to believe that the disclosure officer has not discharged the obligation in paragraph 8 to inspect, view or listen to material, they must at once raise the matter with the disclosure officer and, if it is believed that the officer has not inspected, viewed or listened to the material, request that it be done.

16. When the prosecutor or disclosure officer believes that material might undermine the prosecution case or assist the defence case, for instance in the case of records of previous statements by witnesses, prosecutors must always inspect, view or listen to the material and satisfy themselves that the prosecution can properly be continued. Their judgement as to what other material to inspect, view or listen to will depend on the circumstances of each case.

17. Prosecutors should inform the investigator if, in their view, reasonable and relevant lines of further inquiry exist.

18. Prosecutors should not adduce evidence of the contents of a defence statement other than in the circumstances envisaged by section 11 of the Act or to rebut alibi evidence. Where evidence may be adduced in these circumstances, this can be done through cross-examination as well as through the introduction of evidence. There may be occasions when a defence

statement points the prosecution to other lines of inquiry. Further investigation in these circumstances is possible and evidence obtained as a result of inquiring into a defence statement may be used as part of the prosecution case or to rebut the defence.

19. Prosecutors must ensure that they record in writing all actions and decisions they make in discharging their disclosure responsibilities, and this information is to be made available to the prosecution advocate if requested or if relevant to an issue.

20. In deciding what material should be disclosed (at any stage of the proceedings) prosecutors should resolve any doubt they may have in favour of disclosure, unless the material is on the sensitive schedule and will be placed before the court for the issue of disclosure to be determined.

21. If prosecutors are satisfied that a fair trial cannot take place because of a failure to disclose which cannot or will not be remedied, they must not continue with the case.

22. Prosecution advocates should use their best endeavours to ensure that all material that ought properly to be made available is either presented by the prosecution or disclosed to the defence. However, the prosecution cannot be expected to disclose material if they are not aware of its existence.

As far as is possible, prosecution advocates must place themselves in a fully informed position to enable them to make decisions on The prosecution advocate must continue to keep under review until the conclusion of the trial decisions regarding disclosure. The prosecution advocate must in every case specifically consider whether he or she can satisfactorily discharge the duty of continuing review on the basis of the material supplied already, or whether it is necessary to inspect further material or to reconsider material already inspected. 22 Prosecution advocates should use their best endeavours to ensure that all material that ought properly to be made available is either presented by the prosecution or disclosed to the defence. However, the prosecution cannot be expected to disclose material if they are not aware of its existence. As far as is possible, prosecution advocates must place themselves in a fully informed position to enable them to make decisions on disclosure.

23. Upon receipt of instructions, prosecution advocates should consider as a priority all the information provided regarding disclosure of material. Prosecution advocates should consider, in every case, whether they can be satisfied that they are in possession of all relevant documentation and that they have been instructed fully regarding disclosure matters. Decisions already made regarding disclosure should be reviewed. If as a result the advocate considers that further information or action is required, written advice should be promptly provided setting out the aspects that need clarification or action. If necessary and where appropriate a conference should be held to determine what is required.

24. The prosecution advocate must continue to keep under review until the conclusion of the trial decisions regarding disclosure. The prosecution advocate must in every case specifically consider whether he or she can satisfactorily discharge the duty of continuing review on the basis of the material supplied already, or

whether it is necessary to inspect further material or to reconsider material already inspected.

25. Prior to the commencement of a trial, the prosecuting advocate should always make decisions on disclosure in consultation with those instructing him and it is desirable that the disclosure officer should also be consulted. After a trial has started, it is recognised that in practice consultation on disclosure issues may not be practicable; it continues to be desirable, however, whenever this can be achieved without affecting unduly the conduct of the trial.

26. The practice of "counsel to counsel" disclosure should cease: it isi nconsistent with the requirement of transparency in the prosecution process.

27. A defence statement should set out the nature of the defence, the matters on which issue is taken and the reasons for taking issue. A comprehensive defence statement assists the participants in the trial to ensure that it is fair. It provides information that the prosecutor needs to identify any remaining material that falls to be disclosed at the secondary stage. The more detail a defence statement contains the more likely it is that the prosecutor will make a properly informed decision about whether any remaining material might assist the defence case, or whether to advise the investigator to undertake further inquiries. It also helps in the management of the trial by narrowing down and focussing the issues in dispute. It may result in the prosecution discontinuing the case. Defence practitioners should be aware of these considerations in advising their clients.

28. Defence solicitors should ensure that statements are agreed by the accused before being served. Wherever possible, the accused should sign the defence statement to evidence his or her agreement.

29. Where it appears to an investigator, disclosure officer or prosecutor that a Government department or other Crown body has material that may be relevant to an issue in the case, reasonable steps should be taken to identify and consider such material. Although what is reasonable will vary from case to case, prosecutors should inform the department or other body of the nature of its case and of relevant issues in the case in respect of which the department or body might possess material, and ask whether it has any such material. Departments in England and Wales have established Enquiry Points to deal with issues concerning the disclosure of information in criminal proceedings. Further guidance for prosecutors and investigators seeking information (including documents) from Government departments or other Crown bodies may be found in the pamphlet "Giving Evidence or Information about suspected crimes: Guidance for Departments and Investigators" (March, 1997, Cabinet Office).

30. There may be cases where the investigator, disclosure officer or prosecutor suspects that a non-government agency or other third party (for example, a local authority, a social services department, a hospital, a doctor, a school, providers of forensic services) has material or information which might be disclosable if it were if it were in the possession of the prosecution. In such cases consideration should be given as to whether it is appropriate to seek access to the material or information and if so, steps should be taken by the

prosecution to obtain such material or information. It will be important to do so if the material or information is likely to undermine the prosecution case, or assist a known defence.

31. If the investigator, disclosure officer or prosecutor seeks access to the material or information but the third party declines or refuses to allow access to it, the matter should not be left. If despite any reasons offered by the third party it is still believed that it is reasonable to seek production of the material or information, and the requirements of section 2 of the Criminal Procedure (Attendance of Witnesses) Act 1965 or as appropriate section 97 of the Magistrates Courts Act 1980 are satisfied, then the prosecutor or investigator should apply for a witness summons causing a representative of the third party to produce the material to the Court.

32. Information which might be discloseable if it were in the possession of the prosecution which comes to the knowledge of investigators or prosecutors as a result of liaison with third parties should be recorded by the investigator or prosecutor in a durable or retrievable form(for example potentially relevant information revealed in discussions at a child protection conference attended by police officers).

33. Where information comes into the possession of the prosecution in the circumstances set out in paragraphs 30- 32 above, consultation with the other agency should take place before disclosure is made: there may be public interest reasons which justify withholding disclosure and which would require the issue of disclosure of the information to be placed before the court.

34. Prosecutors must always be alive to the need, in the interests of justice and fairness in the particular circumstances of any case, to make disclosure of material after the commencement of proceedings but before the prosecutor's duty arises under the Act. For instance, disclosure ought to be made of significant information that might affect a bail decision or that might enable the defence to contest the committal proceedings.

35. Where the need for such disclosure is not apparent to the prosecutor, any disclosure will depend on what the defendant chooses to reveal about the defence. Clearly, such disclosure will not normally exceed that which is obtainable after the duties under the "Act" arise.

36. Generally, material can be considered to potentially undermine the prosecution case if it has an adverse effect on the strength of the prosecution case. This will include anything that tends to show a fact inconsistent with the elements of the case that must be proved by the prosecution. Material can have an adverse effect on the strength of the prosecution case:

    (i) by the use made of it in cross-examination; and by its capacity to suggest any potential submissions that could lead to: (ii) the exclusion of evidence and a stay of proceedings;(iii) a court or tribunal finding that any public authority had acted incompatibly with the defendant's rights under the ECHR.

37. In deciding what material might undermine the prosecution case, the prosecution should pay particular attention to material that has potential to weaken the

prosecution case or is inconsistent with it. Examples are:

(i) Any material casting doubt upon the accuracy of any prosecution evidence.

(ii) Any material which may point to another person, whether charged or not (including a co-accused) having involvement in the commission of the offence.

(iii) Any material which may cast doubt upon the reliability of a confession.

(iv) Any material that might go to the credibility of a prosecution witness.

(v) Any material that might support a defence that is either raised by the defence or apparent from the prosecution papers. If the material might undermine the prosecution case it should be disclosed at this stage even though it suggests a defence inconsistent with or alternative to one already advanced by the accused or his solicitor.

(vi) Any material which may have a bearing on the admissibility of any prosecution evidence. It should also be borne in mind that while items of material viewed in isolation may not be considered to potentially undermine the prosecution case, several items together can have that effect.

38. Experience suggests that any item which relates to the defendant's mental or physical health, his intellectual capacity, or to any ill-treatment which the defendant may have suffered when in the investigator's custody is likely to have the potential for casting doubt on the reliability of an accused's purported confession, and prosecutors should pay particular attention to any such item in the possession of the prosecution.

39. Prosecutors should be open, alert and promptly responsive to requests for disclosure of material supported by the comprehensive defence statement. Conversely, if no defence statement has been served or if the prosecutor considers that the defence statement is lacking specific and/or clarity, a letter should be sent to the defence indicating that secondary disclosure will not take place or will be limited (as appropriate), and inviting the defence to specify and/or clarify the accused's case. The prosecutor should consider raising the issue at a preliminary hearing if the position is not resolved satisfactorily to enable the court to give directions.

40. Experience suggests that material of the description set out below might reasonably be expected to be disclosed to the defence where it relates to the defence being put forward. Accordingly, following the delivery of a defence statement and on receipt of a request specifically linking the material sought with the defence being put forward, such linked material should be disclosed unless there is good reason not to do so. However, if defences put forward in a defence statement are inconsistent within the meaning of section 11 of the Act, then the preceding guidance set out in this paragraph will not apply. Conversely, if material of the description set out below might undermine the prosecution case, and does not justify an application to the court to withhold disclosure, prosecutors must disclose it at the primary stage. The material is:-those recorded scientific or scenes of crime findings retained by the investigator which relate to the defendant; and are linked to the

point at issue; and have not previously been disclosed. Where identification is or may be in issue, all previous descriptions of suspects, however recorded, together with all records of identification procedures in respect of the offence(s) and photographs of the accused taken by the investigator around the time of his arrest; Information that any prosecution witness has received, has been promised or has requested any payment or reward in connection with the case. Plans of crime scenes or video recordings made by investigators of crime scenes; names, within the knowledge of investigators, of individuals who may have relevant information and whom investigators do not intend to interview; records which the investigator has made of information which may be relevant, provided by any individual (such information would include, but not be limited to, records of conversation and interviews with any such person); and disclosure of video recordings or scientific findings by means of supplying copies may well involve delay or otherwise not be practicable or desirable, in which case the investigator should make reasonable arrangements for the video, recordings or scientific findings to be viewed by the defence.

41. Before making an application to the court to withhold material which would otherwise fall to be disclosed, on the basis that to disclose would not be in the public interest, a prosecutor should aim to disclose as much of the material as he properly can (by giving the defence redacted or edited copies of summaries).

42. Prior to or at the hearing, the court must be provided with full and accurate information. The prosecution advocate must examine all material which is the subject matter of the application and make any necessary

enquiries of the prosecutor and/or investigator. The prosecutor (or representative) and/or investigator should attend such applications.

43. The prosecutor should, in addition to complying with the obligations under the CPIA, provide to the defence all evidence upon which the Crown proposes to rely in a summary trial. Such provision should allow the accused or their legal advisers sufficient time properly to consider the evidence before it is called. Exceptionally, statements may be withheld for the protection of witnesses or to avoid interference with the course of justice.

44. In all cases the prosecutor must consider disclosing in the interests of justice any material which is relevant to sentence (eg. information which might mitigate the seriousness of the offence or assist the accused to lay blame in whole or in part upon a co-accused or another person).

45. These guidelines should be adopted with immediate effect in relation to all cases submitted in future to the prosecuting authorities in receipt of these guidelines. They should also be adopted as regards cases already submitted to which the Act applies, so far as they relate to stages in the proceedings that have not yet been reached.

14.17. Confidentiality of Market Sensitive Information

Confidentiality issues arise in relation to inside information about companies whose securities are listed, particularly up to the stage at which an SFO/BERR investigation is announced or otherwise becomes public. It is not possible to consider every circumstance or eventuality that might arise. Therefore when considering particular situations SFO staff should use common sense, paying particular attention to the possibility that confidential activity may become public knowledge and the way in which official acknowledgement is given to actions which have hitherto been confidential.

14.18. Definition of Inside Information

"Inside Information" for the purposes sections 56 and 57 Criminal Justice Act 1993 ("CJA 93") means information which: relates to particular securities or to a particular issuer of securities or to particular issuers of securities and not to securities generally or to issuers of securities generally; is specific or precise; has not been made public; and if it were made public would be likely to have a significant effect on the price of any securities. For the purposes of this Part, securities are "price-affected securities" in relation to inside information and inside information is "price-sensitive information" in relation to securities if and only if the information would, if made public, be likely to have a significant effect on the price (i.e. value) of the security.

14.19. Information Gateways

S3 CJA 87 sets out those authorities the SFO may disclose information to and the circumstances in which the information may pass. When providing information under this section the written authority of the Director is required. When considering s3 disclosure of information you should have regard to the Court of Appeal judgment in *Kent Pharmaceuticals and Ors v The Director of the SFO and Ors* [2004] EWCA (Civ) 1494 concerning whether the SFO should give advance notice to the owner of the information of its intention to use the statutory gateway. The Court gave guidance as to when an opportunity to make representations should be given. Key points are that the Director of SFO should decide on notification of disclosure on a case by case basis and that as general rule notification of impending disclosure should be given in sufficient time to enable the document owner to raise any objection e.g. because of commercial sensitivity. Sometimes, it will be inappropriate to notify because the documents are simply being passed to another investigating/prosecuting authority or are required for an investigation which may be hampered if the owner is aware. Sometimes it may be inappropriate or impracticable to give notice of proposed disclosure or, within sufficient time to allow a response e.g. where the documents are required urgently elsewhere or where to do so would hamper investigations. In such circumstances if no notice was given *prior* to disclosure, the Director must consider whether to do so *after* disclosure has taken place. The final point is that the SFO should not allow itself to be drawn into satellite litigation.

When you are providing background information to the Director you should ensure that you specifically address the issue of whether advance notice may be required. This will ensure that the Director is properly informed when exercising his discretion as to whether disclosure should take place and, if so, the procedure that should be adopted. S3 (4) CJA 87 also allows the Director to enter into an agreement for the supply of information to or by him. S3 (5) CJA 87 and the Data Protection Act 1998 entitles SFO staff members authorised by the Director to disclose information to any government department. Many authorities with which the SFO has regular dealing with will have corresponding information gateways allowing for disclosure of information to the SFO.

Fraud Investigation: Criminal Procedure and Investigation

14.20. Obtaining Confidential Information from HMRC

With effect from 18th April 2005 the services of the Inland Revenue and HM Customs & Excise were integrated to form Her Majesty's Revenue & Customs. "HMRC"). The information gateways in place prior to the formation of HMRC remain in place for the moment. Section 1 7(2) Anti-Terrorism, Crime & Security Act 2001 ("ATCSA") provides for the disclosure of confidential revenue information by HMRC for any of the following purposes:

(i) any criminal investigation whatever which is being or may be carried out in the UK or elsewhere;

(ii) any criminal proceedings whatever which have been or may be initiated in UK or elsewhere;

(iii) initiating or bringing to an end any such investigation or proceedings;

(iv) Facilitating the determination of the above.

The SFO is thus no longer limited to requests and constraints under s3 (1) CJA 1987.

14.21. Disclosure overseas

Only the Secretary of State (Home Office) may direct that revenue information may be disclosed overseas. The SFO cannot share information obtained from HMRC without their consent. There may in due course be some blanket "directions", e.g. for EU countries; but meanwhile specific case by cases consent (or even a formal Order) will be needed. The preconditions are in s1 8(3) ATCSA.

14.22. Supporting Documents

A Code has been published and the SFO is bound by it. Please read it carefully alongside the individual Memoranda of Understanding (MOUs) the SFO signed with both revenue departments prior to their integration. The SFO signed separate MOUs with Customs and Inland Revenue. These MOUs remain in effect following the integration of the departments and set out the practical basis on which disclosure will be made and the procedure for making requests. A list of SFO staff allowed to authorise requests is maintained by the Policy Division.

14.23. Procedure for making a request to HMRC

(i) Written requests must be authorised by a member of staff from the list of authorised staff.

(ii) Requests must be on the appropriate form, which can be found as the last page of the Memorandum of Understanding for each Revenue Department.

(iii) The form can be completed by any investigator.

(iv) A request can relate to more than one legal person.

(v) Give brief details of the SFO investigation ("nature of enquiry").

(vi) Case Controllers must be satisfied that the disclosure requested will be for one of the permitted purposes set out in sec 17(2) above; necessary for the prevention or detection of crime (Art 8 – HRA); proportionate to the purpose for which it is requested (i.e. reflects the nature of the crime and the needs of the investigation).

(vii) The request must indicate the protective marking appropriate to the sensitivity of the information requested or provided.

14.24. Legal Issue-Bankruptcy

Under Council Regulation 1346/2000/EC (the regulation) on insolvency proceedings (see 155 NLJ 7202, p 1819) a court has exclusive jurisdiction over the insolvency of a debtor, provided two conditions are satisfied. The first, in accordance with Art 3, is that the court is in the territory where the debtor has his "centre of main interests". The second is that the court has handed down "a judgment opening insolvency proceedings". In that case all other member states are obliged to recognise the court's jurisdiction from the date the judgment becomes effective (see Art 16). This is subject to a public policy exception (see Art 26). Both these conditions are problematic. Both were the subject of the European Court of Justice's (ECJ's) recent judgment in *Eurofood IFSC Ltd, Re: C-341/04* [2006] All ER (D) 20 (May)**.**

14.25. Bankruptcy Order

A bankruptcy order can be made if:-

thirteen specific types of conduct that the court must take into account in considering whether to make a BRO. These are as follows:

(i) failing to keep records which account for a loss of property by the bankrupt, or by a business carried on by him, where the loss occurred in the period beginning two years before petition and ending with the date of the application;

(ii)   failing to produce records of that kind on demand by the official receiver or the trustee;

(iii) entering into a transaction at an undervalue;

(iv)   giving a preference;

(v)   making an excessive pension contribution;

(vi)   a failure to supply goods or services which were wholly or partly paid for which gave rise to a claim provable in the bankruptcy;

(vii) trading at a time before commencement of the bankruptcy when the bankrupt knew or ought to have known that he was [himself to be] unable to pay his debts;

(viii) Incurring, before commencement of the bankruptcy, a debt which the bankrupt had no reasonable expectation of being able to pay; failing to account satisfactorily to the court, the official receiver or the trustee for a loss of property or for an insufficiency of property to meet bankruptcy debts; carrying on any gambling, rash and hazardous speculation or unreasonable extravagance which may have materially contributed to or increased the extent of the bankruptcy or which took place between presentation of the petition and commencement of the bankruptcy; neglect of business affairs of a kind which may have materially contributed to or increased the extent of the bankruptcy; fraud or fraudulent breach of trust and failing to co-operate with the official receiver or the trustee.

14.26. Conclusion

All acquisitive crimes generally cover some of the most commonly encountered criminal activity in England and Wales. This area of criminal law has significant impact on the work of all policing personnel and it is only logical that policies and procedures are in place to protect all parties.

The purpose of investigation is to find the truth and to collect evidence. Evidence law is a body of rules which prescribe the way in which evidence s presented in a criminal trial. These rules regulate how the prosecution proves its case to the court and to ensure that the accused receives a fair trial.

For the most part the prosecution bears the legal burden of proving a defendant's guilt beyond reasonable doubt. For these reasons the police have extensive statutory powers with regard to the investigation of a criminal offence, these powers governed by the 198 Police and Criminal Evidence Act, the Serious Organised Crime and Police Act 2005, the Serious Crimes Act 2007 and the Regulation of Investigatory Powers Act 2000, Proceeds of Crime Act 2002, relevant to the crime of fraud.

The SFO has a distinctive way of investigating and prosecuting serious fraud. Unravelling major fraud involves the examination of vast quantities of documents, often left deliberately in an obscure and fragmented form and polices and management strategies are stated above are important in order to make a proper evaluation of the information especially because the documents need to be seen by a variety of experts- police, accountants, lawyers, bankers, stockbrokers and computer specialists, with a view to producing a compact and coherent form for presentation in court.

Further reading for Chapter Thirteen

J. Albanese, *White Collar Crime in America*, (Prentice Hall, New Jersey 1995).

A. Alvesalo, "Economic crime investigators at work", Policing and Society, vol 13, 2003.

I. Ayres and J. Braithwaite, *Responsive Regulation: Transcending the Deregulation Debate*, (OUP, Oxford 1982)

J. Black, *Rules and Regulators*, (OUP, Oxford 1997).

J. Braithwaite *Corporate Crime in the Pharmaceutical Industry*, (Routledge, London 1984).

A.P. Carr and A.J. Turner, *Stone's Justice Manual 2008*, (LexisNexis, London 2008)

G. Hutton and G. Mc Kinnon, *Blackstone's Police Manual, Volume 4- General Police Duties*, (OUP, Oxford 2008)

N. Chomsky, *Profit Over People: Neo-liberalism and Global Order*, (Seven Stories Press, New York 1999).

D. Friedrichs, *Trusted Criminals: White Collar Crime in Contemporary Society*, (Wadsworth, Belmont 1996).

J. Gobert and M. Punch, *Rethinking Corporate Crime*, (Butterworths, London 2002).

R. Harris and S. Milkis, *The Politics of Regulatory Change: A Tale of Two Agencies*, (OUP, Oxford 1989).

F. Hayek,*The Road to Serfdom*, (Routledge, London 1944).

N. Hertz, *The Silent Takeover: Global Capitalism and the Death of Democracy*, (Arrow Books, London 2001).

S. Lukes, *Power: A Radical View*,(Macmillan, London 1974).

F. Pearce and S. Tombs, (1998) *Toxic Capitalism: Corporate Crime in the Chemical Industry*, (Ashgate, Aldergate 1998).

M. Punch, *Dirty Business: Exploring Corporate Misconduct*, (Sage, London 1996).

S. Simpson, *Corporate Crime, Law and Social Control*, (OUP, Oxford 2002).

R. Walters, *Deviant Knowledge: Criminology, Politics and Policy,* (Willan, Cullompton 2003).

CHAPTER 15 - SENTENCING IN FRAUD CASES

15.1. Sentencing Guidelines

Sentencing is governed by the Sentencing Guidelines. A court when passing sentence must state in open court, in ordinary language and in general terms, its reasons for choosing that particular sentence, its effect, the effect of non compliance with any requirements it may contain, any power to vary or review the sentence on the application of the offender or any other person, and, in the case of a fine, the effect of failure to pay. Where the sentence is of a different kind, or outside the range indicated by guidelines issued by the Sentencing Guidelines Council, the court must state the reason for the departure.

The court must state any aggravating or mitigating or aggravating factors that it has regarded as being of particular importance, and if it has reduced the sentence on account of a guilty plea it must state that fact. If the sentence is a custodial sentence or a community sentence the court must usually state why it is of the opinion required for the imposition of such a sentence. Model explanations for the imposition of custodial sentences have been provided·

15.2. Sentencing Decision

Justices should announce publicly their decision to convict before inquiring into previous convictions. Thereafter, the defendant's full record should be produced; "spent" convictions should be marked; all other previous convictions should be read from the record by the person giving antecedents to the court.

15.3. Previous Offences

In considering the seriousness of an offence committed by an offender who has one or more previous convictions, the court must treat each previous conviction by a court within the United Kingdom or a previous finding of guilt in service disciplinary proceedings as an aggravating factor if the court considers that it can reasonably be so treated having regard to the nature of the offence to which it relates, its relevance to the current offence and the time that has elapsed since the conviction. A previous conviction by a court outside the United Kingdom may be treated as an aggravating factor if the court considers it appropriate to do so. Both the justices and the clerk of the court should have the opportunity of looking at the full record. The defendant should be given the opportunity of challenging or explaining previous convictions. In passing sentence the court should refer to a "spent" conviction only when it is necessary to explain the sentence to be passed.

After conviction or finding of guilt, the court will look to the prosecution and the defence in turn for information enabling it to decide sentence. The prosecution must state the facts in open court to enable the press and the public to know the circumstances of the offences for which the defendant is to be sentenced. Consideration of pre-sentence reports should precede any address in mitigation. Information from prosecution or defence is presented in the form of unsworn statements, although either side may call evidence after conviction in order to clarify issues of fact which have not been resolved by the plea and which are relevant to the determination of sentence and the court itself may likewise call for evidence.

15.4. Legislation on sentencing- The Criminal Justice Act 2003

In every case where the offender is aged 18 or over at the time of conviction, the court must have regard to the five purposes of sentencing contained in section 142(1) Criminal Justice Act 2003. The five purposes of sentencing are the punishment of offenders; the reduction of crime (including its reduction by deterrence); the reform and rehabilitation of offenders; the protection of the public and the making of reparation by offenders to persons affected by their offence

The Criminal Justice Act 2003 does not indicate that any one purpose should be more important than any other and in practice they may all be relevant to a greater or lesser degree in any individual case. The sentencer has the task of determining the manner in which they apply.

The sentencer must consider the seriousness of the offence, the assessment of which will determine which of the sentencing thresholds has been crossed; indicate whether a custodial, community or other sentence is the most appropriate; be the key factor in deciding the length of a custodial sentence, the onerousness of requirements to be incorporated in a community sentence and the amount of any fine imposed.

Section 143(1) Criminal Justice Act 2003 provides that "in considering the seriousness of any offence, the court must consider the offender's culpability in committing the offence and any harm which the offence caused, was intended to cause or might foreseeably have caused."

The Criminal Justice Act 2003 (Sentencing) (Transitory Provisions) Order 2005 (S.I. 2005 No. 643) by inserting the words "or detention in a young offender institution" after the words "a sentence of imprisonment".

The CJA 2003 provides for the repeal of provisions of the PCC(S) A 2000 which allowed for the suspension of a prison sentence of not more than two years (ss.118-125). The 2003 Act introduces an entirely new form of suspended sentence. The repeal of the former provisions and the commencement of the new provisions took effect on April 4, 2005.

Section 181 of the CJA 2003, not yet in force, provides for a new system for dealing with sentences of imprisonment for a term of less than 12 months. The term of the sentence must be expressed in weeks, must not be less than 28 weeks, and must not be more than 51 weeks in respect of any one offence. When passing such a sentence, the court must specify a period (the "custodial period") at the end of which the offender is to be released on licence, and by order (to be known as a "custody plus order") require the licence to be granted on condition that the offender complies during the remainder of the term or any part of it with such requirements as the court may specify. The requirements that may be a specified are listed in section 182 and are substantially similar to the requirements that may be made in connection with a community order, although some of the requirements that may be made under a community order may not be made by virtue of an order under this section (viz. a residence requirement, a mental health requirement, a drug rehabilitation requirement and an alcohol treatment requirement). When making a custody plus order, the court will be required to give the explanations required by section 174.

Section 189 provides that a court which passes a sentence, for a term of at least 28 weeks but not more than 51 weeks, may order the offender to comply during a specified "supervision period" with one or more requirements (s.189(1)), and order that the sentence of imprisonment is not to take effect unless either the offender fails to comply with any requirement, or the offender commits another offence (whether or not punishable with imprisonment) during the "operational period" (to be specified by the court). Where two or more sentences are imposed consecutively there is no power to suspend the sentence unless the aggregate is less than 65 weeks (s.189 (2)).

15.5. Fraud Act 2006 guidelines on sentencing

The Fraud Act contains a transitional provision to ensure the lower maximum penalty for summary cases applies in any case involving an offence committed before the commencement of section 154(1) of the Criminal Justice Act 2003.

The previous (lower) penalty is preserved for cases of fraudulent trading under the company's legislation in which the events occurred before the commencement of this Act, i.e. 17 January 2007.

15.6. Culpability for sentencing purposes

There are levels of criminal culpability for sentencing purposes:

Where the offender

(i) has the intention to cause harm, with the highest culpability when an offence is planned. The worse the harm intended, the greater the seriousness.

(ii) is reckless as to whether harm is caused, that is, where the offender appreciates at least some harm would be caused but proceeds giving no thought to the consequences even though the extent of the risk would be obvious to most people.

(iii) has knowledge of the specific risks entailed by his actions even though he does not intend to cause the harm that results.

(iv) is guilty of negligence.

15.7. Crown Prosecution Service recommendations

The CPS gives guidance as to charges and sentences depend on the charges brought. The charging standard gives guidance concerning the charge which should be preferred if the criteria set out in the Code for Crown Prosecutors are met. The purpose of charging standards is to make sure that the most appropriate charge is selected, in the light of the facts, which can be proved, at the earliest possible opportunity. The CPS Sentencing Manual on theft can be read at website

http://www.cps.gov.uk/legal/section15/chapter_p_16_17.html.

Basically, the CPS use caselaw to indicate the level of sentencing for similar offences, as follows:

15.8. Relevant Sentencing Case Law

> **Caselaw**
>
> ***R v Mason* [1991] 12 Cr.App.R. (S.) 737**
> Pleaded guilty to five counts of procuring the execution of a valuable security by deception, three of obtaining property by deception and one of obtaining services by deception. The defendant took out a £56K mortgage, a £64K mortgage and a £80K mortgage and secured loans on a property using a false name and details. Liability £36K. Carefully thought through scheme over an extended period which required considerable skill.
> Sentence-3 years.

Caselaw

***R v Callen* [1992] 13 Cr.App.R. (S.) 60**
Convicted of conspiracy. The appellant was a mortgage broker. Over a period of four years he conspired with surveyors and accountants to obtain £2 million from mortgages by the provision of false descriptions of the property concerned and false accounts. The defendant earned £50K commission. Sentence-4 years.

Caselaw

***R v Luxon and Others* [1992] 13 Cr.App.R. (S.) 138**
Convicted or pleaded guilty to various offences of procuring the execution of a valuable security by deception, obtaining property by deception, and obtaining services by deception. They were concerned in a series of fraudulent mortgage transactions involving a large number of properties. A total of about £600,000 was obtained, and the lenders sustained losses of about £225,000.
Sentence-18 months to 3 ½ years.

Caselaw

***R v Weinberg* [1993] 14 Cr.App.R. (S.) 381**
Pleaded guilty to procuring the execution of a valuable security by deception. The defendant, a financial services consultant, concealed his debts and applied for a mortgage advance of £292K to enable him to purchase a flat for resale.
Sentence-12 months.

Fraud Investigation: Criminal Procedure and Investigation

> **Caselaw**
>
> ***R v Rice*** **[1993] 14 Cr.App.R. (S.) 231**
> Pleaded guilty to 11 counts of procuring the execution of a valuable security. The defendant, in conjunction with others, obtained seven building society mortgages by giving false particulars of occupation, name and salary. A total of £600K was obtained. The defendant admitted his part in the offences when challenged and offered to give evidence against his accomplices.
> Sentence-2 years.

> **Caselaw**
>
> ***R v Harling and Hayden*** **[1992] 13 Cr.App.R. (S.) 672**
> Pleaded guilty to three offences of obtaining property by deception and one of conspiracy to procure the execution of a valuable security. He was involved in obtaining mortgages in respect of four properties by various false representations, principally relating to sales to fictitious individuals. The total amount involved in the frauds was about £171K all the money was repaid before the offences were discovered
> Sentence-2 years.

R v Harjit Singh Samra **[1991] 13 Cr.App.R. (S.) 168**
Pleaded guilty to two offences of procuring the execution of a valuable security by deception. The defendant obtained mortgages on two houses (£165K) bought to let by making false representations about his income and his circumstances and intentions.
Sentence-9 months.

Caselaw

R v Evans **[1992] 13 Cr.App.R. (S.) 413**
Convicted of two counts of obtaining by deception. The defendant was an estate agent and obtained a mortgage advance of £52K by making false representations in relation to his employment and earnings, and a second advance of £87K relating to a different property by similar false representations. "All too frequently the defendants include people with professional qualifications or with business experience in property dealing."
Sentence-12 months with 3 months suspended.

Caselaw

R v Rolls **[1993] 14 Cr.App.R. (S.) 304**
Pleaded guilty to three counts of procuring the execution of a valuable security by deception. On three occasions the defendant who was in financial difficulties obtained mortgages by pretending to sell his house. Sales were based on genuine valuation. No intention to cause any loss.
Sentence-9 months.

> **Caselaw**
>
> *R v Ozair Ahmed* [1994] 15 Cr.App.R. (S.) 286
> Pleaded guilty to three counts of procuring the execution of a valuable security by deception. The defendant secured three mortgages on domestic premises by false representations about his income. One property was occupied by the defendant; the other two were let out. The total amount of the mortgages was £100K. Previous good character, mortgage payments up to date.
> Sentence- 9 months.

15.9. Sentence depends on CPS Charge

The guidance set out in the charging standard should not be used in the determination of any investigatory decision, such as the decision to arrest; does not override any guidance issued on the use of appropriate alternative forms of disposal short of charge, such as cautioning, or conditional cautioning; does not override the principles set out in the Code for Crown Prosecutors. Each case is to be considered on its individual merits and must not fetter the discretion to charge and to prosecute the most appropriate offence depending on the particular facts of the case.

Sentencing is also guided by Powers of Criminal Courts (Sentencing) Act 2000. Other caselaw is analysed below to demonstrate how the sentencing decision was reached. The sentences must comply with Current Sentences Practice. The CPS Charging Standard correlates with the Home Office Counting Rules which treat the offences below as countable offences relating to fraud:-

False statements by Company Directors
Common law offence of conspiracy to defraud

Insider dealing under the Criminal Justice Act 1993

Fraudulent trading under s 993 Companies Act 2006

Fraudulent misappropriation of funds under the Proceeds of Crime Act 2002

Engaging in a course of conduct which creates a false or misleading impression as to the market in or the price or value of investments, contrary to section 47(2) Financial Services Act17

Obtaining a money transfer by cheque or credit card fraud

Fraudulent issue of money orders by Post Office employee, under the section 22 Post Office Act 1953

Frauds in connection with sale of land, etc, under section 183 Law of Property Act 1925

Making off without payment, under the section 3 Theft Act 1978

Assisting another to retain the benefit of criminal conduct, under section 93A Criminal Justice Act 1988

Acquisition, possession or use of proceeds of criminal conduct, under section 93B Criminal Justice Act 1988

Concealing or transferring proceeds of criminal conduct, under section 93C Criminal Justice Act 1988

Cartel offences, under sections 183 and 185 Enterprise Act 2002

Forgery, under Forgery and Counterfeiting Act 1981 section 1

Copying a false instrument, under section 2 Forgery and Counterfeiting Act

Failure to hand over a Euro note or coin believing it to be counterfeit, under the Protection of the Euro against Counterfeiting Regulations 2001

Counterfeiting, etc of dies and marks, under the section 6(1) Hallmarking Act 1973

False Accounting under the section 17(1) Theft Act 1968

Caselaw is a useful indication of what sentence a certain offence might carry and below are some examples.

15.10. Illustrations of sentencing rational

> **Caselaw**
>
> ***R v Roach* [2002] 1 Cr.App.R.(S) 12.**
> Obtaining money transfer by deception.
> Guidelines in *R v Clark* [1998] 2 Cr.App.R.(S) 95 and *R v Barrick* (1985) 7 Cr.App.R.(S) 142 were not relevant to offending of the kind under consideration. The distinctive feature of this case was that it involved the exploitation of pitifully vulnerable people, whether due to age or infirmity or a combination of both. 18 months' imprisonment considered an entirely correct and appropriate sentence for this offending in the circumstances of this case.

> **Caselaw**
>
> ***R v Stuart Creggy*, CA, 14 February 2008.**
> **Assisting another to retain the benefit of criminal conduct**
> The imposition of an order disqualifying a director for seven years following a plea of guilty to an offence of assisting another to retain the benefit of criminal conduct and a sentence of 18 months' imprisonment, suspended for two years.
> *R v Goodman (Ivor Michael)* (1993) 2 All ER 789 CA (Crim Div) applied.
> The offending behaviour had a relevant factual

connection with the management of the company in question. C, a retiring solicitor, had facilitated the obtaining of benefit by others of a sum of £916,750. The operation could not have been undertaken by those involved in the overall fraud without C's participation.

C did not accept any money or benefit from the fraud.

C had previously been convicted of conspiracy to defraud and falsifying business accounts in the United States.

Caselaw

***R v Feld* [1999] 1 Cr.App.R.(S) 1.**
Fraud-Company management.
Legislation:-Financial Services Act 1986
In relation to offences of raising money by means of false statements relating to the financial position of a company, factors relevant to sentence include: the amount of the fraud; the manner in which it was carried out; the period over which the fraud was carried out; the persistence with which it was carried out; the position of the offender in the company and his measure of control over it; any abuse of trust; the consequences of the fraud; the effect on public confidence in the City and integrity of commercial life; the loss to small investors; the personal benefit to the offender; the plea, age and character of the offender.,

> **Caselaw**
>
> ***R v Palk and Smith*** **[1997] 2 Cr.App.R.(S) 167.**
> Fraudulent Trading.
> There is no doubt that, because of the wide spectrum covered by fraudulent trading offences, in relation to both the amount and the level of criminality on the part of the offender, a wide spectrum of sentences may also be appropriate.
> In broad terms, it is right to say that a charge of fraudulent trading resulting in a substantial total deficiency to creditors is less seriously regarded than a specific charge of theft or fraud to an equivalent amount.
> Current Sentencing Practice Reference: B6-3.3E

> **Caselaw**
>
> ***R v Stevens and others*** **(1993) 14 Cr.App.R.(S) 372.**
> Mortgage Fraud
> One hundred and twenty-eight mortgage applications made in relation to 90 different properties. A total of £1.8 million obtained over a period of 8 years (and attempts made in relation to a further £2.5 million).
> The Court made the following observations: An important consideration is the part played by any given offender – anything between prime mover and nominee. It is an aggravating feature to recruit others to participate in the commission of the fraud. Of relevance also, is the length of involvement in the fraud by a particular offender, as well as the extent of the personal benefit. It is important to bear in mind whether any particular offender is a professional person or a quasi-professional person (breach of trust).

Finally, the nature and the timing of a guilty plea is of consequence where there has been a delay; and, in cases of this kind, as in other types of fraud, the court must pay particular regard to the character of the perpetrator as well as to age when a party to it.

Caselaw

AG's Ref. Nos. 87 and 86 of 1999 (Webb and Simpson) [2001] 1 Cr.App.R.(S) 505.
Fraud- Tax evasion.
Where, over a period of time, an offender has evaded tax, they must not only pay the tax and pay a financial penalty but a custodial sentence should also be imposed. The length of the sentence will depend on a number of factors including: the amount of tax evaded; the period of time during which the evasion took place; whether others were drawn in and corrupted; the character of the offender; the extent (if known) of his personal gain; whether the offender pleaded guilty; the amount recovered.

Caselaw

***R v Graham and Whatley* [2004] EWCA Crim 2755.**
Benefit Fraud.
The Court reviewed the authorities in relation to cases of benefit fraud, as set out in
R v Stewart and others (1987) 9 Cr.App.R. (S) 135, given the increasing prevalence of benefit fraud.
Guidelines
R v Stewart should continue to apply but the figure of

> £10,000 should be updated for inflation. The Court referred to an inflation table that indicates that £1.00 at the time the case of Stewart was heard is approximately equivalent to £1.80 in the present day. Accordingly, where imprisonment is necessary, short terms of up to about nine to 12 months will usually be sufficient, after a trial, where the over payment is less than £20,000
>
> The Court endorsed the aggravating and mitigating features as identified in *R v Stewart*.
>
> Due to the increasing prevalence of social security fraud, and the fact that the offences are easy to commit and expensive to detect, contrary to R v Stewart, there will be cases where courts will be justified in imposing a sentence which contains a deterrent element, for example *Armour and Sherlock* [1997] 2 Cr.App.R.(S) 240.

15.11. Conclusion

For fraud offences committed after 15th January 2007, the date the Fraud Act 2006 came into force, the maximum penalty on indictment and conviction is 10 years but as explained above, sentence on conviction and indictment depends on various factors.

Further Reading for Chapter Fifteen

S. Creighton and V. King, *Prisoners and the Law*, (Tottel, London 2003)

N. Padfield, Editor, *Archbold Magistrates' Courts Criminal Practice*, (Thomson, London 2008)

http://www.cps.gov.uk/legal/section15/chapter_p_16.html

Court of Appeal Guidelines

BIBLIOGRAPHY

Books

W.S Albrecht & G.W Wernz, *Fraud: Bringing the light and dark side of Business* (Irwin, 1995).

A. Arlidge, Japery and I. Gatt, *Arlidge & Parry on Fraud* (2nd edn, Sweet & Maxwell, London 1998)

M. Ashton and C. Richmond, Lollardy *and the Gentry in the Later Middle Ages* (Stroud and New York 1997).

A. Ashworth and B. Emmerson, *Human rights and Criminal Justice* (Sweet & Maxwell, London 2001)

A. Ashworth, *The Criminal Process* (Clarendon Press, London 1995)

A. Ashworth, *Principles of Criminal Law* (Clarendon Press. London 1991)

A. Ashworth, *Principles of Criminal Law* (Sweet & Maxwell, London 1999)

R. A. Atkins and P. H. Rubin, *Effects of Criminal Procedure on Crime Rates*
(Emory University, Atlanta 1998)

J. Austin, *The Province of Jurisprudence Determined* (Clarendon Press, London 1932)

I. Ayres and J. Braithwaite, *Responsive Regulation: Transcending the Regulation Debate*, (Oxford University Press, Oxford 1995)

J. Baldwin and T. Moloney, *The Conduct of Police Investigations: Records of Interview, the Defence Lawyer's Role and Standards of Supervision* (HMSO, London 1992)

M. Balen, *A very English Deceit* (Fourth Estate, London 2002)

D. Barchard, *Asil Nadir and the Rise and Fall of Polly Peck* (Victor Gollancz Ltd, London 1992)

Bar Council, *The Quality of Justice* (Butterworths, London 1989)

E. Barker, *Aristotle: Politics* (Oxford 1946)

N. Barrett, *Digital Crime: Policing the Cybernation*, Kogan Page Limited, London 1997.

J. Bell and S. Boyron, *Principles of French Law* (Oxford University Press, Oxford 1998).

S. I. Benn, *A Theory of Freedom*, Cambridge University Press, Cambridge 1986.

J. Bentham, *An Introduction to the Principles of Morals and Legislation* (Oxford University Press, Oxford 1970).

S. Berger and R. Dore, *National Diversity and Global Capitalism* (Cornell University Press, Ithaca 1996)

V. Bevan and K. Lidstone, *Investigation of Crime* (Butterworths London 1991)

P. Birks, *Pressing Problems in the Law, Volume 1*, (Oxford University Press, Oxford 1995)

Born and Westin, *International Civil Litigation in United States Court*, (3rd edn Kluwler Law International, The Hague 1996)

S. Bower, *Actionable Misrepresentation* (4th edn Butterworths, London 2000)

A. Brown, *Criminal Evidence and Procedure* (2nd edn Butterworths, London 2002)

T. Bower, *Maxwell – the Final Verdict* (Harper Collins, London 1996)

J. Braithwaite, *Crime, shame and reintegration*, Cambridge University Press, Cambridge 1989.

K. Calavita, H. N. Pontell and R. H. Tillman, *Big Money Crime* (University of California Press, Berkeley 1997)

A. B. L. Cheung and I. Scott (edn), *Governance and Public Sector Reform in Asia: Paradigm Shifts or Business as Usual?* (Routledge Curzon, London 2003)

A. Chinhengo, *Essential Jurisprudence* (Cavendish, Manchester 1995)

Cachou, *Evidence* (Longmans, London 1998)

Civil Liberties Trust, *Justice on Trial*, (Civil Liberties Trust, London 1992)

M. Clark, *Business Crime: Its nature and control*, (Polity Press, Cambridge 1990).

R. Clark (edn), *Situational crime prevention: Successful case studies*, (Harrow & Heston, New York, 1997)

M. B. Clinard and P. C. Yeager, *Corporate Crime* (Free Press, New York 1980)

M. R. Cohen, *Reason and Law* (Collier Books, New York 1961)

J. W. Coleman, *The Criminal Elite: Understanding White Collar Crime*, (St Martin's Press, New York 1998)

M .J. Comer, *Corporate Fraud*, (McGraw-Hill Book Company, Berkshire 1985)

H. Croall, *White Collar Crime* (Open University, Milton Keynes 1992),

L.B. Curzon, *Cases in Criminal Law* (Macdonald and Evans, Baintree Mass 1974)

D. Danziger and J. Gillingham, *The Year of Magna Carta* (Hodder and Stoughton, London 2003).

G. Deleuze, *Difference and Repetition*, (New York: Columbia University Press, 1994)

A.V.S.De Reuck and R. Porter, *The Mentally Abnormal Offender* (Little, Brown, Boston, 1968)

P. Devlin, *The Enforcement of Morals* (Oxford Press, Oxford 1965)

P. Dobson and E. Phillips, *Law Relating to Theft* (Cavendish, Manchester 2001)

A. Duff and D. Garland, *A Reader in Punishment* (Oxford University Press, Oxford 1997),

M. A. Elliot, *Crime in Modern Society* (Harper & Brothers, New York 1952)

D. Epstein and G. Weissenberger, *New York Evidence Courtroom Manual* (Anderson Publishing, Ottawa 2004)

H. J. Eysenck, *Crime and Personality* (Paladin, London 1970).

M. Felson, *Crime and everyday life*, (Pine Forge Press, Thousand Oaks, 1998)

S.Field and P. D. Thomas, *Justice and Efficiency* (Blackwell, London 1994)

C. Fields and R. Moore, *Comparative Criminal Justice: Traditional and Non-Traditional Systems of Law and Control* (Waveland Press, Illinois 1996)

H. Fisher, *The German Legal System* (Cavendish Publishing, London 2002)

J. C. Flugel, *The psychoanalytic study of the family* (Hogarth Press, London 1950)

P. Fletcher, *Rethinking Criminal Law* (Oxford University Press, Oxford 2000)

A. Flew, *Crime or Disease* (Harper & Row, USA 1973)

P. Franklin, *Profits of Deceit* (Heinmann, London 1990)

L. Freidman, *History of American Law* (New York Press, 1973)

T. Gabor, *Everybody Does It! Crime by the Public*, (University of Toronto Press, Toronto 1994)

Hagen, *Paths to Justice* (Hart Publishing, Oregon 1999)

M. Giandomenico, *Regulating Europe* (London, Routledge 1996)

D. Gibbons, *Talking about crime and criminals, problems and issues in theory development in criminology,* (Prentice Hall, New Jersey, 1994)

M. Gilbert, *Fraudsters,* Constable, London 1986)

F. T. Giles, *The Criminal Law* (Pelican Books, London 1954)

M. Gillard, *In the Name of Charity* (Chatty and Windups, London 1987)

P. R .Glaze brook, *Statutes in Criminal Law* (Blackstone Press, Oxford 1989)

E.Glover, *The Roots of Crime* (International University Press, Guildford CT USA 1960)

P. Grabosky and J. Braithwaite, *Of Manners Gentle: Enforcement strategies of Australian Business Regulatory Agencies*, Oxford University Press, Melbourne 1986)

E. J. Green, *Psychology of Law Enforcement* (Wiley, Hoboken NJ 1976)

J. M. Greenwald, *Document Fraud* (Loompanics Ltd, Port Townsend Washington 1997)

G. Geis, R. F. Meir and L.M.Salinger, *White-Collar Crime* (3rd edn Free Press, New York 1995)

M. Gottfredson and T.Hirschi, *A general theory of crime*, (Stanford University Press, Stanford 1990)

N. Gunningham and P.Grabosky, *Smart Regulation: Designing Environmental Policy*, (Oxford University Press, Oxford 1998)

Halsbury, *Halsbury's Laws of England*, Volume 26, (3rd edn. Butterworths, London 1959)

J. G. Hall, *The Expert Witness*, (Barry Rose Publishers, London, 1992)

H. L. A. Hart, *The Concept of Law* (Oxford University Press, 1961)

R. H. Helmolz et al, *The Privilege against Self-In crimination* (University of Chicago Press, 1997)

D. Hetdon, *Evidence* (Butterworths, London 1996)
T.Hirschi, *Causes of delinquency*, (University of California Press, Berkeley, 1969)
L. T. Hobhouse, *The Elements of Social Justice* (Faber and Faber, London (1922)
D. Hobson, *The National Wealth* (Harper Collins, London 1999)
T. Hodgkinson, *Expert evidence: Law and Practice*, (Sweet & Maxwell, London 1999)
C. R. Hollin, *Psychology and Crime* (Routledge, London 1989),
Chord, *The Art of the State: Culture, Rhetoric, and Public Management* (Oxford University Press, 1998)
C. Hood, *The Limits of Administration* (John Wiley, London 1976)
I. Huntington, *Fraud: Prevention and Detection* (Butterworths 1992)
J. Iannacci and R.Morris, *Access Device Fraud and Related Financial Crime*, (CRC Press, London 2000)
J. A .Inciardi and H.A.Siega, *Crime –Emerging Issues* (Praeger Publications, Boston MA 1977),
H. B. Irving, *Last Studies in Criminology* (W Collins and Sons, London 1921)
F.G.Jacobs, *Criminal Responsibility* (Weidenfield and Nicolson, London 1971)
M. W. Jackson, *Matters of Justice* (Croom Helm, 1986)
F. Anechiarico and J.B.Jacobs, The *Pursuit of Absolute Integrity: How Corruption Control Makes Government Ineffective*, (Chicago Press, 1996.)
K. M. Jameson, *The Organisation of Corporate Crime* (Sage Publications, Thousand Oaks, CA 1994)
H. Jones, *Crime in a Changing Society* (Penguin, London 1971)

H. Jones, *Crime and the Penal System* (University Tutorial Press, London 1956)

V. Jupp, *Methods of Criminological Research* (Routledge, London 1989)

E.D.Kapstein, *Governing the Global Economy, International Finance and the State* (Harvard University Press, Cambridge MA 1994)

M. Killick, *Fraudbusters* (Indigo Press, London 1998)

D. N. Kirk and A. Woodcock, *Serious Fraud – Investigation and Trial* (3rd edn Butterworths, London 2002)

U. Kothari and M.Minogue (ends), *Development Theory and Practice: Critical Perspectives* (Palgrave, Basingstoke 2002)

N. Lacey, *A Reader in Criminal Justice* (Oxford University Press, 1994)

M. Levi, *Fraud: Organisation, Motivation and Control* (Ashgate Publishing, Aldershot 1999)

R. Leifmann, *Cartels, Concerns and Trusts*, (New York Press, New York, 1999)

D. Lewis and P. Hughmam, *Just how Just?*, (Secker and Warburg, USA, 1975)

T. Matthews, *Privatising Criminal Justice* (Sage Publications, Thousand Oaks, CA, 1989)

J. B. Mays, *Crime and the Social Structure* (Faber and Faber, London 1963)

R. May, *Criminal Evidence*, (Blackstone Press, London, 1999)

G. Mars *Cheats at work: An anthropology of Workplace Crime,* (Dartmouth, Aldershot, 1994)

D.McLean, *International Co-operation in Civil and Criminal Matters* (2nd edn Oxford University Press, 2002)

Lord McClusky Lord, *Justice and Democracy* (Sweet and Maxwell, London 1986)

M. McConville, *Standing Accused* (Oxford University Press, 1994)

J.McEwan, *Evidence and the Adversarial Process* (Blackstone Press, Oxford 1998)

R. Merton, *Social Theory and social structure*, (Free Press, Glencoe, Illinois, 1957)

J. Muncie and E. McLaughlin, *The problems of crime: Crime, Order and Social Control*, (Sage Publications, London, 2001)

D. Nelkon, *White Collar Crime*, (Dartmouth, Aldershot, 1994)

W.L.Neustatter, *Psychological Disorder and Crime* (Christopher Johnson, London 1953)

B. Pettet, *Company Law*, (Pearson Education Ltd, London, 2001)

L. Radzinowicz, *In Search of Criminology* (Heinemann, London 1961)

S.Ramage, *Serious Fraud and Current Issues* (iUniverse, New York 2004)

S.Ramage, *Fraud and The Serious Fraud Office* (iUniverse, New York 2005

J. Rawls, *A Theory of Justice* (Oxford University Press, 1972)

R. Rex, *The Lollards* (Palgrave Press, Basingstoke 2002)

J. R. Richards, *Transnational Criminal Organisations, Cybercrime and Money-Laundering*, (CRC Press, Boca Raton, 1999)

V. Ruggerio, *Crime and Markets*, (Oxford University Press, Oxford, UK, 2000)

D.R.Somin, *Elite Deviance*, (Allyn & Bacon, Boston, 1999)

I. Sinclair, *Essentials of Computer Security* (Bernard Banabi Books, London 1997)

J. C. Smith, *Criminal Case and Comment* (Sweet and Maxwell, London 1960)

J. C. Smith, *The Law of Theft* (Butterworths, London 1997)

P. G. Smith, *The Crime Explosion* (Macdonald, London 1970)

R. G. Steigman, *Illinois Evidence Manual* (Lawyers Cooperative Publishing, 1995)

E.A.Sutherland, *White Collar Crime* (Holt, Rinehart & Winston, Austin Texas 1949)

J. A. F. Thompson, *The later Lollards* (Oxford University Press, 1968)

J. J. Tobias, *Crime and Industrial 19th Century* (Pelican Books, London (1967)

J. Waldron, *Law and Disagreement* (Oxford University Press, 1999)

C. Walker and K. Starner, *Miscarriages of Justice* (Blackstone Press, Oxford 1999)

D.Wasserman and R. Wachbroit, *Genetics and Criminal Behaviour* (Cambridge University Press, 2001),

D.Weisburd, S. Wheeler, E. Waring and N. Bode, *Crimes of the Middle-Classes: White Collar Offenders in the Federal Courts*, (Yale University Press, New Haven, 1991)

M. G. Welham, *Corporate Killing* (Butterworths, London 2002)

A. West and Y. Desdevises, *The French Legal System* (Butterworths, London 1998)

B. Widlake, *Serious Fraud Office* (Warner, London 1994)

J. H. Wigmore, *A treatise of Anglo-American System of Evidence*, (Boston Press, USA,, 1940)

J. H. Wigmore, *Evidence at trials at Common Law*, (Boston Press, USA, 1990)

D. Wolchover, *Silence and Guilt* (Lion Court Lawyers, London 2001)

R. Youngs, *Sourcebook of German Law* (Cavendish Publishing, London 2002)

G. Gilboorg, *The Psychology of the Criminal Act and Punishment* (The Hogarth Press, London 1955)
A. Zukerman, *The Principles of Criminal Evidence* (Oxford University Press, 1989)

Articles and other materials

E.I. Altman, "Financial Ratios, Discriminant Analysis and The Prediction of Corporate Bankruptcy", Journal of Finance, September, 1968.

M. Anderson, "Attack of the quantum worms", New Scientist, 29 October 2005.

T. Anderson and W. Twining, "Analysis of Evidence", 1991, Weidenfeld and Nicholson

Archbold, *Magistrates Courts Criminal Practice*, (Sweet, & Maxwell, London 2007)

Association of Chief Police Officers, "The Right of Silence: Briefing Paper", 1993, ACPO

AFG, "FRANCE- Country Report1. Economic and Financial Background 2003"
http://www.afg-asffi.com

J. Aimes, "Boosting Police Station Skills" Law Society Gazette Vol 91, 2004.

A. Amar and R. Lettow, "Fifth Amendment First Principles: Self–Incrimination Clause": Michigan Law Review, March 1995

A. Amar and V.D. Amar, "The new regulation allowing Federal Agents to monitor Attorney-Client conversations: Why it threatens Fourth Amendment Values.", FINDLAW, Friday, November 16th 2001
http://www.findlaw.com

Amicus Journal, Volume 8, 2003.

M. Atherton and G. Gilmore, "Watchdog in pursuit of rogue advisors", Times Newspapers, September 4th, 2004.

P. Aucoin, "Administrative reform in public management", (1990), Governance 3, 2, 115-37.

Authorite des Marches Financiers, "Modernising the Supervisory Authorities", February 2003.

J. A. Barth, G.Caprio and R. Levine, "Financial regulation and performance: cross-country evidence" (1998), World Bank, Washington DC

BBC, "Huge DVD piracy factory uncovered", 7 April 2006, BBC, http://news.bbc.co.uk

D. Bedlow, 'Ready (or not)', 27 May 0204, Legal Week/Kroll Ontrack Insight into electronic disclosure.

M. Beeson, 'Japan's Reluctant Performers and the Legacy of the Developmental State' in Cheung and Scott, (2003a), 25-43, 2003

S. Bhandari and F.Gillett, "Fraud Watch", (2003) New Law Journal, Vol 153, No 7091,

A. Bidwell, "Wall Street to Newgate" (1987) True Life Crime

C. Biever, ' Beat cybercrime, switch to a virtual wallet', New Scientist ,11 April 2006, London, UK.

Bloomberg News, "Ex-KPMG partner pleads guilty in tax-shelter case", 27 March 2006

W. Bromberg, "Crime and the Mind" (1966) 44 Texas L. Rev. 595

H. Brooke, 'Guns On the table', December 2005, Journalist, London, UK Charity Commission, "Transparency and Accountability"http://www.charity-commission.gov.uk/publications/rs8annexs.asp

Bundesbank – Press Centre: Press Releases from 1999 to 2005
http://www.bundesbank.de/presse_pressenotizen_2005.en.php

Bureau of Justice, "Sourcebook of Criminal Justice Statistics" (1994)

L. Chong, "Liquidators of BCCI under fire over 'farce', Times, 13 April 2006.

S.Claessens and D. Kilingebiel, "Alternative frameworks for the provision of financial services" (1999) World Bank, Washington DC

Clifford Chance Solicitors, "France Overhauls canvassing and financial advice regime laws", Newsletter, Sept/October 2003.

Recommend "Accounting for Administrative Change in Three Asia-Pacific States" (1999) Public Management 1, 3, 429-38

R.Common, "The New Public Management and Policy Transfer: the Role of International Organisations" (1988) in M Minogue, C Polidano and D. Hulme, pp59-75

P. Cornelius, 'Corporate Practices and Notional Governance Systems: What to Country Rankings Tell Us – Part I/II', 1 March 2005, German Law Journal.

Compliance Week, Editorial, 'Are Those Who Aid Fraud Liable As "Primary Violators"?' December 2005, Compliance Week, USA.

R. Deeg and S.Lutz, "Internationalisation and Financial Federalism" (1998) discussion paper Max-Planck Institute, Germany

Deloitte Touche Tohmatsu, "Futuristic Presentation of the Balance Sheet of Insurance Group under future IAS" (2001)

A. Demirguc-Kunt and R. Levine, "Bank-Based and Market-Based Financial Systems: Cross-Country Comparisons" (1999) World Bank, Washington DC

DFID, "Governance and Poverty Strategy" (2000) Department for International Development, London

Denton Wilde Sapte, "UNCITRAL Model Law to transform cross-border insolvency", International Law Online, 25th August 2006

Directorate General 1 – Legal Affairs, "Compliance Report on France", Strasbourg, 2003
http://66.102.9.104/search?q=cache:TYnLUnfXR2YJ:www.greco.coe.int/evaluations/cy

M. Dobler, "National and International Developments in Risk Reporting: May the German Accounting Standard 5 lead the way internationally?" (2005) German Law Journal 1191
http://www.germanlawjournal.com

D.P.Dolowitz and D. Marsh, "Policy Transfer: a Framework for Comparative Analysis" (1998) in Minogue, Polidano and Hulme pp.38-58

D. Donaldson and I. Watt, "Guinness plc. Investigation under sections 432(2) and 442 of the Companies Act 1985" (BERR Report, HMSO, London 1997)

J. Doran, "Reinventing the Wheeler Dealer after a Ban" (31 May 2004) Times Newspaper.

Dept. of Trade and Industry, Press Notices200-2005
http://www.BERR.gov.uk/cld/press2000.htm

J. Duckett, "Bureaucrats in Business Chinese Style: The Lessons of Market Reform and State Entrepreneurialism in the People's Republic of China" (2001) World Development 29,

P.J.Dunleavy and C. Hood, "From Old Public Administration to New Public Management" (1994) Public Money and Management 14, 3, 9-16

Economist, "Bosses behind bars" (12 June 2004)

A. Edlin and A. Schwartz, "Optimal penalties in contracts", 22 International Review of Law and Economics, 381 (2002)

Economist, Book Review, "The Company of Strangers" (14 August 2004)

G.Edmonson and D. Fairlamb, "The milk just keeps on spilling at Parmalat. It's a tale of globalisation gone wrong:

Bankers across Europe harboured doubts about company numbers for years, yet no one blew the whistle", Business Week Online, January 26th 2004
http://www.businessweek.com/print/magazine/content/04_04/b3867074_mz054.htm?ch

G. Elliehausen, "The Cost of Bank Regulation: a Review of Evidence" (April 1998) Federal Reserve Bulletin

A. Edgar and A. Jiwaji, "Legal Week" (10 July 2003) Vol 5 No 26

European Parliament, "Background Briefing Document on Combating Fraud and Corruption in the European Union", 25th September 2002.

European Parliament, "Draft Report on the Commission Green Paper on Criminal –law Protection of the financial interests of the Community and the establishment of a European Prosecutor", 19th September 2002.

Europol, "Work Programme 2007", The Hague, 31st March 2006

R. A. Farrell and V. L. Swigert, "The Corporation in Criminology: New Directions for Research", (1985) Journal of Research in Crime & Delinquency, 83-94

D. Feldman, "The Impact of the Human Rights Act 1998 on English Public Law", BIICL, 7 October 2005

E. Fennell, 'The rot set in as soon as the record speeches began', 8 November 2005, Times, London UK.

G. Ferrarini, "Parmalat", University of Genoa, Centre for Law and Finance, Paper Submitted to European Corporate Governance Institute, No.40, 2005.

J. Fleming, "Stripping away Assets – as the Scale of Fraud around the World increases, both the Law and the Lawyers are running hard to keep up" (Nov 2000) Law Society Gazette, UK.

Florida Annotated Statutes, LexisNexis, 204.

S. Fluendy, "Troubles mount at Sea Containers", Mail on Sunday Newspapers, 9 April 2006

S. Fluendy, "Ofwat: There may be more water frauds", pg 5, Mail on Sunday Newspapers, 9 April 2006.

L .Foley and J. Foley, "Identity theft: The aftermath 2004, 18 September 2005.http://www.ftc.gov/bcp/conline/pubs/credit/affidavit.pdf

D. Fraser, *A land fit for criminals*, (Book Guild Publishing, London 2006)

Fraud Trials Committee Report 1986, HMSO

Freshfields, 'EU measures to combat piracy and counterfeiting', October 2003, Freshfields Bruckhaus Deringer, "The Financial Services Sector in Europe-regulatory Investigation and Enforcement Issues in Germany", Newsletter, September 2002.

N. Garoupa, "The economics of Organised Crime and Optimal Law Enforcement", Stanford Law School, December 1997

GIGALAW, "Internet company sued for selling e-mail addresses", 23March 2006 http://by112fd.bay112.hotmail.msn.com/cgi-bin/getmsg?a=e16a6f600ef742d932484d062e36

Professor Gilmore, "Financial fraud speech", 2006, The 4th International Financial Fraud Convention, UK.

Global Risk Management,' Easier-to-follow accenting rules wanted', 27November 2004, Global Risk Management.

S. Goff, 'Regulator opens doors to the exclusive club', 12 April 2006, the Financial Times, London, UK.

N. Goteiner and J.Mann, "Electronic Evidence Discovery", IPFRONTLINE, 25 August, 2005 http://www.ipfrontline.com/depts/article.asp?id=5417&deptid=3

G. Green and S. Howley, "The new disclosure rules for listed companies", 6th June 2005, CMS Cameron McKenna Solicitors Newsletter.

G. Hall and G. D. Smith, *The Expert Witness*, (Barry Rose Law Pub., London 1992)

G. Hazard and E.B. Rock, "A new player in the boardroom: the emergence of the Independent Director Counsel", Paper 6, University of Pennsylvania Law School, 2004

A. Heaton-Armstrong, E. Shepherd and D. Wolchover, *Analysing Witness Testimony*, (Blackstone Press, London 1999)

J. D. Heydon, *Evidence: Cases and Materials*, (Butterworths, London 2000)

Herbert Smith LLP, "Public access to court documents: Retrospective effect suspended", International Law Online, 24th October 2006.

HMSO, "Davie Report" (1995), HMSO

HMSO, "Graham Report", (1994), HMSO

G. Hall and G. D. Smith, *The Expert Witness*, (Barry Rose Law Publishers, London 1992)

Herbert Smith LLP, "Public access to court documents: Retrospective effect suspended", International Law Online, 24th October 2006.

IMF, "Germany: Report on the Observance of Standards and Code: FATF Recommendations for anti-money laundering and combating the financing of terrorism", September 2004 http://66.102.9.104/search?q=cache:jychBeNas2Yj:www.imf.org/external/pubs/ft/scr/2.

J. Hodgson and M. McConville, "Silence and the Suspect", (1993) New Law Journal, Vol 143

T. Hodgkinson, *Expert evidence: Law and Practice*, (Sweet & Maxwell, London 1999)

I.C. Renfrewshire, "Broker\ facing jail for fraud", 30th October 2006 http://icrenfrewshire.icnetwork.co.uk/tm_headline=broker-facing-jail-for-fraud&method=full&objectid=18012680&siteid=63858-name_page.htm

Identity Theft Resource Centre, Fact Sheet 120: Identity theft and Children, 2005

IOCE, "International Principles for Computer Evidence", 1995.

R. Irving, "Fragility of market confidence exposed", pg 52, Times Newspapers, 19 October 2005.

R. Irving, "Merlin admits SFO inquiry", pg 53, Times, 15 April 2006

Irwin Mitchell, "Inland Revenue Investigations and Raids", 19 July 2004

A. Jamieson, "One in ten Britons suffers ID theft", BBC News, July 2006

Jane's Police Review, "Law and update", Issue 10th November 2006, Jane's Information Group, Surrey, 2006.

Derivatives Week, USA. Justice, Annual Report 2005, Justice, UK

M. Mack, "When does a document become evidence?" Fios Inc., E-Discovery Advisor Magazine, 31 August 2005

R. Jacques, "Man arrested over Webcam Spy Trojan ", VNUNET.com, 19th January 2005.

Justice Bulletin Autumn (2003), Justice.

Justice Annual Report (2003), Justice.

J. Kersnar, "Pay now, pay later- Sarbannes-Oxley Section 404", Chief Finance Officer Journal, April 2005
http://www.cfoeurope.com/displayStory.cfm/3350531

M. Khan, "State Failure in Developing Countries and Strategies of Institutional Reform" (June 2003) Paper to the World Bank ABCDE Conference, Oslo,

M. Knight-John and A. Perumal, "Regulatory Impact Assessment in Sri Lanka: Bridges that have to be Crossed"

(October 2003) Paper to CRC-NCPAG Conference in Manila

Law Commission Consultation Paper, "Legislating the Criminal Code: Fraud and Deception" (April 1998)

Law Commission Report on Double Jeopardy, 2001

Law Commission, "Evidence in Criminal Proceedings: Hearsay and related topics", Report Number 245, 1997.

London Stock Exchange- Annual Reports 1998-2005

M. R. T. McNairy, "The Early Development of Privilege against Self-Incrimination" (1990) Oxford Journal of Legal Studies

G. Majone, "The regulatory state and its legitimacy problems", (1999) West European Politics22, 1, 1-24

T. Maloney, Royal Commission on Criminal Justice, Research Study 2, 3, 4: 'Conduct of Police Investigations: Records of Interview, the Defence Lawyer's Role and Standards of Supervision', (1994) HMSO.

M. Markley, "Who shall Guard the Guards? How can Auditor Independence be guaranteed?" Houston News, Texas, USA, 17th October 2003.

W. McCourt and M Minogue, eds., "The Internationalisation of Public Management: Reinventing the Third World State" (2001) Cheltenham, Edward Elgar

M. Minogue, "Power to the People? Good Governance and the Reshaping of the State" (2002) in Kothari and Minogue, 117-35

M. Minogue, "Getting the Ideas Right: Public Management, Corruption and Development" (June 2002) Paper to World Bank ABCDE Conference, Oslo

M. Minogue, "Should Flawed Models of Public Management be exported?" (2001) in McCourt and Minogue, 20-43

M. Minogue, "Changing the State: Concepts and Practice in the Reform of the Public Sector" (1998) in M Minogue, C Polidano and D Hulme pp 17-37

G. R. Montinola, "Politicians, Parties, and the Persistence of Weak States: Lessons from the Philippines" (1999) Development and Change 30, 739-44

S. Moston and G. M. Stephenson, Royal Commission on Criminal Justice, Research Study 22, "Questioning and Interviewing of Suspects Outside the Police Station" (1993) HMSO.

OECD: France-Phase 2. Report on the Application of the Convention for Combating Bribery of Foreign Officials in International Business Transactions.2004 http://66.102.9.104/search?q=cache:Fuwg2oDHJO8J:www.oecd.org/dataoecd/36/36/262.

J. Murray, "Employers leave gap for in-house fraudsters", IT Week, 24th November 2005.

J. Murray, "Stop staff fraudsters and save billions", IT Week, 2nd December 2005.

A. Ogus. "Corruption and Regulatory Structures" (2003) paper delivered to CRC/CARR Workshop on Risk Regulation, Accountability and Development, Manchester University, June 2000

F. Page, "What is fraud?" New Law Journal,(1997) LexisNexis Publishers, 28th February 1997.

D. Parker, "Policy Transfer and Policy Inertia: Privatisation in Taiwan" (2005) Asia Pacific Business Review 6.

G. Pendell, "Three Rivers-everything you need to know", CMS McKenna Newsletter, 25th November 2004.

C. Polidano, "Administrative Reform in Core Civil Services: Application and Applicability of the New Public Management" (2001) in McCourt and Minogue (2001)

Record Commission, "Statutes of the Realm" (1827) London

S. Ramage, "True or False?" (2003) Accounting Technician, McMillan Scott Publishers, London, September 2003,
S. Ramage, "The Serious Fraud Office", (2004) Accounting Technician, McMillan Scott Publishers, London, July 2004.
S. Ramage, "Crooks and culpability – a study of fraud and fraudsters", (2005), The Criminal Lawyer Journal, Tottel Publishers, London, Vol 159, December 2005.
S. Ramage, "Intercountry or Transnational Organised Crimes", (2006) The Criminal Lawyer Journal, Tottel Publishers, Vol. 166, London, June 2006.
S. Ramage, "The Fraud Offence Bill – A critical Analysis", (2005) The Criminal Lawyer, Tottel Publishers, London, Vol152, May 2005.
S. Ramage, "Misrepresentation", (2005) Accounting Technician, McMillan Scott Publishers, July 2005.
S. Ramage, "The test for deception", (2004) The Criminal Lawyer Journal, Tottel Publishers, London, Vol.147, December 2004.
S. Ramage, "The ex-Chief Executive Officer of Enron", Findlaw, July 2006
S. Ramage, "Obtaining pecuniary advantage by deception- to be classed as a fraud per the Fraud Act", (2006), The Criminal Lawyer Journal, Vol 165, Tottel Publishing, London.
http:// lawcrawler.findlaw.com/scripts/lc.pl?coun=&entry=Enron&sites=wlegal
A. Reid, "Obtaining a money transfer by deception", (2005) The Criminal Lawyer Journal, Tottel Publishing, London, Vol.151, April 2005.
Royal Commission on Capital Punishment, (1953), HMSO London
Royal Commission on the Law relating to Mental Illness and Mental Deficiency, (1957), HMSO London

A. Schick, "Why most Developing Countries should not try New Zealand's Reforms" (1998) World Bank Research Observer 13, 1, 123-31
Serious Fraud Office Annual Reports (1995), (1996), (1997), (1998), (1999), (2000), (2001), (2002), (2003), HMSO.
S. Shaefer and C. T. McCormack, "Law and Future: Evidence" (1956) New York University Law Review
R. G. Smith, "Best practice in fraud prevention", (1998) Trends and Issues in Crime and Criminal Justice, 100.
R. G. Smith, "Electronic Medicare Fraud: Current and future risks", (1999) Trends and Issues in Crime and Criminal Justice, 114.
R. G. Smith, "Defrauding governments in the twenty-first century" (1999) Trends and Issues in Crime and Criminal Justice, 132.
R. G. Smith, "Identity-related crime: Risks and Countermeasures", (1999), Trends and Issues in Crime and Criminology, 129.
J. R. Spencer, "Morality and the Evidence of Absent Witnesses" (1994) Crim LR
S. Sozen and I. Shaw "The International Applicability of New Public Management: Lessons from Turkey" (2002) International Journal of Public Sector Management 15, 4, 475-86
G. Staple, "International Co-Operation in Evidence Gathering", (July 1996) New Law Journal
J. D. Straussman and M. Wong "Chinese Administrative Reforms in International Perspective" (2001) International Journal of Public Sector Management 14, 5, 411-22UNDP (1998) Governance for Sustainable Human Development, New York, United Nations Development Programme
W. Stuetzle, J. Hamre, C. Koch-Weser and C. F. Bergsten, "Transatlantic Responses to Global Challenges: the Way

Forward" (17 July 2003) Centre for Applied Policy Research discussion

W. Stuntz, "Self-Incrimination and Excuse" (1988) Colombia Law Review, Vol 88

J. Sumners, (19 June 2003) Legal Week Vol 5 No 23

M. Taylor and A. Fleming, "Integrated financial supervision" (1999) Mimeo, World Bank

Times, "Keeping the Profession's Name Clean" (23 September 2003)

P. Thornton, "The Prejudiced Defendant: Unfairness Suffered by a Defendant in a Joint Trial" (2003) Criminal Law Review

W. Twining, "Rethinking Evidence: Exploratory Essays" (1990) Oxford University

T. Tyler, "Examining physician suggests British Home Secretary misled Parliament in bid to release Pinochet" (18th January, 2000) articled published by International Committee of the Fourth International

http://www.wsws.org/articles/2000/jan2000/pino-j18.shtml

United Kingdom Fraud Bill 2005, HMSO.

United States Title 18-Part 1- Chapter 47-USA PENAL Codes-Fraud Offences

United Nations, "Global Report on Crime and Justice" (1999) Oxford University Press.

US Sentencing Commission, "Sentencing Guidelines Manual" (1995)

US Securities and Exchange Commission, "The Investor's Advocate: how the SEC protects investors and maintains market integrity", 28th April 2004.

http://www.sec.gov/about/whatwedo.shtml

SEC Annual Reports 1998 to 2004Serious Fraud Office –United Kingdom: annual Reports 1988 to 2005

J. Van Brauman, "Foreign Evidence Gathering and Discovery for US Civil Tax Determination" (1996) American Journal of International Law

J. Van Brauman, "Discovery Abroad: the Perspective of the US Practitioner" (1984) New York University, Journal of International Law and Politics.

J. Van Brauman "Discovery of Documentary and other Evidence in a Foreign Country" (1983), American Journal of International Law

M. Wald, "Interrogations in New Haven: the Impact of Miranda" (1976) Yale Law Review

M. Waller, "The Fraudster may be the Boss, not the PA" (26 April 2004) the Times

J. Wallis and B. Dollery "Government Failure, Social Capital and the Appropriateness of the New Zealand Model for Public Sector Reform in Developing Countries" (2001) World Development 29, 2, 245-63

Washington Post, "Charged over Tax Shelters in KPMG Case", August 30th 2005.

T. Waters, "Fraud in prospect and hindsight", Fraud Intelligence, Informa Publications, January 2002.

D. Wolchover, "Should Judges Sum up on the Facts?" (1989) 781, Crim LR

World Bank, "Guidelines for financial sector development" (1997) Mimeo.

M. Zander, "How will the Right of Silence be abolished?" (1993) New Law Journal, Vol 143

Zukerman, A, "The principles of criminal evidence", 1989, Oxford University Press

J. Karaian, "A mountain to climb", CFO Europe, 2005
http://www.cfoeurope.com/displayStory.cfm/3599490

E. Klein, 'Internal Control Weakness Disclosures Filed In October', VOLUME 63, December 2004, Compliance Week, USA.

M. C. S. Lange, "Keeping your head", Corporate Counsel Magazine, April 2003.

B. McLannahan, "What lies beneath", CFO Europe, 2005 http://www.cfoeurope.com/displayStory.cfm/3713740

Law Commission, "Law Commission Consultation Paper No. 164- Registration of Security Interests: Common Charges and Property other than Land", 2003, HMSO.

Legal Week "Lawyers throw support behind Goldsmith's UK fraud review", July 2006

J. Lewis, "Watchdog to examine expenses black hole", Mail on Sunday Newspapers, 9 April 2006

Lovells Solicitors, "Credit card issuers liable for defective goods supplied abroad", International Law Online, 24th August 2006.

M. Mack, "When does a document become evidence?" E-Discovery Advisor Magazine, 31 August

Martin Kenney & Co, "The Language of Hiding", 6October 2003

B. E Mayn , C. Jeng-Chung and K. Wei Wen, 'The Differences of Regulatory Models and Interne Regulations in the European Union and the United States', Information & Communications Technology Law, Carfax Publishing, vol 13, No 3 October 2004, Canterbury, UK.

J. C. Murray, "Defeasance Provision in Securitized-Loan Document" 2003, http://216.239.59.104/search.

G. D. Nokes, "An introduction to evidence", 1962, Sweet & Maxwell

Northern Business News, "On the trail of white collar crooks!" The Journal, UK, 21st August 2006,

H. Nugent and I. MacKinnon, "Couple made millions from spy virus", pg 12, Times, 1 April, 2006.

T. Nunn, "Pending amendments to the Federal rules should provide guidance to handling metadata", Law & Technology News, January 2006.

K. Paxton-Doggett, 'When and inspector calls', 28 July 2005, the Law Society Gazette 103/30, London, UK.

Penningtons Solicitors LLP, "Accumulation and Maintenance Trusts", International Law Online, 2nd November 2006

Planned Giving Design Centre LLC, "Anderson to pay $217 million to Baptist Foundation- Tax analysts summary" 8May 2002

http://www.pgdc.com/phil/itemID=52474

J. Richards, "Revealed: how credit cards are plundered on the net", pg 1, 6, 7, Times Newspapers, 15 April, 2006.

L. Schlesinger, "'Greedy' fraudsters jailed in loan scam", 27 June 2003.

J. Summers, 'WorldCom and Tyco prove that complex trials do work', 5 July 2005, Times, London, UK.

M. Smith and L. Pritchard, "Top CPS Official is charged with drug dealing and sex attacks", pg 15, Mail on Sunday Newspapers, 9 April 2006.

SOCA, The United Kingdom Threat Assessment of Serious Organised Crime, (HMSO 2006)

M. Stone, *Cross-examination in Criminal Trials*, (Butterworths, London 1995)

J. Summers, "WorldCom and Tyco prove that complex trials do work", Pg 5, The Times, 6 July 2005

E. Shoudt, "Identity theft: victims "cry out" for reform", 52 Am.U.L.Rev.339, 346-7 (2002)

A. Taylor and A. Owens, "Slipping through their fingers", Professional Pensions, 16.2.2006

C. Taylor, "Public Interest Immunity and Police Informants", Journal of Criminal Law, 65, 435, Vathek Publishing 2001.

S. Taub, 'Did Governance Raters Foresee March AIG?' December 2004, Compliance Week, USA.

Taipei News, "Telegram exposes UK-Saudi arms deal", 29th October 2006http://www.taipeitimes.com/News/world/archives/2006/10/29/2003333866,

A. Taylor and A. Owens, "Slipping through their fingers", Professional Pensions, 16.2.2006

Washington Times, "Dog gets carded", January 30, 2004. http://washingtontimes.com/upi-breaking/20040129-031535-6234r.htm

D. Turnbull, "Revealed: How Labour's £2.3 million donor was arrested in drugs swoop", Mail on Sunday Newspapers, 9 April 2006

W. Twining, *Theories of Evidence: Bentham & Wigmore*, (George Weidenfeld and Nicholson, US 1985)

Vox Online, "Lottery fraud", Oct 27, 2006 http://www.vox.gi/index.php?news=1303>

M. Woodcock, "Three arrests over Carriage-works sale 'multi-million fraud'", 30th October 2006, York Press, York, UK.<http://www.thisisyork.co.uk/display.var.992820.0.three_arrests_over_carriageworks_sale_multimillion_fraud.php>

Washington Times, "Dog gets carded", January 30, 2004. http://washingtontimes.com/upi-breaking/20040129-031535-6234r.htm

Rawhide, 'Company lawyers call on Lords to give e-mails the same status as business letters.

Law gets tough on directors' reasonable duties to inform', 8 April 2005, New Law Journal, London,

P. Zumbansen, "Globalisation and the law: Deciphering the message of Translational Human Rights Litigation", German Law Journal, Vol 5 No 12, 1 December 2004

P. Zumbansen, "Piercing the legal veil: Commercial Abitration and Transnational Law", 8, European Law Journal, 400-432 (2002)

United Kingdom Legislation

http://www.legislation.hmso.gov.uk

www.bigcharts.com

www.enron.com

www.financialtimes.com

E. Barraclough, "China to jail more IP cheats", February 2005

www.managingip.com

BizReport, "Secret Service: Fraud threatens economy"

http://www.bizreport.com/news/8691/

L. Brett & P.Sampson, "UK: A payment revolution: the first viable alternative to small, change", 11May 05

http://www.mondaq.com

Deloitte, "The Arm's Length Standard", 5.5.05

http://www.mondaq.com

Dorda Brugger & Jordic

Website of law firm, which represents major fraud cases

Economist- Financial Services Authority

http://www.economist.com/research/backgrounders/

E-Government News, "SFO plans to use IT as key future cornerstone", 11th Aug 2004

http://www.publictechnology.net/print.php?sid=1572

Electronic Commerce Working Group, "Computer crime and IP section", 2006

http://www.cybercrime.gov/ecommerce.html

Fargo Electronics Inc., "Reducing your Identity-related Security Vulnerabilities", 2005.

http://www.fargo.com

M. D. Ford, "Identity Authentication and E-Commerce"
http://www2.warwick.ac.uk/fac/soc/law/elj/jilt/1998_3/ford/
GIGALAW News
http://www.gigalaw.com/newsarchives/
N. A .Goteiner and J. C. Mann, "Electronic evidence discovery", 25.8.05
http://www.ipfrontline.com/depts/article.asp?id=5417&deptid=3
G. Hazard and E. B. Rock, "A new player in the Boardroom: the emergence of the independent directors' counsel", (2004)
http://lsr.nellco.org/upenn/wps/papers/6
J. Karaian, "A mountain to climb", 22.04.06
http://www.cfoeurope.com/displayStory.cfm/3599490
Identity Theft Resource Centre
http://www.idtheftcenter.org
International Centre for Commercial Law
Electra v KPMG:
http://www.icclaw.com/devs/uk/ma/ukma_076.htm
P. Lilley, MP. "Identity Crisis" 2005
http://www.bowgroup.org
PGDC, "Anderson Accountants to pay $217 million to Baptist Foundation", 8.5.02
http://www.pgdc.com/phil/item/?itemID=52474
P. Sales, "Auditors' Negligence Cases"
http://www.11-kbw.law.co.uk/Articles/Commercial%Law/Auditors%20Negligence.html
P. Sikka, "Resisting the auditing industry: the case of Sound Diffusion Group"
http://www3.bus.osaka-cu.ac.jp/ipa97/papers/89.html
R. Tomasic, "Auditors, and the reporting of illegality and financial fraud"
http://www.aic.gov.au/publications/proceedings/10/tomasic.html